STUDIES IN
ANCIENT GREEK SOCIETY

STUDIES IN ANCIENT GREEK SOCIETY

THE FIRST PHILOSOPHERS

GEORGE THOMSON

LAWRENCE & WISHART

LONDON

First published 1955
Second edition 1961
Reprinted with corrections 1972
Reprinted 1977

Copyright © George Thomson 1955

ISBN 0 85315 406 6

Printed in Great Britain by
The Camelot Press Ltd, Southampton

To

MANOLIS GLEZOS

hero of the Greek resistance

In May 1941, at the age of nineteen, he climbed the Acropolis and tore down the swastika, which had been hoisted a few days before by the Nazis as they entered Athens. Arrested and sentenced to death, he escaped and joined the resistance. After the war he was re-arrested and in 1948 again sentenced to death. In response to world-wide protests the sentence was commuted to imprisonment for life, and in July 1954 he was released, suffering from tuberculosis. In December 1958 he was re-arrested.

Μάθε· ἡ προκοπὴ γιὰ τοὺς ἐλεύτερους, γιὰ μᾶς!

PREFACE

THIS second volume follows the same plan as the first. It is a further expansion of *Æschylus and Athens*, dealing with the growth of slavery and the origin of science.

I have not attempted a systematic study of slavery. That is a task for collective research based on all the material now available. It becomes increasingly clear that such a study will never be undertaken by bourgeois scholars, whose acquiescence in colonial oppression renders them incapable of understanding the degradation either of the slave or still more of the slave-owner. I hope, however, that enough has been said to show that Greek civilisation cannot be understood without it.

Nor have I investigated the technical origins of Greek science. That too is a matter for specialists. My aim has been to examine the ideas underlying the work of the natural philosophers, which forms a link between primitive thought and scientific knowledge. When studying the economic basis of tragedy, with the results given in *Æschylus and Athens*, I realised that my conclusions must apply equally to other ideological products of ancient democracy. Accordingly, in the present volume, I have examined the part played by commodity production and the circulation of money in the growth of Greek philosophy.

In this I am greatly indebted to Dr. Alfred Sohn-Rethel, whose study of Kant had led him independently to similar conclusions, to be published in his *Intellectual and Manual Labour*. Not only has he permitted me to read his book in manuscript, but in discussing my own he has helped me to appreciate the profound philosophical importance of the opening chapters of *Capital*.

The chapter on China is a tentative approach to a comparative study of Greek and Chinese philosophy, which I hope to pursue in the third volume. I had intended to say something also about Indian philosophy, but was deterred by the chronological difficulties of Indian history. It is to be expected that, with the spread of Marxism in India, these problems will be solved.

My thanks are due to Professor Benjamin Farrington and Mr. Maurice Cornforth for their criticisms, and also to my colleagues in the Department of Classical Philology at the Charles University, Prague, to whom, after participating with them in many long and lively discussions, I owe more than I can say.

Birmingham, January 1955   GEORGE THOMSON

PREFACE TO THE SECOND EDITION

THIS book has been widely discussed among Marxists, some of whom are not yet convinced of its main thesis, concerning the role of commodity production. Whatever the final conclusion may be on this and other disputed questions, the book has, I believe, drawn attention to the need for a less dogmatic, more dialectical approach to the history of philosophy.

In bourgeois circles, where new ideas are not so welcome, its influence has been less apparent. It seems that most university teachers either ignore it or (less prudently) denounce it; but this has not saved the library copies available to students from becoming dog-eared. Moreover, in recent discussions on slavery some of the ideas put forward in Chapter IX have been reproduced, albeit without acknowledgement. The preceding volume has been treated in the same way, especially the chapters on Homer. I take this as a compliment.

This edition includes a number of additions and corrections, which have already been incorporated in the Czech, Russian, Spanish and German editions, but not the Japanese.

Birmingham, 1961   GEORGE THOMSON

CONTENTS

9

PART THREE
FROM BABYLON TO MILETOS

Chapter V. The Greek Calendar

Chapter VI. The Kadmeioi

Chapter VII. The Greek Theogony

Chapter VIII. The Milesian School

PART FOUR
THE NEW REPUBLICS

Chapter IX. The Economic Basis

PART FIVE

PURE REASON

INTRODUCTION

IN the introduction to Volume I a brief sketch was given of the evolution of class society in Mesopotamia, Egypt, and the eastern Mediterranean, to serve as a background to the study of the prehistoric Ægean. Since then there has been published in *Vestnik drevnei istorii* a proposed scheme for the periodisation of ancient history as part of a draft plan for a new history of the world.[1] In introducing the present volume, I shall reproduce part of this scheme in an abridged form and draw attention to some points which seem to me to need further consideration.

The relevant part of the scheme may be summarised as follows.

That section of the *World History* which deals with primitive communism must reveal the basic features of its development, common to all peoples. Its basis in the social ownership of the means of production must be clearly brought out, and at the same time it is necessary to explain the limitations inherent in this system, which distinguish it from socialist ownership. These limitations are due to the low level of development of the productive forces and to the small size and isolation of the primitive communes. The slow but steady development of the productive forces must be analysed in such a way as to explain the advance from the primitive commune of the earlier type to the tribal commune.

In the chalcolithic period, in which tools were made from copper as well as stone, we find great advances in the valleys of the Nile, Euphrates and Tigris, and Indus. Here we may observe, for the first time, the dissolution of primitive communism, the growth of slavery and of the class struggle, and the formation of the state.

Two stages may be distinguished in the growth of slave society—early and mature. In the early stage, slavery is patriarchal and directed towards the satisfaction of immediate needs rather than the production of commodities. Trade is poorly developed. There is widespread enslavement for debt,

[1] VDI, 1952, 1.

and a considerable class of small producers, consisting mainly of peasants not yet driven from the land. Property is of the oriental type. The state takes the characteristic form of the despotism, and cultural development is slow. In the mature stage, thanks to further developments in the productive forces, slavery is directed towards commodity production, and in the main spheres of production free labour is replaced by slave labour. The small producers are impoverished, and, with the further growth of trade, money relations, and private property, the number of privately owned slaves increases and predominates over the other categories. The characteristic form of state is the *pólis*, culminating in slave-owning democracy. Cultural development is rapid, leading to knowledge in the true sense of the word.

In distinguishing these two stages we must not treat them as though they were sharply separated from one another. On the contrary, mature slave society coexisted with early slave society, just as early slave society coexisted with primitive communism, which continued to prevail in many adjacent areas. Nor must we expect to find them with all the above-mentioned characteristics developed everywhere to the same degree. As typical examples we may cite, for the early stage, Egypt and Mesopotamia, and, for the mature stage, Athens after Solon.

Reviewing the whole history of slave society, we may distinguish six periods.

In the first period (thirtieth–sixteenth centuries B.C.) the slave states of Egypt, Mesopotamia, and the Indus came into being. In China of this period, that is, prior to the Yin or Shang Dynasty, we observe the dissolution of primitive communism, but not yet the rise of a slave state. In the latter part of this period the rise of the Middle Kingdom in Egypt and of the Amorite kingdoms in Mesopotamia coincided with the flowering of Egyptian and Babylonian culture. Through contact with these centres primitive tribes in northern Mesopotamia, Syria, and Cappadocia were drawn into the orbit of slave society, and forms of class society began to develop in Palestine, Phœnicia, and the Ægean. In the meantime the use of metals was transmitted to the primitive peoples of the Eurasian steppes. There it led, not to the formation of slave society, but to the rapid consolidation of ethnic groups of nomadic pastoral tribes. In the early part of the period Indo-European nomads appeared in Hither Asia (the Hittites), and later they penetrated as far as India (the Aryans).

In the middle of the second millennium the slave states of the Near East entered upon a crisis, which was brought about, on the one hand, by the growth of debt slavery and the intensified exploitation of the village communes, and, on the other, by the surrounding tribes, which, having had their primitive communal relations dissolved through contact with these centres, were driven to invade them in quest of plunder.

The second period (sixteenth–seventh centuries B.C.) is marked by the territorial expansion of early slave society, effected partly by the rise of military states administering extensive areas (Assyria, Mitanni, the Hittite kingdom) and partly by the formation of new slave-owning communities in the eastern Mediterranean. Early slave society reached its zenith in Crete (Late Minoan) and began to develop on the Greek mainland (Mycenæ). Later, the Dorians and other Hellenic tribes from the north-west, set in motion by the dissolution of their primitive communal relations, overran Greece and Crete and put an end to Mycenean civilisation. This is the beginning of Greek history proper, marked by the decay of primitive communism, the growth of slavery and of inequalities of property, and the rise of the *pólis*. In the Far East, the Shang Dynasty was overthrown during the twelfth century by the Chou tribes, and succeeded by the Chou Dynasty, under which an early slave-owning state developed in the Yellow River basin. After the eighth century, weakened by the rise of a slave-owning nobility, the Chou empire broke up into a number of independent states (the Warring States).

In the third period (seventh–fourth centuries B.C.) we see in Greece the emergence of mature slave society, based on a rapid development of the productive forces, leading to the growth of trade and the invention of the coinage. The introduction of the coinage resulted at first in a sharp increase of debt slavery, but in the most advanced communities this was soon done away with (Solon's laws) and replaced by the enslavement of barbarians. This was necessary for the growth of chattel slavery; for, so long as freemen were liable to be enslaved, there was a danger that they might combine with the slaves against the exploiting class. Slave society established itself at several centres in Italy, North Africa, and Spain, but, except in the Greek colonies, mainly in its early form. In Mesopotamia and Egypt some features of mature slave society had already appeared at the time of the Persian conquest, but on the whole the early stage of slave-owning relations was maintained under Persian rule.

In Greece, with the further development of mature slave society, the small producers were ruined, and there began a concentration of landownership. Many citizens lost their land, and, having no opportunity of acquiring slaves, sank to the level of lumpen-proletariat. In this way, being no longer a civil community of slave-owning landholders, the political form represented by the *pólis* ceased to correspond to the social content. The result was that, after a period of destructive civil strife, the Greek city-states were subjugated by the Macedonians, who, just because of their backwardness, had preserved a free and prosperous peasantry.

The draft plan goes on to deal with the three remaining periods of ancient history, which lie beyond the scope of the present volume.

The scheme proposed in the plan is correct in the main, but is open to criticism at certain points, of which the most important are the following.

The development of commodity production in the early slave states was greater than the draft plan allows. In many of these states the actual volume of goods produced for export was considerable, especially in Babylonia; but this trade remained firmly in the hands of the ruling class, which was in control of irrigation. It was based on the surplus surrendered as tribute by the peasants, and both they and the merchants, who acted as middlemen, remained dependent on the ruling class of landowners. The class structure of these states was a barrier to the further development of commodity production and of money relations.

Further, the plan does not deal with iron-working. It was the introduction of iron which, by raising the productivity of the small producers, both farmers and artisans, enabled them to become independent. Commodity production developed to the point at which the invention of coined money became possible and necessary, and, thus assisted, it expanded more rapidly than ever, penetrating all ranks of society and dissolving all that remained of the old communal relations. Among the most profitable of the new commodities were human beings, and hence at this stage patriarchal slavery, in which the slave is a use-value, is superseded by chattel slavery, in which the slave is an exchange value, and slavery begins to 'seize on production in earnest'.

Finally, the forms assumed by the class struggle during the transition from early to mature slave society are not clearly defined; and at Athens the emergence of mature slave society should be placed, not in the time of Solon, but more than half a century later, in the time of Kleisthenes; or rather, the whole course of events from Solon to Kleisthenes must be regarded as a single process, in which gradual changes in the relations of production culminated in a political revolution. This is clear from Engels's account of the rise of the Athenian state, which gives a more coherent picture of the process than is contained in the draft plan. The main points are as follows.

In the first place, the key to the whole process is the growth of commodity production:

The rise of private property in herds and articles of luxury led to exchange between individuals, to the transformation of products into *commodities*. And here lie the seeds of the whole subsequent upheaval. When the producers no longer directly consumed their product themselves, but let it pass out of their hands in the act of exchange, they lost control of it. They no longer knew what became of it; the possibility existed that one day it would be used against the producer to exploit and oppress him. For this reason no society can permanently retain the mastery of its own production and the control over the social effects of its process of production unless it abolishes exchange between individuals.

The Athenians were soon to learn how rapidly the product asserts its mastery over the producer when once exchange between individuals has begun and products have been transformed into commodities. With the coming of commodity production, individuals began to cultivate the soil on their own account, which soon led to individual ownership of land. Money followed, the general commodity with which all others were exchangeable.[2]

Engels goes on to describe the reforms of Solon. Their effect was to weaken, but not to destroy, the old gentile constitution. Its final destruction was only brought about at the end of the century through the further development of commodity production, the further growth of slavery, and the rise of an independent merchant class:

> Movable property, wealth in the form of money, slaves and ships, conti-nually increased, but it was no longer merely a means to the acquisition of landed property, as in the old slow days; it had become an end in itself. On the one hand, the old power of the aristocracy had now to contend with successful competition from the new class of rich industrialists and mer-chants; on the other hand, the ground was also cut away from beneath the last remains of the old gentile constitution. . . . Meanwhile, the fight went on between the parties. The nobility tried to win back their former privileges, and for a moment regained the upper hand, until the revolution of Kleisthenes (509 B.C.) overthrew them finally, and with them also the last remnants of the gentile constitution.[3]

And then, after describing the 'revolution of Kleisthenes':

> Now complete in its main features, the state was perfectly adapted to the new social conditions of the Athenians, as is shown by the rapid growth of wealth, commerce and industry. The class opposition on which the social and political institutions rested was no longer that of nobility and common-people, but of slaves and freemen, of protected persons and citizens.[4]

This is the process which underlies the history of Greek philosophy. Anaximander reveals the same class outlook as Solon; Pythagoras expresses the outlook of 'the new class of rich industrialists and merchants' during the brief period in which the class conflict between nobility and common-people had been apparently resolved; Herakleitos, the outlook of the old nobility as modified by the new conditions; and in the work of their successors, from Parmenides onwards, we can trace the further development of the class struggle among the citizens as determined by the fundamental antagonism between freemen and slaves.

[2] Engels OF 124.   [3] Ib. 129.   [4] Ib. 132.

Part One

THE TRIBAL WORLD

Man is the helper and interpreter of Nature. He can only act and understand in so far as by working upon her or observing her he has come to perceive her order. Beyond this he has neither knowledge nor power.

BACON

I
SPEECH AND THOUGHT

1. *Man and the Animals*

'THE first premiss of all human history is of course the existence of living human individuals. Thus, the first fact to be established is the physical organisation of these individuals and their consequent relation to the rest of nature.' So Marx and Engels wrote in their first full statement of Marxism[1]. 'Thought and consciousness', wrote Engels many years later, 'are products of the human brain.'[2] The truth of these statements is so plain that it might almost seem to be obvious; yet philosophers have piled tome upon tome in order to deny, distort, or obscure it.

In one of his dialogues Plato puts into the mouth of Protagoras a fable about the origin of man.[3] Living creatures were made by the gods out of earth and fire. After they had been created, Prometheus and his brother Epimetheus bestowed on them their appropriate faculties, giving them hoofs or wings or underground dwellings, so that each species might have the means of self-defence; wrapping them in furs and skins for shelter against the cold; ordaining that some should be the natural prey of others and at the same time ensuring their survival by making them exceptionally prolific. All this was done by Epimetheus under his brother's direction, but at the end of his task he found that he had inadvertently bestowed all the available faculties on the animals, leaving none for man. In order to save man from extinction Prometheus gave him fire.

This is a myth. The question, what a myth is, will arise later. No myth is true in the form in which it is presented, but many myths contain truth. In the present instance, man did not receive fire as a gift from Prometheus or any other god. He discovered it for himself by his own wits. The Greeks themselves recognised this, for they interpreted the figure of Prometheus as a symbol of human intelligence. Moreover, they recognised that intelligence was inseparable from another faculty, also distinctively human, the faculty of speech. Man

[1] Marx-Engels GI 7.   [2] Engels AD 44.   [3] Pl. *Prt.* 320–2.

differs from the animals in possessing *lógòs*, which is reason, understanding, and also speech. It is this that has made him the lord of creation, the master of nature, swifter than the eagle and stronger than the lion. How did he get it? The answer given in the myth is that he got it because he was deficient in those bodily developments, offensive and defensive, possessed by other animals. Lacking these, he was faced with extinction, and so forced to develop as he did. This, the kernel of the myth, is a scientific truth.

In general, the various forms of animal life have evolved over an immense period of time by natural selection, through which they have become differentiated by adapting themselves, with varying degrees of success, to different environments and to successive changes of environment. Not only do climatic conditions differ in different parts of the earth, but in all parts they have undergone a long series of more or less profound changes. No species of animal can ever be perfectly adapted to its environment, because the environment changes; and a species which has adapted itself exceptionally well to the conditions of a given period may later be incapacitated for that very reason, while other species, less highly specialised, increase and multiply.

Man is one of the primates, the highest order of animals, which includes, besides him, the apes and monkeys.[4] Other mammalian orders are the carnivora, including the dog and cat, and the ungulates, including the horse and cattle. The earliest mammals lived in trees. From this ancestral stock the ungulates and carnivora branched off by adapting themselves in various ways to living on the ground. Losing the finer articulation of their limbs, they learnt to stand firmly and move rapidly on all fours, and they developed various offensive and defensive organs, such as horns, hoofs, spines, tusks, teeth for chewing grass or for tearing flesh, and long snouts for smelling at a distance. Meanwhile another group, ancestors of the primates, remained in the trees and so preserved on the whole the primitive mammalian structure. Their conditions of life required good eyesight rather than a keen scent, agility and cunning rather than speed and strength, and their diet of fruit and leaves made no great demands on the teeth. The snout dwindled,

4 Le Gros Clark 7–31.

while the eyes developed full stereoscopic vision. The claws shrank into flattened nails imbedded in sensitive pads; the digits became more flexible, with the thumb and big toe moving in opposition to the others, so that they could grasp and handle small objects; and finally, in keeping with these developments, the brain became larger and more complex. Since the function of the brain is to control the other bodily organs in their interaction with the external world, it is the one organ whose growth is free from the risks of over-specialisation. Thus, the primates evolved in such a way as to become more, not less, adaptable.

Man's nearest living relatives are the anthropoid apes. From these he differs in his upright gait and posture and his larger brain. In certain features he is actually more primitive than they. Their long arms, short legs, small hindquarters, and stub-like thumbs are comparatively recent developments due to their habit of swinging from bough to bough.[5] These features are absent from the fossil types discovered in Kenya, from which the large anthropoids of the present day are believed to be descended, and they are absent also from the Australopithecus of South Africa. This is a closely related group of fossil types, which have comparatively small brains and heavy jaws, like the apes, but resemble man not only in the absence of the above-mentioned characters, but also in their upright posture, indicating that they were accustomed to walking on open ground; and this is confirmed by geological evidence, which suggests that their habitat was not densely wooded. Whether they had tools of any sort is still an open question.[6]

Even more important are the remains of Pithecanthropus, especially those discovered near Peking. Here again the brain is comparatively small and the skull has many ape-like features, but the body is of human shape. It has been established that these primitive men dwelt in caves, hunted deer, made tools of quartz, and were well acquainted with the use of fire.[7]

It seems, therefore, that the first step in the differentiation of man from the animals was taken when, in response to some change of environment which has not yet been defined, some of

[5] *Ib.* 33–4.   [6] *Ib.* 63–5.
[7] *Ib.* 80–3; see further Pei Wen-chung NLPM.

the apes abandoned their arboreal habits and began living on the ground. This is what the first ancestors of the carnivora and ungulates had done millions of years before; but, when man followed their example, he did so at a far higher evolutionary level, and hence the consequences of the change were entirely different. He was already, as we have seen, in possession of a better brain than any other animal; and in learning to walk on the ground he committed himself to a way of life in which his only chance of survival lay in further development of his brain. At this point we are reminded of another myth:

> There wanted yet the master-work, the end
> Of all yet done—a creature who, not prone
> And brute as other creatures, but endued
> With sanctity of reason, might erect
> His stature, and upright with front serene
> Govern the rest, self-knowing. . . .[8]

2. Hand and Brain

The animals are part of nature. The interaction that takes place between them and their environment is, on their part, entirely passive and adaptive. In this respect there is no difference in quality between them and the lower forms of organic life. It is true that they react on nature, as when the flora of some region is transformed by the depredations of grazing herds of cattle; but the animals themselves are no more conscious of what they are doing than the rivers which carve out valleys in their course. Beehives, birds' nests, and beavers' dams are no exception. Such activities are forms of adaptation biologically inherited.

Nevertheless, there are differences of degree between the lowest animals and the highest. They are more or less adaptable. The non-human primates, the highest of the animals, owe their superiority to the fact that, thanks to the relatively large size of the brain, rendered possible by lack of specialisation in the other organs, they became, of all animals, the most adaptable. They were able to evolve in this way because they lived in trees, which provided them with food ready to hand and a refuge from their enemies.

[8] Milton *Paradise Lost* 7. 505.

When man's first ancestors abandoned these natural advantages, there opened a new stage in the evolution of organic life, in which the relation between animal and nature underwent a qualitative change. In respect of teeth, arms, legs, they were utterly defenceless; and, had they been dependent on them, they would certainly have perished. But they were endowed with a brain, which, though smaller than ours, was larger than those of the anthropoid apes; and moreover, thanks to their erect posture, they had a pair of hands, which, guided by the brain, enabled them to adapt nature consciously to their needs instead of merely adapting themselves to natural conditions. Unlike the animals, man is 'self-knowing', and accordingly his relation with nature is not merely passive, but active, a relation between subject and object. As Engels wrote:

In short, the animal merely *uses* external nature, and effects changes in it merely by his presence. Man changes it so as to make it serve his ends; he *masters* it.[9]

Having thrown the whole weight of his body on his feet, man lost the prehensility of his toes, but, with his hands free, his fingers became capable of the most delicate movements. This was a gradual process. The first effect of the new posture was to relieve the pressure on the jaws by transferring from them to the hands such tasks as tearing and crushing food and other objects. Accordingly, the jaws began to contract, thus leaving room for further expansion of the brain; and, as the brain expanded, so it became capable of subjecting the hands to an ever closer control.

It is to this parallel development of hand and brain that we must look for the physiological origin of man's two cardinal characteristics—the use of tools, and speech. The non-human primates can manipulate natural objects, and even use them as missiles; but only man has learnt how to fashion them into tools. Tool-making requires both manual dexterity and intelligence, or rather, as we shall see later, a new sort of intelligence, inseparable from speech. Now, the motor organs of the hand and the speech organs are controlled from two adjacent areas of the brain.[10] For this reason we commonly find what is called a

[9] Engels DN 291.   [10] Winton 432–3.

'spread' from one area to the other. Children learning to write roll the tongue, or even pronounce the words aloud, in the concentrated effort necessary to control the movements of the hand; and, conversely, they tend to gesticulate more freely than adults when they are talking. These are primitive characteristics. Among savages gesticulation is lavish and elaborate. In some languages it is so closely bound up with speech that words are hardly capable of conveying their full meaning without the appropriate gesture.[11] Indeed, we have only to watch ourselves talking to see that the 'spread' has never been completely eliminated. From this we may infer that the manual operations of early man were accompanied to a greater or lesser degree, in proportion to their difficulty, by a reflex action of the vocal organs. Later, in collective labour, these vocal movements were developed consciously as a means of directing the manual operations; and finally they emerged as an independent medium of communication, supplemented by reflex movements of the hands.

3. Consciousness

In the course of evolution the various forms of animal life have adapted themselves structurally and functionally to their changing natural environment; and the highest of them are marked off from the rest by the size and complexity of the brain, which enables them to react to their environment with greater versatility: in a word, they are more intelligent.

To equate intelligence with brain power might seem to be common sense; yet the point needs to be insisted on, or we shall find ourselves ascribing intelligence where it does not belong. Certain species of bees, wasps, ants, and termites live in highly organised communities, which behave with so much apparent intelligence that they have often been compared to human society. On examination, however, we find that their so-called intelligence does not rest on brain power at all, but on an elaborate division of purely physiological functions. In the higher animals these functions, apart from sexual reproduction, are combined in each individual of the species; in these insects they are distributed and co-ordinated in a system of behaviour

[11] Vol. I, p. 446, n. 3; Cassirer I. 130.

which bears a superficial resemblance to social relations, but differs from them in the absence of the activity which we call production.[12] Again, the migration of birds reveals a sense of direction, which, if it were a feat of intelligence, would be superhuman; but it is really nothing more than a crude and wasteful form of physiological adaptation to the environment.

It may be said that the working of the brain is also a physiological process. This is true, but of all such processes it is the most subtle and refined. It is an instrument which enables the members of a species to react to their environment as individuals. Confronted with a difficult situation, different individuals of the species deal with it with greater or less success by using their brains. This can be seen in the behaviour of the higher mammals. Placed in the same situation, any two fowls will behave in exactly the same way; but some dogs are plainly more intelligent than others. Such individual differences are even more conspicuous among the apes. Thanks to their brains, the non-human primates stand, as it were, on the threshold of an active relation to their environment.

But they cannot speak. Speech is peculiar to man. The difference does not lie in the structure of the vocal organs. Most apes and monkeys have a wide phonetic range amply sufficient for a language. They chatter volubly, and their cries are undoubtedly expressive, but only of passive or subjective attitudes, such as hunger, misery, fear, anger, desire, satisfaction. They are incapable of using sounds as words to designate an object.[13] And, since they are unable to express ideas in articulate speech, we may infer that they are unable to form any definite ideas inside their heads. Incapable of speech, they are also incapable of thought.

As the controlling organ of the body, the brain is the mechanism which receives messages from the other organs, such as the eyes and ears and hands, and co-ordinates them in such a way as to initiate the appropriate reaction. Its power of co-ordination depends on the complexity of its structure. Now, if the human brain is compared with an ape's, the greatest expansion is seen to have taken place in the cortex, which controls the higher nervous system, including speech. It should, therefore, be

[12] Wheeler 308, Prenant 27–30.   [13] Köhler 305.

possible to learn something about the physiological mechanism of speech and thought by investigating the behaviour of the higher animals. This study was taken up more than fifty years ago by Pavlov, who conducted a series of observations under controlled conditions. The results, formulated in his theory of conditioned reflexes, have proved the correctness of the Marxist theory of consciousness and more particularly of Lenin's theory of reflection.[14] In bourgeois circles, the importance of his work is acknowledged by physiologists, but our psychologists and philosophers still shut their eyes to it. The subject is too technical to be treated here, except in general terms sufficient to lay a foundation for the ensuing argument.

A reflex, as Pavlov used the term, is a reaction to a stimulus. When food is admitted into our mouths it becomes enveloped in saliva, which lubricates it and so makes it easier to swallow. By a series of systematic observations carried out on dogs he showed that the contact of food with the mouth starts a chain of movements passing along the nerve fibres to the brain and back to the mouth, where it sets in motion the salivary glands.

Reflexes are conditioned or unconditioned. The example just given is unconditioned. An unconditioned reflex is inborn. The conditions requisite for its development are present in every normal individual of the species from birth. A chick does not learn to peck; a child does not learn to suck. These are unconditioned reflexes. They correspond broadly to what psychologists call instincts, which are ill-defined groups of reflexes. The difference is that for the psychologist an instinct is a process whose real nature is unknown, whereas, when a neurologist speaks of a reflex, he refers to a process which can be recorded like any other material phenomenon. The term reflex is the better of the two, because, as Pavlov said, 'it has had from the beginning a purely scientific connotation'.[15]

The saliva can be made to flow without actual contact. As we know, the sight or smell of food is sometimes enough to 'make

[14] Lenin MEC chap. i. In 1894 Lenin wrote: 'You cannot argue about the soul without having explained the psychical processes in particular; here progress must consist in abandoning general theories and philosophical constructions about the nature of the soul, and in being able to put the study of the facts on a scientific footing' (WFPA).
[15] Pavlov ICR 276.

the mouth water'. A reflex of this kind is conditioned. There are certain sights or smells which we have learnt to associate with food. What do we mean by 'learnt'? One of Pavlov's dogs was fed at regular intervals, and, after it had become accustomed to the procedure, a bell was rung just before each feeding-time. It was then found that the salivation took place at the sound of the bell. The stimulus had been transferred to the sound in accordance with the conditions created by the experiment. In the next stage, the bell was sounded, but no food was given, and in time the salivation ceased. It had been inhibited: that is, a contrary stimulus had been set up, corresponding to the new conditions, and the reflex previously established was suppressed. Pavlov showed that such conditioned reflexes did not operate in the absence of a properly functioning cortex. Further research has confirmed his conclusions, and progress has been made in recording the nervous processes involved.

It has just been said that, in contrast to unconditioned reflexes, which are inborn, conditioned reflexes are acquired. The distinction is not absolute. It is valid for the life of the individual, but not for the evolution of the species. The habit of sucking, which characterises the young of mammals, is inborn in the individual, and has been inborn in innumerable generations of individuals, but it was none the less acquired by the first mammalian species in emerging from the premammalian stage. In the course of evolution conditioned reflexes have become unconditioned. It is the acquisition of such reflexes, together with their cumulative effects on the structure of the organism as a whole, under the influence of natural selection, that constitutes the evolutionary process. Lysenko, whose views are in full agreement with Pavlov's, has put the matter thus:

Changes in heredity, the acquisition of new characters and their augmentation and accumulation in successive generations are always determined by the conditions of life of the organism. Heredity changes and increases in complexity through the accumulation of new characters and properties acquired by organisms in successive generations.[16]

The earliest invertebrates made their appearance on earth more than 500 million years ago; the fishes, nearly 400 million;

[16] Lysenko 34.

the reptiles, about 250 million; the mammals, less than 200 million; man, 1 million.[17] We see from these figures that the rate of accumulation of new characters increases as we ascend the evolutionary scale, at the head of which stands man, the lordly parvenu. His appearance is marked by an increase in the rate of evolution so rapid that it can only be explained as the result of a qualitative change. It was Pavlov's crowning achievement to show how this change can be analysed in terms of the actual functioning of the brain.

The aggregate of unconditioned and conditioned reflexes in a given animal constitutes an organic unity of the type which Pavlov called the primary signalling system. This is the system characteristic of the animals, more or less developed according to their evolutionary level. In man it became so complex as to create the basis for reflexes of an entirely new kind, which, operating together with the rest, constitute the secondary signalling system.

One of his pupils conducted the following experiment.[18] An electric current was applied to a child's finger. The child withdrew its finger. The procedure was repeated. After a time, before the current was applied, a bell was rung; and when this had been repeated, the child withdrew its finger at the sound of the bell. Next, instead of ringing the bell, the experimenter uttered the word 'bell'; and the child withdrew its finger instantly at the sound of the word. Then, instead of uttering the word, he showed it written on a card; and the child withdrew its finger at the sight of the word. Finally the child was made to withdraw its finger at the mere thought of a bell. These results have been confirmed by hundreds of experiments conducted in all parts of the world.[19]

This experiment began with an unconditioned reflex—the withdrawal of the finger in response to the stimulus of the electric charge; and it proceeded to a conditioned reflex—the withdrawal of the finger at the sound of the bell. These were passive responses, arising from external associations. But when the child reacted to the sound, sight, and thought of the *word*, the responses were of a different order. In these cases, through the use of the word, the child has generalised actively,

[17] Le Gros Clark 13–6.   [18] Hollitscher TP 23.   [19] McPherson 2.

'electively'. The word is not merely another signal; it is 'a signal of signals'. As Pavlov wrote:

The word is for man just as much a real conditioned response as all the other responses which he has in common with the animals. At the same time this response is more complex than any other, and in that respect cannot be compared, qualitatively or quantitatively, with the conditioned responses of animals. Words, which are bound up with the whole of the mature person, with all the external and internal stimuli which affect the cerebral cortex, signify all these, take their place, and cause the organism to react in the same way as to the original stimuli themselves.[20]

In this way man developed, on the basis of the primary signalling system, common to him and the animals, a secondary signalling system, which we call speech. This differs from the other in that its characteristic stimulus is not an objective natural phenomenon acting on the sense organs but an artificial sound invested socially with a subjective value.

'Speech', said Marx, 'is the direct reality of thought.'[21] It is true that deaf mutes can be taught to think by means of sign language, which serves as a substitute for speech, but only if they have a normally developed cortex. Thought is an internal process which takes place on the basis of the cortical movements established normally by the development of speech, and it is communicated externally by means of speech, or else by writing, which is speech in visible form. Speech and thought both rest on a complex process of synthesis and analysis operating through an intricate network of cortical nerve connections. How complex the process is may be judged from the fact that,

[20] Hollitscher 21. Pavlov's theory of conditioned reflexes was based on Descartes (Pavlov SW 178). It was also anticipated by Spinoza, *Ethics*, Part II, Prop. xviii: 'If the human body has once been affected at the same time by two or more bodies, when the mind afterwards remembers any one of them it will straightway remember the others. . . . And hence we can clearly understand why the mind from the thought of one thing should immediately fall upon the thought of another which has no likeness to the first; e.g. from the thought of the word *pomum* a Roman immediately began to think about fruit, which has no likeness to that articulate sound nor anything in common, save that the body of that man was often affected by these two, that is, the man frequently heard the word *pomum* while looking at the fruit; and thus one passes from the thought of one thing to the thought of another according as his habit arranged the images of things in his body.'
[21] Stalin ML 29.

whereas the latest mechanical calculator contains 23,000 valves, the human cortex contains nearly 15,000,000,000 cells.[22] We are only beginning to understand how the system works, but its general character is becoming clear. As Plekhanov said, 'consciousness is an internal state of matter'.[23]

In the primary signalling system the stimuli are material phenomena which in particular conditions set up conditioned reflexes. Words, too, are physical stimuli, but of a different kind.

In the first place, as we have remarked, the material form of a word is determined, not naturally, but socially. The same is true of its content. The word *bell* signifies, besides the sound of a bell, the shape of a bell and the function of a bell, and not only of this or that bell, but of all bells; it signifies the sum-total of common properties abstracted from the concrete properties of particular bells. Of words, as 'signals of signals', Pavlov wrote:

> They represent an abstraction of reality and admit of generalisation, which is our compound, specifically human, higher form of thought, which first makes possible common human experience and then science itself, the instrument for perfecting human orientation in the environment and in itself.[24]

In the second place, as this observation of Pavlov's implies, the word serves to organise our sense impressions, not only in relation to previous impressions of the same kind, but in relation to the collective experience of society accumulated and transmitted through speech. The human consciousness is far more than a simple relation between the individual and his natural environment; it is, even in its simplest forms, a social product—the relation between society and its environment as reflected in the individual. It has been observed that, when a small child is drawing or painting an object, it tends to omit those parts of it which it cannot name; and similarly, persons born blind and subsequently cured find difficulty at first in distinguishing even the most obvious shapes and colours.[25] In both cases certain features are missed because they have not yet acquired for the observer a social value.

[22] Young 37.
[23] Lenin MEC 151.
[24] Hollitscher 23.
[25] Young 91.

As Marx wrote: 'It is not the consciousness of men that determines their being, but on the contrary it is their social being that determines their consciousness.'[26]

4. Co-operation

Another characteristic of the higher animals, connected with the expansion of the brain, is the lengthening of the period of immaturity.[27] Most of the ungulates grow very fast. A young hartebest can follow its mother a few hours after birth, a young elephant when it is two days old. The carnivora, on the other hand, are born helpless and remain dependent for several months. Among the primates, the gibbon remains clinging to its mother's body for seven months; the orang-utang spends the first month on its back, then slowly learns to walk, becomes independent at three years, and full-grown at ten or eleven. The human baby takes about a month to learn how to focus the eyes, and can seldom walk before the end of the first year.

Not only do the primates grow more slowly than the lower mammals, but of all their bodily organs the slowest in growth is the brain.[28] In man this disparity is even greater. His brain puts on weight after birth more rapidly and for a longer time than the rest of the body; and the increase is mainly due to the growth of a network of fibres connecting the cells of the cortex, especially the two areas which control, first, the hands and fingers, and, second, the tongue and lips. These areas are very large in proportion to the other motor areas, and much larger than the corresponding areas in the non-human primates. It is the communications established by these fibres in the cortex that constitute the signalling system, and it is during the period of immaturity, when they are being formed, that the most vital and enduring of the conditioned reflexes are established. Thus, the human organism has evolved in such a way as to enjoy exceptional opportunities for the accumulation and elaboration of conditioned reflexes. We have already remarked that, apart from his brain, early man was almost destitute of bodily defences, and to this we must now add the exceptionally prolonged period during which the adults were occupied in

[26] Marx CCPE.   [27] Briffault I. 96–110.   [28] *Ib.* I. 100–3.

rearing helpless infants. It seems probable that this condition both necessitated and assisted the development of collective labour, involving tools and speech.

The formation of conditioned reflexes is, as we have seen, a description in physiological terms of what we call learning. A young animal learns by imitation. It clings to its mother, follows its mother, copies its mother. It acquires by this means many habits which are commonly supposed to be hereditary. For example, a puppy brought up on milk does not salivate when meat is offered to it for the first time.[29] If puppies normally eat meat, it is because they have learnt to do so from their mothers. Among animals the capacity to learn is limited, for the most part, to the period of immaturity. When they have grown up, they are much slower to learn even simple things, and many things which they could have learnt earlier are beyond them.

To this rule there is one important exception. Monkeys are proverbially imitative. The extent to which the animals are capable of conscious imitation has been much discussed. After a careful investigation Chalmers Mitchell concluded:

Notwithstanding the innumerable anecdotes about the intelligence of other animals, and the great difficulty of describing or even thinking over one's personal experience in taming and training animals without slipping into language that implies conscious imitation, I do not think there is any real evidence of it outside the group of monkeys.[30]

The development of this faculty among the primates was no doubt assisted by their habit of living together in bands, composed usually of the females and their offspring.

Conscious imitation is the first step towards co-operation, as can be seen in children. After imitating the action of an adult for its own sake, as though it were an end in itself, the child comprehends in time the purpose of the action, modifies its imitation accordingly, and so learns to co-operate. It might be supposed, therefore, that, after the faculty of conscious imitation had been acquired, co-operation would follow almost as a matter of course. But this is not the case. Apes and monkeys are great mimics, but, except casually and ineffectually, they do not co-operate.[31]

[29] Young 115.   [30] Mitchell 253.   [31] Köhler 169.

From this we may infer that the development of co-operation was closely connected with those two faculties which we have already recognised as distinctively human—the use of tools, and speech. Without co-operation there could have been no speech, which is its medium. What, then, was the function of co-operation? The answer is, quite simply, that many brains are better than one. Having advanced so far in developing the brain as to adopt the upright posture, our ape-like ancestors entered on a new stage, in which their only prospect of survival lay exclusively in the further development of that organ. They had to go forward or perish; and, as the archæological record shows, many breeds of them did perish. They were driven by the struggle for existence to expand their brain power beyond its natural limits. They organised it collectively. This gave them a new weapon. Instead of merely changing themselves so as to conform to their environment, they began slowly but surely to change their environment according to their needs by *producing* their means of subsistence. Thus, the three characteristics we have distinguished—tools, speech, co-operation—are parts of a single process, the labour of production. This process is distinctively human, and its organising unit is society.

5. *The Sentence*

'First came labour; after it, and then side by side with it, articulate speech.' So Engels.[32] In Volume I (XIV, 2) it was shown that the human sense of rhythm is derived through the labour song from the labour cry, which is in its simplest form a twofold signal co-ordinating the muscular efforts of a group of labourers. The question to be considered now is whether the elements of the labour process can be discovered in the structure of articulate speech.

It is characteristic of production, as of other forms of co-operation, that the actions of the individual labourers are integrated as parts of a whole, the labour process, which, accordingly, can only be carried out if the labourers maintain the appropriate relations with one another. This is true, even where a particular process may be performed by a single labourer; for

[32] Engels DN 284.

in such cases the requisite degree of skill has only been reached
by division of labour, which is a wider form of co-operation.
Thus, in production, man's action on nature is not simple and
direct but mediated through his relations with his fellow
labourers. The principle has been explained by Marx:

> In production men act not only on nature but on one another. They
> produce only by co-operating in a certain way and mutually exchanging their
> activities. In order to produce, they enter into definite connections and
> relations with one another, and it is only within these social connections and
> relations that their action on nature, production, takes place.[33]

These relations are maintained by means of the secondary
signalling system, which as we have observed, differs from the
primary signalling system precisely in this, that the interaction
between the individual organism and the natural environment
is mediated through social relations.

A further characteristic of production is the use of tools. To
quote again from Marx:

> An instrument of labour is a thing, or a complex of things, which the
> labourer interposes between himself and the subject of his labour, and which
> serves as the conductor of his activity. He makes use of the mechanical,
> physical and chemical properties of some substances in order to make other
> substances subservient to his aims.[34]

A tool is a natural object which man has taken and shaped
deliberately to be operated by his hands as an artificial hand for
the more effective control of his environment:

> Thus, nature becomes one of the organs of his activity, one that he annexes
> to his own bodily organs, adding stature to himself in spite of the Bible.

In production, therefore, not only is the labour process as a
whole a complex of social relations, mediated by speech, but
each labourer's part in it, his individual action on nature, is
also indirect, being mediated by instruments whose use and
manufacture presuppose a body of knowledge such as could only
have been accumulated by means of social relations.

Accordingly, we may say that there exists between speech and
production an intrinsic connection, pointing to their common
origin in the moment at which man's relation to nature became

[33] Marx WLC (SW 1. 264).   [34] Marx C 1. 158.

social, and so ceased to be merely natural. Production made man human.

Marx identified three elements in the labour process: first, work, the personal activity of the labourer; secondly, the subject of labour, which consists in its simplest form of the earth and its natural products; and thirdly, the instruments of labour.[35] Let us consider what relation, if any, can be traced between this process and the structure of the simple sentence.

The languages of the world are so bewildering in their diversity that some philologists have despaired of finding the clue to the origin of speech. The explanation is that the essential constituents of speech were formed long before the oldest of our linguistic records. Man is about a million years old; the earliest written documents are less than six thousand years old, and the great majority of languages are known to us over only a fraction of that period. All the linguistic changes that we can trace have arisen from changes in social relations, not from the origin of society itself. For light on the origin of speech we must concentrate our attention on those basic features which all languages have in common.

The principles of grammar have been the subject of prolonged discussion among philologists, much of it vitiated by a tendency to invest the principles peculiar to a particular language, or group of languages, usually the philologist's own, with an absolute validity. In particular, many European scholars of the last century treated the structure of Greek and Latin as a universal ideal or norm, by which other languages were measured and judged to be immature or decadent. In recent years, however, thanks to the development of comparative linguistics, much has been done to clear the ground.

Of the eight parts of speech distinguished by the classical grammarians, only two are now regarded as fundamental, the noun and the verb.[36] Apart from them, there are only interjections and morphemes, which, strictly speaking, are not words at all. Let us begin with these.

Interjections are characterised by the fact that they have no place in the morphological or syntactical structure of the language, and some of them stand outside the phonetic system

[35] *Ib.* I. 157.   [36] Vendryes 115–24.

as well. They are inarticulate cries. Those which are purely affective, such as cries of pain, are indistinguishable in principle from animal cries. They belong to the primary signalling system. They are the raw material from which speech was made.

Many of them have an active function, like 'Ssh!' used as a call for silence; and, just as 'Ssh!' may be replaced by a word, such as 'Quiet!' or 'Silence!', so it has been fashioned into a word, *hush*. Other words of similar origin are *boo, pop, tick, quack, tick-tock, quack-quack, pooh-pooh, ding-dong, see-saw*, etc.

As these examples show, many interjections are onòmatopœic, that is, imitated from natural sounds, and many are reduplicated. Further, they are specially common in baby talk and in the languages of primitive peoples. This is not an accident. Just as the growth of the embryo reveals a sequence corresponding to successive phases in the evolution of the species, so baby talk reproduces certain features of primitive speech.[37]

The early philologists were right in recognising onomatopœia as a prolific source of word material, but, for the most part, they failed to see that the medium through which this material was fashioned into speech was labour. Reduplication, which we have just noted as characteristic of interjections, is deeply imbedded in the structure of the Indo-European languages, and indeed of all languages,[38] and it has an elementary function. For the child, a disyllable composed of two identical or similar sounds is easier to pronounce and to remember than a mono-syllable, because it is rhythmical; and, as we have seen, the human sense of rhythm can be traced back to the labour cry, which in its typical form is disyllabic. Standing as it does on the fringes of articulate speech, the interjection has preserved two features which point back to the origin of speech.

Let us now turn to the morpheme. If the interjection has a purely concrete function, not grammatical at all, the morpheme is purely abstract, a mere grammatical instrument. In the expression 'John's father' the suffix -*s* is a morpheme, marking the syntactical relation. So, in 'father of John', is the element *of*. This *of* is conventionally treated as a word; yet it serves the same function as the suffix and is equally devoid of concrete meaning. They are both morphemes.

[37] Le Gros Clark 7, Engels DN 291.   [38] Cassirer 1. 143–4.

The English *I am*, Latin *sum*, Greek *eimi*, have a common ending *-m* or *-mi*. In English it is a meaningless vestige, but in Latin and Greek it was still active as a morpheme marking the first person singular of the verb; and it was originally identical with the pronoun *me*. It is probable that most morphemes originated in this way, that is, in the agglutination and absorption of independent words.[39] Such formations are common in all languages, and can still be followed in our own: *like a man, man-like, manly*. The process is very clear in Chinese, in which most of the morphemes, or 'empty words' as they are called, are also used as 'full words'. For example, the word *kei* serves, according to the context, either as a verb, the English *give*, or as a morpheme, the English *to* or *for*. The 'full word' is converted into a morpheme by being 'emptied' of its concrete meaning.

It must, however, be noted that morphemes, being derived from full words, belong of necessity to an advanced stage in the development of speech. Sentences can be formed without them, the syntactical relations being indicated by position: 'Sheep eat grass.' Different languages construct their sentences in different ways, but in all the organic unit is the sentence. It is the arrangement of words in sentences that constitutes articulate speech.

There are two types of simple sentence, nominal and verbal. The nominal sentence is composed, in English, of two nouns connected by the copula: 'The stream is full.' The verbal sentence consists of a noun and a verb or of two nouns connected by a verb: 'The stream rises,' 'The stream floods the field.' Even this distinction is partly arbitrary. A slight change, introducing the copula, will bring the last two examples into line with the first: 'The stream is rising,' 'The stream is flooding the field.' In other languages this variation is not possible. In some, however, such as Greek, the nominal sentence, in its simplest form, has no copula: 'Full the stream.' This shows that the copula is not indispensable; it is only a morpheme.[40] If we want to reduce these sentences to their essential elements, we must get rid of all the morphemes: 'Stream full,' 'Stream rise,' 'Stream flood field.' These expressions are quite

[39] Vendryes 170.   [40] *Ib.* 22.

intelligible in English, and they represent the normal form of the simple sentence in many languages, such as Chinese.

At this point, with the removal of the morphemes, even the distinction between noun and verb begins to disappear. In languages with few inflections or none, such as English and Chinese, nouns may be used as verbs and verbs as nouns: 'to stream past', 'paid in full', 'to get a rise', 'in flood', 'they field well'.[41] Even in languages so highly inflected as Latin and Greek, the vocative singular of the noun and the imperative singular of the verb are uninflected, that is, have no morphemes. Why did these two forms remain in this rudimentary condition? Their form is rudimentary because their function is rudimentary. They are, in origin, interjections, the one a call to attention, the other a call to action.

We are left with a sentence of two terms, connected either by simple juxtaposition or by a third term; and these two types of sentence correspond to the two types of musical form, binary and ternary (Vol. I, pp. 450–1). The distinction between the verbal sentence and the nominal sentence is reduced to this, that in the former our attention is concentrated on the action or process, in the latter on the state or result. The idea of change is inherent in both, but in the second it is implied rather than expressed.

It is true, of course, that we habitually use simple sentences from which all idea of change is excluded: 'The earth is round.' But these are abstract notions, and therefore not primitive. There is ample evidence to show that historically the abstract has been preceded by the concrete, which, moreover, is constantly reasserting itself. Even in our own language, such abstract ideas as rest, dependence, expectation, obedience, virtue, wicked, heavy, round, bear on the face of them the marks of their concrete origin: to rest is to resist movement, to depend is to hang on, to expect is to watch out for, to obey is to listen to, virtue is manliness, wicked is bewitched, heavy is hard to lift, round is wheel-like. In the Tasmanian languages there were no words for such simple qualities as round and hard, these ideas being conveyed by reference to

[41] In the Arunta language there is no distinction between noun and verb: Sommerfelt 109.

concrete objects—'like the moon', 'like a stone'—accompanied by appropriate gestures.[42]

We are now at the conclusion of our argument. In the first place, production is co-operation in the use of tools, which serve as conductors, transmitting the labourers' activity to the subject of their labour:

> In the labour process, man's activity, with the help of the instruments of production, effects an alteration, designed from the commencement, in the material worked upon. The process disappears in the product; the latter is a use-value, nature's material adapted by a change of form to the wants of man. Labour has incorporated itself with its subject: the former is materialised, the latter is transformed.[43]

In the second place, just as the instruments of production are interposed between the labourer and the subject of his labour as conductors of his activity, so speech is interposed between him and his fellow labourers as a medium of communication effecting those mutual exchanges of activity without which production cannot take place. Consequently, it may be suggested that, as a reflection of the external world acquired through social production, and as the organic unit of articulate speech, the sentence, in its elementary forms of two terms, the one being incorporated in the other, or of three terms, the third mediating the action of the first upon the second, embodies in its structure the three elements of the labour process—the personal activity of the labourer, the subject of his labour, and its instruments.

[42] Smyth 2. 413, cf. Dawson l–lxvii.   [43] Marx C 1. 160.

II
TRIBAL COSMOLOGY

1. *Natural and Social Relations*

IN the present chapter we have to consider the social relations into which men entered with one another in the initial stages of production.

Thought and speech constitute the distinctive activities of the secondary signalling system, which evolved out of the primary signalling system, common to man and the animals. One of the conditions for this development was, as we have seen, the protraction of the period of immaturity, during which the individual remained susceptible to the formation of conditioned reflexes. This may be expressed in non-physiological language by saying that the faculty of conscious imitation, characteristic of the primates, was developed in man so as to form the basis for a new kind of relationship, which was not natural but social, being mediated by speech.

There are two types of natural relations, sexual and parental, and among the higher animals they tend to be mutually exclusive. The female is averse to sexual intercourse during gestation and lactation, and the male plays little or no part in feeding and tending the young. This is true of the mammals in general, including the apes, and, if it was also true of man's ape-like ancestors, it follows that the advance from imitation to co-operation was effected by the development of parental relations, and, more particularly, of the relations between mothers and their offspring. It may be suggested, therefore, that one condition for the development of production was the extension and transformation of those habits of co-operation, based on imitation, which characterised the relations between mothers and offspring in the transition from ape to man. In man the maternal relation, which among the apes is replaced at maturity by the sexual, was gradually prolonged until it comprehended all members of the group in a non-sexual, social relationship. In this way they acquired a sense of kinship, a consciousness of mutual obligations and attachments springing from the natural affinity between a mother and her children. Thus, there is real truth in the Khasi proverb, 'From the woman sprang the clan' (Vol. I, p. 153).

The earliest divisions of labour had, as Marx observed, a physiological foundation, being based on sex and age.[1] The women were less mobile than the men; the infants and the aged were unable to fend for themselves. The invention of the spear opened up a new form of activity, hunting, which fell naturally to the men, who wandered far afield in quest of game, while the women continued the work of food-gathering in the vicinity of the settlement. With this division of labour are probably to be associated the first steps in the regulation of sexual relations.

At this stage the clan was necessarily endogamous. Brothers and sisters mated freely. If, however, we ask whether parents mated with their offspring, the answer must be, in accordance with the conditions we have postulated, that they did not; for, had there been free intercourse between the women of one generation and the men of the next, there would have been no scope for the development of non-sexual co-operation. We must suppose, therefore, that intercourse was restricted to men and women of the same generation. This agrees with our analysis of the classificatory system of relationship, which in its simplest and most primitive form served to distinguish between successive generations and between the two sexes of the speaker's generation (Vol. I, pp. 61–4).

The next step was the bisection of this original group into two exogamous and intermarrying clans. The men of the one clan mated with the women of the other, and at the same time handed over to them a portion of their produce. This new unit, a tribe of two clans, was more efficient than the old. In order to explain it, however, it is not enough to point to this advantage. We look for some factor within the endogamous clan which impelled it to form an alliance with another clan; in other words, we are forced to suppose that the previous form of organisation had developed an internal contradiction which could be resolved in no other way.

Morgan's solution of the problem, adopted by Engels, rested on the assumption, accepted without question in their day, that

[1] Marx-Engels GI 20; see Vol. I, p. 42, n. 24–5.

continuous inbreeding results in physical deterioration of the species. This assumption is now known to be incorrect. But, while endogamy cannot have been physically injurious, it may still have been socially injurious; and, if we follow the line of reasoning by which we have explained the emergence of social relations out of natural relations, that is the conclusion to which it leads. The development of co-operation necessitated the banning of sexual intercourse between successive generations. Social relations grew by negating sexual relations, production by negating reproduction; yet clearly, unless this negation was itself negated, the clan was doomed to perish. The contradiction inherent in its development could be resolved on one condition only, that it ceased to be a self-sufficing reproductive unit. This condition was met by the institution of exogamy. Sexual relations were brought under social control by being excluded from the clan; and at the same time by forging a link between clans, they created the basis for a higher form of social organisation.

The bond between two intermarrying clans, resting as it did on that very relationship which had been excluded from the clan, was the opposite of that which bound together members of the same clan. In the union between the men of the one clan and the women of the other the internal relations of the clan were negated. For this reason such unions did not, and could not, constitute a bond of kinship. The children belonged to their mother's clan, to which the father was a stranger; and he, on his part, had no obligation to them or interest in them. They were not his kin. With the evolution of the tribal system by the subdivision of the two original clans into two exogamous groups of clans, or moieties, this contradiction was extended and elaborated, the two moieties being ranged in opposition to one another. With the development of individual marriage, in place of group marriage, the elements were created for the formation of a new unit, the family, in which the opposition between sexual and economic relations was destined eventually to be overcome; but, since this development could only be brought about by the dissolution of the clan, it was resisted by all those sentiments and traditions that sprang from the solidarity of the clan. The internal unity of each clan was maintained by restricting its external relations to the one relation requisite for its survival; and hence for a long time sexual intercourse, subject only to the negative rule of exogamy, retained a pre-social character. It is true that the men brought food to the women with whom they mated, so that, objectively, the two clans were economically interdependent, and in the higher phases of tribal society these economic relations developed into divisions of labour; but, subjectively, the primary and most persistent relationship between clans was one of antagonism, ranging from friendly rivalry to open hostility. They were united as members of the same tribe, but divided by their internal solidarity. The tribe was a unity of opposites.

This contradiction, inherent in tribal society, was only resolved when the clan broke up into families and the tribe was merged into a larger community divided into antagonistic classes.

2. *Magic and Myth*

The secondary signalling system is a mechanism peculiar to man for regulating the interaction between organism and environment in such a way as to bring the latter under human control; and its starting-point was the formation of a new habit, also peculiar to man, the habit of production, which supplemented and superseded the animal habit of simply appropriating the means of subsistence. Or, to put it the other way round, the development of production necessitated the formation within the group of a new type of relations, neither sexual nor parental but social, mediated by a new system of communication, which formed the basis of speech and thought.

It follows that man's consciousness of the external world was determined from the outset, not by the relations between the individual and his natural environment, but by the relations which he had established with his fellows in the development of production. Man and the animals live in the same world, which impresses itself upon our senses; yet our consciousness of it is infinitely more profound than theirs, because in us the sensory impressions are instantly subjected to a complex process of synthesis and analysis which we owe entirely to our social relations with one another. Only in this way is it possible to explain why the external world should appear so differently to peoples standing at different levels of culture. The surviving Amerindian tribes retain a tribal outlook; yet the American negroes, whose ancestors were kidnapped by European slave-traders from tribal Africa, are to-day as civilised as the rest of the American people. Similarly, the formerly backward peoples of the Soviet Union, the so-called 'aborigines' of Siberia, were till recently a subject of special interest to ethnologists by reason of their shamanistic practices and beliefs; yet to-day, with opportunities for higher education at the most advanced universities in the world, their sons and daughters are more scientific and humane in their outlook on life than the bourgeois ethnologists who used to study them.[2] Such developments only become intelligible when we understand that man's consciousness of the world around him is a *social* image, a product of society.

Applying these considerations to the origin of man, we may say that the human consciousness was generated within the labour process through the use of tools and speech; and consequently the form in which the earth and its natural products—the subject of his labour—presented themselves to his consciousness was determined by his social relations of production.

In this connection let us return to the subject of primitive magic, discussed in Volume I (Chapter I), where it was shown that the life of savages is dominated by magical practices and beliefs. A magical act is essentially mimetic. The participants mimic the fulfilment of the desired reality, in the belief that by this means nature can be compelled to do what is required of her. Now, it has just been shown that, as a development of that conscious imitation which man inherited from the primates, labour was inherently mimetic; and therefore we may say that magic originated in the labour process as its subjective aspect. So long as labour remained collective, the process was necessarily incomprehensible to the individual participants. As an organic sequence of collective and concerted bodily movements, it presented itself to the individual consciousness as a combined act of will, which achieved in the end of the process its natural and necessary result; and, if it failed, as it often did, its failure

[2] Rytkheu TDT.

seemed to arise from resistance on the part of the subject of labour, which had a will of its own, too strong to be overcome. In these conditions the process assumed the form of a conflict, in which the labourers endeavoured by a mimetic act to impose their will on the subject of their labour. In the course of generations they learnt to recognise the objectivity of certain processes, and hence to distinguish in some degree between the real technique of labour and the illusory technique of magic. With this distinction, the magical rite began to emerge as an independent process, either assuming the form of a rehearsal in preparation for the real task, as in the dances associated with hunting, planting, and other kinds of labour, or else directed more or less consciously to some supernatural end.

As labour emancipated itself from magic, there emerged two further distinctions. Within the labour process, the vocal accompaniment ceased to be an actual part of it and became a traditional incantation conveying the appropriate directions to the labourers (Vol. I, pp. 446–9); and in this way there was gradually accumulated a body of craft lore. Within the magical rite, the vocal part served as a directive commentary on the performance, which, being no longer part of the labour process, was not self-explanatory; and in this way there arose a body of myths. In reality, of course, the distinctions were not drawn so sharply. Labour and magic continued to overlap; craft lore was steeped in mythical beliefs; and the myths bore a recognisable, though remote, relation to the labour of production.

Such, in brief, so far as we can reconstruct them at present, are the basic features of pre-class ideology, belonging to the stage of primitive communism. It is characterised, in contrast to mere animal existence, by a consciousness, in some degree, of the objectivity of the world external to man; but this consciousness is entirely practical. In comparison with the ideology of class society, its most striking feature is its deficiency in the power of abstraction. This limitation is determined by its economic basis. It is the ideology of a society based on common ownership and a very low level of production, which is confined to the production of use values. So long as goods were produced for use, and not for exchange, the aspect in which they presented themselves to the consciousness of the producers was predominantly qualitative and subjective. This is a point of fundamental importance, to which we shall return later. In the meantime, in order to give substance to the observations that have just been made, let us take a concrete example.[3]

The art of pottery was invented by the women as an adjunct to water-carrying and cooking. It started with clay models of gourds and other natural receptacles, assisted by the technique of basket-making. Damp clay is plastic, but hardens as the water is expelled from it. After being cleansed, moistened to the right consistency, and mixed with sand or grit, it was kneaded, built up in concentric rings or hollowed out with the fingers, shaped with a scraper, dried in the sun, and finally baked in an open fire or oven.

This was quite an elaborate technique, involving the control of several chemical processes. But that is not how the potters regarded it. To them it was an act of creation—a women's mystery, at which no man might be present. When one of them finished a model she held it up for the others to admire, and called it a 'created being'. After drying it in the sun, she tapped it with her scraper, and it chimed. This was the creature speaking. When she put it in the oven, she laid food beside it. If it cracked in the firing—as it did, if there was not enough sand or grit in it—the loud clang was the creature's cry as it escaped. This was shown by the fact that a cracked jar never chimed again. Hence, in striking contrast to their usual practice, the women never sang at this work for fear that these creatures they had brought into being might be tempted to respond and so break the pots. To them, therefore, the finished article was something more than a pot. It was a living vessel with a voice and a will of its own. Further, since it was to be used as a receptacle for life-giving water and the fruits of the earth, and perhaps ultimately as a coffin for a child, it became in the minds of its makers a symbol of the womb, of female fertility, of the divine mother, the source of life—Pandora, giver of all things, whom the fire-god fashioned from earth and water and filled with a human voice.[4]

Meanwhile, the wheel was invented. The base on which the

---

[3] Karsten 34–5, 240–1, 251–2; Briffault 1, 466–77.
[4] Hes. *Op.* 60–82.

clay was modelled was made to revolve. To shape a big jar by hand takes several days. On the wheel it can be done in a few minutes. Wheel-made pottery was the first form of mass production. This technical advance prompted changes in the relations of production. Pottery ceased to be a domestic craft, carried on by women, and passed into the hands of male artisans producing for the village or later for the open market.

With these changes the myth of the jar-mother had been cut off at the root; and accordingly it was reinterpreted. Pandora, the woman in the form of a jar, became a woman with a jar, the oppressed woman of patriarchal society, seductive, deceitful, the root of evil, and her jar was filled with curses. The myth became a moral fable, told and re-told throughout the community without any recollection of its origin; and meanwhile, disencumbered of myth and magic, the potters acquired a deeper understanding of the objective processes involved, and so increased their mastery of the craft.

3. The Tribal Order and the Natural Order

In *Capital* Marx wrote:

Co-operation, such as we find it at the dawn of human development, among races that live by the chase, or, say, in the agriculture of Indian communities, is based, on the one hand, on the ownership in common of the means of production, and, on the other hand, on the fact that in those cases the individual has no more torn himself off from the navel-string of his tribe or community than each bee has freed itself from connection with the hive.[5]

Earlier he had written:

The tribal commune, or, if one prefers, the primitive herd, based on community of blood, language, customs, etc., is the first condition for the appropriation of the objective necessities of life and for the reproductive and productive activities of its members as herdsmen, hunters, tillers of the soil, etc. The earth is the great laboratory or arsenal which supplies the working tool as well as the working material; it is the seat, the basis, of the community. At this stage the people regard the earth naïvely as being the property of their community in its process of production and reproduction through their labour. The individual has a share in this property only as a member of the community; it is solely in this capacity that he is owner

[5] Marx C 1. 325.

and occupier of the earth. The actual appropriation through the labour process is effected on the basis of these prior conditions, which are not the product of labour but appear as its underlying natural and divine foundation.[6]

Marx reached these conclusions in the course of his work on political economy. All that has been discovered since about totemism confirms them.

In the stage of lower savagery, not only has the individual failed to tear himself from the navel-string of his tribe, but his tribe is still tied in the same way to mother earth. The individuals who compose a clan are not conscious of their kinship with one another as an objective human relationship, but only as one aspect of a wider relationship, in which they identify themselves with a particular species of animal or plant. It is recorded of an Arunta man, in Southern Australia, that, on being shown a photograph of himself, he said, 'That one is just the same as me; so is a kangaroo.'[7] The kangaroo was his clan totem. His sense of kinship with his fellow clansmen expressed itself in the belief that they were all kangaroos.

In my previous discussion of this subject I argued that the totemic clan originated as a small nomadic band attracted to the breeding ground of a particular species of animal or plant, on which it fed (Vol. I, p. 38). After reconsidering this conclusion I think that it should be re-stated as follows. The original diet of the clan consisted of the various animals and plants obtainable in a particular locality; and, when a permanent relationship was established between two such clans, it was based on exchanges of food, each supplying what the other lacked. In the initial stage, it may be presumed, the clan had identified itself with *all* the species on which it fed, that is to say, it had no consciousness of itself as distinct from the rest of nature; but, with the development of economic and social relations between two clans, each asserted its distinctive identity in opposition to the other by identifying itself with the species which formed its distinctive contribution to the common food supply.

For this conclusion there is positive evidence from the Australian tribes. With the totem of a given clan there are commonly associated a number of sub-totems, corresponding in many cases to divisions within the clan. Thus, in the Arunta

6 Marx FKPV 6–7.   7 Spencer A 80.

tribe, the kangaroo was associated with a certain species of cockatoo, because the two animals were frequently found together, and the frog with the gum-tree, in the holes of which it nested.[8] Similarly, according to a tradition of the Unmatjera tribe, the first ancestors of the beetle-grub clan had lived on beetle-grubs, because at that time there was nothing in the world except beetle-grubs and a little white bird of the species known as *thippa-thippa*. The presence of the little white bird is explained when we find that the natives used it as a guide in their search for grubs.[9] From these and other examples that might be cited, it is evident that the original basis for totemic classification was economic. Different species of animal and plant were grouped together because they were encountered together in the quest for food.

As the pair of clans evolved into a tribe divided into moieties, phratries, clans, and sub-clans, these totemic associations expanded likewise until they formed a cosmological system embracing the whole of the known world (Vol. I, p. 40). It would be a mistake to say that the natural order was modelled on the social order, because that implies some degree of conscious differentiation between the two. Nature and society were one. There was no society apart from nature, and nature was only known to the extent that it had been drawn into the orbit of social relations through the labour of production. Granted the identity of man and totem, every relation between persons was also a relation between things. The tribal order and the natural order were parts of one another. Thus, totemism is the ideology of savagery, the lowest stage in the evolution of human society.

Long before the discovery of totemism, the characteristics of savage ideology were understood by Marx and Engels. In one of their earliest works, after explaining that 'consciousness is from the very beginning a social product and remains so as long as men exist at all', they wrote:

The identity of nature and man appears in such a way that the restricted relation of men to nature determined their restricted relation to one another, and their restricted relation to one another determined their restricted relation to nature, just because nature is as yet hardly modified historically.

[8] Spencer NTCA 352–4, 448.
[9] *Ib.* 324, 449; see further Durkheim FPC 31.

On the other hand, man's consciousness of the necessity of associating with the individuals around him is the beginning of the consciousness that he is living in society at all. This beginning is as animal as social life itself at this stage. It is mere herd consciousness, and at this point man is only distinguished from sheep by the fact that with him consciousness takes the place of instinct or that his instinct is a conscious one.[10]

4. Amerindian Cosmogonies

According to the aborigines of northern Victoria the world was created by the eagle and the crow, who for a long time waged war on one another, but eventually made peace, and the people were divided into the two moieties that bear their names.[11] The tribesmen of the Lower Darling River had another version. Their first ancestor arrived at the river with two wives, named Eagle and Crow. The eagle's sons married the crow's daughters, and their children were called crows; the eagle's daughters married the crow's sons, and their children were called eagles. Later the eagles divided into kangaroos and opossums, the crows into emus and ducks.[12] Other variants of the myth are recorded from other parts of Victoria and from New South Wales.[13]

In parts of New Guinea the clans were divided between the moieties according as their totems were land animals or sea animals. In the first moiety, called the People of the Great Totem, were the clans of the crocodile, cassowary, snake, and dog. In the second, the People of the Little Totem, the clans were the dugong, ray, skate, shark, and turtle. Referring to the latter, a native said, 'They all belong to the water; they are all friends.'[14] The clans of New Britain (Melanesia) were divided into two moieties, named after To Kabinana and To Kovuvuru, the joint creators of the world. To Kabinana created the fertile land, discovered useful inventions, and established all good customs; To Kovuvuru created the barren land and mountains, and to him was attributed everything misshapen or badly made.[15] Of the Melanesians in general Codrington wrote:

In the native view of mankind ... nothing seems more fundamental than the division of the people into two or more classes, which are exogamous and in which descent is counted through the mother. This seems to stand

[10] Marx-Engels GI 19–20. [11] Smyth 1. 423–4. [12] Curr 2. 165–6.
[13] Mathew 19. [14] Frazer TE 2. 5. [15] Ib. 2. 119–20.

foremost as the native looks out upon his fellow men; the knowledge of it forms probably the first social conception which shapes itself in the mind of the young Melanesian of either sex, and it is not too much to say that this division is the foundation on which the fabric of native society is built up.[16]

In America, as in Australia, the tribal camp is a diagram of the tribal system, taking the form of a circle divided into semicircles and quarters according to the divisions of the tribe (Vol. I, pp. 352–3). Thus, with each totemic clan assigned to its proper place, the camp reproduces the world of nature as conceived by the tribe; or rather, it represents the social reality which is reflected ideologically in the tribal conception of the world. In one respect, however, the Amerindian systems mark an advance on the Australian. In Australia, as we have seen, the totemic species are classified subjectively with reference to the concrete conditions in which they are found by man. This is in keeping with what is known of the Australian languages, which are extremely deficient in words denoting abstract ideas. Thus, the Tasmanians had names for the different species of tree, but no word for tree; the natives of Victoria had no words for plant, flower, fish, animal.[17] In America, on the other hand, we find that among many tribes the totems were classified with some recognition of their objective natural affinities. Among the Mohegans, for example, there were three phratries, the Wolf, Turtle, and Turkey; and the clans were grouped as follows: (1) Wolf, Bear, Dog, Opossum; (2) Little Turtle, Mud Turtle, Great Turtle, Yellow Eel; (3) Turkey, Crane, Chicken.[18] Among the Sioux, the Thatada clan was divided into four sub-clans, with the following totems: (1) black bear, grizzly bear, racoon, porcupine; (2) hawks, black birds, dark grey birds, owls; (3) three species of eagle; (4) four species of tortoise.[19] This classification reveals a level of abstraction far superior to the Australian; and in other tribes the level was higher still.

The Winnebago tribe of Wisconsin was divided into two exogamous phratries, Those Above and Those Below.[20] The clan totems of Those Above were birds; the clan totems of Those

[16] Codrington 21.   [17] Smyth 2. 27, 70, 413.
[18] Morgan AS 178.   [19] Frazer TE 3. 95–6.
[20] Frazer T 501–7.

Below were land and sea animals. The leading clan of Those Above was the Thunderbird, which was the clan of peace. In its lodge the tribal chief presided, and disputes were settled. The leading clan of Those Below was the Bear, which was the clan of war. In its lodge offenders were punished and captives put to death. The bipartite division of the tribe was also reflected in the arrangement of the camp, when it was on the war-path, and in the lay-out of its villages. According to tradition the superior status of Those Above had been decided by the animal ancestors of the tribe at a game of lacrosse, in which the birds defeated the other animals; and, when the tribe plays ceremonial lacrosse, the two phratries are always ranged against one another. In this, as among other Sioux and Central Algonquin tribes, the animal world is divided into five classes— empyrean, celestial, terrestrial, aquatic, sub-aquatic. It is believed that this classification, which rests on the same principle as the tribal organisation, was elaborated under the influence of the medicine-men in charge of the tribal festivals.[21]

The Ponkas of the Missouri were a tribe of two moieties, four phratries, and eight clans.[22] The camp was a circle with the entrance usually on the west side. In the first quarter, on the left of the entrance, was the phratry of fire, and behind it, in the second quarter, the phratry of wind; in the third quarter, on the right of the entrance, was the phratry of water, and behind it, in the fourth quarter, the phratry of earth. The clans were associated with the black bear, wild cat, elk, buffalo, snake, and other animals, but not grouped together on any recognisable principle, such as we have just noted among the Mohegans and Winnebagos. In this example we see the ideology of totemism in process of being transformed into a more abstract and objective, though still mythical, outlook on the world.

The Zuñis of New Mexico occupied a single village on the river that bears their name. At the end of the last century they were organised, according to Cushing,[23] in seven village wards or phratries, each containing three clans, except the seventh, which consisted of a single clan, thus:

[21] Radin 185.   [22] Dorsey 228.   [23] Cushing 367-70.

1. North: Crane, Grouse, Yellow-wood.
2. South: Tobacco, Maize, Badger.
3. East: Deer, Antelope, Turkey.
4. West: Bear, Coyote, Spring-herb.
5. Zenith: Sun, Sky, Eagle.
6. Nadir: Water, Rattlesnake, Frog.
7. Centre: Macaw.

The north was associated with wind, winter, and war; the south with fire, summer, and tillage; the east with frost, autumn, and magic; the west with water, spring, and peace; the north was yellow, the south red, the east white, the west blue. There is evidence that in earlier times there had been six phratries, not seven, and still earlier only four. This is confirmed by the Zuñi myth of creation. In the beginning there was a magician, who presented the newly created race of men with two pairs of eggs. One pair was blue, like the sky; the other was red, like the earth. Some men chose the blue eggs, others the red. From the blue eggs was hatched the crow, which flew away to the cold north; from the red eggs was hatched the macaw, which belonged to the warm south. The people were divided accordingly into moieties, which together comprised the whole of space and time, the one the north and winter, the other the south and summer.

The advance to be observed in the last two examples lies in this: that, whereas totemism survives at the clan level, the higher units are organised systematically on the basis of abstract ideas of substance, quality, space, and time. The ideological superstructure has developed to the point of reacting on the social organisation out of which it has grown. We ask how this has come about.

Both these tribes practised garden tillage, and the Zuñis had adopted a sedentary mode of life. In other words, they had advanced beyond savagery to the lower stage of barbarism. Their development of the productive forces left them with a surplus, which rendered possible divisions of labour, including a rudimentary division between manual and mental labour. The economic basis of primitive communism was being undermined. Further, both tribes were dominated by magical fraternities, headed by hereditary, or partly hereditary, chiefs and priests. Admission was by initiation; but, whereas in savage society initiation is open to all, the higher ranks in these fraternities were reserved for those who could pay the necessary fees, and so formed the nucleus of a ruling class. The fraternities conducted elaborate ceremonies, public and private, in connection with hunting, tillage, and public health, and preserved the myths relating to the history of the tribe. As specialists in these magical techniques, which were partly but not wholly illusory, the chiefs and priests, exempt from the labour of production, elaborated, in the form of mystical secrets, those abstract notions of space and time which had grown out of the tribal organisation.

These developments were carried still further by the Aztecs, from whom indeed the more northerly tribes may have borrowed some features through cultural contact.[24] The Aztec tribes overran the ancient agrarian culture of the Mayas, and one of them, the Tenochcas, established in the fifteenth century A.D. a military kingdom in central Mexico, with its capital at Tenochtitlan. The city was divided into four wards, corresponding to the four phratries, each of which contained twenty clans. Each clan elected its own chief, and the clan chiefs constituted the tribal council, from which the officers of state were appointed. These were the war chief and the high priest, both confined to certain families, and four officers in command of the contingents contributed by the phratries to the army, which was highly organised as a public force separate from the people.

The Aztecs had a pictographic script and a solar calendar. The year was divided into eighteen months of twenty days each, making a total of 360 days, with five additional days inserted annually and probably a sixth in each leap year. The month was divided into four pentads, that is, five-day weeks. The first days of the four pentads were named after the rabbit, house, flint, and cane. The years were grouped in 'knots', 'bonds', and eras. Thirteen years made one 'knot'; four 'knots' made one 'bond'; and two 'bonds' made an era. The successive years in each 'knot' were designated by the above-mentioned signs—rabbit, house, flint, and cane—in such a way that a given number coincided

[24] Spinden 34, 213, 234; Vaillant, 97, 115, 121; Bancroft 2. 173.

with a given sign—say, Year 13 flint—only once in fifty-two years.

The four signs had other applications. The rabbit was associated with the north, black, winter, air; the flint with the south, blue, summer, fire; the house with the east, white, autumn, earth; the cane with the west, red, spring, water. In addition to the four cardinal points, there were three others— the centre, zenith, and nadir. The numbers 4, 5, 6, and 7 were magical. Just as the calendar cycle was regulated by the four signs, so there was a cosmic cycle of four epochs, each beginning with the creation of a new world and ending with its destruction.

If, as has been shown, the conception of the four horizontal points is tribal, it is equally clear that the idea of vertical extension, represented by the three additional points, is hierarchical; for the Aztecs divided the universe into three levels—the upper world of the gods, the middle world of the living, and the lower world of the dead. As Vaillant remarks, 'the vertical arrangement of the heavens had more to do with rank and order than with a realisation of natural phenomena'.[25] It will be seen in the following chapters that the fifth point, the centre, at which the horizontal and vertical lines of extension intersect, has a special importance. It represents the chieftaincy or kingship, which serves ostensibly to mediate between gods and men but actually to maintain the illusion of tribal equality after the division of society into classes and the formation of the state.

Finally, this Aztec universe was maintained in being by a perpetual strife of opposites:

An eternal war was fought symbolically between light and darkness, heat and cold, north and south, rising and setting sun. Even the stars were grouped into armies of the east and west. Gladiatorial combats, often to the death, expressed this idea in ritual; and the great warrior orders, the Eagle Knights of Huitzilopochtli and the Ocelot Knights of Tezcatlipoca, likewise reflected the conflict between day and night. This sacred war permeated the ritual and philosophy of the Aztec religion.[26]

From all this we see that among the Aztecs, at the time of the Spanish conquest, the old tribal ideas were being

[25] Vaillant 172.   [26] Ib. 175.

transformed along with the transformation of the old tribal society:

> Division of labour only becomes truly such from the moment when a division of material and mental labour appears. From this moment onwards consciousness *can* really flatter itself that it is something other than consciousness of existing practice, that it is *really* conceiving something without conceiving something real; from now on consciousness is in a position to emancipate itself from the world and proceed to the formation of 'pure' theory, theology, philosophy, ethics, etc.[27]

We must now leave the Amerindians and turn to other peoples which had the opportunity of carrying this emancipation forward to its conclusion.

[27] Marx-Engels GI 20.

Part Two

THE ORIENTAL DESPOTISM

As soon as heaven and earth came into being, there was a distinction between upper and lower; and when the first king established the state, society was divided. Two nobles cannot serve one another, nor can two commoners set one another to work. This is the mathematics of heaven.

HSUN CH'ING

III

CHINA

1. *Greece and China*

If we compare Greek history with Chinese, we see some striking parallels. The written records of both languages date from the second millennium B.C. Both languages have survived with relatively little change down to the present day. Modern Greek differs from Classical Greek, but the Greek people still regards Plato's language as its own. Modern Chinese differs from Classical Chinese, but the Chinese people still regards the language of Confucius as its own. Thus, Greek may be described as the oldest of the European languages, Chinese as the oldest of the Asiatic. This linguistic continuity reflects in both cases a continuity of culture. The history of Greece, from the earliest times down to the present day, is the history of a single people, which has never lost its identity or the remembrance of its past; and the same is true of the Chinese people. Furthermore, both peoples excelled at an exceptionally early period in philosophy and poetry, and both have exercised a lasting influence over neighbouring peoples, in the Far West and in the Far East.

There are also important differences. At the present day, Chinese is spoken by some 600 millions, Greek by only eight millions. This is likely to have far-reaching consequences for the future; but from the standpoint of their past history the main difference lies in the circumstances in which the two cultures took shape. The technical basis of Greek civilisation, including the use of metals, the calendar, and the script, was not created by the Greeks themselves but borrowed from the older civilisations of the Near East; in the Far East there was no civilisation older than the Chinese, which, so far as we know, was not indebted for its fundamental features to any external source. This aspect of Greek culture will be treated in a later chapter.

The present chapter, as the fruit of only two years' study, is necessarily brief. Its purpose is twofold. First, a brief account will be given of the cosmological ideas underlying the work of the classical Chinese philosophers. It will be seen that they cannot be dissociated from those we have just discussed. Secondly, attention will be drawn to certain resemblances between the work of the philosophers themselves and that of the early Greek philosophers. These resemblances have often been commented on, but never yet explained.

The written history of China down to 1949 falls into two main epochs, divided by the transitional period of the Warring States, which ended with the consolidation of the Empire under the Ch'in Dynasty in 221 B.C. It is the earlier epoch that concerns us here.[1]

The beginning of the Bronze Age in China cannot yet be dated, but it must be placed well before the Shang Dynasty, which was founded not later than the middle of the second millennium B.C. In China, as elsewhere, by promoting the concentration of wealth, the use of bronze favoured the rise of a chieftaincy, based on military force. Such was the Chou Dynasty, which succeeded the Shang near the end of the second millennium B.C. The conquered territory was distributed among a large number of local chieftains related or allied to the ruling house. The economic unit was the village commune, or clan settlement, based on local handicrafts and common ownership of the soil. The peasants were subject to tributes in kind, labour service, and military conscription, but, in comparison with the later epoch, their yoke was not a heavy one, and within these limits they enjoyed local autonomy under the village elders. There was, in addition, a considerable slave population, owned by the state and employed largely on the land.

The decline of the Chou Dynasty dates from the seventh century B.C. and was brought about by the introduction of iron. With the invention of an iron plough, tillage improved, the cultivated area expanded, the population increased, and there was greater freedom of movement from one district to another, leading to the growth of trade. There was thus brought into being a class of merchants, whose interests lay in the further development of commodity production and in removing restrictions

[1] Wu Ta-kun ICEH.

on the sale of land. In 524 B.C. a copper coinage was introduced. The change that followed has been described as 'the
most momentous in Chinese history and indeed the only major
turning-point before the nineteenth century'.[2] For three hundred years the country was torn by internecine strife between
rival chiefs, each endeavouring to establish himself as tyrant
(*pa*) with the support of the merchant class. About 350 B.C.
Shang Yang, prime minister to the king of Ch'in, introduced
the reform known by his name. The rights of private property
in slaves and land were recognised at law, and the old land
system, based on the village commune, was destroyed. These
measures proved so effective that in 221 B.C. the king of Ch'in
succeeded in establishing himself as the first Emperor, the first
ruler of a unified China. He rewarded the merchants who had
helped him to power by incorporating them among the landowners, with whom they merged into a new ruling class,
composed, on the one hand, of the official bureaucracy, directly
responsible to the Emperor, and, on the other, of the landed
families from which the officials were recruited; and at the same
time, by establishing a state monopoly of all metals, including
iron, he was able to forestall, once and for all, the rise of an
independent merchant class.

This period of the Warring States coincides with the classical
period of Chinese philosophy.

2. *The Great Society*

The historical reality of the Shang Dynasty, which according
to tradition preceded the Chou, has been proved by recent
archæological discoveries. Under this dynasty women played a
more active part in public life than they did in later times, and
the village communes were exogamous. At the spring festivals
the boys and girls of neighbouring villages met and mated in
the fields without constraint, and they married at the following
autumn festival if the girls were with child.[3] These equinoctial
festivals marked the two great turning-points of the year.
During the summer the peasants were engaged continuously in
the fields; during the winter they were confined to the village.

[2] *Ib.* 4.   [3] Granet CC 164, Fitzgerald 45.

Each village had its own phallic cult of a local earth god. The ritual surrounding the kingship was also connected with the fertility of the soil. Under the Chou the classical Chinese conception of the king as Son of Heaven was elaborated and systematised in a form that survived with very little change for more than two thousand years. According to this conception the king was responsible both for the good government of his people and for the ordering of the physical universe. Society and nature were one, and centred in him. This idea of the kingship is not by any means peculiar to China. We find it also in ancient Egypt and Mesopotamia. But its Chinese form is particularly instructive, because we can follow it in detail down to the abolition of the monarchy in 1911, and its tribal origin is abundantly clear. The work of Confucius and Tzu Ssu has been rightly described as marking the transition 'from tribal religion to philosophical enquiry'.[4] It will therefore be worth while to consider briefly the Chinese conception of kingship, showing how it provided the framework for a remarkably coherent and comprehensive theory of nature and man.

The Chinese name for China (Chung Kuo) means the Middle Kingdom, that is, the middle of the world. In the middle of this kingdom lay the imperial capital, containing the Altar of the Sun and the Hall of Destiny. The Altar of the Sun was a square mound, representing space, for the earth and space were imagined in the form of a square. It was covered on top with yellow earth, yellow being the colour of the centre. Its four sides faced the four cardinal points, and were coloured red (south), green (east), white (west), and black (north). When a prince was invested by the Emperor with the lordship of a domain, he took from the mound a clod of earth, red, green, white, or black, according to the quarter in which the domain was situated. The kingdom was imagined as consisting of a central square surrounded by four rectangular bands arranged like Chinese boxes, with their sides facing the four cardinal points. The central region was the capital, where the Emperor resided; the next three regions belonged to the princes, divided into three grades; the fifth was the frontier region, beyond

[4] Hughes 1.

which lay the lands of the four barbarian tribes and the four seas.[5]

During four years out of every five the Emperor was visited by the princes of each region in succession, coming to pay him homage. In the fifth year he made a state tour of the realm. At the beginning of the year, in spring, he visited the eastern quarter and held a court there, robed in green; in summer he passed on to the southern quarter, where he held a court, robed in red; in autumn to the western quarter, with a court in white; in winter to the northern quarter, with a court in black; and so back to the capital. In this way he maintained the unity of the Empire in space and time.

The Hall of Destiny had a square base and a round roof. It represented earth and heaven, or the universe as extended in space and time, for heaven and time were imagined in the form of a circle. During the four years when he was not on tour the Emperor paid regular visits to the hall and performed an annual round of ceremonies, facing east in spring, south in summer, west in autumn, and north in winter, thus inaugurating the months and seasons of the year. In the third summer month he took his stand in the middle of the hall, robed in yellow. In this way he gave a centre to the year.[6]

The conduct of government was required to be in harmony with the movement of the universe. On this subject Tung Chung-shu (second century B.C.) wrote:

In Heaven's course, the warm spring brings to bud, the hot summer nourishes, the cool autumn withers, and the cold winter stores away. Warmth, heat, cool, and cold are different from one another but do the same work, being Heaven's means of completing the year. And the movements of Heaven are followed by the Sage in the conduct of his government, reproducing spring warmth by his beneficence, summer heat by conferring rewards, autumn coolness by punishments, winter cold by executions. His benefits, rewards, punishments, and executions are different from one another but do the same work, being the means whereby the King completes his virtue.[7]

Elaborating these traditional ideas, the philosophers of the Han Dynasty recognised a fivefold division of the world, kept in motion by the interaction of opposites. They distinguished

[5] Granet PC 90–4.   [6] *Ib.* 102–3.   [7] Fung Yu-lan 2. 48.

five elements (wood, fire, earth, metal, water), five classes of animal (scaled, feathered, skinned, furred, shelled), five sense organs (eyes, tongue, mouth, nose, ears), five internal organs (spleen, lung, heart, liver, kidney), five passions (anger, joy, will, sorrow, fear), five musical notes (C, D, E, G, A), and five elemental numbers (8, 7, 5, 9, 6). The two opposites were *yang*, representing all that was male, light, warm, dry, hard, active, and *yin*, representing all that was female, dark, cold, moist, soft, passive. Heaven and Earth stood in the relation of *yang* and *yin*. The odd numbers from 1 to 9 were assigned to Heaven, and the even numbers from 2 to 10 to Earth.[8]

The interaction of the opposites is described as follows:

> The constant course of Heaven is such that opposites cannot arise together. Therefore it is called oneness; it is single, not double; such is the movement of Heaven. The opposites are the *yin* and the *yang*. When the one expands, the other contracts; when the one is to the left, the other is to the right. In spring they both move south, in autumn north; in summer they meet in front, in winter behind. They move alongside one another but not on the same path; they meet, and each in turn takes control. Such is their rhythm.[9]

If the Emperor failed to govern in harmony with the movement of Heaven, evil omens appeared and society fell into disorder. At the same time his good government of society was a necessary condition for maintaining the natural order. The two movements were interdependent. The statesman Ch'ien P'ing, who died in 179 B.C., is reported to have said that 'the prime minister's duty is to help the Son of Heaven to regulate the *yin* and *yang*, to see that the four seasons follow their proper courses, and to conform to what is fitting in all things'.[10]

The year was divided into twelve lunar months, three to each season, corresponding to the twelve signs of the zodiac. A month was intercalated in every third and fifth year, whenever it was found that the sun was in the same sign at the end of a month as it had been at the beginning. The years were grouped in cycles of sixty years. Each of these sexagenary cycles was composed of two sub-cycles, known as the Ten

---

[8] Granet PC 376; Fung Yu-lan 2. 15. The Chinese for 'element' (*hsing*) means properly a 'motive force' or 'agent': Fung Yu-lan 2. 21.

[9] Fung Yu-lan 2. 23–4.   [10] *Ib.* 2. 10.

Heavenly Stems and the Twelve Earthly Branches. The Ten Heavenly Stems consisted of five pairs, corresponding to the five elements, the members of each pair being *yang* and *yin*. The Twelve Earthly Branches were named after the rat, ox, tiger, hare, dragon, snake, horse, sheep, monkey, cock, dog, and pig. The two sub-cycles ran concurrently, and the year was designated by reference to the appropriate member of each. After six revolutions of the one sub-cycle, and five of the other, the sexagenary cycle was complete. This calendar, which originated under the Shang Dynasty, remained in official use until 1911.[11]

History too was believed to move in cycles. According to tradition the Chou Dynasty had been preceded by three (or sometimes five) sages. In the reign of the first, named Huang Ti, the Yellow Emperor, Heaven had made earth-worms appear, and accordingly he declared that earth was in the ascendancy and adopted yellow as his colour. Huang Ti was succeeded by Yü. In his time grass and trees appeared, signifying that wood was in the ascendancy, and he adopted green as his colour. Yü was succeeded by T'ang, founder of the Shang Dynasty. In his reign Heaven made swords appear in water, signifying that metal was in the ascendancy, and he adopted white as his colour. With the accession of the next king, Wen, founder of the Chou Dynasty, fire appeared, and a red bird with a red book in its beak perched on the Altar of Earth, signifying that fire was in the ascendancy. Accordingly, the kings of Chou adopted red as their colour.[12] Theoretically, the next dynasty, the Ch'in, should have been associated with water and black; but the writer who has preserved for us this version of the story lived under the first Emperor of Ch'in, who had not yet announced his decision; and so, since black was unlucky, he was afraid that the obvious conclusion might be unacceptable to his majesty, and added:

Fire must be replaced by water, and Heaven will first reveal water in the ascendancy. The approved colour will then be black; but, should water have already made its appearance without being recognised, then, the cycle being complete, there will be a reversion to earth.[13]

[11] Hastings 3. 82.   [12] Hughes 220.
[13] *Ib*. 220–1; Fung Yu-lan 2. 58–62.

The loyal philosopher found himself confronted with the fact that what he regarded as a law of nature was really a reflection of the social institution which it served to protect:

> Was ihr den Geist der Zeiten heisst,
> Dass ist im Grund der Herren eigner Geist.[14]

In the form in which they have come down to us, these ideas date for the most part from the Early Han Dynasty (206 B.C.– A.D. 24), but they can be traced as philosophical doctrines back to the fourth century B.C., and the ideas themselves are imbedded in the origins of Chinese society. As has been pointed out by Granet, the principle of the centre is not primitive, being a reflection of the centralisation of power in the chieftaincy or kingship;[15] and when this has been removed, we are left with a quartered circle, which corresponds to a tribe of two moieties:

> If the Yin and the Yang form a pair and seem to preside jointly over the rhythm of the world order, it is because these ideas are derived from an earlier age in which the principle of rotation had sufficed to regulate a society divided into two complementary groups. . . . In fact we know that a new era was inaugurated by a festival consisting of a mock battle between two chiefs, each supported by two seconds. The two sides represented the two moieties which had shared the control of society by exercising it alternately.[16]

3. Natural Philosophy

The reader will have observed that these Chinese ideas bear a remarkable resemblance to those of the early Greek philosophers. The parallel has been pointed out by Fung Yu-lan, who compares the numerological teachings of the Yin-yang school with the Pythagorean theory of number, remarking that it is so close as to 'arouse surprise';[17] and in fact it extends much further than this comparison suggests.

In the year A.D. 79 a conference of Confucian scholars was held in the White Tiger Hall in the capital city of Ch'ang An to discuss various problems connected with the interpretation of the classics, and a report of the proceedings has been preserved under the title Po Hu T'ung. In it we read:

[14] Goethe Faust 1. 544.   [15] Granet PC 103–4.
[16] Ib. 26, 105–6.   [17] Fung Yu-lan 2. 93–6; Needham 154–7.

Why do the five elements come to rule successively? Because they give birth successively to one another. Hence each has its end and its beginning. Wood gives birth to fire, fire to earth, earth to metal, metal to water, and water to wood. . . . That they may also injure one another is due to the nature of the universe, which is such that the more abundant overcomes the less, and therefore water overcomes fire; the rarefied overcomes the condensed, and therefore fire overcomes metal; the hard overcomes the soft, and therefore metal overcomes wood, the compact overcomes the diffused, and therefore wood overcomes earth; the solid overcomes the liquid, and therefore earth overcomes water.[18]

We are reminded of Herakleitos:

Fire lives the death of air, and air lives the death of fire; water lives the death of earth, and earth lives the death of water.

The cold warms and the warm cools; the wet dries and the parched is moistened.[19]

Herakleitos also said:

It is the same thing in us that is living and dead, asleep and awake, young and old; each changes place and becomes the other.

We step and we do not step into the same stream; we are and we are not.[20]

Hui Shih, who died at the end of the fourth century B.C., said:

The sky is as low as the earth; mountains are level with marshes.

The sun is just setting at noon; each creature is just dying at birth.[21]

These are not random quotations. The Chinese sayings are just as characteristic of the early Confucians as the Greek are of the Pre-Socratics. Nor is that all. The Chinese thinkers of this period, like the Greek, were concerned with the whole of life, man as well as nature. Their aim was to achieve by means of rational enquiry a true understanding of the world around them and to live according to the truth. Hence they were concerned with ethics no less than with physics, and sought to apply to both branches of knowledge the same principles. The Confucians, like the Pythagoreans, followed the custom of attributing all their teachings without discrimination to the Master, and consequently many of their theories cannot be

---

[18] Fung Yu-lan. 2. 22–3. [19] Heracl. B 76, B 39.
[20] Ib. B 88, B 49. [21] Hughes 120.

precisely dated. It is believed that the Confucian doctrine of the middle—or the mean, as we should call it—goes back, if not to Confucius himself, who was some twenty years older than Pythagoras, at least to his grandson, Tzu Ssu:

> The Master said: 'Perfect is the middle, and for a long time now few men have been capable of it. . . .'
>
> Tzu Lu enquired about strong men, and the Master said: 'Do you mean strong men of the southern kind or strong men of the northern kind, or perhaps making yourself strong? The strong man of the south is magnanimous and gentle in instruction and takes no revenge for being maltreated. It is the habit of a man of true breeding to be thus. The strong man of the north lives under arms and dies without a murmur. It is the habit of a man of true force to be thus. Hence the man of true breeding, steadfast in his strength, having a spirit of concord and resisting pressure, takes up a middle position, and does not waver this way or that. How steadfast his strength! When there is good government, he does not change his principles, and, when there is bad government, he does not change, even though his life may be at stake.'[22]

No Babylonian or Egyptian ever spoke or thought like this; yet Pythagoras and Sokrates did. If Herodotus had been able to travel as far as China, he would have felt more at home in Loyang than he did in Babylon or Memphis, if only because he could have met there his contemporary, Tzu Ssu, with whom he might have spent many days in congenial company:

> We spent them not in toys, in lusts, or wine,
>   But search of deep philosophy,
>   Wit, eloquence and poetry;
>   Arts which I loved, for they, my friend, were thine.[23]

It may be that the following pages will throw some light on the significance of these affinities between eastern and western thought; but it is to be hoped that the subject will be taken up by someone competent to treat it systematically, explaining both the similarities and the differences in the light of the specific historical conditions. That would be an attractive and instructive task, and a contribution to world peace. There I must leave it.

[22] Hughes 33–4.   [23] Abraham Cowley.

IV

THE NEAR EAST

1. *Agriculture*

IN China the development of large-scale irrigation dates only from the Chou Dynasty, and it never became so important there as it was in Egypt and Mesopotamia. The river valleys of the Nile, Euphrates, and Tigris only became habitable after a beginning had been made in draining the swamps and bringing the floods under control. This was done by means of a large labour force recruited from adjacent villages and organised according to a common plan. In this way the primitive village communities, tribal in origin, were absorbed into larger units corresponding to the irrigational basin or catchment area, that is, the amount of cultivated land that could be controlled, at the given level of production, from a single centre. These developments were only rendered possible by a new division of labour, a division between mental and manual labour, which inaugurated a period of economic, social, and cultural advance more eventful than any the world had yet seen and indeed without parallel down to the sixteenth century A.D. In course of time this division of labour was transformed by the growth of property into a division between two antagonistic classes. The mental labourers, drawn from the chieftains and magicians of the primitive communities, established themselves as a ruling class, which expropriated the surplus produced by the manual labourers whose activities they organised. The primary producers, the peasants, were subjected to tribute, forced labour, and conscription, thus providing the man-power neces-sary for the development of the state; but the ownership of land remained, for the most part, communal.[1] Private property in land was precluded, or at least restricted, by the needs of large-scale irrigation, which was a function of the state; but the land was not common in the sense that all who tilled it enjoyed the fruits of their labour. It belonged to the state, represented for them by the king, who claimed to be god incarnate or god's

[1] Clay TLBA; Frankfort KG 221.

tenant on earth. Economically, the kingship is an expression of
the fact that large-scale irrigation depends on centralised
control; ideologically, it expresses, in the new conditions, the
dependence of the individual on the community. In primitive
communism, as we have seen, it is only as a member of the
tribe that the individual is 'owner and occupier of the earth'
(pp. 49-50), and for that reason his ideas about the physical world
are a projection of his tribal relations. But, with the rise of the
state, on which tillage depends, tribal relations are superseded
by class relations, which it is the function of the state to maintain: the individual owns and occupies the earth, not as a
member of the tribe, but as a subject of the king. Hence all
those ideas which had previously been centred in the tribe now
gather round the kingship; and, if the king is worshipped as
a god, his divinity is an idealisation of the lost tribal unity
effected in men's minds after their social relations have passed
out of their control.

In general, the kingship, or oriental despotism, is the form
of state characteristic of all societies which have advanced
beyond primitive communism on the basis of state-controlled
agriculture. But of course every instance presents specific
features of its own. The two regions which concern us in this
chapter resemble one another in that their agriculture was
wholly dependent on irrigation; but there are also differences
between them, which need to be explained.

In Egypt there is only one river. It is a fine waterway, making
communications easy. Sailing craft may float downstream and
are driven upstream by the prevailing north wind. And it is the
sole source of fertility. There is very little rain in Lower Egypt,
and in Upper Egypt none at all. Everything depends on the
Nile, which flows steadily throughout the year, except for the
flood which takes place regularly in July after the upper reaches
have been swollen by the melted mountain snows. The whole
life of the community hangs on this event and the manner in
which it is controlled. For these reasons the unification of the
country was rapid and complete. It was effected in three stages:
the rise of local chieftaincies which covered areas corresponding
to the provinces (nomoi) of later times; the formation of two
kingdoms, Upper and Lower; and the unification of the

country, before the end of the fourth millennium B.C., in a single kingdom, which maintained itself, with many changes of dynasty but otherwise almost without a break, for three thousand years. Another feature of the country is its geographical isolation. The deserts hemming it in on either side, like a closed corridor, provided a more effective barrier than the Great Wall of China. Almost shut off from the outside world, the kingdom grew up self-contained and eventually stagnated. Nowhere else in the ancient world did local conditions exert so decisive an influence. A conspicuous example is to be found in the worship of the dead, on which was lavished a large portion of the abundant surplus produced by the tillers of the soil. This in itself was not peculiar to Egypt, but it developed there in a peculiar form. The practice of mummification, which is its distinctive feature, was only possible because there was no rain; and this practice gave rise to the illusion that inspired the pyramids, erected as dwelling-places for the dead kings, who lay in state there for all time as though they had never died.

In Mesopotamia there are two rivers, each with a number of tributaries. They are less easy to navigate than the Nile, the Tigris in particular being a turbulent river, and the floods are less regular, for the country is subject to torrential rains. The area that could be irrigated in a single system was limited. Moreover, so far from being isolated, the country was exposed to desert nomads on the west and on the north and east to mountain tribesmen from Armenia and Elam. The basic unit was the city-state. The Mesopotamian cities were constantly at war, and, though they were united from time to time by force of arms, these empires were not lasting. Ur, Babylon, Nineveh rose and fell. The sense of insecurity which is characteristic of Mesopotamian thought is to be explained by these historical conditions, and not by the uncertainties of the weather, as Frankfort and others have supposed.[2] In this way, too, we can account for the different forms assumed by the Egyptian and Mesopotamian kingship.

[2] Frankfort BP 138–9.

2. *The Egyptian Kingship*

The Egyptian ideogram for 'village' was a cross inscribed in a circle.[3] It has been suggested that the cross represents the village streets. That may be so, but it is more important to observe that the sign as a whole—a circle divided into four quarters—corresponds to the tribal structure typical of the primitive village community.

The first settlements in the Nile valley were temporary.[4] As the annual flood subsided, there emerged here and there patches of land, higher than the rest, covered in a thick layer of river mud which glistened in the sunshine. Here the hunters built their huts, sowed and reaped a crop of barley or emmer-wheat, and remained in occupation until the next year's flood forced them to retreat. In time, by combining the labour force of neighbouring villages, they learnt to protect the high places with dikes and embankments, and the settlements became permanent. Later still, a cluster of adjacent villages became organised from a single centre, similar in origin to the other settlements, but larger and containing the residence of a paramount chief. He was probably assisted by clan chiefs from the surrounding villages, who formed a council of elders. Earthenware pots have been excavated on these sites, and on some of them are painted buildings and boats carrying heraldic emblems, which were evidently totemic. The process of unification did not stop there. For the reasons already given it continued until two kingdoms were formed, Upper and Lower Egypt, and shortly before 3000 B.C. the whole country was united under the Ist Dynasty.

The high place of the village, as the first land to have emerged from the flood, was sacred, and the shrine or temple erected on it was believed to commemorate the creation of the world. There the creation was re-enacted ceremonially every year. This conception found its highest architectural expression in the pyramids, so designed as to embody the idea of the primeval hill.[5] Mythically it was expressed in the belief that the dry land had been created out of the waters by the sun; and this myth was used by the kings to consolidate their power. Each king

[3] Gardiner 627.   [4] Frankfort KG 17.   [5] *Ib.* 151–2.

was identified with the sun-god and invested with sovereignty by a rite of coronation in which he was presented as creator of the world. In this way the people were taught to believe that the kingship was an institution which had existed ever since the world began, being the necessary instrument for maintaining order in man and nature alike.

One of the rites of the Sed festival, which was a jubilee re-enactment of the coronation, was called the Dedication of the Field.[6] After a piece of ground had been marked out, the king walked across it four times, facing successively the four points of the compass and wearing the red crown of Lower Egypt; then he did the same again, wearing the white crown of Upper Egypt. By so doing he established his claim to rule not only Egypt but the world. This is clear from another rite, in which he is described as passing through the land and touching its four sides and crossing the ocean to the four sides of heaven. Again, at the same festival, wearing the red crown, he sat between two officials, one on either side of him, who sang a hymn proclaiming his power, then changed places and sang it again, then stood in front of him and then behind him and then changed places again, repeating the hymn in each position, so that each of them made the proclamation to the four points of the compass. Then, wearing the white crown, the king went in procession to two chapels of Horus and Seth, where a priest handed him a bow and arrows. After shooting four arrows, south, north, east, and west, he was enthroned four times, facing in turn the four quarters.[7]

One of his titles was 'King of Upper and of Lower Egypt'. Another was the 'Two Ladies', referring to the cobra goddess of Lower Egypt and the vulture goddess of Upper Egypt. These correspond to the twofold division of the kingdom. For the same reason he had two viziers, two treasurers, and at times two capitals. He was also known as the 'Two Lords', referring to Horus and Seth. These two figures belong to the myth of Osiris, the god who was slain every year by Seth, mourned by his sister Isis, and avenged by his son Horus. It has been suggested that this last title signifies, not merely the unification of the two kingdoms but the reconciliation in the king's person of all

[6] Frankfort KG 85.   [7] Ib. 87–8.

antagonisms, natural and social. The royal office was regarded as dual in its very nature. This is clear from the belief—evidently very old—that every king had a still-born twin brother, represented by his placenta.[8] Moreover, just as the king was identified with the sun, so his twin was believed to have become the moon-god. The duality of the king expressed the duality of the universe.

For these reasons, without denying the political origin of the double kingdom, Frankfort has insisted that this principle of duality, which is so marked a characteristic of the Egyptian monarchy, is something more than a purely political concept:

This extraordinary conception expressed in political form the deeply-rooted Egyptian tendency to understand the world in dualistic terms as a series of pairs of contrasts balanced in unchanging equilibrium. The universe as a whole was referred to as 'heaven and earth'. Within this concept 'earth' was again conceived dualistically as 'north and south', 'the portions of Horus and the portions of Seth', 'the two lands' or 'the two (Nile) banks'. The last of these synonyms demonstrates their non-political character most clearly. Each of them is equivalent to the second member of the more comprehensive pair, 'heaven and earth'; they belong to cosmology, not to politics. Yet each of them was suitable to describe the king's domain, for the whole of mankind and all the lands of the earth were subject to Pharaoh. His realm was often described as 'that which the sun encircles', the earth; and the Greeks . . . rendered 'the Two Lands' by *he oikouméne*, 'the whole inhabited earth'. When Pharaoh assumed dualistic titles or called himself 'Lord of the Two Lands', he emphasised not the divided origin but the universality of his power.[9]

This interpretation is undoubtedly correct, with one reservation. It has been shown in the preceding pages that, so far from being peculiarly Egyptian, the idea of the unity of opposites is fundamental to primitive thought, being in fact as old as society itself. In Egypt, however, it assumed a distinctive form, which can best be understood by comparing it with the Chinese. In China we found, in addition to the four cardinal points, a fifth, the centre, occupied by the king, whose function was to regulate the opposites which by their perpetual interaction kept the world in motion. In Egypt the two opposites are brought to rest in the person of the king. In place of a regulated conflict we

<hr/>

[8] *Ib.* 70.   [9] *Ib.* 19.

have an unchanging equilibrium. For the Egyptians, as Frankfort observes, the universe was static. If we ask why, the reason is to be found in the exceptional stability of the monarchy, determined by the need for unified control of the Nile flood and confirmed by the isolation of the country. After the VIth Dynasty, and again after the XIIth, the monarchy collapsed, and there ensued a period of chaos which was only brought to an end when the central authority was restored. Later, after the formation of the First Empire under the XVIIIth Dynasty, the Pharaohs established relations with foreign monarchs, who had similar pretensions among their own peoples, and so they were no longer able to pass themselves off without qualification as sole rulers of the world. The doctrine of divine kingship became paradoxical.[10] What is remarkable, therefore, about the Egyptian kings is that, thanks to the conditions in which they had risen to power, they were more successful than most in doing what all kings have always tried to do, that is, to use the ideas emanating from the centralisation of power as an instrument for holding the exploited class in spiritual subjection. How this was done has been well explained by Caudwell:

With a highly-developed agricultural civilisation a god-king is formed at the top of the pyramid, and he seems to wield all social power. The slave by himself seems very small compared with the might of social labour wielded by the god-king. In association the slave wields tremendous power, the power of pyramids. But this power does not seem to the slave to be his; it seems to belong to the god-king who directs it. Hence the slave humiliates himself before his own collective power; he deifies the god-king and holds the whole ruling class as sacred. This alienation of self is only a reflection of the alienation of property which has produced it. The slave's humility is the badge, not merely of his slavery, but of the power of society developed to a stage where slavery exists and yields a mighty social power. This power is expressed at the opposite pole to the slave by the divine magnificence of the god-kings of Egypt, China, Japan, and the Sumerian, Babylonian and Accadian city-states. . . . As Marx, studying the phenomenon of religion, had perceived as early as 1844: 'This state, this society, produces religion, —an inverted consciousness of the world, because the world itself is an *inverted world*. Of *this* world religion is the general theory, its encyclopaedic compendium, its logic in popular form, its spiritual *point d'honneur*, its enthusiasm, its moral sanction, its solemn complement, its general consolation and justification. It is the fantastic realisation of man, *because* man possesses no true realisation.'[11]

[10] Frankfort 57.   [11] Caudwell IR 39–40; Marx CHPL.

3. *The Mesopotamian Kingship*

The Mesopotamian communities were similar in origin to
the Egyptian. The nucleus was a small tract of alluvial soil
exposed by the receding waters, which was gradually enlarged
by collective labour in a network of dikes and canals. The
inhabitants were organised in an assembly, open'to all adults,
men and women, and a council of elders, composed of the heads
of families, under a high priest, who was in effect the leader of
the community. He was in charge of the shrine or temple, which
housed the communal granary and implements, and he administered the arable lands, which were owned and worked in
common.[12] It has been suggested that he and his subordinates
formed a magical fraternity, such as we find among the more
advanced tribes of Polynesia and America.[13] The god or goddess
worshipped in the temple symbolised the solidarity of the
community and the authority vested in the priests as organisers
of production.

As these communities expanded, they merged into city-
states. The city was based on a combination of large-scale
agriculture with highly developed handicrafts, including metal-
lurgy, for which the raw materials had to be imported. The
alluvial valleys of the Euphrates and Tigris, like the Nile, are
destitute of metals; but, whereas the Egyptian kings had the
copper mines of Sinai just beyond their frontiers, the Mesopotamian cities had to obtain their supplies from Elam by trading
their surplus grain with the mountain tribes. The demand for
metals promoted the growth of trade.

As a complex of village communities, the city contained
several temples, each with its own god, one of them enjoying
precedence as patron god of the city. The priesthood consolidated itself as a ruling class by usurping the powers of the
council and appropriating the land. A portion of the land was
divided into small holdings belonging to free peasants, but the
greater part belonged to the temples. It was cultivated by slaves
taken in war and by the smallholders, whom the priests subjected to labour service. The craftsmen were exploited in the

[12] Frankfort KG 215, 221; Jacobsen PDAM 163, 172.
[13] Childe WHH 82–3.

same way, being obliged to surrender so much of their labour time or of their products to the priests. The fiction of common ownership was maintained by the doctrine that the temple lands belonged to the god who was worshipped there. In the same way the city as a whole was supposed to be the property of its patron god, leased from him by his high priest, the city governor, who supervised matters of general concern, such as irrigation, trade, and foreign relations. These conditions were more favourable to the development of commodity production than those that prevailed in early Egypt, where the whole country was administered as the king's household; and in fact commodity production did develop to the point of silver ingots being used as a medium of exchange. But there it stopped; for, thanks to the enormous wealth and power derived from their control of irrigation, the priests were strong enough to maintain a virtual monopoly of the metal trade and so to prevent the rise of an independent merchant class.[14] In Mesopotamia and Egypt alike trade was restricted to the ruling landowning class, which turned into commodities a portion of the surplus exacted as tribute from the tillers of the soil.

The relations between neighbouring cities were usually unsettled; for, though they were interdependent in the vital matter of water-supply, the growth of population and of commodity production made them rivals. From early times the ruling class had supplemented its labour force by slave raids into the mountains; and the slaves, owned either by the temples or by private citizens, formed a considerable section of the community. In time of war the city elected a war-chief (*lugal*), who was invested with absolute power for a limited period. The title, literally 'great man', was also used of a landowner or a slave-owner.[15] With the intensification of the class struggle and the growth of warfare, it often happened that the 'great man' elected in an emergency refused to vacate his office after the emergency was over; or the governor of one city, having defeated another, would impose himself on it as its 'great man' or owner. In time some of these kings, as they may now be called, having established their rule over a large portion of the

[14] Childe WHH 117–8, Frankfort KG 223.
[15] Frankfort KG 218.

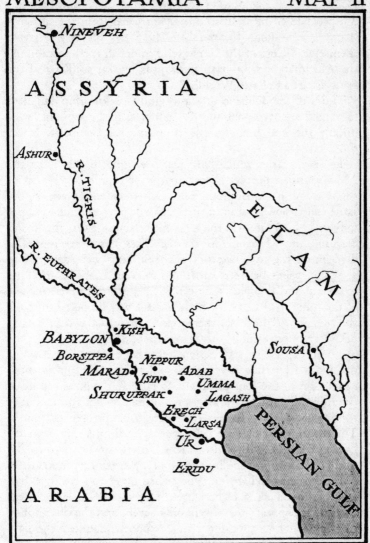

MESOPOTAMIA   MAP II

NINEVEH

ASSYRIA

Ashur

R. TIGRIS

R. EUPHRATES

ELAM

KISH
BABYLON
BORSIPPA
MARAD   NIPPUR
ISIN   ADAB
SHURUPPAK UMMA
LAGASH
ERECH
LARSA
UR
ERIDU

SOUSA

PERSIAN GULF

ARABIA

country, endeavoured to consolidate it by making pretensions
to divinity. This was done by Naram-Sin of Akkad, the IIIrd
Dynasty of Ur, the kings of Isin, and others. The same Naram-
Sin proclaimed himself, in a title borrowed from the sun-god,
'King of the Four Quarters'.[16] The kings of Assyria styled
themselves 'Kings of the Universe', and one of them, combining
the Akkadian and Assyrian titles, was known as 'King of the
Four Quarters of the World'.[17]

Thus, if the doctrine of the divinity of kingship failed to
take hold in Mesopotamia, it was not that the aspirants were
unduly modest, but, on the contrary, the competition was
too keen.

The royal titles which have just been quoted show that the
Mesopotamian peoples shared in the primitive conception of
the universe as a quartered circle. Other evidence points to the
same conclusion. The most distinctive achievement of Mesopotamian architecture was the ziggurat or stage-tower, the 'tower
reaching unto heaven', as the Israelites described it.[18] The
description was apt, because these buildings were designed as
stepping-stones between earth and heaven, enabling the king
to ascend and the god to descend. They were, in fact, models
of the universe. Just as the highest stage was supposed to touch
the sky, so, at the base, there was built into the floor a tank
of water, representing 'the waters beneath the earth'.[19] The
ziggurat of Ashur was designated 'the house of the world
mountain'. The stages were rectangular or square, and oriented
in relation to the four cardinal points.[20] In the present state of
the ruins the number of stages is not easy to determine, but it
seems that in early times they were usually three or four.[21]
Thus the ziggurat of Erech IV, as depicted on a clay cylinder,
had three stages, with three niches in the lowest, two in the
middle, and two in the highest, making seven niches in all.[22]

The ziggurat of Babylon is described by Herodotus, who had
visited it, as having eight stages.[23] From Babylonian sources,
however, it appears there were only seven, and the discrepancy
is explained by supposing that Herodotus counted the base

[16] Frankfort KG 228.
[17] Ib. 230.
[18] Gen. 11. 4.
[19] Langdon in CAH 1. 399.
[20] Parrot 102.
[21] Langdon in CAH 1. 390–1.
[22] Parrot 37.
[23] Hdt. 1. 181.

(*kigal*), which is invisible from the outside, as a separate stage.[24] The ziggurat of Borsippa certainly had seven stages. It was known as 'the house of the seven guides of heaven and earth'. This appellation shows that the stages represented the spheres of the seven 'planets' (Saturn, Jupiter, Mars, Venus, Mercury, and the sun and moon). It is believed that they were originally coloured black, orange, red, white, blue, yellow, gold-and-silver.[25] Thus the structure corresponded to the seven 'planets', the seven great gods, the seven gates of the underworld, the seven winds, and the seven days of the week. In the Sumerian language the idea of the universe was written with the sign for the number seven.[26]

This conception of a sevenfold universe finds its most graphic expression in the design on a cuneiform tablet known as the Babylonian world map, which has been interpreted by Lewy.[27] There are two concentric circles, with the city of Babylon at the centre. The Euphrates is shown in its full length from its source in the mountains to the swamps where it enters the sea. The space between the circles is 'the Bitter River', known to the Greeks as Ocean. The edges of the tablet are damaged, but enough remains to show that the outer circle passed through the bases of seven isosceles triangles arranged at regular intervals, so that the whole presented the appearance of a seven-pointed star. Each of the seven points is, or was, inscribed with the word *na-gu-u*, 'district', and one of them is further defined as 'the place where the sun is not seen'. Lewy goes on to show that these seven triangles are really the seven mountains which are the dwelling-places of the seven winds, described elsewhere as 'the seven gods of the universe'. The peaks of the mountains support the heavens, while their foundations conceal the entrances to the underworld; and together they form a ring round the earth along which the regions of heaven and hell were believed to meet.

There seems to be little doubt that this interpretation is correct. It accords with the fact that the ziggurat, which also served as a link between heaven and hell, was imagined as a mountain. Indeed, Lewy goes further, and, after citing evidence to show that there were seven different kinds of wind, he argues

[24] Parrot 27.   [25] *Ib.* 204.   [26] Lewy 16–7.   [27] *Ib.* 10–1.

that one wind of each kind was believed to have its abode in each of the seven leading cities of the Babylonian period—Ur, Nippur, Eridu, Kullab, Lagash, Kesh, and Shuruppak.[28] Thus the ziggurats of these cities represented the seven mountains of the universe, with their capital, Babylon, at the centre.

We are left with the question, whence the sanctity of the number seven? What, in other words, is the origin of our seven-day week, which we have inherited through Jewish religion from Babylonia? It has sometimes been supposed that the number derived its significance from the four lunar quarters. But, as Nilsson has pointed out, the quadrupartite division of the month cannot have arisen from simple observation: 'it is in its very nature a numerical system'.[29] With this Lewy agrees. The number seven was not obtained by dividing the days of the month; on the contrary, the month was divided by the sacred number. Now, the Babylonian month contained five 'sabbaths' or unlucky days—the 7th, 14th, 19th, 21st, and 28th. The 19th is included because, as Lewy points out, it is the 49th— seven times seven—after the beginning of the preceding month; and from this and other evidence he concludes that the early Assyrian calendar had been based, not on the lunar month at all, but on seven periods of seven weeks, reckoned for convenience at fifty days each.[30]

Turning to the relation between the seven-point system and the four-point system, he cites a number of passages in which the two systems are combined. We read, for example, in a Sumerian exorcism: 'By the seven winds, by the four regions of earth . . .' He maintains that the seven-point system was the older of the two:

Numerous texts know four main winds giving their names to the four principal directions and corresponding approximately to our four points of the compass. However, . . . this division of the horizon into four parts apparently superseded another system in which seven winds defined seven main directions dividing the compass into seven sectors.[31]

What, then, was the origin of the seven-point system? After drawing attention to the Akkadian word for 'day', which means

[28] Lewy 37.   [29] Nilsson PTR 171.   [30] Lewy 51.   [31] Ib. 7–8.

also 'wind', and the Sumerian signs for 'day', which were also
used for 'wind' and 'storm', he produces evidence to show that
in the Near East there is 'a regular daily recurrence of land and
sea winds'. This, he argues, explains the use of a common word
or sign for 'day' and 'wind', and he concludes that the seven-day
week 'was created by dedicating one day to each of the seven
winds'.[32]

This conclusion leaves us still asking, why *seven* winds? The
question we began with has not been answered. Accordingly, we
must retrace our steps. The evidence adduced for giving priority
to the seven-point system is not decisive. This objection applies
to all the passages which he has quoted in this connection, and
above all to the text on which he relies for identifying the seven
kinds of wind. They are defined as follows:

(1) the 'gracious winds' or 'winds of life', depicted in human form;

(2) the 'guardian winds', portrayed with bird faces and wings;

(3) the rain-carrying winds, represented with fish cloaks, to whose water
was attributed a purifying effect;

(4) and (5) rain-carrying winds, likewise depicted with fish cloaks, with
special functions in the growth of vegetation;

(6) and (7) thunderstorms, represented with horns of copper and weapons,
accompanied by lightning and having destructive and devastating qualities.

If we look to the form in which these winds were depicted, we
see that there are only four kinds (men, birds, fish, horns), the
third and fourth being subdivided so as to make seven. The
fourfold division is the older.

Why, then, was the four-point system expanded into a seven-
point system? The answer is to be found in Mexico. The Aztecs
believed in an upper world of the gods, a middle world of
mankind, and a lower world of the dead, and accordingly they
imagined the world as extending from its centre horizontally in
four directions and vertically in two. The Babylonians held a
similar belief, which was embodied in the ziggurat, and above
all in the ziggurat of Babylon itself, the centre of the world.
For them, too, the universe was divided horizontally into four
quarters, radiating from a common centre, and vertically into
three levels, making seven points in all.

[32] *Ib.* 19.

4. *The Babylonian New Year*

The Mesopotamian conception of the cosmos has been characterised by Jacobsen as follows:

> The origin of the world order is seen as a prolonged conflict between two principles, the forces making for activity and the forces making for inactivity.[33]

He qualifies this formulation by saying that he is defining the concept in modern terms. Had he been defining the Chinese concept of the *yang* and *yin*, no such qualification would have been necessary. The Mesopotamian principle is the same as the Chinese, but the form in which it was expressed is less civilised. It is mythical and concrete, not abstract and philosophical. The same difference may be observed in Egyptian thought, as compared with Chinese; but Mesopotamian ideology is more barbaric than Egyptian. It breathes a spirit of aggressiveness and brutality, reflecting the abrupt rise of the ruling class, its insecurity and internal antagonisms, and the violence with which it maintained itself in power.

The form in which the conflict of opposites manifested itself in Mesopotamia may be illustrated by an analysis of the New Year Festival at Babylon.[34]

The festival was celebrated in the month of Nisan, which coincided with the vernal equinox. It lasted eleven days, during which all the ordinary business of the city was suspended.

The opening days were given over to lamentation. While the priests conducted rites of expiation in the temples, the people mourned, saying that the god Marduk was imprisoned in the mountain—in other words, dead and buried. The 'mountain', his supposed place of confinement, was probably the ziggurat. On the evening of the fourth day the priests chanted the *Enuma elish*, or Hymn of Creation. On the fifth the king entered the chapel of Marduk, and there the high priest divested him of his regalia, slapped his face, and pulled his ears. In this way, as Langdon remarked, 'he was for the moment reduced to the rank of layman'.[35] After he had protested his innocence on bended

---

[33] Jacobsen in Frankfort BP 187.
[34] Langdon BEC, Frankfort KG 317.
[35] Langdon BEC 26.

knees, the priest reinvested him and assured him that Marduk would increase his dominion. In the meantime the people continued to lament for their god, hurrying through the streets and asking one another, 'Where is he held captive?'; and a goddess went forth from the city, wailing. It appears that she too was believed to descend into the underworld and to be imprisoned there.

On the sixth day a number of state barges arrived in Babylon from all the principal cities of the kingdom, each carrying a statue of the patron god or goddess of the city. Meanwhile the people engaged in mock battles in the streets. On the seventh Marduk was somehow set free by his son Nabu, the god of Nippur. On the eighth the statues were arranged in order of precedence, under the direction of the king, in a part of the temple known as Ubshu-ukkinna, 'the meeting-place of the gods'. There, according to the interpretation of the ritual, the gods appointed Marduk to be their champion. There followed a rite symbolising a duel between Marduk and the monster Tiamat, in which Marduk was represented by the king.

On the ninth day the king and priests, with all the statues, marched in procession to the Festival Hall outside the city, where it was proclaimed that Marduk had destroyed his enemies. Next day, after the victory had been celebrated at a banquet, the procession returned to the city, and that night the god was united in marriage with the goddess. Whether the king represented him in this rite at Babylon is not certain, but he did so in the corresponding rite at Isin and other cities. On the last day there was a second assembly of the gods, again represented by their statues, at which they 'fixed the fates' for the coming year. Next morning the work of ploughing and sowing was put in hand, and the city resumed its normal life. The new year had begun.

The contents of *Enuma elish*, the hymn chanted on the fourth day, may be summarised as follows. The newly created gods of order were attacked by the powers of chaos, headed by the female monster Tiamat. Overcome with terror, they assembled together and appointed the bravest among them, Marduk, to be their king. Then followed a pitched battle. The enemy was routed and fled, all except Tiamat, whom Marduk engaged in single combat. He threw over her a net held down at the corners by the four winds and shot an arrow into her gaping maw, piercing her heart and killing her. Then he smashed her skull and split her body in two halves like an oyster. He lifted up one half and locked it into position so as to form the sky. Finally, after creating mankind, he received the thanks of the other gods, who built a temple for him, where they might assemble every year to 'fix the fates' for their human worshippers.

The evolution of the festival may be reconstructed as follows.

First, in primitive communism, the young men and women of the two moieties met in spring for a celebration which was at once a collective sexual union, ensuring both the reproduction of the human community and the revival of the fertile powers of nature, and a rite of initiation, implying that the participants died and were born again:

> Initiation was originally an annual summer celebration for a clearly defined and comprehensive age group comprising all those of both sexes who had just reached puberty. The rite of human death and rebirth is thus traced back to a form in which it is inseparable from the death and rebirth of vegetation. Human life moved in unison with nature. The same pulse throbbed in both.[36]

Secondly, in the higher stages of tribal society, with the growth of magical fraternities, initiation became exclusive and tended, especially among the men, to assume the form of a contest or ordeal (Vol. I, p. 48); and at the same time the collective union was replaced by the sacred marriage, a rite which was still designed to revive the powers of nature but was performed in secret on behalf of the community by the magical fraternities.

Thirdly, with the development of agriculture based on irrigation, which required, as we have seen, organised mass labour, the celebration became associated with the calendar. The old lunar calendar of 354 days, resting as it did on simple observation, required no special knowledge, but it was useless for the organisation of agriculture, which depends on the sun. The discovery of the solar year of 365 days was by no means a simple matter. It was a secret of the priests, who, as organisers of

[36] Thomson AA 132.

agriculture, were faced with the problem of co-ordinating the lunar calendar with the solar year. This they did by inserting an interval of eleven days between the end of one lunar year and the beginning of the next. The interval might be inserted at any one of the turning-points in the solar year—the two solstices and the two equinoxes. At Babylon it was done at the vernal equinox, immediately before the ploughing was begun. During these eleven days everything was in suspense, as though the world had come to a stop.

Finally, with the rise of the state, the king was presented as the agent who maintained the world in being by means of an annual contest with the powers of chaos. His period of office, limited initially to one year, became permanent, subject at first to an annual renewal, which was later reduced to a formality; and at the same time his authority was invested with divine sanction through the myth of Marduk, the god who saved his fellow gods from destruction and so became their king and creator of the world. The myth of creation sprang from the reality of kingship, but in the human consciousness, split by the class struggle, this relation was inverted, and the king's part in the ritual was accepted as a commemoration of what the god had done in the beginning. It may be that the rite of the fifth day, in which he was 'reduced to the rank of layman', was intended by the sagacious priests as a reminder to their sovereign that he owed his position, not to himself alone, but to the ruling class whose representative he was. If so, it still remains true that he was as indispensable to them as they were to him. Without him, they could not have maintained their hold over the minds of the people.

5. The Primeval Pair

The *Enuma elish*, as we have it, is written in Akkadian, and dates from about the middle of the second millennium B.C., when the kings of Babylon were in control of the whole country. It is based, however, on an older version, in which the hero had not been Marduk of Babylon but the Sumerian wind-god, Enlil, who belonged to Nippur.[37] If it was the wind-god who cut

[37] Jacobsen in Frankfort BP 183-4.

Tiamat in two and raised up half of her body to form the sky, the incident becomes intelligible; for it is a world-wide belief that heaven and earth, originally one, were forced apart by wind or light.[38] In China, Shang Ti, the god of creation, was parted by one of his children from the mother goddess with whom he was united, and then he went up into the sky to produce the fertilising rain.[39] In Polynesia, Rangi (heaven) and Papa (earth) were locked together in an embrace, until their children, who had never seen the light, tore them apart, 'so that light was made manifest also'.[40] In Egypt the sexes are reversed, presumably because, in the absence of rain, the earth was regarded as the fertilising agent. The sky goddess, Nut, was represented as bending over the recumbent earth-god, Geb, from whom she was separated by their child, Shu, the wind-god.[41]

By restoring Enlil in place of Marduk, we have explained the treatment of Tiamat; but a further anomaly still remains. The story of the separation of heaven and earth has already been told, in another form, at the beginning of the poem. Such reduplications are found in other theogonies. Poems of this kind are composed over a long period by collecting and combining ancient myths whose original significance has in many cases ceased to be understood.

The story told at the beginning of the poem is as follows. At first there was chaos, in which the male Apsu (fresh water) mingled with the female Tiamat (salt water). From these were born Lahmu and Lahamu, representing silt; from these Anshar and Kishar, representing the rim of the sky and the edge of the earth; and from these again Anu and Nudimmut. Anu is the sky-god. Nudimmut is another name for Ea, originally En-ki, 'lord of the earth'. There seems to have been some reconstruction at this point, and it is believed that originally the third pair was An-ki, heaven and earth, who were forced apart by the wind.[42] From them sprang the gods, who brought order into chaos. Similarly, in an Egyptian text we read that in the beginning there were two pairs of snakes, male and female, and two pairs of toads, also male and female, representing the

[38] Marót THE.   [39] Eberhard 19.
[40] Makemson 49–74.   [41] Roscher 2. 1010, 3. 487.
[42] Jacobsen in Frankfort BP 185.

primeval waters and the darkness that lay upon them, and from these emerged the sun-god.[43]

All cosmogonies of this type, which is evidently very primitive, have been classed as 'genealogical', because they are founded on the notion that the physical universe was brought into being by a process of sexual reproduction. This designation may be accepted, with one reservation. To us, familiar with the institution of monogamy and the facts of procreation, the primeval pair appears simply as a projection of the wedded couple. This is a misapprehension. It cannot have appeared in that light to the savages, among whom it originated, for the simple reason that in their society marriage was collective and the idea of physical paternity was unknown. For them the primeval pair was not a pair of individuals but a pair of moieties, represented as male and female because the males of the one moiety mated with the females of the other. In other words, these genealogical cosmogonies are all variations, more or less refined, of the theme contained in the Australian myth of the eaglehawk and crow (p. 52). The idea of sexual reproduction is a *social* image. The evolution and organisation of the universe is presented in a form determined by the evolution and organisation of the tribe.

6. *The Function of the Kingship*

Frankfort writes:

> The ancients, like the modern savages, saw man always as part of society and society as imbedded in nature and dependent on cosmic forces. For them nature and man did not stand in opposition and therefore did not have to be apprehended by different modes of cognition.[44]

This is true, so far as it goes. In the savage consciousness, as we have already pointed out, nature is identified with society because it is only known to the extent that it has been drawn into social relations through the labour of production, which, being at a low level of development, restricts both the relations between men and nature and their relations with one another (p. 51). But these ancients were not savages. Granted that no Babylonian or Egyptian thinkers ever succeeded in regarding

[43] Frankfort KG 184–5.   [44] Frankfort BP 12.

nature objectively as governed by its own laws, independent of man, their thought differs, nevertheless, from savage thought, just as their society marked an advance on primitive communism. If we understand how this advance was achieved, we shall also understand why they failed to achieve more than they did.

These kingdoms of the Near East had arisen, as we have seen, on the basis of a division between mental and manual labour, which resulted, on the one hand, in an extraordinarily rapid development of the productive forces, and, on the other, in a division of society into antagonistic classes, a leisured class and a labouring class. It was only after the division of society against itself that the possibility arose of a distinction being made between society and nature; but in the ancient Near East this possibility was never realised, because the intellectual development of the ruling class was restricted by the contradictions inherent in the conditions of its existence.

In both Babylonia and Egypt there arose, through the development of production and more especially of exchange, the elements of a new class of merchants, intermediate between the ruling class of priests or nobles, who were in control of irrigation, and the exploited class of peasants and slaves. It would appear that in one Sumerian city, Lagash, the merchants actually seized power for a short time under the usurper Urukagina (about 2400 B.C.), but they were overthrown.[45] The reforms of Hammurabi (1792–50 B.C.), of the Ist Dynasty of Babylon, were due to pressure from them, and in Egypt a similar movement can be traced in the rise of the bureaucracy at the end of the XIIth Dynasty; but in neither country did the merchants ever establish themselves in power or even become conscious of themselves as a revolutionary class. They remained economically and ideologically dependent on the landowning class:

The division of labour . . . manifests itself also in the ruling class as the division of mental and material labour, so that inside this class one part appears as the thinkers of the class—its active, conceptive ideologists, who make the perfecting of the illusion of the class about itself their chief source of livelihood,—while the others' attitude to these ideas and illusions is more passive and receptive, because they are in reality the active members of the

[45] Avdiev 54–6.

class and have less time to make up illusions and ideas about themselves. Within this class this cleavage can even develop into a certain opposition and hostility between the two parts, which, however, in the case of a practical collision, in which the class itself is endangered, automatically comes to nothing; in which case also there vanishes the semblance that the ruling ideas were not the ideas of the ruling class and had a power distinct from the power of this class. The existence of revolutionary ideas in a particular period presupposes the existence of a revolutionary class.[46]

Hence, notwithstanding all that had been achieved in the technique of engineering, architecture, chemistry, astronomy, and mathematics, the ideologists of this epoch were forced to subordinate their knowledge to the notion that the existing structure of society was part of the natural order. The perpetuation of this illusion was the special function of the kingship.

The king was indispensable to the ruling class politically and ideologically. Politically, he was commander of the army, the main weapon of state power; ideologically, he embodied in his person what Marx called 'the imaginary substance of the tribe',[47] that is, the illusion of its lost unity and equality. All the paraphernalia of mystification with which the priests surrounded him was designed to present him in this light. Every festival in the calendar was contrived to lead, as Frankfort has expressed it, 'to a reaffirmation of the harmonious interlocking of nature and society in the person of the sovereign'.[48] This idea was reaffirmed so insistently just because it had ceased to correspond with men's understanding of reality. The ideological superstructure which had been thrown up in the transition from primitive communism to class society ended by becoming a dead weight crushing all further development of the productive forces. And hence, for all their technical achievements— their towers reaching unto heaven and their death-defying pyramids—these Bronze Age societies failed to create anything that might be called philosophy. On this point Langdon remarked:

Perhaps the failure to construct a system of philosophy was due to a consistent method of eradicating all views not in keeping with the orthodox

[46] Marx-Engels GI 39-40.   [47] Marx FKPV 8
          [48] Frankfort KG 190.

fatalism. At any rate we hear of no Babylonian thinkers who were persecuted for their views or who ventured to write on any aspect of philosophy except ethics.[49]

Frankfort's judgment is even more categorical:

There are very few passages which show the discipline, the cogency of reasoning, which we associate with thinking.[50]

In passing this judgment, however, we should remind ourselves that the ruling class of this epoch was only doing what every ruling class has done from that day to this. Analysing the bourgeois idea of the individual, which reflected the private enterprise of expanding capitalism, Marx observes that he 'was regarded as a product not of history but of nature', and adds that 'this illusion has been characteristic of every new epoch in the past'.[51] It is revealed very plainly by Frankfort himself in his discussion of the present subject.

Having described the way of thinking characteristic of the ancient Near East as 'an intuitive, an almost visionary, mode of apprehension', to which he gives the name of 'speculative thought', he continues:

In our own time speculative thought finds its scope more severely restricted than it has been at any other period. For we possess in science another instrument for the interpretation of experience, one that has achieved marvels and retains its full fascination. We do not allow speculative thought, under any circumstances, to encroach on the sacred precincts of science. . . . Where, then, is speculative thought allowed to range to-day? Its main concern is with man—his nature and his problems, his values and his destiny. For man does not quite succeed in becoming a scientific object to himself. His need of transcending chaotic experience and conflicting facts leads him to seek a metaphysical hypothesis that may clarify his urgent problems. On the subject of his 'self' man will, most obstinately, speculate —even to-day.[52]

Blind to the reality of his class relations, bewildered by chaotic experience and conflicting facts, man—that is, bourgeois man— seeks for a solution to the mystery, not in science, which has unravelled so many mysteries and made him what he is, but in 'a metaphysical hypothesis', which will somehow, he hopes, bring order out of chaos. And so, although the ziggurats and

[49] Langdon BCL 439.   [50] Frankfort BP 11.
[51] Marx CCPE 267.   [52] Frankfort BP 12.

pyramids are in ruins, the illusion that inspired them is still cherished, most obstinately, even to-day, although already, among a third of the earth's inhabitants, it has been shattered by the working class, which, having recognised man's place in history, is busy reuniting society and transforming nature.

7. *The Hebrew Prophets*

Midway between Egypt and Mesopotamia lay the land of Canaan, less fertile in its soil but endowed with other natural resources which those countries lacked. Some time in the latter half of the second millennium B.C. it was settled by the Hebrews, a league of nomadic tribes from the desert, who under Solomon established a kingdom similar in character, though far less rich and powerful, to its mighty neighbours on the south and east. On the death of Solomon the kingdom split in two, and the Hebrews never recovered their unity and independence. Yet, though politically insignificant, they were destined to win a place in history comparable only with the Greeks. It is a commonplace to say that these two cultures, united in Christianity, constitute the foundation on which European civilisation has been built; and yet, so far as their early history is concerned, they have been treated by most historians in complete isolation from one another, as though nothing were to be gained by considering what they had in common and why their development was so different. All that can be attempted here is to draw attention, in the course of my main argument, to certain features of Jewish history which may serve to illustrate the connection; and the first of these may aptly be introduced in concluding our discussion of the oriental despotism.

Both Egypt and Mesopotamia depended on imports for metals and timber. In Egypt the copper mines of Sinai were near enough to be kept under direct control, but there was no good building timber nearer than Lebanon. Mesopotamia was lacking in stone as well. Copper was imported from Armenia, copper and tin from Syria, copper and silver from Cappadocia, timber from Syria and Palestine, stone from Elam. In exchange, both countries offered from the beginning their surplus of grain, and later, with the growth of handicrafts, a wide range of goods manufactured from the imported raw materials.

The trading relations established in this way introduced the surrounding peoples to the use of bronze and so drew them into the wake of the economic and social developments that had already taken place in the great river valleys. During the second millennium B.C. there arose three major powers: Egypt in the south, Babylonia in the east, and the Cappadocian kingdom of the Hittites in the west. These powers traded and made war with one another, contending for the mastery of the intervening area, with Syria and Palestine as their battleground. In 1288 B.C. the Egyptians were defeated in Syria by the Hittites. A century later the Hittite kingdom collapsed under an attack from the west. Shortly after that Babylon fell to the Assyrians, who campaigned over the whole area and eventually conquered Egypt; then their empire too collapsed, and after a brief interval, in which Babylon recovered her supremacy, the whole of the Near East, from Elam to Ionia and from Egypt to Armenia, fell to the Medes and Persians. The Persian Empire marked an advance on its predecessors in that it was organised systematically under satraps responsible to the central government instead of depending on tribute exacted from recalcitrant native kings.

From these considerations it follows that the intervening region, comprising Syria and Palestine, presents some special features due to the geographical and historical conditions.

In the first place, its long coast has a number of good harbours opening on to the Mediterranean. In the course of the Bronze Age there arose, on or near the coast, a series of commercial city-states. The most important were Ugarit, Byblos, and Alalakh in Syria, and the Phœnician cities of Tyre and Sidon. These states began, like the Egyptian and Mesopotamian, as hieratic kingships based on the land; but, owing to the comparative unimportance of irrigation and the more rapid growth of trade, the merchant class became relatively strong and succeeded, not indeed in overthrowing the kingship, but in using it as an instrument for the encouragement of trade.

In the second place, living under the shadow of such powerful neighbours, none of these cities was able to subjugate the others in a united kingdom covering the whole region. Their internal

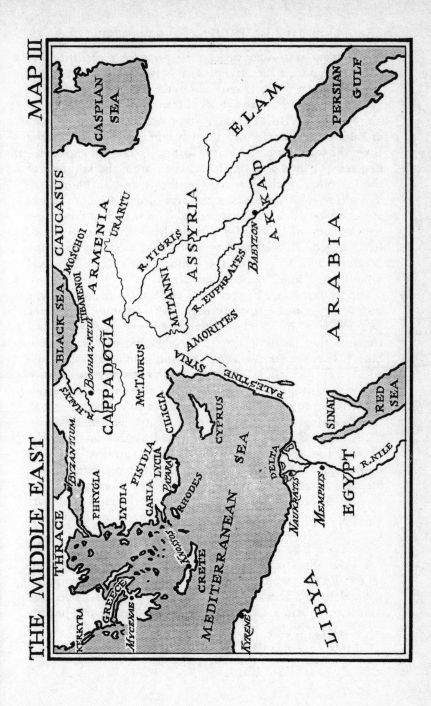

MAP III

THE MIDDLE EAST

CASPIAN SEA

CAUCASUS

ARMENIA

MOSCHOI

TIBARENOI

URARTU

R.TIGRIS

MITANNI

ASSYRIA

R.EUPHRATES

BABYLON

AKKAD

ELAM

PERSIAN GULF

AMORITES

ARABIA

BLACK SEA

R.HALYS

BYZANTIUM

BOGHAZ-KEUI

CAPPADOCIA

Mt.TAURUS

SYRIA

CILICIA

PALESTINE

THRACE

PHRYGIA

LYDIA

PISIDIA

CARIA

LYCIA

PATARA

RHODES

CYPRUS

MEDITERRANEAN SEA

SINAI

RED SEA

DELTA

NAUKRATIS

MEMPHIS

R.NILE

EGYPT

KERKYRA

GREECE

MYCENAE

KNOSSOS

CRETE

KYRENE

LIBYA

development was intensified by the persistence of their local autonomy and the keen competition between them.

We first hear of the Phœnicians in the sixteenth century B.C. as providing warships, and crews to man them, for the Egyptian kings of the XVIIIth Dynasty, who controlled the greater part of Palestine.[53] They formed a loosely knit league of cities strung along the coast north of Mount Carmel. To the east and south, between the coast and the desert, there arose the kingdom of the Hebrews, speaking a language closely akin to Phœnician. The Hebrews had adopted a settled agricultural life, but without abandoning entirely their pastoral habits, and without forgetting their pastoral traditions.[54] Their god, Jehovah, was a tribal god, like the gods of neighbouring tribes, such as Chemosh of the Moabites and Milcam of the Ammonites.[55] Their historical destiny was shaped by two main factors.

On the one hand, the principal trade route between Egypt and Mesopotamia passed through their territory. Merchant caravans were constantly making their way backwards and forwards through the plain of Esdraelon and past the Judæan hills.[56] They were thus drawn from the beginning into the cross-currents of international trade, always in a subordinate capacity but with lasting effects on their social relations.[57] The kings endeavoured to strengthen their position against the priesthood by promoting commerce, but their efforts were nullified by their weakness in the international field. Again and again the plain of Esdraelon was traversed by foreign armies, looting as they went, and the people were subjected to repeated invasions, massacres, plantations, and deportations. No other country was exposed so helplessly and continuously to the ravages of war; and yet, owing to its central position between the contending powers, it was never permanently subdued. It was the cockpit of the Near East.

On the other hand, the great desert stretching from Gilead to the Persian Gulf remained an inexhaustible reservoir of pastoral tribes. These nomads were always on the move, and from time to time some of them settled among the Judæan

[53] Schaeffer 14–5.   [54] Robinson 1. 49.
[55] S. A. Cook in CAH 3. 429.   [56] Robinson 1. 29.
              [57] Ib. 1. 353–4, 363.

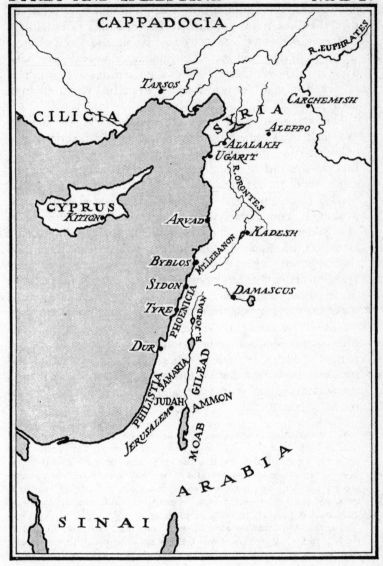

hills.[58] Thanks to this continual contact with their own ancestral
institutions, the common people of Israel not only preserved
their tribal traditions but cherished them with a fierce tenacity
as they saw them threatened by economic and social changes
arising from trade and war. Their spokesmen were the prophets,
who, it has been observed, were 'the inheritors and guardians
of that democratic principle which Israel had preserved from
nomad days'.[59]

This combination of historical circumstances was unique.
We shall meet something like it in Hesiod's Bœotia and in
Solon's Attica; but nowhere else in the ancient world do we
find, as in Israel of the ninth and eighth centuries B.C., the
sufferings of the exploited masses recorded in their own words.
Hesiod was a small farmer, who urged the workers to go on
working in spite of everything and consoled them with stories
of a golden age far back in the irrevocable past.[60] Amos was a
herdsman, who spoke for the workers, not to them, threatened
their oppressors with Jehovah's anger, and promised them a new
age of plenty in the years to come. The Attic peasants of Solon's
day must have suffered almost as much, but their only recorded
spokesman was a nobleman, who used their grievances as a
means of promoting the interests of his own class. In the
Hebrew prophets, for the first time in history, the dispossessed
peasantry found a voice—a voice preserved in writing and
treasured from that day to this by generations of European
peasants struggling against the same wrongs and inspired with
the same hopes:

Also Amaziah said unto Amos, O thou seer, go, flee thou away unto the
land of Judah, and there eat bread, and prophesy there; but prophesy not
again any more at Bethel; for it is the king's sanctuary, and it is the royal
house. Then answered Amos and said to Amaziah, I was no prophet, neither
was I a prophet's son, but I was an herdsman and a dresser of sycamore-
trees, and the Lord took me from following the flock, and the Lord said
unto me, Go, prophesy unto my people Israel. . . .[61]
Hear this, O ye that would swallow up the needy, and cause the poor of
the land to fail, saying, When will the new moon be gone, that we may sell
corn? and the sabbath, that we may set forth wheat? making the ephah small,
and the shekel great, and dealing falsely with balances of deceit; that we may

[58] Robinson 1. 345–6, Cook in CAH 3. 433.   [59] Robinson 1. 325.
[60] Thomson AA 68.   [61] Amos 7. 12.

buy the poor for silver, and the needy for a pair of shoes, and sell the refuse
of the wheat. The Lord hath sworn by the excellency of Jacob, Surely I will
never forget any of their works. . . .[62]

Behold, the days come, saith the Lord, that the plowman shall overtake
the reaper, and the treader of grapes him that soweth seed; and the mountains
shall drop sweet wine, and all the hills shall melt.[63]

At last, after nearly three thousand years, the prophecy of Amos
is coming true.

If Solomon had been able to consolidate his kingdom, the
prophets would have been suppressed. As it was, they preserved
the ideal of tribal unity in a form determined by the special
history of their people. Like the kingship, Hebrew monotheism
embodies 'the imaginary substance of the tribe', but in a different and purer form. The idea of kingship was imposed on
the people by the ruling class as a means of consolidating its
power. The idea of Jehovah was created by the people themselves as a symbol of their memories and aspirations. Its moral
nobility springs from its historical origin as a vision of the
classless society that had passed away and was to come again.

[62] Amos 8. 4.   [63] Amos 9. 13.

Part Three

FROM BABYLON TO MILETOS

Nations borrow only what they are nearly in a condition to have invented themselves.

FERGUSON

V

THE GREEK CALENDAR

1. *Syria and Crete*

IN Egypt and Mesopotamia the rise of the state was determined by two developments in the productive forces—bronze-working and irrigation. Irrigation would have been impossible without bronze tools, and without irrigation there would have been no large-scale agriculture. The agricultural surplus appropriated by the ruling class was immense. Its disposal involved a system of accounting, which was a form of intellectual labour as highly skilled as the engineering of irrigation. It was used partly for the production of commodities, and in Mesopotamia a rudimentary form of silver money was evolved. It is important, however, to observe that, apart from foodstuffs, commodity production was limited mainly, even in Mesopotamia, to luxury goods. The surplus was exchanged for metals, timber, and other raw materials not obtainable at home, but the internal economy remained fundamentally a natural one, consisting in the production of simple use values or of values surrendered as tribute and exchanged directly on the local market.

The Mesopotamian cities were driven to expand by the need for raw materials, which they extorted as tribute or purchased in exchange for agricultural products or manufactured articles. Trade of this kind led to the rise of the Hittite kingdom, which controlled the silver mines of Mount Tauros. In the course of the third millennium Mesopotamia, Anatolia, and Egypt were drawn together by a network of caravan routes passing to and fro across the intervening deserts, with access to the sea along the coast of Syria and Palestine.

In these conditions there arose along the Syrian coast a number of small but prosperous city-states, peopled by Phœnicians, Hittites, Hurrites, and Mitannians. The valleys were fertile and the mountains abounded in excellent timber, stone, and tin. There were good harbours, and it was only a short crossing to Cyprus, so named after its wealth of copper. Of these assets the most important for the future were the forests and the harbours.

For the old continental world of Egypt and Mesopotamia these Syrian seaports were the gateway to the Mediterranean, which offered cheap transport and profitable trade in raw materials and luxury goods with the undeveloped countries beyond the sea.

These cities differed from the Mesopotamian in several respects. On the one hand, irrigation played a less important part in agriculture, and the agricultural surplus was smaller. On the other hand, the relative volume of industrial production was greater. In addition to the manufacture of jewellery, cosmetics, and other luxury goods, there were dyeworks for dyeing wool with the sea-purple extracted from the murex shell, copper foundries for smelting the ores imported from Cyprus, workshops for the manufacture of bronze tools, and shipyards, turning out many types of vessel, including transports large enough to accommodate ninety men.[1] Even more important was the carrying trade between Mesopotamia and the Mediterranean. These cities owed their prosperity very largely to the accumulation of merchant capital. From the cuneiform tablets recovered at Ugarit we learn that no less than seven languages were in use in that city. Among the tablets are fragments of a bilingual dictionary, which contained the following entry under the heading 'cost':

The price; high price; low price; poor price; fixed price; good price; stiff price; fair price; town price. . . .[2]

It was in these cities, in response to commercial needs, which required of every merchant a knowledge of several languages and several scripts, that the Phœnician alphabet was invented.

During the same period there arose in Crete a number of similar city-states, which were eventually unified under the rule of Knossos. Lying across the entrance to the Ægean, the island was well placed for trade, and being protected by the sea, these cities were free from heavy expenditure on defence. In their economic and political organisation they closely resembled the Syrian. At the head of the community was a priest-king, who had inherited the traditions of the Mesopotamian kingship, but in a form modified by the development of trade. The commercial character of the Minoan kingship has been noted in the

[1] Schaeffer 38–9.   [2] Ib. 40.

preceding volume (p. 28). Here it only remains to add that these Syrian and Minoan cities maintained close relations with one another, commercial and cultural. The importance of this point for the origin of Greek civilisation is so great that it is worth pausing to hear what the archæologists have to say about it.

Reporting in 1939 on his excavations at Ugarit, Schaeffer writes:

We are convinced that further research on protohistoric sites in Syria and neighbouring regions will throw yet more light on the origins of civilisation in the eastern Mediterranean lands. In particular, as regards the Ægean, it seems necessary to reduce the influence hitherto accorded to predynastic and protodynastic Egypt and to search rather in the direction of Asia. One must not forget that between Crete and Egypt the mariners of those days had to negotiate one of the widest stretches of open sea in the Mediterranean. On the other hand, the numerous islands in the Ægean Sea, the southern coast of Asia Minor and Cyprus, all served as links between Crete and Syria and its immediate Mesopotamian hinterland. This was the oldest and most important trade route between east and west, and Ugarit was one of the principal stopping-places on it from the fourth millennium onwards.[3]

Woolley reached a similar conclusion ten years later after his excavations at Alalakh:

There can be no doubt but that Crete owes the best of its architecture, and its frescoes, to the Asiatic mainland. And we can say more than this. The exchange of goods by international trade is one thing, and a most important thing, but it has its limits. One cannot export a palace on board ship, nor is the 'art and mystery' of fresco-working a form of merchandise. These professional techniques require direct contacts, and we are bound to believe that trained experts, members of the architects' and painters' guilds, were invited to travel overseas from Asia (possibly from Alalakh itself, seeing that it had its Mediterranean harbour) to build and decorate the palaces of the Cretan rulers.[4]

Later still, as a result of further expansion, there arose a number of small states on the Greek mainland, and one of these, Mycenæ, eventually wrested the lead from Knossos and for a short time dominated the Mediterranean carrying trade. Of the rest the most powerful, according to ancient tradition, were Sparta, Pylos, Thebes, and Orchomenos. Through this movement of commercial expansion the technical achievements

[3] Ib. 3.   [4] Woolley FK 77.

of the Near East, and the ideas and customs associated with them, were transmitted to Greece.

To what extent were these cities of the late Bronze Age dependent on slave labour? It is not yet possible to give a precise answer to this question. We know that merchants' capital has been associated with piracy and kidnapping in all ages, and that the Phœnicians and Ionians of the ensuing epoch were notorious slave-raiders. It is probable, therefore, that the slave traffic kept pace with other forms of trade. We know that there were slaves in Ugarit, public and private, and it is likely that in Syria and Greece, as in Babylonia, the typical form of the institution, employing the largest number, was temple slavery, recruited not so much from slave-dealers as from defaulting debtors, kidnapped children, and above all prisoners of war.

In general, however, it seems that throughout the Bronze Age the mass labour required for the execution of public works was obtained by conscripting the free peasantry. The Great Pyramid, according to Herodotus, was built by successive gangs of 100,000 men, each gang working for three months at a stretch, and the whole project, including the construction of roads from the quarries to the site, took twenty years to complete.[5] The workers are described as Egyptians and therefore were not slaves. Similarly, in our account of Solomon's building of the temple at Jerusalem, the two categories of forced labour and slave labour are carefully distinguished:

And king Solomon raised a levy out of all Israel; and the levy was thirty thousand men. And he sent them to Lebanon, ten thousand a month by courses: a month they were in Lebanon and two months at home; and Adoniram was over the levy. And Solomon had threescore and ten thousand that bare burdens, and fourscore thousand that were hewers in the mountains, besides Solomon's chief officers that were over the work, three thousand and three hundred, which bare rule over the people that wrought in the work. And the king commanded, and they hewed out great stones, costly stones, to lay the foundation of the house with wrought stone. And Solomon's builders and Hiram's builders and the Gebalites did fashion them, and prepared the timber and the stones to build the house. . . .[6]

As for all the people that were left of the Amorites, the Hittites, the Perizzites, the Hivites and the Jebusites, which were not of the children of Israel; their children that were left after them in the land, whom the children

---

[5] Hdt. 2. 124, cf. D.S. 1. 63.   [6] 1 Kings 5. 13.

of Israel were not able utterly to destroy, of them did Solomon raise a levy of bondservants, unto this day. But of the children of Israel did Solomon make no bondservants; but they were the men of war, and his servants, and his princes, and his captains, and rulers of his chariots and of his horsemen.[7]

Some of these figures are no doubt exaggerated, and in any case it is not likely that so large a labour force was available to the rulers of Knossos or Mycenæ; but there is no reason to suppose that in Greece of this period there was any radical departure from the traditional modes of exploitation.

2. The Egyptian and Mesopotamian Calendars

We know that these city-states of the Bronze Age were governed by kings, probably priest-kings. The cuneiform texts of Ugarit suggest that the kingship there was similar in nature to the Mesopotamian. For precise information about the Minoan kingship we must await the interpretation of the Minoan script, but in the meantime we can do something to fill the gap by investigating the early history of the Greek calendar; for here as elsewhere the development of the calendar was closely associated with the kingship. At the end of our investigation we shall find that some light has been thrown on the origins of Greek philosophy.

Among primitive peoples the calendar is regulated entirely by the moon.[8] The basic unit is the month, corresponding to a complete lunation and divided into two or three parts according to the lunar phases. The lunar (synodic) month contains 29·53 days, and twelve months make the lunar year of 354·36 days. There is thus a difference of approximately eleven days between the lunar year and the solar astronomical year of 365·24 days, which corresponds to the cycle of the seasons. This is an embarrassment even to primitive peoples, but with the development of agriculture it became an imperative necessity to devise some means of co-ordinating the lunar calendar with the solar year. The problem may be solved in two ways. The lunar calendar may be supplemented from time to time by adding a thirteenth month in order to bring it back into step with the solar year. This is the lunisolar calendar. Or the lunar basis

---

[7] 1 Kings 9. 20.   [8] Nilsson PTR 148–223.

may be abandoned. The months are retained, but they are extended or adapted to a period corresponding more or less closely to the seasonal cycle of 365·24 days. This is the solar calendar.

The Egyptians invented a solar calendar early in the third millennium. They divided the year into three seasons and twelve months of thirty days each, with five additional days at the beginning, which was fixed with reference to the rising of Sirius in July. This calendar was used in civil administration, but the religious festivals continued to follow the old lunar calendar, with the result that they fell behind the solar calendar at the rate of eleven days a year. In order to obviate this inconvenience a lunisolar calendar was introduced about 2500 B.C. It was tied to the solar calendar by intercalating a thirteenth month in nine years out of every twenty-five.[9] This is the twenty-five-year cycle: $(25 \times 365) = (16 \times 354 \cdot 36) + (9 \times 383 \cdot 89) = 9125$.

In Mesopotamia, according to Neugebauer, the calendar remained strictly lunar, without any systematic intercalation, until the fifth century B.C.[10] A lunisolar calendar was then constructed by intercalating a thirteenth month in seven years out of every nineteen. This is the nineteen-year cycle: $(19 \times 365 \cdot 24) = (12 \times 354 \cdot 36) + (7 \times 383 \cdot 89) = 6939 \cdot 5$. If this view is correct—and it is not quite certain—the backwardness of the Mesopotamian calendar, as compared with the Egyptian, is probably to be explained by the administrative autonomy of the city-states.

In Greece, too, the calendar was regulated independently by each state, but its structure seems to have been everywhere the same.[11] The year was divided into twelve months alternating in length between twenty-nine and thirty days, and the deficit of eleven days was made good by intercalating a thirteenth month in three years out of every eight. This is the octennial cycle: $(8 \times 365) = (8 \times 354) + (2 \times 29) + 30 = 2920$. It will be understood that, since the true lunar year contains 354·36 days, not 354, the phases of the moon did not actually coincide with those days of the calendar month to which they were

---

[9] Parker CAE.   [10] Neugebauer 97, 101, 123.
[11] L. Bischoff in Pauly-Wissowa *s.v.* Kalender; Nilsson ERBGK, SS.

traditionally assigned; and hence it was customary for Greek writers to distinguish, when circumstances required, between the actual new moon and the nominal new moon.[12]

The main question for this chapter is whether this lunisolar calendar was invented independently by the Greeks, and, if not, whence and how did they acquire it?

3. *The Greek Calendar: its Ultimate Origin*

There are numerous correspondences between Greek and Babylonian festivals which suggest that the two calendars had a common basis.

In Babylonia offerings to the dead were made in the month of Teshrit, the first of the second half-year (September–October); at Athens the Genesia, a feast of ancestors, fell in the corresponding month of Boedromion. In the month of Kislev (November–December) drink-offerings were made to Eresh-kigal, goddess of the underworld, to fructify the earth; the Attic Haloa, an agrarian feast of Demeter, was held in the month of Poseideon (December–January). These parallels were pointed out by Langdon.[13] There are many others.

There was great diversity in Greece with regard to the beginning of the calendar year.[14] In Athens and Delphi it began at the first new moon after the summer solstice; in Bœotia and Delos after the winter solstice. In Chios, on the other hand, it began with the vernal equinox; in Sparta, Rhodes, Crete, and Miletos with the autumnal equinox. These variations have not been explained. They may have been determined by local factors, or they may have been inherent in the Greek calendar from the outset. At Babylon, as we have seen, the New Year Festival took place at the vernal equinox, but at Erech and Ur it was repeated at the beginning of the second half-year, that is, at the autumnal equinox,[15] and there is evidence that the old Sumerian year had begun at the winter solstice.[16] Notwithstanding these

---

[12] Th. 2. 28. That is why, in the last section of the *Works and Days* (765–828), dealing with the traditional associations of particular days, all of which had their *origin* in the lunar phases, there is no mention of the moon.

[13] Langdon BMSC 86–7.   [14] Pauly-Wissowa *s.v.* Kalender.

[15] C. J. Gadd in Hooke MR 46.   [16] Langdon in CAH 1. 462.

discrepancies, we find all over Greece traces of a bipartite year divided, as in Babylonia, at the equinox.

The tribal federation known as the Amphiktyones met at Delphi twice a year, in spring and autumn.[17] When Theseus set out for Crete to slay the Minotaur (Vol. I, p. 383), he left Athens on the 6th of Mounychion (April–May) and returned six months later on the 7th of Pyanopsion (October–November).[18] In the cult of Apollo at Delos oracles were delivered only in the six summer months; in the cult of the same god at Patara in Lycia they were delivered only in the six winter months.[19] The tie between these two centres was very old. The Delians possessed some ancient hymns to Apollo which they attributed to Olen of Lycia (Vol. I, p. 483), and the founders of Ionia chose members of the Glaukidai, a Greek family from Xanthos, to be their kings (Vol. I, p. 165). It will be observed that at Delos the oracular season cuts across the calendar year, which began in the historical period with the winter solstice.

At Athens the youths ready for initiation (épheboi) began their training in Boedromion (September–October), and they had important duties to discharge in Elaphebolion (March–April). In that month, under the direction of the árchon, they sacrificed a bull to Dionysus.[20] At Magnesia-on-the-Maiandros a bull was presented to Zeus Sosipolis at the new moon of Kronion (October–November) with prayers for the safety of the city, peace, plenty, and a good harvest, and after being fattened through the winter it was sacrificed on the 12th of Artemision (April–May).[21] The sacrifice was performed by the stephanephóros, a priest whom we find in several Ionian cities. He was entitled to wear a crown, and also apparently purple, as a mark of royalty,[22] and he gave his name to the year.[23] He may be

---

[17] Str. 420, cf. D. 18. 154–5.   [18] Plu. Thes. 18, 22.

[19] Serv. ad Verg. A. 4. 143, cf. Hdt. 1. 182, D.S. 2. 47.

[20] Mommsen FSA 176, CIA 2. 471 (IG 2. 471), cf. CIA 4. 318b (IG. 2. 478).

[21] SIG 589. Kronion is identified with Pyanepsion by the fact that it coincided with the sowing, while the equation of Artemision with Mounychion may be inferred from the position of Artemision at Delos, Artamitios at Rhodes, Kos and elsewhere, and Artemisios in the Macedonian calendar.

[22] Str. 648, cf. 633.   [23] SIG 589. 1.

equated, therefore, with the Athenian *árchon basileús*, who exercised the sacral functions derived from the prehistoric kingship. A similar festival was observed in Miletos.[24]

At Olympia the priests known as Basilai sacrificed to Sosipolis on the Hill of Kronos at the vernal equinox. This rite may have been connected with the Games, which fell six or seven months earlier.[25] We are not told what the victim was, but the origin of the Basilai is betrayed by their name ('kings'), and the parallel with Magnesia is confirmed by the fact that in both cults the god Sosipolis was associated with the snake.[26] The god Dionysus, who was closely connected with Zeus, was worshipped as bull and snake.[27] At Kos a specially selected bull was sacrificed to Zeus Polieus by the *geraphóros basiléon*, whose royal origin is again clear ('bearer of the kings' privileges'), on the 20th of Batromios (probably February–March); but in this case there is no record of a corresponding observance six months earlier.[28]

This evidence suggests that there was in several Greek states an ancient co-ordination of equinoctial rites corresponding to the Mesopotamian New Year Festival observed in Nisan (March–April) and again in Teshrit (September–October). On the fifth day of the festival the king performed a ceremony, signifying the victory of Marduk over his enemies, in the presence of a white bull, which he addressed as 'divine bull of Anu, glorious light which illumines the darkness'. That the bull was subsequently sacrificed is not stated in our records, which are fragmentary, but it was certainly intended to represent the constellation Taurus, in allusion to the fact that the sun was in the sign of Taurus at the vernal equinox when the ceremony was instituted. This was the sun's position at the time of year in question throughout the fourth and third millennia. It moved out of Taurus into Aries about 1900 B.C.[29] The presentation of the bull must therefore have been an ancient feature of the festival. It follows that, if the Greek festivals mentioned above were ultimately of Mesopotamian origin, they must have been brought to Greece in Minoan times, presumably by way of Crete.

[24] Hsch. Διὸς βοῦς.   [25] Paus. 6. 20. 1.   [26] Harrison T 241, fig. 61.
[27] Ib. T 449, PSGR 398–400.   [28] SIG 1025.
[29] C. J. Gadd in Hooke MR 54, Langdon BEC 26.

This conclusion is in keeping with what we know of Minoan religion, in which the bull and the snake were both prominent objects of worship, the bull being associated with the kingship; and also with the evidence from Syria. In the Ugaritic texts the Phœnician god El, corresponding to the Greek Kronos, is described as 'the bull El' (Shor-El), and on a stone carving we see him enthroned beneath a winged sun-disk, which implies that he was connected with the solar year.[30] In the month of Skirophorion, just before the summer solstice, the Athenians sacrificed an ox to Zeus Polieus.[31] In Samos this month was named Kronion, the month of Kronos.[32] At Athens the next month, the first of the new year, in which the feast of Kronos was celebrated, was known in historical times as Hekatombaion, but we are told that it had formerly been called 'the month of Kronos'.[33] It would seem, therefore, that the feast of Kronos was connected with the summer solstice, being held just before it or just after it. All this needs further study, but the evidence at our disposal supports the hypothesis that the cult of a bull associated with the calendar reached Greece through Crete and Syria from Mesopotamia.

4. *The Greek Calendar: its Immediate Origin*

It has been argued by Nilsson, whose *Primitive Time-Reckoning* is the standard work on the early history of the calendar, that the Greek calendar was of non-Greek origin, and that it was introduced not earlier than the seventh century, or at most the eighth, under the supervision of the Delphic priesthood.[34]

The first part of this conclusion is undoubtedly correct in the sense that the Greek calendar did not belong to the indigenous tradition of the Greek-speaking immigrants into the Ægean. They took it over from the cultures with which they came in contact. But when? If it was a religious product, as Nilsson believes, there is a strong presumption that, like so much else in Greek religion, it was a heritage from the Minoan age, and there are positive reasons for believing that it was older and less dependent on Delphi than he allows.

[30] Schaeffer 60, Pl. 31.   [31] Mommsen 512.   [32] *SIG* 976.
[33] Plu. *Thes.* 12.   [34] Nilsson ERBGK 29, PTR 365.

If it had been constructed in comparatively recent times at Delphi, we should expect to find some degree of uniformity in the beginning of the calendar year and in the names of the months. But this is not the case. Only at Athens and Samos does the year begin, as at Delphi, with the summer solstice. The names of five of the Delphic months occur sporadically elsewhere, but the rest are unique.[35] Moreover, a comparison of the Attic-Ionic and Doric names suggests that their history followed that of the dialects themselves.

The Attic nomenclature agrees closely with the Delian,[36] pointing to an Attic-Ionic prototype older than the Ionian migration. We turn naturally to Bœotia. There we find a month Lenaion, mentioned by Hesiod, which recurs in Delos and all over Ionia. At Athens the feast of Lenaia was kept in the same month, and there is no doubt that, like other cults of Dionysus, it reached Athens from Bœotia. Similarly, Poseideon, found only in the Ionic calendars, recalls the Panionic cult of Poseidon Helikonios, which, as the name shows, originated in Bœotia.

ATHENS	DELOS	RHODES	DELPHI
*Hekatombaion	Hekatombaion	Panamos	*Apellaios
Metageitnion	Metageitnion	Karneios	Boukatios
Boedromion	Bouphonion	Dalios	Boathoos
Pyanopsion	Apatourion	*Thesmophorios	Heraios
Maimakterion	Aresion	Sminthios	Daidophorios
Poseideon	Poseideon	Diosthyos	Poitropios
Gamelion	*Lenaion	Theudaisios	Amalios
Anthesterion	Hieros	Pedageitnyos	Bysios
Elaphebolion	Galaxion	Badromios	Theoxenios
Mounychion	Artemision	Artamitios	Endyspoitropios
Thargelion	Thargelion	Agrianios	Herakleios
Skirophorion	Panemos	Hyakinthios	Ilaios

* First month of the calendar year.

The Doric nomenclature is different but within itself remarkably uniform. Karneios and Hyakinthios, referring to

[35] Some are difficult to explain, e.g. Amalios, Bysios, Ilaios. The Attic for Endyspoitropios would be Endoprostropaios, but what does it mean?

[36] In addition to the actual homonyms, the Delian Apatourion, Lenaion, and Galaxion all correspond to Attic feasts. Panamos (Panemos) is Macedonian.

ancient Dorian festivals, are almost universal. The same is true of Pedageitnyos, Badromios, and Theudaisios. The first two of these, though differently placed, are the same names as the Attic-Ionic Metageitnion and Boedromion; and Badromios or Boedromion corresponds in meaning to the Delphic Boathoos. But their different positions in the calendar make it difficult to suppose that they were borrowed from Delphi as late as the eighth or seventh century. And finally, the Doric Agrianios, which occurs at Aigina, Sparta, Rhodes, Kos, Kalymnos, and Byzantium, is found nowhere else except in Thebes and three other towns of Bœotia (Chaironeia, Lebadeia, Oropos). Similarly, the feast of Agriania is recorded only in Bœotia and Argos (Vol. I, pp. 195–6), and it is clear that it reached Argos from Bœotia. At Argos it was associated with the Proitides, who reduplicate the Minyades of Orchomenos, and with Melampous, who was descended from Minyas (Vol. I, p. 226). Where and when did this month get into the Doric calendar? Not in Argos, because that would leave unexplained its wide distribution in other Dorian communities. It seems they must have picked it up in Bœotia before they entered the Peloponnese.

If the Attic-Ionic and Doric calendars go back to a common source in Bœotia, their origin must be placed in the Minoan age. This confronts us with a further question. What was the relation between the Bœotian and Delphic calendars? Here we are at a loss, because the Bœotian material is fragmentary. If they go back to the Minoan age, there is no reason to give Delphi priority over Thebes and Orchomenos. All we can safely say is that the Attic-Ionic and Doric calendars are derived from a prehistoric original located in Central Greece.

If this hypothesis is accepted, it provides us at once with the oriental connection we have been looking for. Kadmos, the founder of Thebes, was a Phœnician, connected through Europa with Minos of Knossos. It will be remembered that Europa was carried off from Phœnicia by Zeus in the shape of a bull, and that in one of the religious texts from Ugarit we are told how the bull-god El mated with the mother-goddess Asherat (Vol. I, pp. 376–7).

If the Greek calendar was of Minoan origin, how, it may be asked, does it come about that only one month is mentioned by

name in Hesiod's *Works and Days*, a poem devoted to the agricultural labours of the year, and none at all in Homer? In regard
to Hesiod, the answer is that, owing to the Greek system of
intercalation, which will be discussed in the next section, the
calendar months were useless for his purpose, which was to
prescribe the exact time of year at which the farmer must begin
his various tasks. That could only be done by reference to the
solar year as revealed in the annual motion of the stars. In regard
to Homer, it is a mistake to suppose, as Nilsson has done,[37] that
the Homeric Greeks had no names for the months just because
they are not mentioned in the poems. Since their aim was to
present an idealised picture of the heroic past, the epic poets
avoided all mention of institutions that had only a local or
contemporary interest; and on this principle allusions to the
calendar were excluded, because its nomenclature varied from
city to city.[38]

We shall find in the *Works and Days* positive support for the
hypothesis that the Greek calendars, as we know them, are
derived from prehistoric Bœotia; but before pursuing this
matter we must examine the Greek system of intercalation.

5. *Intercalation*

When did the Greeks begin to intercalate systematically?
I have already mentioned Neugebauer's view that in Mesopotamia there is no evidence of systematic intercalation before
the fifth century B.C. In this he follows Kugler, who denied
that there was systematic intercalation in Mesopotamia before
528 B.C.[39] Accepting this view, and assuming that the Babylonians must have worked out a system before the Greeks,

---

[37] Nilsson PTR 345-6.

[38] There is, it appears, one allusion to a calendar feast in the *Odyssey*.
Odysseus landed in Ithaca 'at the turn of the month' (14. 162, 19. 306)
when there was no moon (14. 457), and five days later the town-criers
announced a festival at which a hecatomb was to be offered to Apollo of
the New Moon (20. 276-8, 21. 258-9 sch.). This must have been the
Hekatombaia, which was observed at Athens on the 7th of Hekatombaion
(*SIG* 615) and also at Delphi (*CIG* 1715). That is why Odysseus prays to
Apollo to direct his aim against the suitors (22. 7), who, since there were
108 of them (16. 247-61), made a symbolic hecatomb.

[39] Neugebauer 97; see Nilsson PTR 260.

Fotheringham and Langdon concluded that there was no systematic intercalation in Greece before the fourth century.[40]

Having no knowledge of the Sumerian and Akkadian languages, I cannot discuss the Babylonian evidence, and will merely utter a word of caution. Every system of intercalation based on the month as the intercalary unit is at best a clumsy expedient. Let us take the octennial cycle. The proper place for Lenaion, the first month of the Delian year, was the lunation following the winter solstice. After falling there in a given year, it would fall eleven days earlier in the next year, and in the third year, if there was no intercalation, it would fall twenty-two days too early. On the other hand, if a month was intercalated in the second year, it would fall in the third seven days too late. The inconvenience of these recurrent deviations is obvious, and it must sometimes have been found expedient to depart from the regular course of intercalation for the sake of particular occasions. We know that Agesilaos of Sparta intercalated a thirteenth month irregularly in order to increase the annual revenue,[41] and that at Rome the republican calendar was thrown into confusion by persistent interferences of this kind.[42] The same temptation must have presented itself to the Mesopotamian priesthood. The fact that an intercalary system was not consistently operated does not prove that it was unknown.

Let us return to Greece. Here we are on firmer ground. Herodotus writes:

> The Greeks intercalate a month every two or three years for the sake of the seasons; the Egyptians have twelve months of thirty days each with five extra days added every year, so that the cycle of the seasons is brought round to its starting-point.[43]

In the Egyptian solar calendar, which is here described correctly, there are no intermittent additions to the year. Appreciating the convenience of this arrangement, Herodotus contrasts it with the Greek method of intercalating a month 'every two or three years' (dia trítou éteos). This passage, which Fotheringham and Langdon overlooked, proves that systematic intercalation, based

[40] Fotheringham 179, Langdon BMSC 109.

[41] Plu. Agis 16. The Egyptian kings swore an oath at coronation never to tamper with the year: Parker 54.

[42] Fowler RF 4.   [43] Hdt. 2 . 4 . 1.

on the octennial cycle, was general in Greece in the fifth century B.C. Can it be traced further back?

Hesiod describes Lenaion as a midwinter month.[44] This was the position of the Attic Gamelion in the fifth century and the Delian Lenaion in the third. If this verse is genuine, there was a stable relation between the calendar and the seasons, and therefore a system of regular intercalation, in Hesiod's time.

Some scholars have denied that it is genuine. It is rejected by Nilsson as 'a later interpolation'.[45] The termination *-ón*, we are told, is Attic-Ionic, not Bœotian; no Bœotian month named after the Lenaia was known to Plutarch; and this is the only mention of a calendar month in the poem. There is very little force in these objections. The Ionic termination is dictated by the epic dialect. The other Bœotian data are many centuries later than Hesiod, and the names of the months were subject to change. The reason why this month is singled out for mention may well be that, as the first after the winter solstice, it marked the beginning of the Bœotian year. Furthermore, if we expunge this verse, we must do the same with vv. 557–8, where the same month is mentioned again, and then the whole of the intervening passage, which contains some characteristic Hesiodic conceits, will be left in the air. There is really no case for rejecting the verse at all.

In early Greece, according to the Hellenistic astronomer Geminos, the practice had been to intercalate a month in every other year.[46] It may be conjectured that this is the principle underlying the Greek festivals held every three years, which were associated almost exclusively with Demeter and Dionysus, that is, with agriculture and viticulture.[47] But on this system

---

[44] Hes. *Op.* 504. The convention of the *héne kai néa*, designed originally to neutralise the 30th of the 'full' months so as to adjust them to the true lunar month of 29·5 days, is said to have been introduced at Athens by Solon (D.L. 1. 57, Plu. *Sol.* 25); but it was already known to Hesiod (*Op.* 771, cf. Nilsson ERBGK 27) and probably to Homer (*Od.* 14. 162, 19. 306). This shows that the Greek calendar year of $12 \times 29\frac{1}{2}$ days was at least as old as the eighth century.

[45] Nilsson ERBGK 41, cf. SDA 1–5.   [46] Gem. 8. 26, cf. 8. 33.

[47] Paus. 2. 4. 1, 4. 34. 9, 6. 26. 2, 8. 15. 2, 8. 23. 1, 8. 29. 1, 10. 4. 3, Ael. *VH.* 13, D.S. 4. 3, Ov. *F.* 1. 393, *Met.* 9. 640, *Rem. Am.* 593, Prob. *ad* Verg. *G.* 3. 43, Firm. Mat. 84, *CIG. Sept.* 3. 282, *CIG. I.M. Aeg.* 1089, Hom. *H.* 7. 11, *Od.* 5. 125; Roscher *s.v.* Triptolemos, Prott-Ziehen 26.

the intercalations are excessive. After eight years the calendar will have gained a whole month over the solar year. Accordingly, it was modified by omitting one of the four intercalations in each octennium. The intercalations then fell at successive intervals of three, two, and three years—for example, in the third, fifth, and eighth years; or, in other words, one and two months were inserted alternately in each quadrennium. This is the system described by Herodotus.

In addition to the three-year festivals mentioned above, we hear of four festivals celebrated in every ninth year, and all four are located in the very region which we have just identified as the earliest home of the Greek calendar. They are the Daphnaphoria at Thebes, and the Charila, Stepteria, and Herois at Delphi.[48] Further, we are informed that the Pythian Games of Delphi, which we know as quadrennial, had once been a festival of this type. This eight-year period was termed indifferently an *oktaetería* or an *ennaetería*, because, as Censorinus explains, a new period began in every ninth year.[49] It corresponds to the octennial intercalary cycle.

Here we encounter an apparent contradiction in the ancient authorities, which Fotheringham used to discredit them. Censorinus says that the octennial cycle was invented by Kleostratos of Tenedos, who was a younger contemporary, possibly a pupil, of Thales. The eight-year festivals just mentioned must have been older than that. 'If', it is argued, 'Censorinus was right in explaining the eight-yearly festivals by the *oktaetería*, he is wrong in attributing the *oktaetería* to Kleostratos.' The first alternative is accordingly dismissed as 'the fancy of a later age'.[50] This does not follow. It may be that Kleostratos was the first to state the mathematical formula for

---

[48] Procl. *Chr.* 26, Paus. 9. 10. 4, Plu. *M.* 293c, 418a, Ael. *VH.* 3. 1.

[49] Cens. *ND.* 18. 4–6. The Pythia began as a musical festival (Str. 481) correlated with the Stepteria (*FHG.* 2. 189, 4. 359, Ael. *VH.* 3. 1). There was an eight-year festival in Pisidia as late as II–IIIrd century A.D. (ABS 16.117). The Pythia was probably made quadrennial in 582 B.C., the date of the first Pythiad: Nilsson PTR 364–5.

[50] Fotheringham 176. He adds: 'And in fact it is easier to explain the festival periods as mere powers of two. We have two-year festivals and four-year festivals and eight-year festivals.' This explanation explains nothing.

the octennial cycle, which had long been operated but only by rule of thumb. Further, Censorinus says there were several forms of the cycle, differing from one another in the distribution of the intercalary months, and he ascribes them to various authorities, one of whom is Kleostratos. Thus we may accept him as the author of what became the standard form of the cycle without denying that it had been known in other forms long before.

The hypothesis that the octennial cycle goes back to the Minoan age enables us to solve one of the most vexed problems of the Greek calendar—the arrangement of the Olympic Games.

The Pythian Games were held every four years on the 7th of Boukatios.[51] Since the octennium contains ninety-nine months, they must have fallen at alternate intervals of forty-nine and fifty months; and in order to keep them in the same calendar month it was necessary that one month should be intercalated in the quadrennium of forty-nine months and two in the quadrennium of fifty months. The reason why they were held on the 7th is of course that this day, marking the first lunar quarter, was sacred to Apollo (Vol. I, p. 293). In practice, however, owing to the difference between the Greek calendar month of twenty-nine or thirty days and the true lunar month of 29·53 days, the lunations did not coincide with the calendar months. The connection of the 7th with the first quarter was therefore nominal.

The Olympic Games were also held at intervals of forty-nine and fifty months,[52] but they differed from the Pythia in two respects.

First we are told that they lasted five days, from the 11th to the 16th, and that they were held at full moon, which fell nominally on the 15th. Pindar speaks of the full moon shining when the first race was run by their founder, Herakles.[53] It is probable, therefore, that they were held at the actual full moon, like the Spartan Karneia,[54] the dates mentioned being nominal. For a panhellenic event this arrangement would have the

[51] Farnell CGS 4. 421.
[52] Porph. ad Il. 10. 252, Ba. 7. 2–3, Pi. O. 3. 33 sch., 5. 14 sch.
[53] Pi. O. 3. 17–22.   [54] E. Alc. 445–51.

advantage that its date could be calculated without reference to the local calendars.

Secondly, instead of keeping to the same month, like the Pythian Games, they fell alternately in Apollonios and Parthenios. Apollonios was the eighth month after the winter solstice, and Parthenios must have been the ninth, because we are told that these two months correspond to Mesori and Thoth, which were consecutive months in the Egyptian calendar. Apollonios was therefore the Delphic Boukatios and the Attic Metageitnion.

Weniger's explanation of this rule, adopted by Cornford, is well known.[55] It is that, if the Games had been held regularly in Apollonios, they would have interfered with an older quadrennial festival, the Heraia, which was fixed at the new moon of Parthenios. To obviate this difficulty they were placed a fortnight before and a fortnight after the Heraia in alternate quadrennia. In my *Æschylus and Athens* I accepted this solution of the problem,[56] but I am now convinced that it is untenable. It may be conceded that Parthenios is named after Hera Parthenos (Vol. I, p. 282), and, though we have no information on this point, that this was the month of the Heraia; but the only support for the further assumption that the feast was held at the new moon is a statement to the effect that the new moon was sacred to Juno at Rome.[57] The truth is that the date of the Heraia is unknown; and, even if it were as Weniger supposed, it would still be necessary to explain why the juxtaposition of the two feasts, if it caused any difficulty, was not avoided by the simple expedient of arranging the quadrennia so that they never fell in the same year.[58]

[55] Weniger HZO, Cornford OOG.

[56] Thomson AA 115-6.

[57] Jo. Lyd. *de mens.* 36.

[58] Fotheringham supposed that the alternation of forty-nine and fifty moons was not a regular procedure but 'merely meant that there was sometimes an intercalation between Thosythias and the Games and sometimes not' (178). This is impossible. Not only is it contradicted by Porphyry, but, if intercalation had been unsystematic, as he was trying to prove, the normal interval between two celebrations would not have been forty-nine or fifty months but forty-eight. Nilsson rejected Fotheringham's view, and his own solution, although confused, is on the right lines (PTR 365); see Thomson GC 60-1.

It may be presumed that the Games had existed in some form long before 776 B.C., which was the traditional date of their foundation (Vol. I, p. 369). It is true that hitherto the site has yielded only very scanty Mycenean remains, but this negative evidence is not decisive, and there are two considerations to be set against it. According to the local tradition the Games were founded by the Idæan Herakles, who came from Crete (Vol. I, pp. 288-9). Pindar, on the other hand, says they were founded by the Dorian Herakles from Argos.[59] On the former hypothesis it is easy to see how after the Dorian conquest, and still more after the Argive hegemony of Pheidon (Vol. I, p. 561), the credit might have been transferred from the Cretan to the Dorian Herakles; but on the alternative view it is very hard to explain how this full-blooded hero was induced to withdraw in favour of the faded partner of the Minoan mother-goddess. Further, the Idæan Cave on the Hill of Kronos, the Hill of Kronos itself with its priest-kings, the Basilai, and its cult of Eileithyia and the snake—all these point to the Minoan age and particularly to Crete, and they are paralleled in various parts of Arcadia by a number of local cults referring to Rhea and the birth of Zeus.[60]

Since the Pythian Games were originally octennial, they must have been a calendar feast, with no functional relation to the agricultural year. But there is no reason to suppose that the Olympic Games had ever been octennial. Their dependence on the octennial cycle is due simply to the fact that this cycle formed the basis of the calendar. Now it is quite intelligible that an octennial feast should have been instituted to mark the completion of an octennial cycle, but there was no such thing as a quadrennial cycle, and consequently no basis in the calendar for a quadrennial feast. The quadrennial character of the Olympic Games must therefore have been determined by some extraneous factor. If the festival was to attract competitors from other states, there was an obvious objection to holding it every year. It would have clashed constantly with other local events of the same kind. The Spartan Karneia, for example, took place

[59] Pi. O. 3.
[60] Paus. 8. 28. 2, 8. 38. 2, 8. 41. 2, Str. 387, cf. Paus. 4. 31. 9, 4. 33. 1. They may have been brought to Greece by the Kydones: Str. 348, Od. 19. 176.

at the same full moon.[61] Accordingly, I believe that the Games began as an annual seasonal feast, and were made quadrennial in 776 B.C., the year from which the Olympiads were counted, in order to give them a panhellenic status.[62]

Apollonios was the month of the fruit harvest, which falls normally towards the end of August. The Olympic prize of victory was a crown of wild olive plucked from the sacred trees that grew in the precincts and it was said that the Idæan Herakles and his companions used to rest after their exercises on beds of olive leaves.[63] For these reasons it is probable that the primitive nucleus of the festival was an initiation ceremony connected with the fruit harvest.

The Games were administered by two priestly clans, the Iamidai and the Klytidai. The Iamidai can be traced to north-west Anatolia.[64] The Klytidai claimed descent from Melampous, which means that they had come from the Bœotian Orchomenos (Vol. I, p. 191). It may be supposed that the calendar, too, was administered, and perhaps introduced, by them.

Since the octennial cycle was designed to reconcile the calendar with the solar year, it must, when first instituted, have proceeded from what was regarded as the proper relation between the two. Let us suppose that a month is intercalated at the end of the third, fifth, and eighth years, and see how a festival fixed by the calendar will change its position in the solar year. Assuming that in the first year the harvest moon is full on August 22, we get the following dates for the harvest festival in the ensuing years of the octennium: (2) August 11, (3) August 1, (4) August 18, (5) August 7, (6) August 27, (7) August 16, (8) August 4.[65] In the second, third, fifth, and

[61] Nilsson GF 118.

[62] An intermediate stage in the same process may be seen in the Lesser (annual) and Greater (quadrennial) Panathenaia.

[63] Paus. 5. 7. 7, 5. 15. 3, Str. 353; Thomson AA 115.

[64] Iamos was a son of Euadna daughter of Pitana (Pi. O. 6, 28–30, cf. Paus. 6. 2. 5), daughter of Eurotas, son of Lelex, king of the Spartan Leleges (Apld. 3. 10. 13, Paus. 3. 1. 1); see Vol. I, pp. 332, 429.

[65] The dates, which are given *exempli gratia*, are taken from Weniger's table (21). I have chosen the 3–5–8 form of the cycle because that appears to have been the one in general use (Gem. 8. 33), but the other variants would serve just as well.

eighth years the festival falls 11, 21, 15, and 18 days before the harvest is normally ready. This difficulty could have been surmounted by applying the principle of the movable feast, which must have been familiar in the days when there had been no systematic intercalation at all. In these years the festival was postponed till the next full moon. If this was the practice established at Olympia when the Games were made quadrennial, the result of that reorganisation would have been the Olympic rule as we know it:

	Apollonios	Parthenios	
1.	August 22		
5.		September 6	50th month
9.	August 22		49th month

Stated in more general terms, our solution of the problem is simply this. When the Olympic festival was made quadrennial, it had, for the reasons given, fluctuated between the two months for so long that both were regarded as consecrated to it, and therefore it was divided between them.[66]

If the octennial cycle was in operation at Olympia in 776 B.C. on the basis of a hieratic tradition which was derived in part from prehistoric Bœotia, there is no difficulty in supposing that it was known to Hesiod.

6. *The Farmer's Almanac*

Hesiod's *Works and Days* is a farmer's almanac, containing a guide to the seasons, which may be summarised as follows:

Begin the harvest when the Pleiads are rising and the ploughing when they are about to set (383–4).
When Sirius is passing overhead, hew your timber (417–22).
Sixty days after the winter solstice Arcturus begins to rise at dusk: prune the vines (564–70).
When the Pleiads rise, sharpen your sickles and get ready for the harvest (571–5).
The appearance of Orion is the time for threshing (597–9).
When Orion and Sirius come into mid-sky, gather the grapes (609–11).
When Orion and the Pleiads set, remember to plough, and the year is completed.

---

[66] The month in which the Games were held, whether Apollonios or Parthenios, was also called Olympikos: Weniger 8.

These directions may be set beside the Hippocratic treatise *On Regimen*:

> According to the recognised practice I divide the year into four parts: winter, from the setting of the Pleiads till the vernal equinox; spring, from the equinox till the rising of the Pleiads; summer, from then till the rising of Arcturus; autumn, till the setting of the Pleiads.[67]

	Setting of Pleiads	Nov. 7
	43 days	
WINTER	Winter solstice	Dec. 21
	92 days	
————	Vernal equinox ———————	Mar. 21
SPRING	48 days	
————	Rising of Pleiads ———————	May 8
	43 days	
SUMMER	Summer solstice	June 21
	92 days	
————	Autumnal equinox ———————	Sept. 21
AUTUMN	48 days	
	Setting of Pleiads	Nov. 7

Further details supplied later in the treatise enable us to reconstruct the whole scheme, which is the same as Hesiod's.

With this tradition of a year divided into four seasons was associated another, which played an important part in Greek cosmology—the concept of a universe composed of four elements:

> Light and darkness, hot and cold, dry and wet have equal shares in the universe. The prevalence of the hot produces summer; of the cold, winter; of the dry, spring; of the wet, autumn.[68]

Again, we learn from another Hippocratic treatise, *On Human Nature*, that the body contains four humours which predominate in rotation with the seasons of the year. And, lastly, we are told by Aristotle that the four Attic-Ionic tribes corresponded to the four seasons, implying that they had seasonal functions to perform in turn (Vol. I, p. 105). Thus, all these ideas—calendrical, cosmological, physiological—rested on a tribal basis, such as we have found underlying similar ideas in other parts of the world.

[67] Hp. *Acut.* 3. 68 (Littré 6. 594).

[68] D.L. 8. 24, Hp. *Nat. Hom.* 7. Common Indo-European had names for only three seasons: Nilsson PTR 71.

To return to Hesiod, the prestige and popularity enjoyed by the *Works and Days* was derived partly from its ideological value. As the son of an immigrant (Vol. I, p. 566), who had acquired a private holding separate from the village commune, Hesiod voiced the individualistic outlook of the new type of farmer at a time when the old clan ties were being dissolved. But the poem also served a practical purpose. In the old days the soil had been tilled collectively under the supervision of the chief, who was conversant with the calendar; but, with the abolition of collective tillage, the farmer needed to be his own astronomer. Moreover, the official calendar was useless for his purpose, even if it was known to him, because it was always deviating from the solar year. His requirements could only be met by a knowledge of the stars. This is what Hesiod provided. He collected and presented in a form easily remembered and accessible to all the astronomical lore which had previously been used for the regulation of the calendar by the priest-kings of Thebes, Orchomenos, and Delphi.

7. *The Octennium and the Kingship*

We are now free to accept without reserve the numerous indications in Greek mythology of a connection between the octennium and the kingship.

Every eight years the tenure of the Spartan kings was confirmed by the ephors after inspecting the stars.[69] This was doubtless an ancient custom which they had brought with them from central Greece; for they claimed descent both from Hyllos, son of Herakles, who was born at Thebes, and from Kadmos.

Every eight years Minos, king of Knossos, used to retire to the Cave of Zeus to commune with his god.[70] Every eight years the Athenians used to send him a sacrificial tribute of seven boys and seven girls—an obligation from which they were freed by Theseus, who went to Crete and slew the Minotaur.[71] The myth of Theseus and the Minotaur was enacted in the Crane

[69] Plu. *Agis* 11.
[70] *Od.* 19. 178–9, Pl. *Min.* 319c, *Lg.* 624a–b, Str. 476, 482, D.S. 5. 78.
[71] Plu. *Thes.* 15.

Dance, imitating the windings of the Labyrinth, before the horned altar of Apollo at Delos.[72] The date of the dance is not given, but it probably took place on the 7th of Thargelion during the festival which celebrated the birth of Apollo and Artemis.[73] That would explain the number of the victims, seven for Apollo and seven for Artemis; and the 6th of Thargelion was the day on which the Athenians dispatched their annual pilgrimage to Delos in commemoration of their deliverance from the tribute.[74] At Athens too a festival began on the 6th. This was the Thargelia, in which two human victims were put to death, one on behalf of the men, the other on behalf of the women; and according to tradition this rite was instituted to expiate the death of Androgeos, who was a son of Minos.[75]

The octennial festivals of Thebes and Delphi were connected with both the calendar and the kingship. At the Daphnaphoria the girls carried in procession an olive trunk hung with balls symbolising the sun, moon, and stars, and 365 chaplets representing the days of the solar year.[76] At the Stepteria there was a rite enacting Apollo's slaughter of the Delphic dragon (Vol. I, p. 216), and it took place in a hut which was supposed to represent a royal palace.[77] This reminds us of Kadmos and his slaughter of the Theban dragon—a myth which will be dealt with in the next chapter.

There are many indications that nine was a sacred number in Minoan religion. The excavations at Pergamos have revealed, adjacent to the temple of Demeter, a terrace of nine steps. Another terrace of nine steps has been found outside the temple of the same goddess at Lykosoura. At Lato in Crete there is yet another terrace of nine steps, and here it is in the market-place.[78] In Minòan Crete such terraces were always contiguous to the king's palace, which usually faced on to the market-place, like Priam's palace at Troy and the Royal Porch (stoâ basíleios) at Athens.[79] What their purpose was is not yet known. Perhaps they served to accommodate groups of priests at choral

[72] Plu. Thes. 21, Call. Del. 307–13, Il. 18. 590–606.
[73] Hsch. θαργήλια, D.L. 2. 44, Anon. VPlat. 6 Cobet, Plu. M. 717d.
[74] X. Mem. 4. 8. 2, Pl. Phdo 58a–b.
[75] D.L. 2. 44, Phot. Lex. φαρμακός, Suid. φαρμακούς, Phot. Bibl. 534.
[76] Procl. Chr. 26, cf. Paus. 9. 10. 4.   [77] Plu. M. 418a.
[78] Tritsch AE 18, 100.   [79] Il. 2. 788–9; Tritsch 98, 102.

performances, like the nine umpires (*aisymnétai*) who directed the dance in the market-place in Phæacia (Vol. I, p. 479). Whether these officials stood in any definite relation to the kingship is not clear, but it may be inferred that, at least in Minoan times, their number had a functional value; for it can hardly be an accident that they are paralleled by the nine *hellanodíkai* who umpired the Olympic Games and the nine *árchontes* who succeeded to the Athenian kingship.[80]

Again, when Telemachos landed at Pylos, Nestor and his people were engaged in sacrificing nine groups of nine bulls, corresponding to the nine territories of his kingdom (Vol. I, pp. 361–2). These were probably tribal divisions, like the 'ninths' (*enátai*) into which each of the Dorian tribes was divided at Kos and Sparta. At Kos the bull sacrificed to Zeus Polieus was selected from twenty-seven bulls presented by the tribes, three from each 'ninth'.[81] At the Spartan Karneia nine huts were erected, each accommodating nine men, three from each phratry.[82]

In other cases the number has no functional value, being chosen simply for the sake of its traditional associations. No further explanation is needed for the nine Muses, the nine Kouretes who tended the infant Zeus in Crete,[83] the nine days' purification at Lemnos, or the nine boys and nine girls who headed the procession when the bull was presented to Zeus Sosipolis at Magnesia;[84] and, when we read that Bellerophon was feasted in Lycia for nine days on nine oxen, and that animals were selected for sacrifice at the age of nine years,[85] the inference is that the perfect number was regarded as appropriate to a perfect feast or a perfect sacrifice.

Lastly, since at the end of the octennium the sun, moon, and stars were back where they had been at the beginning, the octennial period, or 'great year' as it was called, became a symbol of universal renewal and regeneration, a world cycle of birth, death, and resurrection. Herakles laboured for eight years

---

[80] The *hellanodíkai* are expressly described as *epóptai* of the Games (Paus. 5. 9. 5); and this accords with my interpretation of the latter term (AA 125–6, WC 10).

[81] *SIG* 1025.

[82] Ath. 141e–f.

[83] Str. 473.

[84] Philost. *Her.* 740, *SIG* 589.

[85] *Il.* 6. 174, *Od.* 10.19, 390, cf. *Il.* 18, 351, Theoc. 26. 29, Hes. *Op.* 436.

to expiate the murder of his children.[86] Kadmos served a penance of eight years for the slaughter of the Theban dragon.[87] In the ninth year Persephone released the souls of the dead, who were born again to be 'exalted as wise men, athletes and kings, and to be remembered on earth as sanctified heroes for ever'.[88]

Granted that the octennial cycle goes back to the Minoan age, we are still left with the question, when and where was it invented? Not in Egypt, nor, it would seem, in Mesopotamia; for, even if an intercalary system was known there in early times, it can hardly have been the octennial cycle, or we should find some trace of it in mythology and religion. There the sacred number was not eight or nine, but seven, which reappears in Greece in the cult of Apollo. An answer to the question may be forthcoming when further excavation in Syria has yielded up a calendar. In the meantime we can only say that the Minoans may have acquired it through Syria from the Hittites, among whom we find traces of an octennial cycle in connection with the kingship.[89]

[86] Apld. 2. 5. 11.
[87] Ib. 3. 4. 2, cf. Serv. ad Verg. A. 7. 761, Hes. Th. 801.
[88] Pi. fr. 133, cf. Orph. fr. 295; Rohde 2. 211.
[89] See p. 145.

VI

THE KADMEIOI

1. *The Origins of Greek Rhetoric*

IN his *From Religion to Philosophy*, published in 1912, Cornford examined the teachings of the early Greek philosophers in the light of the evidence collected by Durkheim and others regarding the nature of primitive thought, and he reached the conclusion that the philosophers were working on certain religious ideas which had their roots in the structure of tribal society. At the end of his life he took up the problem again with results that will be considered in the next chapter.

Meanwhile another scholar had approached the problem from a different point of view. In his *Agnostos Theos*, published in 1913, Norden made a study of the Sermon on the Areopagus and showed that the Greek and Latin authors employed, in poetry and prose, certain forms of speech, liturgical in origin, which can be traced independently in the Old Testament. The two streams, the Hellenic and the Hebrew, drawn from Mesopotamia and Egypt, were reunited in Christianity, notably by St. Paul, who, in virtue of his birth and upbringing, was well versed in both. Later, in the Byzantine liturgy, they were reinforced by a third stream, the Syrian, of the same ultimate origin.[1]

These two works, which appeared simultaneously, are complementary. Cornford was concerned with the content of Greek thought, Norden with the form; and both reached the same conclusion. The roots of Greek philosophy lie in the ancient religions of the Near East. In the present chapter, by way of introduction to Cornford's work, I shall summarise some of Norden's main conclusions and show how they agree with his in pointing to a hieratic origin.

The earliest of the philosophers whose writings have survived in sufficient quantity to give an impression of his style is Herakleitos of Ephesos; and he was famous for his style. The

[1] Norden AT 207, 260–1, Cantarella 2. 28–37.

central doctrine of his philosophy is contained in what he calls the *lógos*, which he presents as though it were indeed a mystery, like the Eleusinian *legómena* and the Orphic *hieroi lógoi*. It may be defined in modern terms as the principle of the interpenetration of opposites, and it gives the key to his style. Just as his thought is dialectical, so his style is antithetical. Words and clauses are abruptly counterposed so as to lay bare the contradictions in the ideas which they convey. The effect, as described by Plato, is like a series of volleys from a band of archers.[2] In a highly inflected language like Greek such a style is necessarily accompanied by constant rhymes and assonances, and to these Herakleitos adds the use of puns—a universal characteristic of primitive speech, designed to invest it with a magical or mystical significance. Being so closely wedded to the subject, it cannot be described as rhetorical, and yet it exhibits all those features which later became so familiar in the schools that technical terms were invented for them: *antíthesis*, *asýndeton* (clauses juxtaposed without connecting words), *parísosis* (clauses with the same number of syllables), *paromoíosis* (assonance), *paronomasía* (punning).[3] It may be called, for short, 'the antithetical style' (Norden's *Satzparallelismus*).

The founder of Greek rhetoric, in the accepted view, was Gorgias of Leontinoi, who visited Athens in 428 B.C. and created a sensation by his flamboyant oratory. In his style he resembles Herakleitos, only it is more elaborate. In Herakleitos form and content are in perfect unity; in Gorgias the form has been elaborated for its own sake. He made a profound impression on his Athenian contemporaries, as we can see from the speech which Plato puts into the mouth of Agathon in his *Symposium*. In Thucydides, too, his influence is strong, especially in the speeches, but in Plato's own style it is much less so. The same is true of Xenophon, Isokrates, Demosthenes, and all the Attic orators. They made occasional use of 'Gorgiastic figures', as they were called, but with discrimination. In the meantime, however, in the third century B.C., the so-called 'Asiatic style' was introduced in Ionia and flourished for several centuries, especially in the Hellenised cities of the Near East.

[2] Pl. *Tht.* 180a.
[3] Arist. *Rh.* 3. 9, Demetr. 192, Cic. *Or.* 2. 63. 256.

It is simpler than that of Gorgias, but essentially the same. And lastly, the same style, with further modifications but still recognisably the same, reappears in parts of the New Testament and blossoms later into the distinctive idiom of the Byzantine liturgy. Perhaps it is worth while to quote a passage from the First Epistle to the Corinthians, which gives, even in English, some impression of its quality:

Behold, now is the accepted time; behold, now is the day of salvation: giving no occasion of stumbling in anything, that our ministration be not blamed; but in everything commending ourselves, as ministers of God, in much patience, in afflictions, in necessities, in distresses, in stripes, in imprisonments, in tumults, in labours, in watchings, in fastings, in pureness, in knowledge, in long-suffering, in kindness, in the Holy Ghost, in love unfeigned, in the word of truth, in the power of God; by the armour of righteousness on the right hand and on the left, by glory and dishonour, by evil report and good report; as deceivers, and yet true; as unknown, and yet well known; as dying, and behold, we live; as chastened, and not killed; as sorrowful, yet always rejoicing; as poor, yet making many rich; as having nothing, and yet possessing all things.[4]

What was the origin of this style? Norden believed that Gorgias modelled himself on Herakleitos, but this is unlikely. Gorgias was not the founder of the Sicilian school of rhetoric. He had been preceded by Empedokles of Akragas and Korax and Teisias of Syracuse.[5] The alternative is to suppose that all were drawing on a common liturgical source. Gorgias and his predecessors did for rhetoric what Stesichoros did for choral lyric (Vol. I, p. 466): they took over the ancient liturgical form, divested it of its ritual setting, and secularised it as an art form.

One of the surviving fragments of Gorgias is from a funeral oration, and this yields some valuable evidence. The funeral oration (*epitáphios*) was related to the dirge (*thrênos*), from which it differed in being spoken, not sung, and to the encomium (*enkómion*), which was a speech in praise of the living; and the encomium was related to the hymn (*hýmnos*), from which it differed in being spoken, not sung, and addressed to a man, not a god.[6] These forms rest on a common ritual basis. Running

---

[4] 2 Cor. 6. 2; see Thomson FRP 79–81.
[5] D.L. 8. 58–9, Quint. 3. 1. 8.
[6] Aristid. *Ars Rh.* 1. 160 (*Rh. Gr.* 5. 60).

through them all we find a number of ideas which were evidently traditional. The most frequent are the following. First, the speaker expresses anxiety lest he may fail to find words adequate to the occasion.[7] Secondly, this initial hesitancy often takes the form of a question.[8] Thirdly, the hesitation is attributed to the belief that praise may provoke envy.[9] Fourth, after these preliminaries the speaker opens his main theme by referring to the ancestry of the persons concerned.[10] Fifth, the person concerned is addressed or described in a series of arresting images.[11] And, lastly, it is said that the memory of the dead is imperishable, or simply that the dead live.[12]

Reading the funeral oration of Gorgias, we see at once that it is made up of these traditional ideas. Its content has been taken from ritual. So with its form. If we study the extant examples of funeral orations, dirges, encomia, and hymns, we find that they exhibit in an exceptional degree the features of that antithetical style which is so conspicuous in Gorgias and Herakleitos.[13] Indeed, it is noticeable that in some of the dirges

[7] Gorg. 6, Pl. Sym. 180d, 194e, Mnx. 236e, Th. 2. 35. 2, D. 60. 1, Isoc. 10. 12–3, Liban. Laud. Const. 5.

[8] D. 60. 15, Pl. Mnx. 236e, Lys. 2. 1–2, A. Ch. 854=855, cf. 314=315, 417–8, Ag. 775–8=783–6, 1490–1, Theoc. 17. 11, Eumath. 10. 11, Anaximenes Ars Rh. 35, Menandrus 11. 17, Liban. Laud. 3. 1, Andreas Cretensis Megas Kanon (Cantarella 1. 100–1), Cantarella no. 41 (1. 77). These passages may be compared with many hymns, which begin with the singer at a loss to find the right name for invoking the god: Norden AT 144–7.

[9] Pl. Lg. 802a (cf. Hdt. 1. 32. 7), Gorg. 6, Pl. Hp. Ma. 282a, A. Ag. 894=904, Ba. 3. 67, 5. 187, 12. 199, Pi. O. 8. 54, Th. 2. 35. 2, D. 60. 14.

[10] Th. 2. 36. 1, Lys. 2. 3, Isoc. 10. 16, 11. 10, Pl. Mnx. 237a–b, Sym. 178b, Liban. Laud. 3. 1, cf. 2. 1, 3. 2, 4. 1, Aphthon. Progym. 8.

[11] Pl. Sym. 197d–e, A. Ag. 887–90=896–9, E. And. 891, Antoniadis 354, Valetas 1. 88–9, IS 37.

[12] Gorg. 6, Lys. 2. 79–80, Simon. 121, A. Ch. 502=504, IS 124. Note especially the last example, which is as forceful as Herakleitos himself: 'O Lord my God, I will sing unto thee a funeral hymn and a burial song; for by thy burial thou hast opened unto me the gateway to life and by thy death thou hast put Death to death.'

[13] The following passages are a few among many that might be added to those already cited: Th. 2. 40. 1, D. 60. 37, Simon. 5, Ach. Tat. 1. 13, Eumath. 7. 9, Lucian. de luctu 13, Liban. Mon. de Nicom. 12, A. Ch. 326=328, Th. 91–3=93–5, Per. 702+4=700–2, S. Tr. 947, El. 197, E. Ba. 1153.

the antithetical structure is not merely formal, as in Gorgias, but determined by the content, as in Herakleitos.[14]

Turning to the Eleusinian Mysteries, we find that, although only a few liturgical phrases have survived, they all conform, some of them strikingly, to the antithetical style.[15]

Finally, there are two facts concerning Herakleitos himself that deserve attention. We know that he had disciples, the Herakleiteioi,[16] and we may presume that they were organised in a religious society, like the Orphics, Pythagoreans, and other philosophical schools. We also know that he belonged to the royal family of Ephesos, descended from the founder, Androklos, whose father, Kodros, had been king of Athens (Vol. I, pp. 191-2, 544). He would have been king himself, had he not resigned the office in favour of his brother.[17] One of the royal privileges was the priesthood of Demeter Eleusinia. This, we may suppose, had been acquired by his ancestors as kings of Athens; for the Athenian officer responsible for the Eleusinian Mysteries was the *árchon basileús*.[18] So Herakleitos came of an ancient royal family. He was himself by right of birth a priest-king. That is why he wrote in a hieratic style.

2. The Thelidai

Early in the second century B.C. the citizens of Miletos built a new town hall.[19] In it they placed a statue of Anaximandros —evidently the great philosopher of that name. It was an old statue of the sixth century, which they had removed from its original site on the Sacred Way running from the city to the great temple of Apollo at Branchidai, which was known throughout the Greek world as an oracular shrine. Branchos is described as a descendant of Delphos.[20] The meaning of this tradition is probably that the shrine at Branchidai was reorganised by the

---

[14] A. *Th.* 941-5=961-4, S. *Aj.* 394. This seems to be the origin of the figure of speech known as oxymoron (a self-contradictory expression) which is a conspicuous feature of the style of Æschylus, reflecting his profound sense of dialectics.

[15] Clem. *Pr.* 2. 14, Firm. Mat. 18, D. 18. 259, Plu. *Prov.* 16, Procl. *ad* Pl. *Tim.* 293c, Hippol. *Ref. Omn. Her.* 5. 7.

[16] Pl. *Tht.* 180a, D.L. 9. 6.   [17] D.L. 9. 6.

[18] Str. 633; Arist. *AR.* 57. 1.   [19] *SIG.* 3.   [20] Str. 421

Ionian settlers at Miletos under Delphic supervision; for we are told elsewhere that the cult was older than the Ionian colonisation.[21] Miletos itself, according to tradition, was founded from Milatos in Crete by Sarpedon, son of Zeus and Europa and brother of Minos.[22]

Several other statues of the sixth century have been discovered on the Sacred Way. One is a marble lion dedicated to Apollo by Thales, Pasikles, Hegesandros, a fourth whose name is illegible, and Anaxileos, all sons of Archegos, son of Python; another is dedicated by the sons of Anaximandros, son of Mandromachos; a third, also to Apollo, by Histiaios.[23]

The Thales and Anaximandros of these inscriptions cannot have been the philosophers, but their names suggest that they belonged to the same clan. Anaximander the philosopher was a son of Praxiades and a kinsman of his master, Thales.[24] Thales, a son of Examyes by Kleoboulines, belonged to the clan Thelidai.[25] Who were the Thelidai? We are told by Diogenes of Laerte that they were a branch of the Kadmeioi.[26] This is confirmed by Herodotus, who says that Thales was 'of Phœnician extraction', referring to the Phœnician origin of Kadmos.[27] That this is his meaning is clear from another passage, in which he describes the Gephyraioi, another branch of the Kadmeioi, as 'Phœnicians who came with Kadmos to the country now called Bœotia' (Vol. I, pp. 123–4). In further confirmation we may recall that Kadmeioi from Thebes had taken part in the colonisation of Ionia (Vol. I, pp. 390–1). Priene, across the bay from Miletos, was settled by Philotas with a contingent from Thebes,[28] which must have included some Kadmeioi, because we are told that the city was sometimes called Kadme in his honour.[29] These traditions may have been derived from Kadmos of Miletos, who was remembered as an early historian of the city and whose name speaks for itself.[30] At Mykale, across the bay, there was a cult of the Potniai—that is, Demeter and Persephone—which had

[21] Paus. 7. 2. 6.   [22] Eph. 32=Str. 941.
[23] SIG. 3. For the name Pasikles cf. Hdt. 9. 97. For other names in mandro, see SIG. 3g, SEG. 4. 461. 4, Apul. Fl. 18, SIG. 960. 5. 1079, 1068. 3, Hdt. 4. 88.
[24] Str. 7, D.L. 2. 1, Suid. s.v.   [25] D.L. 1. 22.   [26] Ib.
[27] Hdt. 1. 170. 3.   [28] Str. 633.
[29] Ib. 636, Hell. 95. Philotas himself belonged to the Boiotoi: Paus. 7.2.3.
[30] Suid. s.v.

evidently been brought there from Potniai near Thebes.[31] The Theban cult of Demeter had once been a palace cult of the Kadmeioi (Vol. I, pp. 125, 193). And finally, in view of their ancestral ties with the Delphic Apollo, the Thelidai may well have held a special place in the worship of the other Apollo at Branchidai. That would explain why their statues were erected along the Sacred Way.

Thus Thales and Anaximander, founders of the Milesian school of philosophy, also belonged to an ancient family of priest-kings.

3. Prehistoric Bœotia

The main interests of Thales and Anaximander were astronomy and cosmology, and they were descended from the Kadmeioi, the prehistoric priest-kings of Bœotian Thebes. The *Works and Days* of Hesiod is largely concerned with astronomy, the *Theogony* with the origin of the gods and of the world. Hesiod was born at Askra, and his memory was preserved at Thespiai by a religious society that bore his name (Vol. I, p. 485). Askra and Thespiai are only a few miles from Thebes. Thus, even if his poems had been lost, making a detailed comparison between his work and Anaximander's impossible, we might still have concluded from the external evidence that they were drawing on a common tradition derived from Minoan Crete and ultimately from Syria.

It is true, of course, that, when Herodotus speaks of Kadmos as a Phœnician, he is thinking of the Phœnicians of his day, who dwelt, not in Syria, but farther down the coast in Tyre and Sidon; but these Phœnicians were descended from the people, sometimes called Proto-Phœnician, which, along with other peoples, had occupied Syria in the Bronze Age. It must also be remembered that, although regarded as a Phœnician, Kadmos had ties with Minoan Crete, his sister being Europa, mother of Minos; and if these latter ties are less prominent in the tradition, it is simply because they had been broken by the Dorian occupation of that island (Vol. I, p. 384). Kadmos stands for the Minoan kingship, which, as we now know, was

---

[31] Hdt. 9. 97.

closely connected with the Syrian. This is borne out by other details of his story. Before reaching Bœotia he travelled all round the Ægean,[32] and is said to have discovered the gold-mines of Mount Pangaion in Thrace.[33] It is in Bœotia, however, that he left the most abiding impression, no doubt because his descendants there were among the most powerful of the Minoan dynasties. If we examine the local traditions recorded from this part of Greece, we find there many more Minoan-Phœnician connections, some of them linked with Kadmos or his sister Europa, others with the Hesiodic *Theogony*.

Aphrodite, whose Minoan-Phœnician affinities are well known (Vol. I, p. 512), was worshipped at Thebes in the form of wooden effigies said to have been carved from the timbers of the ships that had brought the Kadmeioi to Bœotia.[34] She had another cult at Tanagra.[35] At Thespiai there was a cult of Eros (Love).[36] Other cults of Eros are recorded from Leuktra in Laconia, founded from the Bœotian Leuktra (Vol. I, p. 395), and from Parion, founded from Erythrai, which was one of the original Ionian colonies and named presumably after the Bœotian Erythrai.[37] Both Aphrodite and Eros are prominent in the Hesiodic *Theogony*, and the latter reappears, under the name Pothos (Desire), in the Phœnician cosmogony.

Demeter, another Minoan goddess, was associated with the Kadmeioi at Thebes and elsewhere in Bœotia; and at Lebadeia she was worshipped as Demeter Europa (Vol. I, p. 124). On the road from Thebes to Mykalessos there was a village called Teumesos at which Europa was said to have been hidden by Zeus.[38] This is evidently a local variant of the legend that deposited her in Crete. On the road from Thebes to Thespiai, and again at Anthedon, there were joint cults of Demeter and the Kabeiroi.[39] The same cult was established in Lemnos and Samothraike, where Kadmos is said to have been initiated into it.[40] The name of the Kabeiroi has been referred to the Semitic base *kbr*, which means 'great'. This is only a conjecture, but

[32] Roscher *s.v.*
[33] Clem. *Str.* 1. 307b, Plin. *NH.* 7. 57. 197, cf. Hdt. 6. 47.
[34] Paus. 9. 16. 3.   [35] *Ib.* 9. 22.1.   [36] *Ib.* 9. 27. 1, 9. 31. 3.
[37] *Ib.* 9. 27. 1.   [38] *Ib.* 9. 19. 1.   [39] *Ib.* 9. 25. 5, 9. 22. 5.
[40] Roscher *s.v.* Megaloi Theoi.

it is supported by the fact that in Greek they were also known
as the Megaloi Theoi, the 'great gods'.

Apollo slew the Delphic dragon; Kadmos slew the Theban
dragon; Zeus slew the monster Typho. All these are variants of
the same theme. In one tradition, known apparently to Hesiod,
the fight between Zeus and Typho is said to have taken place
on a hill called Typhaonion near Thebes.[41] In another it is
located on Mount Kasios, which overlooks Ugarit, and we are
told that Zeus was only saved by Kadmos coming to his rescue.[42]
In the cuneiform texts from Ugarit we read how Baal, son of El,
slew the seven-headed serpent Lotan, which is the Hebrew
Leviathan.[43] All these traditions are derived from a common
original, which has been preserved in the *Enuma elish*.

Lastly, it will be recalled that Rhea saved the new-born Zeus
from his father, Kronos, who had devoured all her children, by
giving him a stone wrapped in swaddling clothes, which he
devoured, mistaking it for the infant.[44] In the *Theogony* the
incident is located in Crete, but there were other Bœotian
traditions which placed it at Plataiai and at Chaironeia.[45] The
same theme has recently turned up in the so-called Epic of
Kumarbi, a Hittite-Hurrian cosmogony, which presents a
number of parallels to the *Enuma elish* on the one hand and to
Hesiod on the other. Already, before this was published,
Cornford had argued that the Hesiodic cosmogony had reached
Greece by way of Ugarit and Minoan Crete.

[41] Pi. *O.* 4. 11 sch., Hes. *Sc.* 32, Hsch. Τυφίοι.
[42] Nonn. *D.* 1. 481–534.   [43] Schaeffer 65.
[44] Hes. *Th.* 481–500.   [45] Paus. 9. 41. 6.

THE GREEK THEOGONY

1. *The Evidence*

AT the end of his life Cornford returned to the problem which he had raised in his *From Religion to Philosophy*. In his last work, left unfinished and only published nine years after his death, he made a detailed examination of the Hesiodic *Theogony* in the light of the *Enuma elish*, together with other versions of the same theme, and showed that the ideas which form the content of these poems persist, transformed but still recognisable, in the cosmology of Anaximander. This is undoubtedly his greatest achievement, being a contribution not merely to scholarship but to knowledge. It falls short, as we shall see, of a full solution to the problem, but even so it shows that he was far in advance of any other bourgeois historian of philosophy. Its limitations are the limitations of bourgeois philosophy itself.

Although his general conclusions are clear, the argument on which they rest is complicated by the nature of the evidence. In the first place, the *Enuma elish* raises a number of problems in itself. In its extant form it belongs substantially to the middle of the second millennium B.C., when Babylon was the political and cultural centre of Mesopotamia; and accordingly its hero is Marduk, the patron god of that city. This, however, as we have remarked above (p. 89), was not its original form:

Behind our present version with Marduk as the hero undoubtedly lies a still earlier version wherein, not Marduk, but Enlil of Nippur played the central role. This more original form can be deduced from many indications in the myth itself. The most important of these is the fact that Enlil, although he was always the second most important Mesopotamian deity, seems to play no part whatever in the myth as we have it, while all the other important gods have appropriate roles. Again the role which Marduk plays is not in keeping with the character of the god. Marduk was originally an agricultural or perhaps a solar deity, whereas the central role in the *Enuma elish* is that of a god of the storm such as Enlil was. Indeed, a central feat ascribed to Marduk in the story—the separating of heaven and earth—is the very feat which other mythological material assigns to Enlil, and with right, for it is the wind which, placed between the sky and earth, holds them apart like the two sides of an inflated leather bag. It seems, therefore, that Enlil was the original hero of the story and was replaced by Marduk when our earliest known version was composed around the middle of the second millennium B.C. How far the myth itself goes back, we cannot say with certainty. It contains material and reflects ideas which point backward through the third millennium B.C.[1]

In the second place, the material for reconstructing the intermediate links between the two poems is fragmentary, and raises similar problems. It consists of the cuneiform texts recording the Hittite-Hurrian and Ugaritic myths, the Phœnician theogony as recorded by Philon of Byblos, and the Book of Genesis, together with some other passages from the Old Testament. All these versions emanate from Mesopotamia, but it is not yet possible to determine precisely the relation in which they stand to the *Enuma elish*. And finally there remains the gap which will only be filled if and when we recover the Minoan Cretan version of the myth.

Fortunately there is no need, for our present purpose, to enter into these complications. Apart from incidental references to other material, we shall confine our attention to the two main poems, recapitulating Cornford's thesis, that the Hesiodic *Theogony* is a Greek version of a Mesopotamian myth based on the ritual of the oriental despotism and containing certain ideas which appear as premisses in early Greek philosophy. In some of the details my interpretation differs from his, and account will be taken of evidence which has come to light since his death.

The *Enuma elish* may be divided into six episodes: (1) the birth of the gods; (2) strife breaks out between them; (3) Marduk is made king; (4) the fight between Marduk and Tiamat; (5) the construction of the heavens and the creation of man; (6) the building of the temple and the fixing of fates. These will be summarised in turn and compared with the corresponding episodes in the *Theogony*.

2. The Birth of the Gods

The *Enuma elish* begins by describing how things were in the beginning:

[1] Jacobsen in Frankfort BP 183-4.

> When the sky above had not been mentioned,
> And the name of firm ground below had not been
>   thought of;
> When only primeval Apsu, their begetter,
> And Mummu and Tiamat, she who gave birth to
>   them all,
> Were mingling their waters together;
> When no marsh had formed and no island was to
>   be found;
> When no god at all had appeared,
> Had been named by name, and had his lot deter-
>   mined:
> Then were gods created in the midst of them;
> Lahmu and Lahamu appeared and were named.

In the primeval chaos of fresh water (Apsu), salt water (Tiamat), and mist (? Mummu), there was nothing which had any definite shape and therefore nothing which had a name. The opening of the *Tao Te Ching* is very similar:

> When the Tao had no name, that was the beginning of heaven and earth; then, when it had a name, this was the mother of all creation.[2]

The idea is that a thing that is nameless does not exist and is brought into existence by being named. This primitive notion is paralleled in child psychology by the fact that, when learning to draw, small children tend to draw only those features of an object for which they know the names (p. 32). It underlies all primitive beliefs in the magical efficacy of names (Vol. I, pp. 46–7), and it rests on the simple truth that it is only through speech, as the medium of social production, that man has become conscious of the objective reality of the external world. As Malinowski observed:

> The mastery over reality, both technical and social, grows side by side with the knowledge of how to use words. . . . Familiarity with the name of a thing is always the direct outcome of familiarity with the use of that thing. . . . The belief that to know the name of a thing is to get a hold on it is thus empirically true.[3]

The opening of the poem, enumerating the four successive pairs of male and female, has been discussed in an earlier chapter (p. 90), where it was pointed out that the separation of heaven and earth effected by the generation of these pairs is

[2] Hughes 145.   [3] Malinowski CG 2. 233.

repeated later in the poem, when Marduk cuts Tiamat's body in two. The discrepancy is hardly felt, because the two accounts are so different from one another. In the second, which forms the main body of the poem, the protagonists are visualised concretely as living beings, the one human, or rather super-human, and the other a monster such as was imagined to live in the sea. In the first, the divine couples are treated almost impersonally. It is true that Lahamu has a part to play in the sequel, and both he and the others were objects of worship; but in the opening of the poem they almost attain to the level of abstract ideas.

We are reminded of the first two chapters of Genesis. In the first chapter we are told how God created the world in seven days—day and night, heaven and earth, dry land and sea and grass and trees, the heavenly bodies, fishes and birds, and finally the land animals and man and woman. In the second chapter we are told that 'no plant of the field was yet in the earth' and 'the Lord God formed man of the dust of the ground'. Here the contradiction between the two accounts is obvious, and it is agreed that the first, the more abstract, is also the later of the two.

The same reduplication appears in the *Theogony*. In the intro-ductory section we are told how, after Chaos, Earth and later Heaven were born, but the one is described as 'the foundation of all things' and the other as 'an everlasting abode for the blessed gods',[4] as though they were not themselves gods at all; and then, with the beginning of the story, they come to life as a quarrelsome married couple. Here too we shall find grounds for believing that the introductory section is later than the rest; and for that reason it will be deferred for later consideration after we have dealt with the remainder of the poem.

3. Strife between the Gods

The newly created gods come together and dance:

> The divine companions gathered together,
> And as they surged to and fro they disturbed Tiamat,
> Disturbed her belly,
> Dancing within her where the heavens are founded.

[4] Hes. *Th.* 117, 128.

Apsu, too, was disturbed and went to Tiamat with his servant Mummu:

> Apsu began to speak
> And said to pure Tiamat:
> 'Their ways have become hateful to me,
> They give me no rest by day nor sleep by night;
> I will abolish and put an end to their ways,
> That peace may reign once more and we may sleep.'

At this news the gods were thrown into panic; but one of them, Ea, after uttering a spell over Apsu which sent him to sleep, killed him, took from him his crown, and built his dwelling upon him. (This means that the fresh waters are confined to their proper place beneath the earth.) Then he seized Mummu, castrated him, and smashed his skull.

The corresponding episode of the *Theogony* may be summarised as follows.[5] After giving birth to Heaven, and the Hills, and the Sea, Earth lay with Heaven and bore the Titans, including Kronos, who is described as 'the youngest and cleverest of her children, and he hated his father'. There follows the birth of the Kyklopes and the Hundred-handed Giants. Heaven, we are told, hated his children, and, as each was born, hid it within Earth, not suffering it to come up into the light, so that Earth groaned inwardly, being congested. Then she made a sickle and called on her sons to take vengeance on their father; but they were afraid, all except Kronos, who promised to do her bidding. So she gave him the sickle and set him in an ambush:

> And Heaven came, bringing on the night and yearning for love, and spread himself all over Earth and lay upon her; and the son stretched his left hand from his ambush and took in his right the long sickle and lopped his father's privy parts and threw them behind him.[6]

From them sprang Aphrodite.

At first sight these two episodes might appear to be totally unconnected, but they have two points in common: the goddess's children are at first confined within her, and a god is castrated. That these points are significant is clear from other versions.

In the Polynesian cosmogony recorded by Grey, Heaven and

[5] Hes. *Th.* 126–206.   [6] *Ib.* 176–82.

Earth clove together, until their children, confined in darkness, forced them apart, thereby creating light. In another version Heaven's privy parts are severed in the course of the struggle and are turned into pumice-stone.[7] In the Phœnician cosmogony recorded by Philon of Byblos, Earth resisted the embraces of Heaven, and one of her sons, Kronos (El), came to her rescue. Armed with a spear and iron sickle, he gave battle to his father and overthrew him and castrated him 'at a spot which is still shown to this day', and the blood from his amputated parts trickled into the springs and streams. The place in question is probably Aphaka, at the source of the River Adonis, which was said to run with blood in the spring.[8] In the Epic of Kumarbi, Alalu, the first king of heaven, after reigning for nine years, was overthrown by Anu, who also reigned for nine years, and was then overthrown by Kumarbi, who pulled him down from heaven and bit off his privy parts. Anu then said to him, 'Three terrible gods have I planted within thee as fruit of my body'; whereupon Kumarbi spat them out, and they were born from Earth.[9] Finally, in the Egyptian myth of Geb (earth) and Nut (sky) the two parents are forced apart by their offspring Shu (wind).[10]

Returning to the *Enuma elish*, it seems, in the light of these parallels, that this episode, in which the father-god is overthrown by one of his children, who have disturbed their parents by dancing within their mother's belly, is only another rendering, abbreviated and no longer understood, of the separation of heaven and earth.

4. *The King of the Gods*

Marduk, son of Ea, is born, tall, cunning, and terrible to behold, with four eyes and four ears, and fire blazing from his lips. Meanwhile Tiamat prepares revenge. She marshals an army of sea-monsters and places them under the command of her new husband, Kingu, to whom she has entrusted the supreme power, represented by the tablets of destiny which she

[7] Tylor 1. 322. 5, Roscher 2. 1542–3, Cornford PS 205.
[8] Phil. Bybl. 2. 22; E. Burrows in Hooke L 52; *Et. M. s.v.*
[9] Güterbock K; Gurney 190.   [10] Frankfort BP 55, 63.

fastens on his breast. Again the gods are in panic. At length Ea goes out to meet her, hoping to overcome her with a spell, but he returns terrified. Then Anu goes and pronounces against her the agreed command of all the gods, but he achieves nothing. The gods are in despair. At last a proposal is moved and carried that Marduk should be their champion. Marduk accepts, on certain conditions:

> If I am to be your champion,
> To vanquish Tiamat and deliver you,
> Then assemble and proclaim my lot to be supreme . . .
> Let me determine destiny by word of mouth like you,
> So that whatever I will shall not be altered,
> And the command that I speak shall not be changed.

On this passage Jacobsen comments:

> Marduk is a young god. He has abundant strength, the full prowess of youth, and he looks ahead to the physical contest with complete confidence. But, as a young man, he lacks influence. It is for authority on a par with the powerful senior members of the community that he asks. A new and un-heard-of union of powers is here envisaged: his demand foreshadows the coming of the state with its combination of force and authority in the person of the king.[11]

The gods assemble and after a banquet they proclaim Marduk king:

> We have given thee kingship and power over all things;
> Take thy seat in council, and thy word shall prevail.

After overthrowing his father, Kronos had a number of children by his sister Rhea, but he swallowed them all for fear that he in his turn might be overthrown by one of them. Advised by her mother, Rhea gave birth to Zeus in Crete, where he was hidden in a cave, and she presented Kronos with a stone wrapped in swaddling-clothes, which he duly swallowed. Later he was persuaded to disgorge his offspring, including the stone, which was deposited at Delphi. Meanwhile Zeus grew to manhood and released the Kyklopes and Hundred-handed Giants, whom Heaven had bound beneath the earth. He did this because it had been foretold to him that with their aid he would overcome his father and the Titans. Appealing for help to the other gods, he promised them that, if he succeeded in

[11] Jacobsen in Frankfort BP 192.

conquering the Titans, he would confirm all who sided with him in possession of their existing privileges and bestow new privileges on those who had none. The result was that, after the victory, the other gods invited him to become their king. The battle was fought in Thessaly between the two mountains, Olympus and Othrys. It lasted ten years, and ended with the defeat of Kronos and the Titans, who were imprisoned beneath the earth.[12]

Kronos and the Titans correspond to Kingu and his host of sea-monsters, but the latter do not fight. At the sight of Marduk they turn tail and flee, leaving Tiamat to face him alone. Marduk is invested with kingship by the assembled gods before the battle; Zeus becomes king by invitation after the battle is over. The Mesopotamian version preserves the traces of a tribal assembly in full enjoyment of its powers, whereas the rise of Zeus is presented in terms of a deal between chiefs, each of whom has a privileged position in his own tribe or clan. In this the Greek version reflects the actual conditions in which the Achæan chiefs rose to power (Vol. I, pp. 328–31).

The idea of the father being overthrown by the son is absent from the *Enuma elish*; yet Marduk does succeed where his father had failed, and consequently supersedes him. The idea of the father swallowing his children has left no trace at all. In the Epic of Kumarbi, however, the first idea is prominent, as we have seen, and the second appears in a different form: we are told that Kumarbi begot a son made of diorite stone. This agrees with the Phœnician cosmogony, in which one of the sons of Heaven and Earth is named Baitylos: *baitýlos* is a Greek word meaning a meteorite, and we know that it was used of the stone swallowed by Kronos.[13] It may be inferred that this detail is derived from an Anatolian or Syrian cult of a stone fetish.

The remainder of the story need not detain us long. Marduk's encounter with Tiamat and his treatment of her body have already been described (pp. 89–90). After fashioning the sun, moon, and stars, and setting them in their places, the victorious king summons the assembly and indicts Kingu as a rebel. Kingu is bound and executed, and from his blood the gods

[12] Hes. *Th.* 453–506, 617–735.
[13] Barnett, EK; Hsch. *s.v.*, cf. Roscher 1. 747.

fashion human beings to serve them with sacrifices. Then the gods assemble once more and after a banquet confirm the powers which they have bestowed on their king by reciting his fifty names, which define his various functions.

The encounter with Typho follows the same lines, except for the treatment of the body, which is simply cast into Tartarus, where it gives rise to stormy winds. There remains the creation of man. On this point Hesiod is silent. The Orphics had a tradition similar to the Babylonian: man, they said, sprang from the blood of Dionysus after he was slain by the Titans.[14] The reason why Hesiod says nothing about it is that the Greek noble families, with whose origin he is concerned, claimed to be descended from the gods; and so the origin of mankind calls for no further explanation. In this, as in other respects, the Greeks stood much closer to their tribal origins (Vol. I, pp. 499–500).

5. *The Hesiodic Cosmogony*

It has already been pointed out that in the first two chapters of Genesis the creation of mankind is reduplicated, exactly as the separation of heaven and earth is reduplicated in the *Enuma elish*; and the reason is that in both cases alternative renderings of the same theme have been combined in a single narrative after their original significance had been obscured. A similar discrepancy confronts us in the first chapter itself.

The narrative begins as follows:

In the beginning God created the heaven and the earth. And the earth was waste and void; and darkness was on the face of the deep; and the spirit of God moved upon the face of the waters. And God said, Let there be light; and there was light. And God saw the light, that it was good; and God divided the light from the darkness.

That was on the first day. On the fourth day:

And God made the two great lights; the greater light to rule the day, the lesser light to rule the night; and he made the stars also. And God set them in the firmament of the heaven to give light upon the earth and to rule over the day and over the night, and to divide the light from the darkness.

The explanation is simple. In order that the work of creation

[14] Orph. fr. 210–32.

might be fitted into the seven-day week, it was necessary to suppose that the day as a time unit had existed from the outset. The seven-day week was of Babylonian origin, but its association with the creation was a Hebrew idea, intended to sanctify the Sabbath; and the story of the creation was adjusted to accommodate it.

Nor was that the only adjustment. 'In the beginning God created the heaven and the earth.' That was on the first day. On the second day he 'made the firmament' and 'called the firmament Heaven', and on the third day he made the dry land appear and 'called the dry land Earth'. Here we have another reduplication, and here again it is the first of the two passages that has been added. In the primitive tradition there had been nothing in the beginning except 'waste' and 'void' and 'darkness'; and then this amorphous mass was separated by 'the spirit of God'—that is, the wind—into two parts, heaven and earth. The initial event was the separation of heaven and earth.

In Greece the Orphics preserved the primitive tradition unimpaired:

Orpheus sang and told how heaven and earth and sea, which had once been united in one form, were parted by strife; and how the stars and the moon and the course of the sun keep an everlasting sign in the sky; and how the mountains arose, and the babbling streams with the nymphs, and all creeping things.[15]

This is from the Hellenistic period, but the tradition was much older than that, as we learn from these lines of Euripides:

The story is not mine—I had it from my mother—that Heaven and Earth were once one form, and after being parted from one another they gave birth to all things and brought them to light—trees, winged creatures, sea-monsters, and mankind.[16]

The process was also envisaged as the splitting of an egg into two halves. This symbol is prominent in Orphic literature and is also found in the Upanishads:

In the beginning it was not; it came into being; it grew; it turned into an egg; the egg lay for a year; the egg broke open; one half was of silver, the other of gold; the silver half became this earth, the golden the sky. . . . And what was born from it was Aditya, the sun.[17]

---

[15] A.R. 1. 496.   [16] E. fr. 484.   [17] Chàndogya Upanishad 3. 91.

The idea of the world egg does not occur, so far as I know, in Babylonian literature, but it is known that a cosmic egg figured in Egyptian ritual.[18] It has also been suggested that a vestige of the same belief survives in Genesis; for in the sentence, 'the spirit of God *moved upon* the face of the waters', the meaning of the Hebrew text is rather *brooded upon*, referring to the incubation of an egg.[19]

We may now turn to the introductory section of the Hesiodic *Theogony*. It runs as follows:

First of all Chaos came into being, and next broad-bosomed Earth, everlasting foundation of all things, and Love (Eros), fairest among the immortal gods, who loosens the limbs and subdues the sense and will of gods and men alike. From Chaos were born Darkness and black Night, and then from Night Sky and Day, whom she conceived and brought forth after lying with Darkness. And Earth bore, first, starry Heaven, equal to herself, that he might cover her all round and be an everlasting abode for the blessed gods, and then the tall Mountains, lovely haunts of the Nymphs who inhabit the mountain valleys, and the raging deep, the Sea—all these she brought forth without sexual intercourse. And then she lay with Heaven and bore . . .[20]

There follow the names of the Titans and her other children by Heaven, as described above.

This account of the world is much more sophisticated than the story which follows. On the one hand, Chaos and Darkness are impersonal abstractions; on the other, the mountains and sea are natural objects. Earth is described in the same breath as 'broad-bosomed' and as the 'everlasting foundation of all things'. The first designation is mythical; the second is rational, being clearly related to the belief, adopted by Thales, that the earth is like a wooden disk or drum floating on water. Similarly, when we are told that she gave birth to 'the starry Heaven, equal to herself, that he might cover her all round', the reference is to the traditional conception, probably Orphic, of 'starry-kirtled Night': that is, the night sky was regarded as a star-spangled robe enveloping the earth.[21]

[18] Lefebvre ODH 65; Lange 53.
[19] Skinner 18. [20] Hes. *Th.* 116–33.
[21] A. *Pr.* 24, E. *Io.* 1150, Alexis 89, Nonn. *D.* 2. 165–6, 16. 124; Lobeck 379–80, 551.

Nevertheless the primitive kernel is still recognisable, if the passage is compared with other Greek versions of the same theme. Of these the most important is the Orphic cosmogony parodied by Aristophanes:

First there was Chaos and Night and black Darkness and wide Tartarus, but not earth nor air nor heaven; and in the boundless bosom of Darkness black-winged Night laid a wind-egg, from which in the cycle of seasons there sprang much-longed-for Love, like whirls of wind, his golden wings glistening on his back.[22]

Love is here the initial movement (*éros* 'love', *eroé* 'motion') which forced the egg apart and so started the process of differentiation. And his wings glisten, because now there is light. This is very close to the myth. In the beginning heaven and earth were one; then their offspring, wind, forced them apart, thereby creating light. It is not really inconsistent with this that Love, who serves in the beginning to separate things from one another, should afterwards become the force that reunites them; for, after the initial division of things, the impulse which produced it is itself divided into two movements—that which draws things together (Love) and that which drives them apart (Strife).

In starting with Chaos, Aristophanes is following Hesiod. But, as Cornford remarks, the Greek *cháos* did not mean what we understand by the word but rather a 'chasm' or 'gap', and he goes on:

Now, if cosmogony begins with the coming into being of a yawning gap between heaven and earth, this surely implies that previously, in accordance with Euripides's formula, 'Heaven and Earth were once one form', and the first thing that happened was that they were 'separated from one another'. Hesiod can hardly have meant anything else.[23]

It was not Hesiod who meant that, but his predecessors. Hesiod's account is confused, and it is not difficult to see why. In the sequel Heaven and Earth are presented anthropomorphically as human beings, a quarrelsome married couple. This picture of them is incompatible with the idea that they originated as one. Accordingly, that idea is rejected, and instead we are told that Heaven was born from Earth, who in Greek tradition is 'the mother of all things'.[24] This first child was

[22] Ar. *Av.* 692-7.   [23] Cornford PS 195.   [24] A. *Pr.* 90.

fatherless, but that does not raise any difficulty, because such virgin births were familiar to the Greeks, as to other primitive peoples (Vol. I, p. 287). The result of this reconstruction is that Love, the force that parted them, and Chaos, the gap thus made between them, are deprived of their proper place in the sequence of events. Their names are still mentioned out of deference to tradition, but they are no longer functional.

Having explained these anomalies, we have no difficulty in reconciling the Hesiodic version with the primitive form of the myth. In the beginning there was an inchoate mass, like an egg; then something began to move inside it, so that it broke open in two parts, heaven and earth; and between them there was created light. Later the sun, moon, and stars were formed in heaven, creating day and night; and on earth there arose mountains, so that dry land appeared out of the sea.

One further point remains to be accounted for. We remember that in the sequel Heaven hid his children inside Earth, who groaned, being congested; and we recognised here a reference to the original unity of the pair, though in the story as Hesiod tells it this point is no longer understood. Later, after Kronos had prepared his ambush, 'Heaven came, bringing on the night and yearning for love, and spread himself all over Earth and lay upon her'.[25] The implication is clear. During the day-time Heaven and Earth are parted from one another, and therefore there is light; but, when night falls, they come together again, and the light is extinguished. Here the reunion of the sundered pair is used to explain the alternation of day and night. Elsewhere it is applied to the annual cycle of summer and winter, Heaven being the begetter who makes the Earth conceive and bear fruit, as in these lines which Æschylus put into the mouth of Aphrodite:

> The pure Sky yearns with love to wound the Earth,
> And loving Earth yearns likewise to be wed,
> Till from the heavenly bridegroom showers descend
> Upon the bride, who brings forth for mankind
> The grazing cattle and Demeter's corn,
> With precious moisture ripening the fruits
> To autumn fullness. In all this I have part.[26]

[25] Hes. *Th.* 176–8.   [26] A. fr. 44.

Æschylus was probably alluding to the Eleusinian Mysteries, in which, in one of the ceremonies, the initiates looked up to the sky, and cried 'Rain!', and then down to the earth, and cried 'Teem!'[27] We can now understand why Hesiod gives so much prominence to the birth of Aphrodite: the goddess who sprang from the separation of Heaven and Earth represents the force which is to draw them together again.

All this is without parallel in the *Enuma elish*. There love plays no part, although the festival at which the poem was recited included a sacred marriage. In view of the Phœnician affinities of Eros and Aphrodite, we are led to postulate for this element in the Hesiodic tradition a Phœnician origin. This hypothesis is confirmed when we find that, in the Phœnician cosmogony preserved by Philon of Byblos, the beginning of things is described as a dark, windy chaos, which stirred within itself, and from this movement there sprang Desire (Pothos), and the offspring of Desire was Mot.[28] The cosmogony of Philon is admittedly a late compilation, but it contains some undoubtedly ancient elements, and one of these is the god Mot, whose name has turned up in the cuneiform texts from Ugarit.[29]

6. *The Separation of Society and Nature*

We may now summarise our conclusions. The Babylonian, Greek, and Hebrew cosmogonies represent the accumulated product of a long epoch in the evolution of thought, from lowest savagery to the upper levels of barbarism. Their nucleus is a simple myth in which the structure of society is projected on to nature. To the primitive savage, the external world is inseparable from his social relations, through which he has become conscious of it. Just as he is incapable of conceiving of his own existence except as a member of the tribe, so the world of nature is inextricably involved in the tribal relations in which he has his being. Nature and society are one. Hence, in its most primitive form, the myth of the separation of heaven and earth is a simple projection of the basic organisation of the tribe.

[27] Procl. *ad* Pl. *Tim.* 293c, Hippol. *Ref. Omn. Her.* 5. 7.
[28] Phil. Bybl. 2.   [29] Schaeffer 69–75.

With the advance from savagery to barbarism, and still more with the rise of the kingship, whose function is to perpetuate the ideological unity of tribal society after its economic basis has disappeared, the myth ceases to be intelligible in its primitive form and is reinterpreted. In the *Enuma elish* three versions of it are combined in a single narrative. The most primitive is contained in the account of the disturbance which the new-born gods created by dancing in their mother's belly: but this is no longer understood. In the fight between Marduk and Tiamat the idea of the separation is still prominent, being maintained by the ritual to which the poem belonged, but it has been adapted, along with the ritual, so as to present the king as a victorious and omnipotent creator god, with absolute power over his people's welfare. Accordingly, in order to prepare a setting for this episode, which is the climax of the poem, an introduction has been added, consisting of a summary genealogy of divine couples signifying the formation of the physical universe. This is intellectually the most advanced section of the poem, but it still moves within the forms of primitive thought, the evolution of the world being expressed in terms of sexual reproduction.

The *Theogony* and Genesis differ from the *Enuma elish* in being completely detached from ritual. Moreover, in their present form they date from a period when the kingship—never so powerful in Greece or Judah as it had been in Babylonia—has passed away. In them, therefore, the primitive myth is in process of being transformed.

In the *Theogony* the fight between Zeus and Typho has lost all contact with the creation; and similarly the strife between Heaven and Earth is described without any understanding of its original cosmic significance. Both of these are now little more than folk-tales. In the introductory section the idea of sexual reproduction is maintained, but only in a perfunctory fashion. Of the divinities concerned, the majority are, properly speaking, not divinities at all but names of natural phenomena. The features of the physical universe are coming to be recognised for what they are in themselves. Here, therefore, we observe the emergence of a new mode of thought, which marks the first step towards scientific knowledge of the world.

The first chapter of Genesis is, historically speaking, even more advanced. On the one hand, the features of the universe are completely objectified as natural phenomena external to man, and their evolution is described as a material process. On the other hand, this process is not natural but artificial; it is the handiwork of a supreme being who speaks, sees, works, and rests from his labours, just like a man. The subject has been banished from the real world only to reassert itself in fantasy as the idea of god. This Hebrew god who created the world in seven days is not in any sense part of the natural world, like the gods of *Enuma elish* and the *Theogony*, but, on the contrary, is supernatural. Such a distinction is entirely alien to primitive thought. It reflects a cleavage between man's consciousness of himself as man and his consciousness of nature, which springs, as we shall see, from a corresponding cleavage in society.

VIII

THE MILESIAN SCHOOL

1. *Ionian Cosmology*

THALES, Anaximander, and Anaximenes, all of Miletos, are the acknowledged founders of European philosophy. In calling them philosophers, however, we are not using that term in its current sense. They were concerned mainly with what we should call problems of natural science, and not at all with the laws of thought, which had not yet become a subject of investigation. Their field of inquiry was the whole realm of nature in so far as it was known to them. They differed from Hesiod and other poets who devoted themselves to such matters in that, while not denying the existence of gods, they identified the divine with the faculty of motion, which they assumed to be inherent in matter. They recognised no distinction between the natural and the supernatural. For this reason they have sometimes been regarded as the first scientists, and undoubtedly their work was a step towards the development of natural science; but it rests on simple observation, not experiment. The experiments attributed to them are trivial. For these reasons we give it the name, not of science, but of natural philosophy.

Even at the present day, when cosmology is a science, current theories of the origin and evolution of the universe contain a large element of speculation. But, although 'free' from the control of observation and experiment, it does not follow that such speculation is uncontrolled; on the contrary, it is controlled all the more rigorously by preconceptions derived from the structure of society. It has to be remembered, too, that these preconceptions also enter into the interpretation of observed facts and the selection of experiments. They represent the subjective, or ideological, element, in modern science, which cannot be eliminated and can only be controlled to the extent that it is made the subject of a scientific theory of society.[1] If

[1] Cf. Lenin MEC 198: 'From the standpoint of modern materialism, i.e. Marxism, the *limits* of approximation of our knowledge to the objective, absolute truth are historically conditional, but the existence of such truth

this is true of modern science, it is clear that the cosmological speculations of the first natural philosophers belong exclusively to the domain of ideology. That being so, we have to analyse them in the light of the social preconceptions which they reflect; and, when we do that, we find that, while they carry on the mythical tradition which we have investigated, there is a sense in which we can say that they have broken with that tradition. They have preserved the tradition in respect of its content, but broken with it in respect of its form. The old content has been transformed. When we have established this point, we shall be ready to address ourselves to the fundamental question, what were the social and historical conditions by which this transformation was determined? The question is fundamental, because the answer to it will enable us to understand the distinctive character of ancient Greek civilisation.

The *History* of Diodoros opens with a brief account of the origin of the world, which has evidently been taken from the Ionian philosophers:

In the original composition of the universe heaven and earth had one form, their natures being confounded. Later, with the separation of these bodies from one another, it comprised the whole of the visible order. The air acquired the property of continual motion, and, since it is light and buoyant by nature, the fiery part of it gathered together in the uppermost regions, with the result that the sun and other heavenly bodies were caught up in the whirl of the whole. Meanwhile the slimy, muddy part, with the condensation of the wet parts, settled by reason of its weight at the bottom. Then, stirred up and churned over continually, the wet parts formed the sea, while the more solid parts became soft, muddy soil. Congealed by the sun's heat, the earth's surface fermented; and then, in many places, the wet parts formed tumours with putrid discharges covered in fine membranes, such as may still be seen in marshland when very hot air passes suddenly over frozen ground. From these, living creatures were generated by the heat. . . .[2]

is unconditional, and the fact that we are approaching nearer to it is also unconditional. . . . In a word, every ideology is historically conditional, but it is unconditionally true that to every scientific ideology (as distinct, for instance, from religious ideology) there corresponds an objective truth, absolute nature. . . . The materialist dialectics of Marx and Engels certainly does contain relativism, that is, it recognises the relativity of all our knowledge, not in the sense of the denial of objective truth, but in the sense of the historically conditional nature of the limits of the approximation of our knowledge of this truth.'

[2] D.S. 1. 7. 1.

The mythical origin of this theory is evident. Diodoros does not name its author, but it clearly belongs to the Ionian school of thought, and indeed it is reminiscent of Anaximander himself.

2. *Thales and Anaximander*

According to Aristotle the aim of the early Greek philosophers was to discover 'the material principle from which all existing things derive their being . . . and into which they finally pass away, its substance persisting despite changes of conditions';[3] and this view has been followed by many modern writers on the subject. Cornford makes this comment:

Misled by Aristotle's habit of regarding his predecessors as more or less imperfectly anticipating one or more of his own four causes (material, formal, moving and final), the older historians of philosophy accepted his view that the early Ionians were concerned only with 'principles of a material kind', such as water or air. Accordingly, they were represented as putting to themselves the question, what is the one (material) substance of which all things consist? But, if we look at the systems themselves, the question they answer is a different one: how did a manifold and ordered world arise out of the primitive state of things?[4]

This comment is partly, but not entirely, correct. It is true that Aristotle was to some extent misled by the tendency, not uncommon among philosophers, to read into the work of his predecessors anticipations of his own conclusions; and yet, if we follow the evolution of Ionian philosophy, we can recognise in the Milesian school itself a subtle shift of attention from the question, whence did it come into being? to the question, whereof is it made? Presented at first as a genetical process, the world, as they conceive it, becomes gradually self-regulating. This is a significant change. It shows that the work of these philosophers, who revolutionised the *form* of primitive thought, contains also the germ of a new *content*. Again, it is true that they did not think of their first principle explicitly as a material principle, because for them the distinction between material and non-material did not exist; but it is significant that Aristotle, an idealist consciously opposed to the materialists of his day, should describe them in this way. They were primitive materialists.

[3] Arist. *Met.* A 3. 983b. 6.   [4] Cornford PS 159, cf. Cherniss 348.

Of Thales we know little. He is said to have been interested in astronomy, geometry, and engineering, and in commercial as well as philosophical speculation. He held that the world as we know it evolved out of an original state of things in which there was nothing but water, and that the earth floats on water. This is in keeping with the traditional conception of 'the waters that are beneath the earth', the Babylonian *apsu*.

Anaximander made a map of the world, and wrote a book on cosmology, from which a few fragments survive. These, together with what we learn about his views from Aristotle and other writers, enable us to form a general idea of his system, though many of the details escape us.

The beginning of things is defined as 'the unlimited', which is 'immortal and imperishable', that is, endowed with motion and therefore divine. In consequence of this motion, the opposites—the hot, dry, wet, and cold—'separated out' from it as follows. A portion of the unlimited, pregnant with these opposites, separated from the rest, and within it there emerged the hot and the cold. The hot moved outwards, where it formed a sphere of fire; the cold moved inwards and separated into earth and air, the earth being situated in the centre and enveloped by the air. Then, on earth the wet and dry were separated out by the heat from the sphere of fire; and, conversely, the cold broke up the sphere of fire into separate rings, enclosed by air, but containing a number of apertures; and these apertures, through which the fire is visible, are the sun, moon, and stars. Thus the universe is composed of fire, air, sea, and earth, corresponding to the two pairs of opposites—hot and cold, wet and dry. Finally, it is probable, though not certain, that Anaximander held the view that living creatures evolved from the moisture on earth as it was evaporated from the sun.

This theory rests on three preconceived ideas—common origin, perpetual motion, and the conflict of opposites—all of which are derived, as we have seen, from primitive thought, being in origin nothing more than a projection of the structure of the tribe. As if to drive the point home, Anaximander himself, in the only complete sentence of his writings that has survived, says of the unlimited:

From this things come into being, and into it they pass away, according to necessity; for they render satisfaction to one another for their wrongdoing according to the order of time.[5]

The phrase which I have translated 'render satisfaction' (*díken kai tísin didónai*) refers properly to the settlement of disputes between rival clans (Vol. I, p. 134).

Against this it has been urged that we have no right to read so much into what is after all only a metaphor, such as was natural and indeed indispensable at a time when there existed no scientific terminology. It is, however, a fallacy to suppose that scientific terminology is free from metaphor. The term 'natural law', for instance, is a metaphor, taken from social relations, and an inquiry into its origin would show that it is just as firmly rooted in feudal ideology as Anaximander's 'render satisfaction' is in tribal. The truth is that, just as man's consciousness of the external world has been formed through the development of social relations in the labour of production, so his speech, in which that consciousness assumes a material form communicable to others, necessarily reflects its social origin.

Behind this objection lies the blindness of bourgeois empiricists to their own social relations, which determine their own thoughts. They suppose that the individual can acquire knowledge of the world by a 'free' act of immediate apprehension, independent of society, or, if society does intervene, it can only do so as an obstacle to understanding. It is true that in the conditions of class society the acquisition of knowledge may be positively obstructed in this way, as it was in Babylonia and Egypt; but in pre-class society there was no such obstacle, only the limitations imposed by the low level of the productive forces and the consequent simplicity of social relations. The greatness of the Milesians lies precisely in this, that they expressed in a new form, abstract and objective, the fundamental truths which had forced themselves on the consciousness of primitive man, but had previously found expression only in the concrete, subjective form of myths.

It is from this point of view that we must assess the value of the three postulates which Anaximander took over from primitive thought and made the basis of his cosmology.

[5] Diels 9.

All things are of common origin: that is to say, the universe has evolved out of a single undifferentiated mass. This truth was denied by later Greek philosophers, and only reasserted itself in the epoch of modern capitalism, when it was placed on a scientific basis:

Kant began his career by resolving the stable solar system of Newton and its eternal permanence—after the famous initial impulse had once been given—into a historical process: the formation of the sun and of all the planets out of a rotating nebulous mass. With this he already drew the conclusion that, given this origin of the solar system, its ultimate dissolution was also inevitable.[6]

Anaximander, as we shall see, drew the same conclusion.

Again, all things are in continual motion. On this point Cornford observes:

If we would understand the sixth-century philosophers, we must disabuse our minds of the atomistic conception of dead matter in mechanical motion and of the Cartesian dualism of matter and mind. We must go back to the time when motion was an unquestioned symptom of life, and there was no need to look further for a 'moving cause'. Matter or body requires a distinct moving cause only when it has been deprived of its own inherent life.[7]

Here, too, Anaximander's position is essentially the standpoint of modern science:

Motion is the mode of existence of matter. Never anywhere has there been matter without motion, nor can there be. Motion in cosmic space, mechanical motion of small masses on the various celestial bodies, the motion of molecules as heat or as electrical or magnetic currents, chemical decomposition and combination, organic life—at each given moment each individual atom of the world is in one or other of these forms of motion, or in several forms of them at once. All rest, all equilibrium, is only relative, and only has meaning in relation to one or other definite form of motion.[8]

This truth was not recovered without a long and bitter struggle, waged against the ruling class of feudal society, which was determined to suppress it. *E pur si muove.*

Lastly, development consists in a conflict of opposites. This principle has been accepted by bourgeois thinkers in the natural sciences, but resisted, at least in recent times, in the study of society, because of its obvious implications:

[6] Engels AD 29.   [7] Cornford PS 179–80.   [8] Engels AD 70.

The identity of opposites . . . is the recognition, discovery, of the contradictory, mutually exclusive, opposite tendencies in all phenomena and
processes of nature, including mind and society. The condition for the
knowledge of all processes of the world in their 'self-movement', in their
spontaneous development, in their real life, is the knowledge of them as a
unity of opposites. Development is the 'struggle' of opposites. . . .[9]

Classical scholars have often debated with their scientific
colleagues the extent to which the Greek philosophers deserve
credit for having anticipated the discoveries of modern science.
The debate is always inconclusive, because the question is
misconceived. The truth of the matter is, not that these ancient
Greeks anticipated the results of modern science, but that
modern scientists have succeeded in reaffirming certain fundamental but forgotten truths and establishing them securely on
the basis of experimental proof.[10] The early Greek philosophers
stood near the beginning of class society; the modern bourgeois
scientists stand near its end. In the work of Anaximander, the
mythical cosmogony of primitive communism is in process of
being transformed by the 'pure reason' of the new ruling class,
but with its dialectical content still unimpaired; in the work
of Kant, and still more of Hegel, the new dialectical content,
immeasurably richer than the old, is on the point of bursting
the bonds imposed on it by the 'pure reason' of bourgeois
society. The primitive dialectics of these early Greek materialists
stands to the dialectical materialism of the present day in
the same relation as primitive communism stands to modern
communism.

Anaximander regarded the conflict of opposites as a process
in which they encroach periodically on one another and so lose
their identity by becoming reabsorbed into the undifferentiated
form of matter out of which they emerged. That is what he
means when he says that they 'render satisfaction to one another
for their wrongdoing according to the order of time'. The
universe is in perpetual motion, which takes the form of a
series of cyclical movements, the hot and the cold, the wet and
the dry, prevailing alternately over one another, thus producing
summer and winter, spring and autumn, in the cycle of the
year.

[9] Lenin D 81.   [10] Engels LF 79.

All this resembles the Chinese doctrine of the *yang* and the *yin*, whose contradictory movements determined the progress of the seasons; and, just as the Chinese philosophers believed in a fivefold cycle of dynasties, corresponding to their five elements, so Anaximander maintained that the universe was periodically reabsorbed into the unlimited and then re-created as before. This is what he meant when he described the unlimited as 'immortal and imperishable'.

Pursuing the comparison with Chinese cosmology, we notice one significant difference. On the one hand, the Chinese philosophers formulated the conflict of opposites as an abstract idea, the *yin-yang*. This development is related to the kingship, to which was attributed the power of regulating the conflict. In Anaximander's system the opposites are conceived only in their concrete manifestations as the hot and the cold, the wet and the dry, which are treated not as qualities but as things. On the other hand, it is only in Anaximander that we find the principle of periodical dissolution applied to the universe as a whole. We have already met this principle in Aztec cosmology (p. 57), but in ancient China there is no cosmic, only a dynastic, cycle (pp. 67–8). Here again we can see the influence of the kingship, which in China, as in Egypt, purported to be a permanent feature of the natural order.

Now, if Anaximander's world was involved in this eternal cycle of coming into being and passing away, Aristotle was justified in describing his 'beginning' as 'that from which all existing things derive their being and into which they finally pass away, its substance persisting despite changes of conditions'. The idea of change as a cyclical process carries with it the implication that the subject of it returns repeatedly to the state from which it started and hence to that extent remains unchanged. The germ of this idea lay, as we have seen, in the socially organised cycle of the seasons. It was, as Cornford points out, traditional in Greek thought to represent perpetual motion as circular, the circle being 'limitless', that is, having no beginning or end. Nevertheless, in the form which Anaximander gave it, the idea was new; and, moreover, it contained within itself a contradiction, which was the germ of further development. If the world moves through a cycle of eternally repeated changes, then, it might be argued, every 'beginning' is also an 'end': there is no absolute 'beginning', and therefore no evolution. This part of Anaximander's system was developed by some of his successors, notably Herakleitos and Parmenides, in such a way as to negate the primitive premiss of common origin and evolution in time.

3. Anaximenes

Anaximenes, the last original thinker of the Milesian school, chose as his 'beginning', not water or the unlimited, but air, in which he included mist and darkness; and he taught that the world as we know it has evolved by rarefaction and condensation of this primary substance. By rarefaction air became, fire; by condensation it became water and earth. He said: 'Just as the soul, being air, holds us together, so breath or air encompasses the whole world.' We are also told that he associated rarefaction with heat and condensation with cold. From this it seems that, in place of Anaximander's rotation, or 'whirl', he postulated a twofold movement similar to the respiratory process, the one condensing the air into water and earth, the other rarefying it into fire.

In selecting one of the four elements as his primary substance, Anaximenes reverted to the standpoint of Thales, and it has been suggested that this was a retrograde step. In a certain sense this is true. The transition from primitive thought to civilised thought took place by a dialectical process, in which each step forward was also a step back. For the present, however, it is enough to note that in taking this step he was advancing in the general direction in which Greek philosophy was destined to move.

Thales, so far as we know, made no attempt to explain by what process his primary substance evolved into the world that we see. This problem was Anaximander's main concern. Assuming the existence of the four elements, he recognised that these differed quantitatively from one another, being heavier or lighter, and he used this difference to explain their distribution in space. The wet and cold gravitated towards the centre; the dry and hot floated up to the circumference. The result, however, was a qualitative change: the wet and cold became water and earth, the dry and hot became air and fire. Quantitative change led to qualitative change. Anaximander, of course, did not, and could not, think of the matter in such terms; but this is the conception he was groping after when he put forward his hypothesis of the unlimited.

What Anaximenes did was to explain the qualitative aspect of this process by reducing it to quantitative terms. The various parts of the universe are not made of different things, but differ from one another only in containing more or less of the same thing. In this way he weakened the third of the three primitive premisses; for where there are no qualitative distinctions, there can be no conflict of opposites.

This conclusion was not immediately apparent. Both Pythagoras and Herakleitos endeavoured to combine Anaximander's strife of opposites with Anaximenes' principle of quantitative differentiation, but both systems contained this internal contradiction, which was seized on by Parmenides, who denied origin, motion, and change, thus effecting a complete rupture with primitive ideas and directing philosophical speculation along entirely new lines determined by the new developments in the relations of production.

4. Burnet and Cornford

It was Cornford's achievement to reveal the *Enuma elish*, the Hesiodic *Theogony*, and early Greek philosophy as marking stages of a continuous process in the history of thought; and so far my account of the matter has closely followed his. But the point has now been reached at which we must take leave of our guide, and in doing so it is necessary to consider why he failed to pursue his analysis further. Of his books on Greek philosophy all except the first and last are devoted to the study of Plato; yet, so far from being presented as a further stage of the same process, Platonism seems to be divided from it by an unbridgeable gulf. In the last years of his life Cornford turned aside from Plato, and resumed his inquiry into the origins of philosophy, which he sought as before in the development of society. From the conclusion of his *Principium Sapientiæ*, which he left unfinished, it is clear that he was intending to pursue his investigations still further afield into Indian and Chinese philosophy; but not nearer home into Platonism. In this his work on philosophy resembles that of his contemporary, Chadwick, on poetry. Both were great scholars, who threw a flood of light on the prehistory of their subject but none at all on its history. Why does his analysis stop short at the very point at which it promises to yield its most valuable results? This is the negative aspect of his work. In examining it, we must be careful not to obscure its positive aspect, which is still not fully appreciated. Let us begin, therefore, by contrasting his work with a rival's, whose influence in academic circles has been far greater.

Although published as far back as 1912, Cornford's *From Religion to Philosophy* has never been reprinted. Burnet's *Early Greek Philosophy* was first published in 1892; a second edition appeared in 1908, and a third in 1920. The same author's *Greek Philosophy from Thales to Plato* was published in 1914 and has been reprinted several times. It contains no mention of Cornford's work. It opens with a cursory discussion of possible Babylonian and Egyptian influences, which are dismissed as negligible: 'The truth is that we are far more likely to underrate the originality of the Greeks than to exaggerate it.'[11] Indian philosophy is dismissed as inferior and derivative. Chinese is not mentioned. Burnet reaffirmed his standpoint in 1920 as follows:

My aim has been to show that a new thing came into the world with the early Ionian teachers—the thing we call science—and that they first pointed the way which Europe has followed ever since, so that, as I have said elsewhere, it is an adequate description of science to say that it is 'thinking about the world in the Greek way'. That is why science has never existed except among peoples who have come under the influence of Greece.[12]

This, if true, is clearly a fact of great historical importance. How are we to explain it? Burnet's reply to this question is that there is no explanation:

No one will ever succeed in writing a history of philosophy; for philosophies, like works of art, are intensely personal things. It was Plato's belief, indeed, that no philosophical truth could be communicated in writing at all,

[11] Burnet GP 9.   [12] Burnet. EGP v.

it was only by some sort of immediate contact that one soul could kindle the flame in another. . . . It will only, therefore, be in so far as the historian can reproduce the Platonic contact of souls that his work will have value. In some measure this is possible. Religious faith often seems able to break through the barriers of space and time, and so to appreciate its object directly; but such faith is something personal and incommunicable, and in the same way the historian's reconstruction of the past is primarily valid for himself alone. It is not a thing he can hand over ready-made to others. There is nothing mysterious about this aspect either of religious faith or of philological interpretation. On the contrary, all knowledge has the same character. [13]

It is hard to see why, on these premises, the impossibility of writing history should be limited to philosophy and art. The hopes, fears, loves, hates, longings—in a word, the wills—of innumerable human beings are also 'intensely personal things'; and yet it is these, in their totality, that make history:

The social history of men is never anything but the history of their individual development, whether they are conscious of it or not. Their material relations are the basis of all their relations. These material relations are only the necessary forms in which their material and individual activity is realised. [14]

Having reduced 'all knowledge' to 'the Platonic contact of souls', Burnet might justly have claimed to have absolved himself from the obligation of explaining anything at all. He proceeds, however, to offer two reasons why it was the Greek people, and no other, that made this unique contribution to the history of man:

The Greeks achieved what they did, in the first place, because they were born observers. The anatomical accuracy of their sculpture in its best period proves that, though they never say anything about it in their literature, apparently taking it for granted. . . . Further, the Greeks always tried to give a rational explanation of the appearances they had observed. Their reasoning powers were exceptional, as we can see from the mathematical works they have left us. [15]

Thus, they achieved what they did because they were endowed with the innate capacity to achieve it. They were 'born observers'; 'their reasoning powers were exceptional'. Whether

[13] Burnet GP. 1.
[14] Marx to Annenkov 28–12–46 (Marx-Engels C 7).
[15] Burnet GP 10.

this was a gift from God—a divine spark, perhaps—or simply 'in the blood', we are not told.

In my *Æschylus and Athens* I ventured to comment, in another context, on some flaws in Burnet's reasoning, and was duly rebuked for my temerity by an eminent scholar, who wrote:

> I cannot conclude without deprecating the language which Professor Thomson thinks fit to employ of some great scholars of an older generation. He accuses Burnet of 'slipshod thinking, which glides with a deceptive facility past all the crucial issues'—an absurdity to those who knew Burnet well and remember how his rigorously logical mind was at once a tonic and a terror to his friends. [16]

In extenuation of the offence it can only be said that those who did not share this privilege of 'the Platonic contact of souls' have no choice but to judge the master by his works and to express surprise that such reasoning can still commend itself to serious students of the subject.

It is against this background that we have to consider the weaknesses in Cornford's argument.

He begins his *Principium Sapientiæ* by maintaining, against Burnet, that, except in medicine, the Greeks produced nothing that can be called science before the time of Aristotle:

> The question we are concerned with lies outside the field of medicine and of the industrial and fine arts. It is the question whether methods of observation, generalisation and experiment were commonly used by the Ionian philosophers. They were not bringing their ingenuity to bear on healing the sick or driving tunnels or making statues. Their problems were not of the practical kind which daily force upon us the necessity of sharpening our wits to circumvent some mechanical obstacle. They could not be solved by 'experiment' in the loose sense of trial and error; and, as we have seen, the philosophers neglected, to an extent which strikes the mind as astonishing, to check their statements by experiment in the scientific sense of putting to nature a question the answer to which could not be foreseen. [17]

Then, turning to the work of Epicurus, he examines 'the common belief that this final expression of Ionian natural philosophy was pre-eminently scientific', and concludes that 'it was not in fact anything of the kind but a dogmatic structure based on *a priori* premisses'. [18] Later in the book the same test is applied to Anaximander:

[16] A. C. Pickard-Cambridge in CR 56. 26.
[17] Cornford PS 10–1.   [18] *Ib.* 159.

Having now before us some picture of the earliest Ionian system, we can attempt to distinguish those elements in it which could be derived from immediate observation and those which must have been inherited from tradition.

He continues:

Every reader is struck by the rationalism which distinguishes it from mythical cosmogonies. This characteristic must certainly not be under-rated. . . . The Milesian system pushed back to the very beginning of things the operation of processes as familiar and ordinary as a shower of rain. It made the formation of the world no longer a supernatural but a natural event. Thanks to the Ionians, and to no one else, this has become the universal premiss of all modern science. But there is something to be added on the other side. If we give up the idea that philosophy or science is a motherless Athena, an entirely new discipline breaking in from nowhere upon a culture hitherto dominated by poetical and mystical theologians, we shall see that the process of rationalisation had been at work for some time before Thales was born. . . . And when we look more closely at the Milesian scheme, it presents a number of features which cannot be attributed to rational inference based on an open-minded observation of facts. [19]

The last point is reaffirmed:

What we claim to have established so far is that the pattern of Ionian cosmogony, for all its appearance of complete rationalism, is not a free construction of the intellect reasoning from direct observation of the existing world. [20]

Having thus cleared the ground, he proceeds to demonstrate that the ideas underlying the system are derived through Hesiod from the mythical cosmogony of the *Enuma elish*, which was generated as a reflection of the New Year ritual. In this way they are traced back to their origin in a social institution designed to meet a material need.

This conclusion is correct, so far as it goes, and yet it falls short of a solution to the problem. The book leaves us unsatis-fied. This feeling is reflected in the editor's final comments. After summarising some further material from the author's manuscripts, Guthrie writes:

The danger of ending with this inadequate summary is that it may convey the false impression that the earliest Greek philosophers (and of ancient peoples it was only among the Greeks that this transition from myth to philosophy was achieved) did no more than repeat the lessons of myth in a changed terminology. [21]

[19] *Ib*. 187.   [20] *Ib*. 201.   [21] *Ib*. 259.

The same transition was achieved in the same period by the Chinese, as we saw in Chapter III, and it is already clear that this parallel is likely to have an important bearing on the solution of the problem; but, apart from this mistake, the comment is justified. Cornford has not overlooked the fact that in the Ionian systems the content of the old myth has been transformed by being *rationalised*; but, although he has described the process, he has not attempted to explain it. He does not even seem to be aware that an explanation is needed. The truth is, he never got beyond Durkheim.

According to Durkheim, the structure of human thought, including logical categories and classes and the concepts of space, time, force, and causality, consists of 'collective representations', which are projections on to the external world of the structure of human society. Applying this principle to primitive thought, he and his colleagues collected a great deal of useful information showing that it is in all essentials a projection or reflection of the tribal system. So far so good; but, if the development of thought is determined by the development of society, what determines the development of society? And in what relation does civilised thought stand to the structure of civilised society? Faced with these questions, which cannot be answered without recognising the class struggle, Durkheim was utterly at a loss, and only succeeded in confusing the issue, which Marx and Engels had stated so plainly in the preceding generation. Fifty years later it is plainer and sharper than ever.

Far from attempting to overcome Durkheim's limitations, Cornford chose deliberately to work within them. In *From Religion to Philosophy* he wrote:

In certain early phases of social development the structure and behaviour of the world were held to be continuous with—a mere extension or projection of—the structure and behaviour of human society. [22]

No attempt is made to explain what these 'early phases' were, or how they differed from those that followed them; on the contrary, with these words Cornford tacitly excluded the later phases from his field of investigation. That was his position in 1912, and he never modified it. On the contrary, in his later

[22] Cornford FRP 55.

years, as he came to realise that the only alternative was Marxism, he clung to it all the more tenaciously. In relation to the Pre-Socratics he was a materialist, in relation to the Post-Socratics an idealist.

We can now see why the conclusion of *Principium Sapientiæ* is unsatisfactory. In contrast to pre-scientific thought, which is socially determined, scientific thought is held to be a 'free construction' resting on 'immediate' and 'open-minded observation', unimpeded by the intervention of any preconceived ideas. Is there any such thing in human consciousness as 'immediate observation', that is, a simple act of physical perception which is not in any way determined by social relations? The whole of modern physiology teaches us that there is not. As society becomes more complex, so does the process of determination, but it does not cease. Moreover, even if we granted that at a certain stage of its development society by some mysterious change gave rise to 'pure' reason, we should still be left with the problem of explaining why some thinkers failed to take advantage of this heaven-sent opportunity of basking in its light. We are told that the Ionian philosophers 'made the formation of the world a natural and no longer a supernatural event', and that 'this has become the universal premiss of all modern science'; but, if they were capable of this achievement, how is it that some of their successors, including Plato, renounced it and reaffirmed theological doctrines of the supernatural? To these questions Cornford has no answer. His postulate of 'open-minded observation' is not a rational inference but an *a priori* premiss, which is no less dogmatic than those which he detected in Epicurus and shows that his mind was closed on the question of the class struggle.

How then is the rationalism of Ionian natural philosophy to be explained? Farrington's answer is as follows:

The Milesians were not simply observers of nature. They were observers of nature whose eyes had been quickened, whose attention directed, and whose selection of phenomena to be observed, had been conditioned by familiarity with a certain range of techniques. The novelty of their modes of thought is only negatively explained by their rejection of mystical or supernatural intervention. It is its positive content that is decisive. Its positive content is drawn from the techniques of the age.[23]

[23] Farrington GS 1.36–7.

If this were so, we should expect to find the same rationalism prevalent among the early Sumerians and Egyptians, who in technical inventiveness far surpassed the Greeks; but the difference between their mode of thinking and the Greek is precisely that it was lacking in this novelty. The early Greek philosophers owed what was new in their work, not to familiarity with the techniques of production, but to the new developments in the relations of production which by transforming the structure of society had generated a new outlook on the world. As Stalin observed:

The superstructure is not directly connected with production, with man's productive activity. It is connected with production only indirectly, through the economy, through the basis. The superstructure, therefore, reflects changes in the level of development of the productive forces not immediately and directly, but only after changes in the basis, through the prism of the changes effected in the basis by the changes in production. [24]

It is to these changes that we must now turn.

[24] Stalin ML 7.

Part Four

THE NEW REPUBLICS

Thou visible God
That solder'st close impossibilities,
And mak'st them kiss!

SHAKESPEARE

IX

THE ECONOMIC BASIS

1. Commodity Production

IN the closing pages of *The Origin of the Family, Private Property and the State,* Engels defines civilisation as follows:

> Civilisation is, therefore, according to the above analysis, the stage of development in society at which the division of labour, the exchange between individuals arising from it, and the commodity production which combines them both, come to their full growth and revolutionise the whole of previous society.[1]

This definition, it may be noted, is superior to the traditional one, current among bourgeois archæologists, which is that civilisation is 'the culture of cities'.[2] It is true, of course, that some degree of urban development is one of civilisation's general characteristics, but only one out of many, such as the use of writing and the division of society into classes. The merit of Engels's definition is that it is analytical, not merely descriptive. It treats civilisation as the culmination of an organic process of economic and social change.

The division of labour involves the production of a surplus over and above the producers' immediate needs; and this increase in the productivity of labour is due to better tools and greater skill, that is, to development of the productive forces. It is accompanied by corresponding changes in the relations of production. As production becomes more specialised, it becomes less collective; and as with production, so with consumption. In this way the division of labour 'undermines the collectivity of production and appropriation, elevates appropriation by individuals into the general rule, and thus creates exchange between individuals' until 'gradually commodity production becomes the dominant form'.[3]

The growth of commodity production led, in the first place, to the rise of a new class, the merchants. The merchant is one who lives, not by production, but by the exchange

---

[1] Engels OF 198–9.   [2] Clark 89.   [3] Engels OF 199.

of what others have produced, which he buys cheap and sells dear:

> He occupies himself with the exchange of commodities and the operations incidental to it, which are separated from production and performed by a non-producer, and this is merely a means to increase wealth, and at that wealth in its most general social form, exchange value.[4]

In the second place, it tends to dissolve collective relations based on common ownership of the means of production and to replace them with individual relations based on private property:

> Objects in themselves are external to man, and consequently alienable by him. In order that this alienation may be reciprocal, it is only necessary for men, by a tacit understanding, to treat each other as private owners of those alienable objects, and by implication as independent individuals. But such a state of reciprocal independence has no existence in a primitive society based on property in common. . . .[5]
>
> We see here, on the one hand, how the exchange of commodities breaks through all local and personal bonds inseparable from direct barter, and develops the circulation of the products of social labour; and, on the other hand, how it develops a whole network of social relations spontaneous in their growth and entirely beyond the control of the actors.[6]

And, thirdly, it creates the need for the use of a special commodity, consisting of some uniform and durable material, which will serve as a medium of exchange, capable of expressing in itself the values of all other commodities:

> If we bear in mind that the value of commodities has a purely social reality, and that they acquire this reality only in so far as they are expressions or embodiments of one identical social substance, viz. human labour, it follows as a matter of·course that value can only manifest itself in the social relation of commodity to commodity.[7]
>
> Since no commodity can stand in the relation of equivalent to itself, and thus turn its own bodily shape into the expression of its own value, every commodity is compelled to choose some other commodity for its equivalent, and to accept the use-value, that is to say, the bodily shape, of that other commodity as the form of its own value.[8]
>
> The general form of relative value, embracing the whole world of commodities, converts the single commodity that is excluded from the rest and made to play the part of equivalent . . . into the universal equivalent.[9]

[4] Marx C 3. 384.   [5] Ib. 1. 59.   [6] Ib. 1. 86.
[7] Ib. 1. 15.   [8] Ib. 1. 25.   [9] Ib. 1. 37.

In the ancient east, as we have seen, the commodity selected to play the part of universal equivalent was silver, which was weighed out in exchange for other commodities, whose value in relation to one another was expressed in the form of a given quantity of silver. This was a form of money, but only a rudimentary form, because, so long as the metal was not guaranteed to conform to an accepted standard of purity, there still clung to it differences of quality, and to that extent it failed to function as the universal equivalent of other commodities, that is, as 'something common to them all, of which they represent a greater or less quantity'. This condition was only realised in the seventh century B.C. with the invention of the coinage.

Lastly, with the development of commodity production and the division between manual and mental labour there appears the cleavage of society into classes, the exploiters and the exploited:

This cleavage persisted during the whole civilised period. Slavery is the first form of exploitation, the form peculiar to the ancient world; it is succeeded by serfdom in the middle ages and in more recent times by wage labour. These are the three great forms of servitude characteristic of the three great epochs of civilisation.

Engels then proceeds to define more closely the economic basis corresponding to the emergence of civilisation:

The stage of commodity production with which civilisation begins is distinguished economically by the introduction of (1) metal money, and with it money capital, interest and usury; (2) merchants, as the class of inter-mediaries between the producers; (3) private ownership of land and the mortgage system; (4) slave labour as the dominant form of production.[10]

Remembering that Marx and Engels died before the early history of Egypt and Mesopotamia had been recovered by excavation, we ask whether their analysis needs to be modified in the light of subsequent research. Two questions arise in this connection.

First, was slave labour the dominant form of production in the Bronze Age? From the evidence available it would seem that, while slavery had existed in Mesopotamia and Egypt from the earliest times, it was only in the first millennium B.C. that it

[10] Engels OF 201.

developed to the point of dominating production. This was indeed perceived by Marx himself, who recognised that even in the history of Greece and Rome, which as he knew it fell entirely within the first millennium, there was a period in which slavery had not yet 'seized on production in earnest'.[11] It should also be noted that Stalin, in his 'rough picture of the development of the productive forces', passes directly from stone to iron, omitting bronze.[12] It may be inferred that he regarded the discovery of iron as the crucial stage in the advance from stone to metal, bronze being transitional.

Secondly, to what extent were the other characteristics of civilisation, as defined by Engels, present in the Bronze Age? It is not yet possible to give more than a general answer to this question. There was a considerable development of commodity production, but mainly in luxury goods: that is to say, it was confined to a portion of the surplus value which the ruling class extracted from the tillers of the soil. Among the masses of the people the primitive communal relations of production had been converted into tributary relations, but without involving any more radical change.

It may be concluded, therefore, that in the Bronze Age the conditions defined by Engels had not come to their full growth. The final transformation of the economic basis was effected in the Iron Age and first in those regions which offered the best opportunities for exploiting the new developments in the productive forces. These were Greece and Palestine, and more especially Greece. For nearly eight centuries the Greeks and the Phœnicians were competitors for the economic control of the Mediterranean, until, after the Greeks had taken the lead, both

[11] Marx C 1. 325: 'Peasant agriculture on a small scale, and the carrying on of independent handicrafts, which together form the basis of the feudal mode of production, and after the dissolution of that system continue side by side with the capitalist mode, also form the economic foundation of the classical communities at their best, after the primitive form of ownership of land in common had disappeared, and before slavery had seized on production in earnest.' Cf. 3. 937: 'This form of free farmers' property managing their own affairs as the prevailing norm constitutes on the one hand the economic foundation of society during the best times of classical antiquity, and on the other is found among modern nations as one of the forms arising from the dissolution of feudal landlordism.'

[12] Stalin DHM 123.

were subjugated by the Romans, who destroyed Corinth and
Carthage in the same year (146 B.C.).

This conclusion is confirmed by other features of these
Bronze Age states.

2. Basis and Superstructure in the Bronze Age

One of the differences between the bourgeois revolution and
the socialist revolution, according to Lenin, is the following:

> For the bourgeois revolution, which arises out of feudalism, the new
> economic organisations are created gradually in the womb of the old order,
> gradually changing all the aspects of feudal society. The bourgeois revolution
> was confronted by only one task—to sweep away, cast aside, destroy all the
> fetters of the preceding society.[13]

The same point is made by Stalin:

> The bourgeois revolution usually begins when there already exist more or
> less finished forms of the capitalist order, forms which have grown and
> ripened within the womb of feudal society prior to the open revolution;
> whereas the proletarian revolution begins when finished forms of the socialist
> order are either absent or almost completely absent.[14]

From this it follows that in the socialist revolution 'the development of the new relations of production and productive forces
is not a spontaneous process, as under capitalism, but takes
place consciously'.[15]

Going still further back to the transition from ancient
society to feudalism, it could be shown that feudal relations
developed even less consciously, more spontaneously than
capitalist relations in the ensuing epoch; and in the transition
from primitive communism to ancient society the same feature
can be observed to an even greater degree. This gradual and
spontaneous development of the new economic relations is
matched by the equally protracted and tenacious survival of the
old social order and the ideas which cement it. Never having
been challenged or even called in question, the established
institutions and ideas, dating from the very beginnings of
society itself, retard for a long time the development of the
new relations, to which they yield so gradually as to leave the

[13] Lenin WP 285–6.   [14] Stalin PL 123–4.   [15] Glezerman 29.

community scarcely conscious of any change. This explains why in Mesopotamia and Egypt, with the rise of the kingship, the memory of tribal institutions was almost completely obliterated. The Sumerians distinguished themselves from the barbarians by saying that the latter 'knew not a city' and 'had no king'.[16] They did not know that the city had grown out of the tribal camp, nor that the king was descended from the tribal chief. The transition had been effected so slowly as to be imperceptible, and therefore all they could see, when they compared themselves with the barbarians, was not two successive stages of development but two totally unconnected ways of life. Such consciousness of change as there was existed only in the minds of the ruling class, and more particularly in the minds of its leading ideologists, the priests. These were well aware that something had changed, but, since their chief concern was to persuade the people that nothing had changed, or could ever change, they succeeded to some extent in deceiving also themselves. Thus, no matter how important other functions of the kingship might become—administrative, military, judicial— one of its main functions was ideological. It was the institution which, surrounded by every device that might lend it an air of sanctity and inviolability, served, more than any other, to hold the minds of the people in subjection to the ruling class by pretending that, in honouring the king, they were doing what their ancestors had always done and what their descendants would continue to do. This function of the kingship was carried to its extreme point in Egypt, where an immense portion of the wealth produced by the peasantry was interred in royal tombs, the pyramids, erected by the labour of those same peasants who also tilled the soil. These monuments of perverted ingenuity provided the ruling class with a means of absorbing the surplus labour-power of the workers in such a way as to strengthen the institution which held them in bondage. And finally, so long as the kingship could be maintained, it was possible for the class struggle, commodity production, and other features of civilisation to develop, but without that radical transformation of the economic basis which was necessary in order 'to sweep away, cast aside, destroy all the fetters of the preceding society'.

[16] Hooke MR 44.

3. The Phœnicians

The most important inventions forming the technical basis of the early Bronze Age civilisations in the Near East were pottery, spinning, and weaving, the smelting and casting of copper, the manufacture of bronze from copper and tin, the plough, the wheeled cart, the harness, the sailing ship.[17] These were followed, early in the third millennium B.C., by the bellows, the tongs, and the *cire-perdu* process of bronze-casting.[18] In the latter part of the third millennium the rate of invention declined and remained at a low level down to the end of the Bronze Age.[19] The decline is remarkable, because it is clear that the possibilities of development in the inventions already made were far from exhausted. The wheel and the plough were both known, but there were no wheeled ploughs. From a technical point of view, there would have been no difficulty in adapting the harness, which was invented for oxen, so that it could be used on horses without choking them, or in replacing the steering oar, which involves a great expenditure of man-power, by the rudder; but in fact neither of these inventions were made until slave society had given place to feudalism.[20] These simple improvements were not made, because the use of human labour, however wasteful, was cheaper. It is noteworthy that Egypt was more backward than Mesopotamia. The wheeled cart and the bronze bellows and tongs were used in Mesopotamia for several centuries before they were introduced in Egypt.[21]

The art of iron-smelting is believed to have been discovered in Armenia.[22] It was known to the Hittites but not practised extensively.[23] At the close of the second millennium B.C. the new metal was being worked in many places, and iron tools and weapons came rapidly into common use throughout the Near East. The circumstances are obscure, but this great technical

---

[17] Lilley 1–8.

[18] *Ib.* 12–3: 'The extremely ingenious *cire-perdu* process of casting was developed. In this a wax model of the shape required is made. This is then coated with clay and placed in a furnace, where the wax melts and runs away, while the clay is baked hard to form a mould. Molten metal is then run into the mould and after cooling the clay is broken away.'

[19] *Ib.* 14–5.   [20] *Ib.* 16–7.   [21] *Ib.* 18.   [22] *Ib.* 21.

[23] Gurney 82–4.

advance must be connected with the turbulent *Völkerwanderung* which threw the eastern Mediterranean into confusion and in Greece brought the Bronze Age to an end with the Dorian invasion (Vol. I, pp. 29, 401).

Iron is more difficult to smelt than copper, because it requires a higher temperature, but, once the technique of working it had been mastered, it marked a great advance over both copper and bronze. Not only did it make better tools, but it was more widely distributed and therefore cheaper. Bronze had been used mainly for luxuries and weapons. It was only with the introduction of iron that metal became generally available for ploughshares, axes, knives, hammers, and sickles. The result was a fundamental change in the relations between industry and agriculture:

> The greatly increased productivity of agriculture yielded a surplus which could support a large number of specialised craftsmen. The product of the craftsmen became generally available instead of being the monopoly of the wealthy. In particular, the craftsman provided for the farmer those same tools with which the latter increased the productivity of his work. And thus, for the first time, there arose a balanced relationship between industry and agriculture, instead of the former one-sided relationship by which agriculture provided the food for the craftsman, but the craftsman's product went only to a select few.[24]

In addition, by increasing productivity and so rendering possible new divisions of labour, the use of iron carried still further the process of transforming collective production and appropriation into individual production and appropriation. Hence it marked a new stage in the growth of commodity production. The village commune, resting on common ownership and surrendering its surplus in the form of tribute, was succeeded by a community of individual proprietors, each producing independently for the open market (Vol. I, pp. 356–8). Such was the Greek *pólis*, based on the use of iron.

Referring to the end of the Bronze Age in Syria, Woolley writes:

> The great folk-movement of the 'Peoples of the Sea' which overwhelmed Boghazkeui turned southwards into Syria, the main host advancing by land, accompanied by their women and children in heavy two-wheeled ox-carts,

[24] Lilley 21.

the fleet keeping pace with it down the Syrian coast. One by one the cities fell before them and were laid waste, and the survivors of the defeated states swelled the ranks of the invaders. Carchemish was taken, and Aleppo; at Alalakh the burnt ruins of the topmost houses show that the city shared the fate of its more powerful neighbours. This was in the year 1194 B.C.[25]

The invaders were routed by Ramses III on the Egyptian frontier (Vol. I, p. 401). Of the survivors, some took to the sea; others remained in southern Palestine, where they formed the kingdom of Philistia.

The question arises, why did the cities of Syria not recover from this blow? They had survived many previous invasions in the course of their long history. The answer is given by Schaeffer in describing the fall of Ugarit:

There is no doubt that Ugarit did not survive the invasion of the Sea Peoples, and that the town virtually ceased to exist after the twelfth century. Thus the disappearance of Ugarit coincides with the end of the Bronze Age. This is not merely fortuitous. True, the havoc wrought by the invasions at the beginning of the twelfth century gave the last blow to the once prosperous town. But the cause of its decline was also an economic one. Up to that time the importing of copper-bearing minerals from Cyprus and the working of bronze were among the most flourishing industries at Ugarit. But now the consumption of copper began to dwindle, for iron tended more and more to replace copper in the manufacture of weapons and tools.[26]

It is not merely that bronze-working was one of the most flourishing industries in these cities, but the power of the ruling class rested on the monopoly of this expensive metal. Now, with cheap iron available, their power was swept away. There can be no doubt that similar changes were taking place in the Ægean. Mycenæ did not have to face the Peoples of the Sea, but nevertheless her prosperity declined. When the Dorians entered the Peloponnese, they met with little resistance.

The first peoples to exploit the opportunities offered by the new metal were naturally those which enjoyed the greatest freedom for the development of trade. In Egypt and Mesopotamia the old ruling class was, for the reasons given, so firmly entrenched that it was able to absorb the new relations of production without losing power. In Egypt, the Pharaohs entered on their last stage of economic and cultural decline. In Mesopotamia, the Assyrian kings placed all their faith in war. Their

[25] Woolley FK 170.   [26] Schaeffer 28.

conquests were sensational but short-lived. The Persians, who followed them, after a brief interval in which Babylon recovered her supremacy, established their empire on a basis which was better adapted to the new conditions. Trade was permitted and indeed encouraged as a source of revenue, but in such a way as to leave intact the old system of land-tenure, based on a natural economy, the surplus being drawn off as tribute to the central government. In these circumstances, with the mercantile traditions of Knossos and Mycenæ temporarily submerged by the Dorian invasion, the initiative was seized by the Phœnician cities of Tyre and Sidon.

By the ninth century B.C. the Phœnicians had settled in several parts of Cyprus, established a number of trading stations in the Ægean, and founded many colonies in the western Mediterranean. The greatest of these was Carthage.[27] Here the kingship was abolished and replaced by a mercantile oligarchy. There were two executive officers, the *shophetim*, corresponding to the Hebrew judges and responsible to the Senate, which was elected from the heads of families. The popular assembly survived, but seldom met except in times of crisis. The state was controlled by the heads of families, who in a short time gained possession of extensive territories in Africa and Spain, inhabited by primitive peoples and rich in agricultural and mineral resources. Aristotle says that the Carthaginian constitution closely resembled the Spartan.[28] In both cases a conquering people, which had preserved its tribal institutions, adapted them as a means of consolidating itself as a ruling caste. The main difference is that the Carthaginians, like the Romans, had ample scope for extending their conquests. They held their own in the western Mediterranean against the Greeks, and all but crushed the rising power of Rome. They failed, because the Romans had two advantages—a firm basis in the peasantry, and close contact with the Greeks, who by that time had outstripped the Phœnicians.

By the end of the eighth century the Greeks had broken the Phœnician monopoly of the Ægean carrying-trade and were challenging them in the Levant. In the seventh century they planted a large number of colonies in southern Italy and eastern

[27] Weill 192.   [28] Arist. *Pol.* 1272b.

MAP V

THE WESTERN MEDITERRANEAN

Sicily and a few, such as Massalia (Marseille), still farther west. Then, in 549 B.C., the Phœnicians were conquered by the Persians and finally fell out of the race. During the years that followed, the Greeks found themselves confronted with the same danger, but, thanks partly to their geographical situation and still more to their democratic institutions, they met and mastered the Persian menace.

Before leaving the Phœnicians, let us turn to the Book of Ezekiel, which contains a valuable account of Tyrian trade in the early years of the sixth century B.C.:

> Thou, O Tyre, hast said, I am perfect in beauty. Thy borders are in the heart of the seas, thy builders have perfected thy beauty. They have made all thy planks of fir trees from Senir; they have taken 'cedar from Lebanon to make a mast for thee. Of the oaks of Bashan have they made thine oars; they have made thy benches of ivory inlaid with boxwood (?) from the isles of Kittim. Of fine linen with broidered work from Egypt was thy sail, that it might be to thee for an ensign; blue and purple from the isles of Elishah was thine awning. The inhabitants of Sidon and Arvad were thy rowers; thy wise men, O Tyre, were in thee, they were thy pilots. The ancients of Gebal and the wise men thereof were in thee, thy calkers; all the ships of the sea with their mariners were in thee to exchange thy merchandise. . . . Tarshish was thy merchant by reason of the multitude of all kinds of riches; with silver, iron, tin and lead they traded for thy wares. Javan, Tubal and Meshech, they were thy traffickers; they traded the persons of men and metals of brass for thy merchandise. They of the house of Togarmah traded for thy wares with horses and war-horses and mules. The men of Dedan were thy traffickers: many isles were the mart of thine hand; they brought thee in exchange horns of ivory and ebony. Syria was thy merchant by reason of the multitude of thy handiworks; they traded for thy wares with emeralds, purple and broidered work, and fine linen and coral and rubies. Judah, and the land of Israel, they were thy traffickers; they traded for thy merchandise wheat of Minnith and pannag and honey and oil and balm. Damascus was thy merchant for the multitude of thy handiworks, by reason of the multitude of all kinds of riches, with the wine of Helbon and white wool. . . . Dedan was thy trafficker in precious cloths for riding, Arabia and all the princes of Kedar, they were the merchants of thy hand; in lambs and rams and goats, in these were they thy merchants.[29]

Senir is Mount Hermon in the Lebanon. Bashan is the open country stretching east and north-east from the Lake of Galilee. By the 'isles of Kittim', named after Kition in Cyprus,

[29] Ezekiel 27. 3–21. Javan is mentioned as exporting yarn (27. 19) with reference to the wool trade of Miletos (Ath. 540d, 553b). For a commentary on this passage, see Cooke 296–306.

is meant the islands of the Mediterranean. Elishah is believed to
be either Carthage or Sicily. Arvad is Arados (the modern Ruad)
to the north of Sidon. Gebal is Byblos in Syria. Tarshish is
probably Tartessos, a Phœnician colony on the coast of Spain.
Javan is Ionia. Tubal and Meshech are the Tibarenoi and
Moschoi on the Black Sea coast of Anatolia. Togarmah is
Armenia and Dedan Arabia.

This passage has been quoted at length, because there is no
reason to doubt its authenticity (although, needless to say, it has
been doubted) and it gives a fuller picture than any available from
Greek sources of the nature and extent of Mediterranean trade
in the sixth century B.C. The following points may be noted.

In the first place, the Tyrian imports consist mainly of raw
materials and foodstuffs. The exports are 'handiworks', that is,
articles manufactured by Tyrian craftsmen from the imported
raw materials; and these are all luxury goods. Exchange takes
the form of barter; there is no mention of money. The wide
range of their trade, extending to all corners of the Mediterranean, enabled the merchants to take full advantage of local
differences in value, buying cheap and selling dear. Thus,
Tyre was a typical mercantile city, her wealth taking the form
of merchants' capital.

It is important to observe that the growth of merchants' capital
does not by any means presuppose a high level of production:

The circulation of money and commodities may act as an intermediary
between spheres of production of widely differing organisation, whose internal
structure is still predominantly adjusted to the production of use-values.
This independent status of the process of circulation, by which various
spheres of production are connected by means of a third link, expresses two
facts. On the one hand, it shows that circulation has not yet seized hold of
production but still treats it as an existing fact. On the other hand, it shows
that the process of production has not yet absorbed circulation and converted
it into a phase of production.[30]

If this is true of medieval Europe, which Marx has in mind
here, it is still more true of antiquity:

The trade of the first independent and highly developed merchant towns
and nations rested as a purely carrying trade upon the barbarism of the
producing nations between which they intervened.[31]

[30] Marx C 3. 386.   [31] Ib. 3. 388–9.

In the second place, the Ionians are coupled with two peoples of the Black Sea, the Tibarenoi and the Moschoi, which are known to us from other sources as bronze-workers and later as iron-workers.[32] At the time in question the Black Sea coasts had been colonised intensively from Miletos, which controlled the Hellespont and Propontis (Vol. I, p. 545). It is probable, therefore, since the Black Sea was closed to the Phœnicians, that their trade with that region was conducted through the Ionians as intermediaries, and that the slaves whom the Ionian merchants shipped to Tyre had been brought from the northern colonies of Miletos. It so happens that one of our earliest Ionic inscriptions, from the Milesian colony of Kyzikos on the Propontis, records a vote of the people granting to members of a certain family, who bear Phrygian names, exemption from several taxes, including the tax on the use of the public scales, the tax on the sale of horses, and the tax on the sale of slaves.[33] Thus there was a well-established slave trade in the Ægean in the sixth century B.C. Indeed, it seems likely that one of the main incentives to colonisation, Phœnician and Greek alike, was the quest for slaves, who were bought up from kidnappers in backward regions, where their value was low, corresponding to the low level of production, and then transported to the main industrial centres, where their value was correspondingly high.

Finally, the Phœnician alphabet of twenty-two letters, evolved to meet the needs of trade, was a great advance on the Mesopotamian and Egyptian scripts. These were so complicated and clumsy as to require the services of professional scribes, and the scribes were so well organised, under the protection of the state, that they resisted successfully the simplification of their art. The Greeks took over the Phœnician alphabet, probably in the ninth century B.C., and added signs for the vowels.

The invention of the alphabet may be compared with the invention of iron-working. Just as iron made metal implements more widely available, so the new script made it technically possible for everybody to read and write. We have no means of determining the percentage of literacy in the Near East, but in

[32] Dussaud 141–70.   [33] SIG. I. 4.

the Greek democracies it must have included the great majority of the citizens, because the procedure of ostracism, which was a characteristically democratic institution, required them to record their votes in writing. An impressive memorial to this advance in human knowledge is the colossal statue of Ramses II at Abu Simbel in Nubia. Some Ionian mercenaries visited the spot about the year 589 B.C. and in an idle hour scratched their names on his divine majesty's leg.[34]

The alphabet embodied a new principle. The antecedent forms of writing—pictographic and ideographic—were concrete: the written symbol was a visual image of the idea it represented. It was not necessarily pictorial, any more than the spoken word was onomatopœic, but it was concrete. Alphabetic writing, on the other hand, is devoid of visual imagery. The written word is a combination of symbols which are meaningless in themselves, being designed to represent the smallest phonetic elements to which the word can be reduced. In this way the new medium marked an advance in the development of abstract thinking, made it possible for speech and thought to become objects of cognition, and so prepared the way for the sciences of grammar and logic.

4. *The Growth of Greek Trade*

Bourgeois students of the economic history of ancient Greece are divided between two extremes. Beloch and Pöhlmann describe the economic expansion of the eighth and seventh centuries B.C. as though it involved a considerable volume of industrial production with a sufficient degree of specialisation in the leading cities to serve as the basis for a highly organised system of international commerce; and, following Mommsen, they do not hesitate to speak of a capitalist class and a proletariat, and even of socialism, as categories applicable to this historical epoch. Their view has been combated by Hasebroek, who contends that they have misinterpreted the evidence in the light of irrelevant modern analogies.

There is no doubt that on the main issue Hasebroek is right, although he fails to analyse the misconception which lies at the

[34] *Ib.* I. I.

root of such interpretations. This had already been done by Marx. He explained that there can be no capitalism without the existence of a class of free labourers selling their labour power, and consequently capitalism must be sharply distinguished from precapitalist forms of production, which may be highly developed in other respects but lack this basic characteristic:

> If we consider money, its existence implies a definite stage in the exchange of commodities. The particular functions of money which it performs, either as the mere equivalent of commodities, or as means of circulation, or as means of payment, as hoard or as universal money, point, according to the extent and relative preponderance of the one function or the other, to very different stages in the process of social production. Yet we know by experience that a circulation of commodities relatively primitive suffices for the production of all these forms. Otherwise with capital. The historical conditions of its existence are by no means given with the mere circulation of money and commodities. It can spring into life only when the owner of the means of production and subsistence meets in the market with the free labourer selling his labour-power. And this one historical condition comprises a world's history. Capital, therefore, announces from its first appearance a new epoch in the process of social production.[35]

Hence, the mistake made by Mommsen and the rest lay in their assumption that the capitalist mode of production is based on nothing more than the development of merchants' capital:

> In the precapitalist stages of society, commerce rules industry. The reverse is true of modern society. Of course, commerce will have more or less of a reaction on the societies between which it is carried on. It will subject production more and more to exchange value by making enjoyments and subsistence more dependent on sale than on the immediate use of the products. Thereby it dissolves all the old conditions. It increases the circulation of money. It seizes no longer merely upon the surplus of production, but corrodes production more and more, making entire lines of production dependent on it. However, this dissolving effect depends to a large degree on the nature of the producing society. . . .

[35] Marx C 1. 148–9, cf. 146 n. 1: 'In encyclopædias of classical antiquities we find such nonsense as this, that in the ancient world capital was fully developed, "except that the free labourer and the system of credit was wanting"; Mommsen also, in his *History of Rome*, commits, in this respect, one blunder after another.' At the other extreme R. M. Cook falls into an equal absurdity (IG 90): 'The invention of the coinage must have been in part due to chance, since the Lydians and Ionians at that time were not at a higher stage of economic development than had ever been reached by an earlier society.'

To what this process of dissolution will lead, in other words, what new mode of production will take the place of the old, does not depend on commerce, but on the character of the old mode of production itself. In the antique world the effect of commerce and the development of merchants' capital always result in slave economy; or, according to what the point of departure may be, the result may simply turn out to be the transformation of a patriarchal slave system devoted to the production of direct means of subsistence into a similar system devoted to the production of surplus value. However, in the modern world, it results in the capitalist mode of production. From these facts it follows that these results were conditioned by quite other circumstances than the mere influence of the development of merchants' capital.[36]

Hasebroek's own conclusion is as follows:

Let us conclude by summing up our positive knowledge of the conditions of trade during the period preceding the Persian Wars. It was focused in a number of ports and cities which by reason of their geographical situation were specially suitable as commercial centres. Chief among these were Corinth, Aigina and Athens in Greece proper; Miletos in Asia Minor (the *entrepôt* of trade between Asia Minor and the Mediterranean); Naukratis in Egypt (for trade between the Mediterranean and Egypt); and in the west, Carthage and Massalia (Marseille). . . . The commodities dealt in were mostly commodities of value; they were never, so far as we know, articles of everyday need. Chief among them would be gold and silver and ivory, costly metal work (*e.g.* an inlaid sword), valuable vases, woven cloths, ornaments (such as were dear to the warriors of Homeric times) and above all slaves, both men and women. For such commodities the demand was always considerable, and from the earliest times they would be exchanged against each other between nation and nation. The trader bought them in this or that market and from this or that craftsman. If he sold them again at a profit he would return and secure further supplies, and perhaps he might secure for the craftsman valuable raw materials for his work; for besides trading in finished articles he must also have dealt in those natural products which though indispensable are in some places scarce—iron, for example (which the Taphian Mentes exchanged for copper), tin, purple, wood for shipbuilding, oil and wine.[37]

Hasebroek's treatment of the evidence, on which he bases this conclusion, is one-sided and sometimes fallacious; but, so far as the content of Greek trade in this period is concerned, his estimate may be accepted. The reader will observe that it corresponds very closely to the picture given in Ezekiel of Tyrian trade in the same period.

Nevertheless, it suffers from one serious weakness, which

[36] Marx C 3. 389–90.   [37] Hasebroek 68.

demands attention, because it is shared by some Marxist historians, who, parting company with Engels, have tended to underestimate the social and political effects of the commercial expansion which took place in the period prior to the Persian Wars.

In the fourth century B.C. Greek trade was concentrated in the hands of non-citizens and based mainly on moneylenders' capital. This is demonstrated by Hasebroek, though here too his detailed interpretation of the evidence is unsound. In the sixth century, however, the situation was entirely different. The evidence for the earlier period is meagre but unambiguous; and Hasebroek's treatment of it can only be described as capricious. It must therefore be considered in some detail.

Some time in the seventh century a ship from Samos, with Kolaios as captain, was on its way to Egypt when it was driven from its course by an easterly gale and put in at Platea, near Kyrene, where Kolaios left a year's provisions for some emigrants from Thera who were stranded there. From Platea he intended to turn back to Egypt, but the east wind continued and carried him through the Pillars of Herakles (the Straits of Gibraltar) to the port of Tartessos, which no Greek had ever visited before. There he sold his goods for a profit of sixty talents—the largest ever made by any Greek, says Herodotus, 'excepting Sostratos of Aigina'. This adventure was the beginning of friendly relations between Samos and Kyrene.[38]

Without committing ourselves to all the details of this story, we observe that the places mentioned—Samos, Kyrene, Tartessos, Aigina—are known from other sources to have been important commercial centres; and therefore we have no reason to doubt its authenticity. Kolaios of Samos, like Sostratos of Aigina, was a merchant adventurer. In regard to Sostratos, it should be noted that Pindar, two centuries later, mentioned the Bassidai of Aigina as a rich family of sea-captains trading on their own account.[39] Other members of the same class—that is, nobles who had turned to trade—were Charaxos of Lesbos, Sappho's brother, who shipped wine to Naukratis,[40] and Solon of Athens, who according to Aristotle travelled to Egypt 'on

[38] Hdt. 4. 152.   [39] Pi. N. 6. 32–4.
[40] Str. 808, Ath. 596b, Hdt. 2. 135.

business and to see the world'.[41] These instances show that in the seventh and sixth centuries it was not uncommon for members of the nobility to engage in overseas trade. Indeed we may go further. In two instances that have come down to us we find them concerned in the actual process of production. Peisistratos of Athens consolidated his position as tyrant by means of the revenues he drew from his mines in Thrace;[42] and shortly afterwards his rivals, the Alkmeonidai, repaired their fortunes by executing a contract for rebuilding the temple at Delphi, which had been destroyed by fire.[43]

What does Hasebroek make of this evidence, which contradicts his thesis that at no time before the Hellenistic period had Greek trade been in the hands of wealthy citizens? The story of Kolaios is dismissed without argument as 'a fifth-century legend composed in order to give a historical explanation of the friendship between Samos and Kyrene'. Sostratos is mentioned without comment, but we are assured that 'the sea voyages which the noble families of Aigina undertook, and from which, according to Pindar, they won great renown, were plundering expeditions and had nothing to do with commerce at all'.[44] This is a distinction without a difference; for as Marx explained:

Merchants' capital in its supremacy everywhere stands for a system of robbery, and its development among the trading nations of ancient and modern times is always associated with plunder, piracy, slave-snatching and colonial conquest.[45]

Again, we are told that 'Sappho's brother was not a trader, even though he brought wine to Naukratis, nor was his occupation "sea commerce"; he was simply a large-scale Lesbian farmer who sold off the produce of his vineyards in a foreign market'.[46] The truth is, we know nothing of Sappho's family circumstances, and, if we are to indulge in guesswork, the most probable conjecture is that Charaxos was engaged in selling overseas the produce of his family estate and perhaps of other estates as well. It is hard to see how such an occupation falls short of 'sea commerce'. Finally, Hasebroek disposes of

[41] Arist. AR. 2. 6, cf. Plu. Sol. 5. 25.   [42] Hdt. 1. 64.
[43] Philoch. 70.   [44] Hasebroek 69, 21.   [45] Marx C 3. 389–90.
[46] Hasebroek 13–4.

Peisistratos's Thracian revenues and the building operations of the Alkmeonidai by not mentioning them at all. The result is to leave him in an even more vulnerable position than his opponents, who, whatever faults may be found with their interpretations, did at least state the facts.

5. The Coinage

The conclusion to be drawn from the foregoing considerations is that there was in Greece during the seventh and sixth centuries B.C. a movement of commercial expansion, which, though small by modern standards, marked nevertheless a new stage in the evolution of ancient society, characterised by the rise of a merchant class, which in a number of cities won control of the state and established a democratic constitution. The nature of this democratic revolution will be considered later. At present we are concerned with its economic basis.

It was in Greece, in the period in question, that the coinage was invented. According to the Greeks themselves, the first coins were minted by the kings of Lydia, and there is no reason to doubt the truth of their tradition.[47] Lydia was rich in gold and silver, and it lay across the principal caravan routes from the East, which passed down the valleys of the Hermos and Maiandros to Smyrna, Miletos, and the other cities of Ionia. From Ionia the new medium spread across the Ægean to Aigina, Euboia, Corinth, Athens, and a little later to the Greek colonies in Italy and Sicily. Thus Greek society was the first to be based on a monetary economy. The significance of this development has seldom been appreciated.

Hasebroek writes:

> We must hesitate to speak of Greece in this period as having a monetary economy. The precious metals were, indeed, practically everywhere the standards of value, but the coins into which they were made, starting from the seventh century, had at first a purely local currency, and it took a long time before they became the media of international payments.[48]

This is scarcely true as a statement of fact and is misleading in its implications. The difficulty in identifying the exact place of

[47] Hdt. 1. 94.   [48] Hasebroek 71.

origin of the earliest Ionian coins is in itself an indication that
they had more than a local circulation, and on the mainland of
Greece we find from the beginning evidence of keen competition
between the so-called Æginetan and Euboic standards. Further,
even those currencies which did not circulate outside the state
that coined them prove by the very fact of their existence that
commodity production was penetrating more and more deeply
into social relations and thus 'dissolving all the old conditions'.
In a later chapter, after we have examined the old conditions
which were thus dissolved, we shall be in a better position to
appreciate the magnitude of the revolution. Meanwhile let us take
note of the impression it made on the people who lived through it.

The actual invention of the coinage was preserved in popular
memory in the stories of Midas, the Phrygian king who
turned all that he touched into gold, and Gyges of Lydia, who,
with the aid of his gold ring, which had a magical seal, made
himself invisible, stole into the king's palace, killed the king,
and became king himself.[49] 'Man is money.' The meaning of
this proverb, already current in the seventh century B.C., is
clear: there is nothing money cannot buy; there is nothing the
man with money cannot become.[50] The same truth is implicit in
another saying of the period: 'Riches have no limit.'[51] Money
had been invented to facilitate the process of exchange—selling
in order to buy; but it was used very soon for a new purpose—
buying in order to sell: the merchant buys cheap in order to sell
dear.[52] Money-making has ceased to be a means to an end and
become an end in itself; and to this process there is no limit.
The cycle is repeated again and again until eventually, owing
to some unforeseen and uncontrollable cause, such as currency
depreciation, the money-made man finds himself, like Midas,
starving in the midst of his gold.[53] Hence money came to be
recognised as a universal, incalculable, and subversive force:

> Money wins friendship, honour, place and power,
> And sets man next to the proud tyrant's throne.
> All trodden paths and paths untrod before
> Are scaled by nimble riches, where the poor
> Can never hope to win the heart's desire.

[49] Pl. *Rp.* 359d.   [50] Alc. 101.   [51] Sol. 1. 71.
[52] Arist. *Pol.* 1257.   [53] *Ib.* 1257b.

> A man ill-formed by nature and ill-spoken,
> Money shall make him fair to eye and ear;
> Money shall earn him health and happiness,
> And only money can cloak iniquity.[54]

All this—and much more might be quoted to the same effect—shows that Engels's account of the matter is correct:

> The Athenians were soon to learn how rapidly the product asserts its mastery over the producer when once exchange between individuals has begun and products have been transformed into commodities. With the coming of commodity production, individuals began to cultivate the soil on their own account, which soon led to individual ownership of land. Money followed, the general commodity with which all others were exchangeable. When men invented money, they did not realise that they were again creating a new social power, the one general power before which the whole of society must bow. And it was this new power, suddenly sprung to life without the knowledge or will of its creators, which now, in the full brutality of its youth, gave the Athenians the first taste of its might.[55]

What is said here of Athens is equally true of Ionia. As we have seen, commodity production had been developing over a long period in many parts of the Near East, but only now, with the introduction of the coinage, did it 'come to its full growth and revolutionise the whole of previous society'.

6. Slavery

The two centuries preceding the Persian Wars saw the introduction of the sheep-shears, rotary quern, wine-press, and crane. After them no further inventions are recorded before the Hellenistic age.[56] Thus, in industrial as well as commercial progress the fifth century was a turning-point. What was it that brought the movement to a stop? The answer is that this was the century in which 'slavery seized on production in earnest'.

In general, the slave had no incentive to increase production, because the whole of his surplus product was taken from him. On the other hand, so long as the supply was plentiful, he could be worked to death, like the African miner to-day. His cost of reproduction was less than that of the free labourer. His labour power was unskilled but cheap. It was profitable, but

---

[54] S. fr. 85.   [55] Engels OF 125.   [56] Lilley 28.

only at a low level of production. Moreover, being overworked, short-lived and deprived of family life, he was not in a position to acquire or transmit any skill, even if he had been encouraged to do so; and hence slave labour obstructed the improvement of technique. Freemen had no interest in combining with slaves against their common exploiters; rather, their aim was to buy slaves of their own, and this they could hope to do, so long as they were cheap. The main source of supply was kidnapping and conquest. Thus, besides preventing the increase of wealth, slavery promoted its destruction through internecine wars, in which Greek enslaved Greek. In these circumstances it became expedient to kill the adult males because, being trained to arms, they were difficult to manage, and keep only the women and children. This practice was well established in the fifth century B.C.

In spite of these considerations, some historians, anxious to present 'the glory that was Greece' in the most favourable light, have discounted the part played by slave labour and even declared that 'Greek society was not a slave society'.[57] In order to test such statements it is enough to turn the pages of Herodotus and Thucydides.

Of the Greek words for 'slave' some were used loosely, but one had a very definite meaning. The word *andrápodon*, 'chattel slave', means literally a 'man-footed' creature, being formed on the analogy of *tetrápoda*, 'four-footed' cattle. Similarly, *andrapodistés* and *andrapodokápelos* meant 'slave-snatcher' and 'slave-dealer' respectively. In all the passages that follow the reference is to *andrápoda*, that is, to chattel slaves.

The word occurs for the first time in the *Iliad*, where Euneos of Lemnos offers wine in exchange for metals, oxen, hides, and slaves (Vol. I, p. 356). The slaves sold at Kyzikos were *andrápoda* (p. 188). The first Greek city to employ chattel slaves was Chios, where there was a slave market throughout antiquity, and it is noteworthy that as early as 600 B.C. the constitution of this island was democratic.[58] About the same time Periandros, tyrant of Corinth, sent 300 young men from Kerkyra, a Corinthian colony, to Sardeis, where they were to be castrated and

[57] Zimmern 161.
[58] Ath. 265b; Tod I. 2.

serve as eunuchs.[59] A century later we hear, again from Chios, of one Panionios, who made a handsome fortune by procuring good-looking Greek boys, castrating them, and selling them at Ephesos and Sardeis.[60] The people of Arisbe, one of the six original cities of Lesbos, were enslaved by their neighbours of Methymna.[61] Some prisoners from Lesbos were employed in chain gangs by Polykrates, tyrant of Samos, on the fortification of the island.[62] A band of emigrants from Samos, who had settled in Crete, were attacked by the inhabitants together with some seamen from Aigina and enslaved.[63] One of the inducements offered to the Persians for subjugating Naxos, which was then under a democracy, was that the island had a large slave population.[64] When the Persians conquered Ionia the citizens of Samos sailed away to Sicily, where they seized the Greek city of Zankle. This they did with the support of Hippokrates, tyrant of Gela, who in return for his assistance took half the slave population, together with the majority of the citizens, for work in his chain gangs.[65] When the Persians invaded Greece, they were under orders to enslave the inhabitants of Eretria and Athens and dispatch them to Sousa. They were able to carry out the order in respect of the Eretrians, who were eventually settled near the Persian capital; but the Athenians eluded them.[66] It seems that even at this period there already existed in Anatolia large landed estates worked by slave labour; for, when Xerxes entered Phrygia at the head of his army, he was entertained by one Pythios, reputed to be the wealthiest of his subjects, who bestowed on him vast sums in gold and silver, adding that he still had plenty to live on from his farms and slaves.[67]

Following up the victory over Persia, the Athenians captured Eion in Thrace and sold the inhabitants into slavery;[68] then they sailed to Skyros, enslaved the inhabitants, and replaced them with planters from Athens.[69] Meanwhile Gelon, tyrant of Syracuse, had kidnapped the common people of Megara Hyblaia and Euboia, two Greek colonies in Sicily, and sold them for

[59] Hdt. 3. 50.
[60] Ib. 8. 105–6.
[61] Ib. 1. 151.
[62] Ib. 3. 39.
[63] Ib. 3. 59.
[64] Ib. 5. 31.
[65] Ib. 6. 23.
[66] Ib. 6. 94, 119.
[67] Ib. 7. 28.
[68] Th. 1. 98. 1.
[69] Ib. 1. 98. 2.

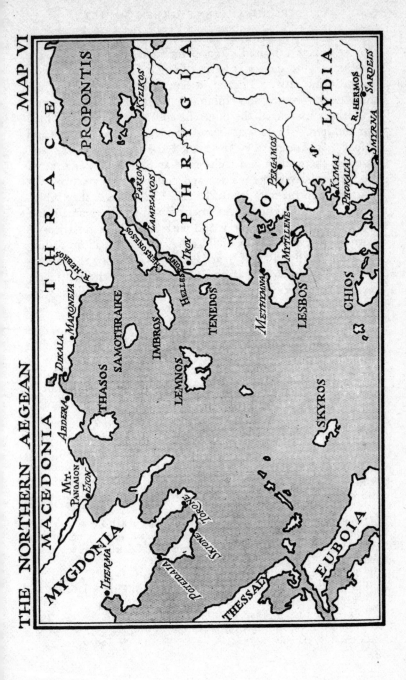

export.[70] In 430 B.C., at the outbreak of the Peloponnesian War, the Athenians captured Argos Amphilochikon and sold the inhabitants into slavery.[71] In 427 B.C. the Thebans stormed the neighbouring city of Plataiai, executed 200 of the men, and enslaved the women and children.[72] In 425 B.C. the democrats of Kerkyra massacred the oligarchs and enslaved their women and children.[73] In 421 B.C. the Athenians captured Torone and Skione. At Torone they dispatched the men to Athens and enslaved the women and children;[74] at Skione they massacred the men, enslaved the women and children, and resettled the territory with planters from Plataiai.[75] In 416 B.C. they subjugated Melos, massacred the men, enslaved the women and children, and resettled the island with planters from Athens.[76] During the campaign in Sicily an Athenian squadron sailing along the north coast put in at Hykkara, kidnapped the inhabitants, and sold them at Katane.[77] After the rout of the Athenians, not less than 7000 prisoners, Athenians and their allies, were thrown into the quarries, where many of them perished, and the survivors were sold into slavery.[78]

These are cases of Greeks enslaving Greeks. Of the regular traffic in barbarians the ancient writers tell us almost nothing, simply taking it for granted; but we learn from Aristophanes and other Attic sources of his time that the slave population of Athens was drawn from countries as distant as Illyria, Thrace, Scythia, the Caucasus, Cappadocia, Phrygia, Lydia, Caria, Syria, Egypt, and Arabia.[79] As to prices, the best evidence is an inscription of the year 414 B.C., from which we learn that sixteen slaves belonging to a resident alien were sold by auction at prices ranging from 70 to 301 *drachmaí*, with an average of 168 *dr.* for males and 147½ *dr.* for females.[80] These sums may

---

[70] Hdt. 7. 156. From an inscription we learn that in 446 B.C. an Athenian expedition into Megaris returned with 2000 *andrápoda* (Tod 1. no. 41). In 432 B.C. the Athenians charged the Megarians with sheltering runaway slaves from Athens (Th. 1. 139. 2).

[71] Th. 2. 68. 7.   [72] *Ib.* 3. 68. 2.   [73] *Ib.* 4. 48. 4.
[74] *Ib.* 5. 3. 4.   [75] *Ib.* 5. 32. 1.   [76] *Ib.* 5.116. 4.
[77] *Ib.* 6. 62.   [78] *Ib.* 7. 86. 3–4, Plu. *Nic.* 29.

[79] Ar. *Th.* 1001, *Lys.* 184, *Ach.* 273, *Ves.* 828, *Pa.* 1138, *Th.* 279, 293, *Pa.* 1146, *Av.* 1133, *Ra.* 1046, *Pa.* 1146, *Av.* 523 sch., *Ves.* 433, *Av.* 762–4, 1244, *Ec.* 867, cf. Hdt. 8. 75. 1.   [80] Tod. 1. no. 79.

be compared with the fees paid to professional teachers for tutoring the sons of the well-to-do. Euenos of Paros offered a course on 'human and political virtue' for what was regarded as the very modest fee of 500 dr.[81]

From this it is clear that in the period under review there was a continuous demand for slave labour. We do not know the size of the slave population. All we can say is that at Athens it seems to have risen sharply during the latter half of the fifth century. Thus Thucydides relates that in the year 458–7 B.C., when the Athenians decided to fortify the city in circumstances that demanded the utmost speed, the whole people turned out on the job, including women and children.[82] He does not mention slaves, as he might be expected to have done, if they had been available in large numbers. The same author records that in 413 B.C. over 20,000 slaves deserted to the Spartans, who had occupied Dekeleia, most of them being manual workers.[83] It may be inferred that they had been employed in the quarries and mines.[84] We know that in this generation Nikias, leader of the ill-fated Sicilian expedition, owned 1000 slaves, whom he hired out for work in the mines at an annual return of about 10 talents.[85] Assuming that he had bought them at an average price of 168 dr. per head (a figure which may well be too high, since only the cheapest slaves would be sent to the mines), it may be reckoned that he received an annual return of at least 35 per cent. So high a return in this field of investment must have tended to maintain high rates of interest in general. It was evidently a common thing for those who owned only a few slaves to employ them in this way, receiving from each a return of an obol or more a day. Apart from the mines, the largest concentration we hear of at Athens is the arms factory of Kephalos, who employed 120 slaves.[86] This was no doubt exceptional. A generation later we hear of a well-to-do family whose property consisted of a house in town, two country farms, and a cobbler's shop employing ten or eleven slaves.[87] Large numbers

[81] Pl. Ap. 20b.   [82] Th. 1. 90. 3.
[83] Ib. 7. 27. 5.   [84] Bury HG 485.
[85] Hipponikos owned 600 slaves and employed them in the same way: X. Vect. 4. 14–5, Mem. 2. 5. 2, Plu. Nic. 4.
[86] And. Caed. Her. 20, Myst. 38, Hyp. fr. 155, Aesch. 1.97: Lys. 1.12.8.
[87] Aesch. 1. 97.

of slaves were employed in domestic service and also in brothels. Glotz has estimated that an ordinary Athenian household might contain from three to twelve slaves.[88] This is no more than a guess, but it is important to note that even the poorer citizens seem to have had one or two slaves. Chremylos, in the *Wealth* of Aristophanes, is a poor peasant; yet he owns several slaves.[89] Slaves and poor citizens were employed in the same conditions on public works. The extent to which slave labour had encroached on free labour at Athens by the end of the fifth century may be judged from the accounts for the Erechtheion, which was built in 408 B.C. Of the seventy-one men engaged on the job, sixteen were slaves, thirty-five were resident aliens, and twenty were citizens.[90] The reason why the third figure is so low is of course that the citizens enjoyed the franchise, which entitled them to earn money as jurors, to partake of the meat and wine which was distributed free at the frequent public festivals, and to put their names down in the lotteries for colonial plantations. They were protected to some extent by democracy.

What then is our conclusion? Ehrenberg writes as follows:

The question of free and slave labour is really the question of manufacturing on a small or on a large scale. Since we do not believe in the predominant economic importance of big *ergastéria*, where slave labour was generally preferred, we do not believe in the predominant role of slave labour in general. It was necessary and needed everywhere, but rather as supplementary and not as part of the foundations of economic life. Free men never felt slave labour as a danger, hardly ever as a disadvantage.[91]

In support of this view he appeals to Westermann, whom he describes as 'the outstanding living expert on all questions of Greek slavery':

[88] Glotz AGW 200.

[89] Ar. *Pl.* 26, 228, 1105. Even in Hesiod, the small farmer's minimum equipment includes a slave woman (*Op.* 405–6). The testimony of Aristophanes is discounted by A. H. M. Jones on the ground that 'comedy was after all written by well-to-do authors, and slaves provided a variety of comic turns'. It might be added that modern accounts of ancient Athens are 'after all' the work of well-to-do historians. Besides reducing Aristophanes to the level of a music-hall comedian, Jones has overlooked the fact that Chremylos owns a number of slaves in addition to the one who does duty on the stage.

[90] *IG.* 1. 373–4.   [91] Ehrenberg 183–4.

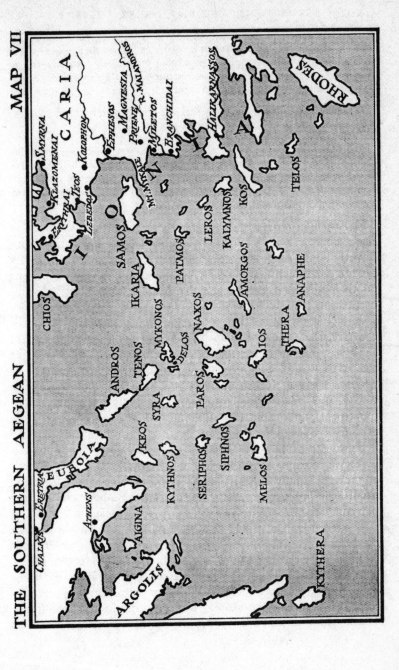

THE SOUTHERN AEGEAN

MAP VII

CHALKIS
ERETRIA
EUBOIA
ATHENS
AIGINA
ARGOLIS

KYTHERA

SMYRNA
KLAZOMENAI
ERYTHRAI
TEOS
LEBEDOS
KOLOPHON
EPHESOS
MAGNESIA
PRIENE
MILETOS
R. MALANDROS
BRANCHIDAI
CARIA

Mt. MYKALE
HALIKARNASSOS

RHODES

CHIOS
SAMOS
IKARIA

PATMOS

LEROS
KALYMNOS
KOS
TELOS

AMORGOS
ANAPHE

ANDROS
TENOS
MYKONOS
DELOS
PAROS
NAXOS
IOS
THERA

SYRA
KEOS
KYTHNOS
SERIPHOS
SIPHNOS
MELOS

The slaves were employed at the same work as the free, usually side by side with them and apparently without prejudice or friction. In any sense which implies either that the enslaved population predominated over the free or that the Greek city-states displayed the mentality of a slave-ridden society, Greek society was not founded on slavery.[92]

There is an axiom of political economy which these scholars have overlooked:

If it is a scientific task to resolve the outward and visible movement into the inward and actual movement, it stands to reason that the conceptions regarding the laws of production which the agents of production and circulation form in their heads will differ widely from the real laws, being merely the conscious expression of the apparent movements.[93]

The Athenian citizens felt no danger or even disadvantage in slave labour, so long as they could exploit it directly or indirectly by the methods mentioned above; and that is what they did. In the fourth century they became a class of *rentiers* living on their unearned income and despising manual labour as an occupation fit only for barbarians and slaves. Of course, they were not conscious of this mentality as slave-ridden; on the contrary, they appealed to the self-evident truth that, since the slave was inferior by nature, it was in his own interest to be treated as a slave. This, like similar sophistries put forward by white settlers and their descendants in Africa and America to-day, was 'merely the conscious expression of the apparent movement', and proves nothing except the capacity of an exploiting class to deceive itself.

If we set aside these ideological factors and turn to the objective relations of production, what remains of Ehrenberg's argument? Simply this: the Athenian economy was based on small-scale production, and therefore slave labour cannot have played a large part in it. The fallacy is obvious.

The truth is that, just because they were based on small-scale production, the Greek city-states, having grown up in conformity with the new developments in the productive forces, especially iron-working and the coinage, were able, under the democracy, to insinuate slave labour surreptitiously into all branches of production, and so create the illusion that it was something ordained by nature. It was then that 'slavery seized

[92] Westermann 470.   [93] Marx C 3. 369.

on production in earnest'. This was the culminating point in the evolution of ancient society, to be followed by a long decline, in which the limitations inherent in a slave economy asserted themselves on an ever-increasing scale, obstructing the further development of the productive forces and diverting the energies of society from the exploitation of nature to the exploitation of man.

7. The Individual

'Many proofs might be given to show that the early Greeks had a manner of life similar to that of barbarians to-day'.[94] This statement is without parallel in the literature of Babylonia and Egypt. It is perhaps not an accident that its author, Thucydides, was by birth both an Athenian nobleman and a barbarian. On his father's side he belonged to the illustrious clan of the Philaidai, who claimed descent from Ajax (Vol. I, p. 121). For several generations his branch of the clan had possessed mining interests in Thrace. One of his paternal ancestors, Miltiades, had been tyrant of the Thracian Chersonesos (Vol. I, p. 572) and had married a Thracian princess. His own father bore a Thracian name, Oloros, and his mother was the daughter of a Thracian chief.[95] Thus, the circumstances of his birth and upbringing may have helped him to see the relation between Greek and barbarian in its true light. But his case is not unique. It is only a striking instance of a general truth. The Greeks had emerged so rapidly out of barbarism that they carried with them into civilisation, fully conscious of their origin, many tribal institutions and ideas; and in these conditions they created a new form of state, the democratic republic, characterised by the adaptation of tribal institutions to the latest developments in the mode of production. The democratic constitution was presented to the people as restoring to them in a new form those principles of tribal equality which their ancestors had enjoyed from time immemorial until they had been robbed of them under the landed aristocracy.[96] This was an illusion— what Marx and Engels called 'the illusion of the epoch';[97] and it was the exact reverse of the reality. Being designed to facilitate

[94] Th. 1. 6. 6.
[95] Th. *Vit.* 1.
[96] Thomson AA 207–8, PR 109.
[97] Marx-Engels GI 30.

the growth of commodity production, the democratic republic created the conditions in which the old tribal, gentile, traditional, patriarchal, personal relations were swept away.

Such was the contradiction that forced itself on the consciousness of the Greeks. Before proceeding to survey the political and ideological forms in which it found conscious expression, let us recapitulate our analysis of its economic basis.

In primitive communism property had been something inseparable from man himself:

> Property means originally nothing but man's relation to his natural conditions of production as belonging to him, as his, as presupposed together with his own existence—his relation to them as the natural pre-condition for himself, forming as it were no more than an extension of his own body. He does not, properly speaking, stand in any relation to his conditions of production, but rather exists himself doubly, subjectively as himself, objectively as these natural, inorganic conditions of his existence. The forms of these natural conditions of production are: first, his existence as a member of a community, and therefore the existence of this community, originally a tribe, or a tribe more or less modified; and secondly, his relation to the land through the community, as his, that is, common ownership of the land, either combined with individual possession or else with only the produce divided, the land itself and cultivation remaining common.[98]

Such relations still persisted in parts of Greece as late as the sixth century B.C. (Vol. I, p. 320). The colonies which the Greeks planted all over the Mediterranean were organised on the same principle, modified to this extent, that they were based, not on common ownership, but on a union of families, each of which held in perpetuity a piece of land inherited from one of the founders (Vol. I, p. 314). The family was inseparable from the soil on which it lived:

> The pre-condition for the appropriation of land is membership of the community; but, as a member of the community, the individual is now a private proprietor. His private property signifies to him both a piece of land and his own status as a member of the community.[99]

His piece of land is, in Greek, his *ousía*, his substance, that in which he and the other members of his family, past and present, have their being, the source both of their material sustenance and of their social status.

[98] Marx FKPV 27–8.   [99] *Ib.* 10–1.

From the beginning, however, the Greek city-state, united within itself, was in strenuous conflict with its neighbours, Greek and non-Greek alike, robbing or robbed, enslaving or enslaved. In this way, with the rapid growth of a monetary economy, its internal unity was negated by the struggle for the land and later by the antagonism between slave-owners and slaves. In each state the citizens were united against the slaves, yet divided against themselves by competition for the surplus value produced by slave labour. Such tendencies had operated in the Bronze Age, but then they had been held in check by theocratic despots. Now they were given free rein. In Greek democracy the individual found himself 'freed' from all relations other than those determined by the mysterious nexus of commodity exchange.

At the same time, in keeping with the lower level of commodity production, this freedom of the individual never reached the level it has attained in modern capitalist society. The citizen body, the slave-owners, endeavoured to maintain their solidarity in face of the growing slave population by excluding the land from the orbit of exchange. At Athens, under the constitution of Kleisthenes and throughout the fifth century, the rights of citizenship were identified, at least nominally, with the rights of landownership, with the result that trade developed in the hands of resident aliens. Only in the following century do we find clear signs that land was becoming freely alienable again, as it had been, to some degree, in the sixth century; and the result was the dissolution of the city-state. We may say therefore, that one of the basic factors determining the development of the city-state, was this internal contradiction between the old system of land-tenure and the new force of commodity production.

X
THE DEMOCRATIC REVOLUTION

1. Ancient Democracy

DEMOCRACY is a form of the state. The state is an organisation for the forcible repression of one class by another. Democracy is that form of state in which recognition is given to the principle of the subordination of the minority to the majority.[1] There are three main types of democracy: ancient or slave-owning democracy, bourgeois democracy, and socialist democracy. Ancient democracy is the dictatorship of the slave-owners; bourgeois democracy is the dictatorship of the bourgeoisie; socialist democracy is the dictatorship of the proletariat. The third differs qualitatively from the other two in that it is a dictatorship of the majority over the minority and leads directly to communism in which the state itself will disappear. The first two types differ from one another in that they rest on slave labour and wage labour respectively. The slaves of ancient society were themselves commodities, entirely devoid of freedom, nominal or real. The wage-labourers of bourgeois society are nominally free, but, since their labour power is a commodity, which they are forced to sell in order to live, they are actually unfree. Despite this fundamental difference, these two types of democracy have certain features in common, which, though superficial, are not for that reason to be dismissed as insignificant. Both are dictatorships of a minority; both were established under the leadership of a new class, whose wealth was derived from industry and trade, supported by the peasantry and opposed by a hereditary landowning oligarchy; and both were established in a period marked by the rapid growth of commodity production.

By the democratic revolution of ancient Greece (it took place nowhere else in the ancient world) we mean the transfer of state power from the landed aristocracy to the new merchant class. It has been objected that the term is too vague, since it might equally well be applied to the bourgeois revolution or the

[1] Lenin SR 80–2.

socialist revolution.[2] This is true, but not very important. The want of a more precise term arises from the lack of a distinctive name for what, in his account of ancient Greece, Engels called 'the new class of rich industrialists and merchants'. Accordingly, when we speak of the democratic revolution, it must be understood that we are referring to the ancient Greeks, who, after all, have some claim to priority, seeing that democracy is still called by their name for it.

The revolution was generally preceded by a transitional phase, known as the tyranny. Thus we may distinguish three stages: oligarchy, or the rule of the landed aristocracy, tyranny, and democracy. This sequence is typical, but of course it did not develop everywhere at the same rate or with the same regularity. In some of the most backward states it was never completed; in some of the most advanced it was arrested or reversed; in the latter years of the fifth century B.C. the struggle between democrats and oligarchs assumed the form of a pan-hellenic war between Athens and Sparta. The earliest tyrants belong to the second half of the seventh century: Kypselos and Periandros at Corinth, Theagenes at Megara, Orthagoras at Sikyon, Thrasyboulos at Miletos, Pythagoras (not the philosopher) at Ephesos. In some cities the tyranny was averted or anticipated by an *aisymnétes* or 'arbitrator' appointed by agreement between the rival factions to exercise dictatorial powers for a limited period. Such were Pittakos of Mytilene and his contemporary Solon of Athens (594 B.C.). In 545 B.C. Polykrates became tyrant of Samos, and five years later, with the assistance of another tyrant, Lygdamis of Naxos, Peisistratos succeeded in consolidating the tyranny at Athens. The earliest democracies known to us were at Chios (600 B.C.) and Megara (590 B.C.). At Megara, a few years later, the oligarchs staged a successful counter-revolution, perhaps with the support of the Bakchidai, who shortly after the death of Periandros had regained power at Corinth. At Miletos the death of Thrasyboulos was followed by two generations of civil war, after which the city recovered her former prosperity under the tyrant Histiaios. In the meantime the tyranny of Lygdamis at Naxos had given place to a democracy; and at Samos, too, after the death of Polykrates (523 B.C.), there was a democratic revolution, but this was defeated by Persian intervention. Everywhere, after their conquest of Ionia (545 B.C.), the Persians had installed tyrants friendly to themselves; and hence, when the Ionians revolted (499 B.C.) and again when the Persians were routed at the Battle of Mykale (479 B.C.), the democracy was generally restored.

In Italy and Sicily the movement began later and had a different outcome. The non-Greek peoples of southern Italy and Sicily were culturally at a much lower level than the Lydians and Carians and hence more open to exploitation. In Syracuse and probably other cities as well the Greeks of the lower classes made common cause with the natives against the landed aristocracy. The struggle was already acute by the middle of the sixth century, but in several cities the tyranny appears, not as a transition to democracy, but rather as an instrument for the forcible unification of neighbouring cities. We hear of Empedokles the philosopher at the head of the democratic party at Akragas about 470 B.C.,[3] and another philosopher, Archytas the Pythagorean, was the elected leader of the democracy at Taras about 400 B.C.[4]

Only at Athens is the course of events recorded with sufficient fullness to form a continuous narrative, and therefore we are obliged to treat the history of this city as being in the main typical of the rest. Having traced the growth of the democratic movement at Athens, we shall examine its reflection in Athenian thought, and, having thus reconstructed in outline the ideology of democracy, we shall apply the results to the work of the first philosophers.

2. Oligarchy

When the Dorians occupied the Peloponnese, their tribal organisation was still largely intact. The Dorian settlement of Sparta derived its distinctive character from the fact that the tribal system, confined to the conquerors, was converted by the act of conquest into a rigidly exclusive ruling caste. Being so few, the Spartans were only able to hold down the serfs by maintaining their military organisation, which was tribal, in a state of constant readiness. That is why, so far from withering

[3] D.L. 8. 66.   [4] Str. 280.

away, as it did elsewhere in Greece, the kingship persisted; and for the same reason, seeking to forestall the disruptive effects of commodity production, they did everything possible to uphold within their own ranks the tribal system of common ownership.

The land was divided into inalienable family estates, cultivated by the serfs, who paid over fifty per cent of the produce and so provided each Spartan with his contribution to the common meals; for, even after marriage, the men continued to live together. They issued no coinage and refused to publish a code of laws, without which organised commerce was impossible. Nevertheless, inequalities did develop. The law against alienation was evaded, and there arose a class of landless Spartans. This problem was solved by a policy of cautious expansion. It had to be cautious, because a military defeat would have presented the serfs with the opportunity for which they were always waiting; and for the same reason Spartan foreign policy was guided by the determination to maintain so far as possible the supremacy of the landowning class in other states.

In Attica the first steps in the formation of the state were traditionally associated with the reign of Theseus (Vol. I, pp. 362–5), and the process was continued without interruption during and after the Dorian invasion of the Peloponnese. It was in this period that the clan chiefs of Attica consolidated themselves as a hereditary oligarchy, the Eupatridai, drawing more and more of the cultivable land into their own hands (Vol. I, pp. 357–8). By loans of seed and stock after a bad season the big landowner became a creditor of the small, increasing his pressure until the latter could only redeem the debt by surrendering his personal liberty. This, too, was the period in which the tribal customs relating to homicide were modified in the interests of the new ruling class. In tribal society the manslayer had been forced to flee and seek protection with a stranger, who received him as a suppliant and adopted him (Vol. I, p. 133); but now the Eupatridai, who had converted the old clan cults into hereditary priesthoods, introduced the practice of purification, which was a modified form of adoption, both being derived from primitive initiation (Vol. I, p. 48). In this way, by arranging that the manslayer should appeal to them, they reserved to themselves full discretion in the treatment of an offence to which the incentives grew with the growth of private property.

SOUTHERN GREECE   MAP VIII

There is evidence that in the period immediately following the Dorian invasions Attica played an active part in the revival of maritime trade;[5] but in the seventh century this movement was checked by competition from Aigina, to the south, and Euboia, to the north, which were better placed on the trans-Ægean trade route. Aigina, in particular, was the first city on the Greek mainland to strike its own coinage, but Chalkis and Eretria, the leading cities of Euboia, were not long in following. The circulation of money exposed the Attic peasantry to further exploitation from merchants and money-lenders, whose rates of

[5] Ure OT 321–31.

interest ranged as high as fifty per cent. At the same time it weakened the ruling class, whose power was based on wealth in land. About 632 B.C. a nobleman named Kylon, who had married a daughter of Theagenes, tyrant of Megara, attempted to seize power at Athens; and, since Theagenes appears to have been connected with the woollen trade, for which Megara was famous, it may be that Kylon too had commercial interests. If so, the Athenian merchants were not yet strong enough to challenge the landowners successfully; for Kylon's attempt was abortive.[6] After taking sanctuary in the temple of Athena Polias, he was put to death at the instigation of Megakles, leader of the Alkmeonidai. Kylon's family were sentenced to perpetual banishment, but his adherents secured the banishment of the Alkmeonidai as well for having violated the sanctuary. A few years later the Eupatridai published a code of laws, drawn up by Drakon; and it is probable that this too was a concession to the new merchant class.

Then, early in the sixth century, came the first crisis. The peasants were on the verge of insurrection, demanding a redivision of the land. The poorest of them were permitted to retain only one-sixth of their produce (Vol. I, pp. 591–2). Many had been forced to sell all, driven overseas as beggars or slaves, while others were homeless in fields once their own.[7] The Eupatridai perceived that, if they were to avert a peasant uprising, they must reach some compromise with the merchants, who were as alarmed as they were at the threat to private property. Accordingly, Solon, a member of the Kodridai who had been actively engaged in trade, was entrusted with dictatorial powers. If Solon had been a revolutionary, he would have made himself tyrant; but, of course, if that had been his intention, he would not have been appointed. The Eupatridai knew their man.

First, he relieved the economic pressure on the peasantry by cancelling outstanding debts and prohibiting enslavement for debt. In this way he evaded the demand for a redivision of the land. He did nothing to restrict current rates of interest. The smallholder was still in danger of being dispossessed by the money-lender. At the same time he took steps to encourage

[6] Hdt. 5. 71, Th. 1. 126.   [7] Sol. 24.

industry and trade. He introduced an official standard of weights and measures, and issued the first Attic currency. It may be inferred that the silver mines of Laurion were first worked at this time. These mines—the richest in Greece, except those of Siphnos, which became exhausted at the end of the century—were the material foundation of Athenian prosperity and power. Further, by prohibiting the export of corn, for which there was a steady demand in Megara and Aigina, he reduced the price of food. All these measures were of direct assistance to the merchants and artisans, and indirectly benefited the peasantry by creating employment for those who had been driven off the land. The size of the slave population at this time is unknown, but it cannot have been large. The only source of supply had been the impoverished peasants, and it is probable that most of these had been exported to Aigina and Megara. Solon himself claimed in later years to have brought home many Athenians who had been sold abroad;[8] and it seems clear that the opportunity arose when, acting on his instigation, the Athenians made war on the Megarians and wrested from them the island of Salamis and the port of Nisaia.[9] It is likely enough that the victors brought back enslaved Megarians as well as liberated Athenians; but, as this was the first war of its kind in Athenian history, the number of foreign captives employed in Attica at this period must have been small.

Secondly, Solon gave the lower classes a voice in the government by reviving the popular assembly. It was this body which elected, partly by vote and partly by lot, the chief officers of state, the *árchontes* (Vol. I, p. 364); and it also met as a court of justice to try cases other than homicide. On the other hand, by the side of the Assembly, Solon created a new body, the Council of Four Hundred, so called because it was composed of a hundred members elected, probably by lot, from each of the four tribes. Aristotle says that the four tribes corresponded to the four seasons (Vol. I, p. 105); and this may be interpreted to mean that their representatives on Solon's new council discharged certain functions by rotation in the course of the year. His motive in instituting this body was to put a check both on the Assembly and on the Council of the Areopagus,

[8] Sol. 24. 8–12.   [9] *Ib.* 2.

which was the name now borne by the old Council of the Eupatridai. The effect, therefore, was to strengthen the new middle class.

Thirdly, Solon abolished the aristocratic claim to serve as *árchontes* by right of birth, and made membership of his new Council, together with the public offices elected from it, open to all citizens who possessed corn, oil, or wine to the value of not less than 200 *médimnoi* of corn. This property qualification excluded the poor peasants and artisans, but not the rich merchants, who were able to acquire land either by purchase or by intermarriage with the nobility. At the same time he introduced three further measures to check the power of the clans. He placed statutory limitations on the amount which might be paid out of public funds for the entertainment of victors at the Olympic Games and also on the scale and cost of private funerals (Vol. I, pp. 480–1); and he made it legal for a man who died without issue to exercise the right of free testamentary disposition instead of leaving his estate to his fellow clansmen, as hitherto he had been obliged to do.

The general effect of Solon's reforms and the intention behind them emerge very clearly from Adcock's remarks on the subject:

> The effect of his limitations on the Assembly was to keep administration and the initiative in policy in the hands of the well-to-do or middle classes. It was true that years of aristocratic government had left the commons politically uneducated, the easy dupes of ambitious leaders, and Solon's poems show him well aware of the dangers of their uninstructed hopes. But the alternative, to deny to the commons all political power, was a greater evil and a greater danger, and Solon might hope that the new economic order would keep the poorer Athenians too busy or too contented to lend themselves to faction. Given that little power which was enough, the people might not be misled into grasping at more. And both policy and justice demanded that, if they did not really govern, they should be protected from misgovernment and injustice.[10]

Solon's hopes were disappointed. In the years that followed, the poorer Athenians rapidly gained sufficient education in political affairs to realise that the only way in which they could obtain protection from misgovernment and injustice was to govern themselves.

[10] F. E. Adcock in CAH 4. 55.

3. Tyranny

During the next thirty years, as money continued to dissolve the old conditions, the landowning nobility began to disintegrate. Solon himself had been an aristocrat who turned to trade, and now other noble families followed suit, notably Megakles of the Alkmeonidai, whose father had established commercial connections with Sardeis,[11] and Peisistratos. They were opposed by Lykourgos of the Boutadai, and at the same time were in competition with one another. The three factions are thus described by Aristotle:

> There were three factions. One was the Coast Party (*parálioi*) under Megakles son of Alkmeon, who seemed to be aiming at a middle-class republic. Another was the Plains Party (*pediakoí*), led by Lykourgos, who wanted an oligarchy; and the third was the Hill Party (*diákrioi*), led by Peisistratos, who seemed the most democratic. Along with the last-mentioned were ranged men who had been impoverished by the loss of debts owed to them and others who were afraid because they were of impure birth. This is shown by the fact that after the overthrow of the tyranny a decree was passed for registering the population on the ground that many possessed the franchise who were not entitled to it. Each party was named after the districts in which its members tilled the soil.[12]

In my *Æschylus and Athens* I adopted the interpretation of this passage which was put forward by P. N. Ure in his *Origin of Tyranny* (1922). Since, however, his views are ignored in the *Cambridge Ancient History* and are not now easily accessible, it is necessary to restate them here.

The Plains Party was based on the big landed estates of the best farming districts, especially the valley north of Athens and the Thriasian Plain north-east of Eleusis. On this there is no disagreement. The Coast Party was based on the *paralía*, which denoted the whole of the Attic seaboard, not merely the south coast.[13] This was the party of the merchants, large and small. Some of them, we may suppose, had bought up farms near the sea in order to produce wine and oil for export; others were

[11] Hdt. 6. 125.

[12] Arist. *AR.* 13. 4. Ure's view has recently been re-examined in a new study of the subject by Oliva (RRT).

[13] Th. 2. 55, Hdt. 5. 81, Str. 395, 400, *CIA.* 2. 1059 (cf. Str. 398), 1194–5, 1206b; Ure OT 313.

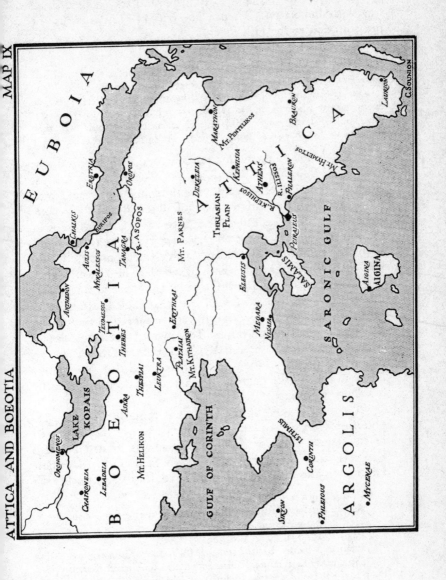

MAP IX

ATTICA AND BOEOTIA

EUBOIA

ATTICA

BOEOTIA

ARGOLIS

SARONIC GULF

GULF OF CORINTH

LAKE KOPAIS

Mt. HELIKON

Mt. KITHAIRON

Mt. PARNES

Mt. PENTELIKOS

Mt. HYMETTOS

Thriasian Plain

SALAMIS

AIGINA

R. ASOPOS

R. KEPHISOS

R. ILISSOS

R. KEPHISOS

EURIPOS

OROPOS

CHALKIS
ERETRIA
AULIS
MYKALESSOS
ANTHEDON
TANAGRA
TEUMESSOS
THEBES
THESPIAI
LEUKTRA
ASKRA
LEBADEIA
CHAIRONEIA
ORCHOMENOS
PLATAIAI
EROTHRAI
MEGARA
NISAIA
ELEUSIS
DEKELEIA
MARATHON
BRAURON
ATHENS
KEPHISIA
PHALERON
PEIRAIEUS
ISTHMIA
CORINTH
SIKYON
PHLEIOUS
MYCENAE
LAUREION
C. SOUNION

smallholders with boats of their own who traded in a small
way with Euboia and Aigina. The crux of the matter is the
identification of the Hill Party.

Adcock has identified it as follows:

> The Hill Country (the Diakria) could share neither in the agricultural
> prosperity of the Plain nor in the commercial progress of the Coast. Here,
> in a tangle of glens, lived shepherds and herdsmen and crofters, many, no
> doubt, men to whom Solon had given freedom but not land. In Peisistratos
> they found a leader who would urge their claims and could win their
> affection so that they stood firmly by him even in failure and exile.[14]

With such a following, no matter how loyal, Peisistratos might
have made himself a Rob Roy, but not ruler of Athens.
Aristotle, it will be observed, says nothing in the passage quoted
about herdsmen and crofters, who, of all sections of the people,
would have had the strongest claim to be regarded as 'sons of
the soil' (Vol. I, p. 266); on the contrary, he refers to semi-
aliens and ruined money-lenders. Such elements as these would
scarcely have congregated in the tangled glens of Attica.[15] They
would have been found where there was a demand for labour.
Accordingly, we conclude, with Ure, that these 'hillmen' who
gave their support to Peisistratos were employed in the *métalla*,
that is, the quarries and mines. There were marble quarries on
Mount Pentelikos, between Kephisia and Marathon, and on
Mount Hymettos, to the east of Athens; and there were silver
mines in the hills of Laurion which reach the sea in the rocky
headland of Sounion.[16]

Ure's identification of the Diakria is confirmed by topogra-
phical evidence. Two villages are known to have been situated
in this region. One of them, Plotheia, was located between
Kephisia and Marathon; the other, Semachidai, lay near
Laurion in the heart of the mining country.[17] Aristotle tells

[14] F. E. Adcock in CAH 4. 62.
[15] As Ure observes, Aristotle insists that of all people farmers and herdsmen are the least revolutionary: Arist. *Pol.* 1318b, 1319a.
[16] Paus. 1. 19. 6, 1. 32. 1, Str. 399.
[17] Plotheia is located by tombstones (AJA 3. 426). An inscription (MDA
35. 286) mentions a mining concession near Laurion and describes it as
lying to the north of the road leading past Rhagon to the Semacheion. The
Semacheion was the shrine of Semachos, eponym of the Semachidai
(Philoch. 78).

how, after he had become tyrant, Peisistratos granted exemption from taxes to a man he met tilling the rocky slopes of Hymettos.[18] He does not say that this crofter also worked in the quarries there, but it is probable that he did. At this period the quarries and mines were worked by dispossessed peasants and immigrant aliens, who had settled as squatters on the adjoining waste lands; and by championing the interests of these *Bergmänner* Peisistratos won the support of the only large concentrations of labour in the country.

These considerations would carry weight, even if Peisistratos were not known to have been interested in the mining industry. On this aspect of the matter we have some direct information.

Peisistratos belonged to one of several Attic clans descended from the Neleidai of Pylos, who fled to Athens after the Dorian invasion (Vol. I, p. 192). His family seat was at Philaidai near Brauron, and therefore he must have had ancestral ties with the clan of that name, whose chief in his time, Miltiades, was one of the most influential noblemen in the country, having won the chariot race at Olympia.[19] He seized power for the first time in 561–560 B.C., supported no doubt by Miltiades. Five years later he was forced to flee the country, Megakles and Lykourgos having combined against him. Where he spent this first exile we are not told, but in 550–549 B.C., having come to terms with Megakles, he returned to Athens, and, according to the story, re-entered the city with a Thracian flower-girl dressed up as Athena beside him in his chariot.[20] Then he quarrelled with Megakles and was driven out again. This time he went to Macedonia, where he founded an urban settlement at a place called Rhaikelos on the Gulf of Therma.[21] His purpose is not stated, but it can hardly be an accident that he had settled so close to the metalliferous hills of Mygdonia; and later he moved east of the river Strymon to the neighbourhood of Mount Pangaion, the richest mining region in Thrace. There he collected money and mercenaries, and, having made alliances

[18] Arist. *AR.* 16. 6. The story is that on the slopes of Hymettos the tyrant came across a man tilling a piece of rocky ground, and sent his slave to ask him how much he got out of it. 'Nothing but toil and trouble,' he replied, 'and of this toil and trouble I have to pay a tithe to Peisistratos.' Pleased with his reply, the tyrant exempted him from the tax.

[19] Hdt. 6. 35.   [20] Arist. *AR.* 14. 4.   [21] *Ib.* 15. 2.

with the Thessalian chiefs and with Lygdamis of Naxos, he returned to Euboia, and landed with his troops at Marathon. His supporters from town and country flocked there to join him, and in a few days, after defeating the oligarchs at Pallene, he was again master of Athens. Thus, in the words of Herodotus, 'he rooted the tyranny by means of his mercenaries and the revenues which he drew from the river Strymon and from Attica itself'.[22]

Not long after this Miltiades left Athens for the Thracian Chersonesos, where he made himself chief of the native tribes and married into the family of Oloros, king of Thrace.[23] There can be little doubt that this was a plan, worked out with Peisistratos, for extending Athenian influence along the whole coast of Thrace and securing control of the Hellespont (Vol. I, pp. 572-3). It is probable that corn was already being exported to Greece from the colonies of the Black Sea; for, when Xerxes reached the Hellespont at the head of his army in 481 B.C., he saw some Greek ships sailing through the straits and was told that they were carrying grain to Aigina.[24] At the same time, with his Thracian connections, he must have had some part in promoting those mining interests which were inherited in the following century by Thucydides (p. 205). Further, since he is known to have had relations with nomad tribes from Scythia, who at one time drove him out of the Chersonesos, it is likely that he was instrumental in conveying to Athens the first consignment of those Scythian slaves who from this time forward constituted the city police.[25] And, lastly, he may have sent miners as well as policemen. One of the mining villages near Laurion was Maroneia. A rich vein was struck here in the year 483 B.C.[26] There was a town of the same name on the Thracian coast, and this was an ancient settlement; for its founder, Maron, is mentioned in the *Odyssey*.[27] Its earliest coins date from the latter part of the sixth century, and their characteristic device is the forepart of a prancing horse,[28] which is found on Attic coins of the same period and has been identified as an

[22] Hdt. 1. 62-4. [23] *Ib.* 6. 36, Th. *Vit.* 1. [24] Hdt. 7. 147. 2.
[25] Scythian policemen first appear on Attic vases in the time of Peisistratos: CAH Plates 1. 282.
[26] Arist. *AR.* 22. 7. [27] Eph. 74, *Od.* 9. 197-8. [28] Head HN 215.

emblem of the Peisistratidai.[29] The Attic village may therefore have derived its name from Thracian miners settled there
under Peisistratos or his sons.

After the Persian War the Attic silver mines were under state
ownership and worked almost entirely by slave labour, the
slaves being privately owned. Thus, Nikias, son of Nikeratos,
hired 1000 slaves to a Thracian named Sosias for work in the
mines.[30] This Sosias was probably himself a slave employed by
the state as a contractor for public works (poletés). From the
evidence reviewed above we may conclude that the mines passed
into the hands of the state under the rule of Peisistratos
and that slave labour began to predominate in the same
period.

It is probable that Peisistratos used the opportunity afforded
by the flight of his oligarchical opponents to solve the agrarian
problem. The peasants were settled on the confiscated estates as
small proprietors.[31] At the same time he ensured the continued
support of the merchants and artisans by developing the coinage,
encouraging the export trade in oil, wine, and pottery, and
embarking on an ambitious programme of public works, including the demolition of the old city wall and the construction of
an aqueduct. He completed the temple of Athena Polias, for
which he imported marble from Paros, and began the great
temple of Zeus Polieus, which he planned on a scale so
ambitious that it was only completed more than six hundred
years afterwards by the Roman emperor, Hadrian. In order to
combat the religious influence of the aristocratic clans he gave
official recognition to the popular cults of Dionysus, and his
sons built a new hall of initiation for the Mysteries at Eleusis,
which were now brought under state control.[32] He reorganised
the City Dionysia as a dramatic festival and instituted public
recitals of the Homeric poems (Vol. I, pp. 571–5).

---

[29] Seltman AHC 30.   [30] X. Vect. 4. 14–5.

[31] It is not stated in our sources that Peisistratos did this, but we know
that the tyrant Kypselos expropriated the Bakchidai (Nic. Dam. 58), and the
redivision of the land was one of the measures traditionally associated with
the tyranny (Pl. Rp. 565–6). It is possible that Peisistratos gave land to his
followers, the Diakrioi, at a time when they were being ousted from the
mines by slave labour.

[32] Robertson 169.

Peisistratos died in 528–527 B.C. and was succeeded by his sons, Hipparchos and Hippias. Hipparchos was assassinated nine years later by Harmodios and Aristogeiton of the Gephyraioi (Vol. I, p. 123). Athenian aristocrats of the next century gave currency to the story that the assassins were responsible for overthrowing the tyranny and so for establishing the democracy; but in point of fact Hippias remained in power for another eight years. His growing unpopularity during the latter part of his reign was due primarily to the changes which had taken place in the balance of political forces. In strengthening 'the new class of rich industrialists and merchants', Peisistratos had done his work so well that they now felt strong enough to dispense with a protective dictatorship. Consequently, they grew increasingly impatient of the expenses which it entailed, while Hippias became involved in financial difficulties, which he could only meet by further exactions. Thus, having begun as a progressive force, the tyranny ended by becoming an obstacle to progress. The final blow came in 512–511 B.C., when the Persian conquest of Thrace deprived Hippias of his main source of revenue. He was expelled two years later.

The function of the tyranny was transitional. By forcing and holding a breach in the rule of the landed aristocracy, it enabled the middle class to consolidate its forces for the final stage in the democratic revolution, which involved the overthrow of the tyranny itself. That is why, in Greek tradition, it was almost unanimously condemned. It was denounced in advance by the oligarchs because it was progressive and in retrospect by the democrats because it had become reactionary. In the case of Peisistratos, however, there was a popular tradition, preserved by Aristotle, that his reign was a return to the age of Kronos.[33] This legend of the golden age of Kronos, when all men had lived contentedly without having to win their bread in the sweat of their brows, was a folk memory of primitive communism;[34] and its association with the rule of Peisistratos is a striking testimony to the strength and breadth of his popular support.

The violent resistance which the democratic movement had

[33] Arist. AR. 16. 7.   [34] Roscher s.v. Kronos.

to overcome is mirrored in the poetry of Theognis of Megara, an aristocratic *bon vivant*, who, true to type, identified civilisation with the privileges of his class:

Shame has perished; pride and insolence have conquered justice and possess the earth . . .

The city is still a city, but the populace has changed; once they knew nothing of laws, wrapped their flanks in goatskins, and dwelt like deer outside the walls; but now they are the nobles and the one-time nobles base—O who can bear the sight? . . .

Grind them hard and let their yoke be heavy: that is the way to make them love their masters . . .

The mass of the people knows one virtue, wealth; nothing else avails . . .

Not to be born is best nor look upon the sunshine; or once born to pass as soon as maybe through the gates of death and lie beneath a heap of earth.[35]

Because the old caste system dating from the Bronze Age had broken down; because the serfs were no longer content to be burdened like asses; because, too, the old unwritten code of personal allegiance and patriarchal liberality had been translated into cash—therefore, civilisation had perished. But civilisation did not wait for Theognis. The old culture was breaking up, but new aspirations, new values, new ideas were bursting into life.

4. *The Revolution of Kleisthenes*

The overthrow of Hippias was effected by the combined opposition of Kleisthenes, the son of his father's enemy, Megakles, who was playing his own hand, and the other exiled oligarchs, who saw in the weakening of the tyranny an opportunity for a counter-revolution. During their exile the Alkmeonidai had been repairing their fortunes. It was in these years that they rebuilt the temple at Delphi (p. 193), and they used their influence there to break the friendly relations which Peisistratos had cultivated with Sparta. In 510–509 B.C. Kleisthenes entered Attica with the Spartan king at the head of a Spartan army. It was evidently the intention of the Spartans that the fall of Hippias should be followed by a restoration of the oligarchy; but Kleisthenes aimed at taking his place, and, when this became apparent, the oligarchical leader Isagoras appealed to Sparta to intervene a second time.

[35] Theog. 291., 53, 847, 699, 425.

Kleisthenes replied by appealing to the people. Learning a lesson from Peisistratos, he put through in the teeth of the oligarchs a number of democratic reforms and enfranchised hundreds of resident aliens and slaves. The result was that, when the Spartan king reappeared in Attica to restore the *ancien régime*, with Isagoras acting for him as informer, he was shut up together with his troops in the Akropolis and only released after undertaking to desist from further intervention. It was a great victory for the people.

The constitutional struggle had centred in the franchise. The qualification for citizenship was membership of a phratry; and, since the phratries were groups of clans, this meant that the citizen body was still nominally a tribal community, composed of the old Attic clans. It is probable that a large part of the peasantry had never been included in these clans (Vol. I, p. 113); but, so long as they had only peasants to deal with, the nobles were able to hold their own. Now, however, thanks to the policy of commercial expansion pursued by Solon and Peisistratos, a considerable number of artisans had settled in Attica; and a law had been passed stipulating that membership of the phratries should be open to non-clansmen (Vol. I, p. 107). It is clear, however, that the oligarchs had succeeded to a large extent in defeating the purpose of this measure, because, as we have seen, the supporters of Peisistratos included many immigrants, who had either been excluded from the phratries or else were afraid of being expelled from them. How much this class owed to the tyranny is shown by the fact that, when it fell, one of the first acts of Isagoras was to disfranchise a large number of citizens who were unable to prove pure Athenian descent; and shortly afterwards, when the Spartans invaded Attica, no less than seven hundred families were expelled. It is clear therefore that oligarchical influence in the phratries was still strong; and hence, in the new constitution of Kleisthenes, the political functions of the phratries were abolished once and for all.

The way in which this was done was characteristic. Tribal reorganisation was nothing new. It had been carried out in other Greek states (Vol. I, p. 319) and in Attica itself after the Dorian invasion of the Peloponnese (Vol. I, p. 392). Yet the imprint on men's minds of the social structure under which their ancestors had lived since human society had first taken shape was so deep that it was still accepted without question as the natural and necessary foundation of any social order. Accordingly, in Attica, as elsewhere in Greece, when the primitive tribal system was superseded, the external features of the old order were faithfully reproduced in the new; and when a modern historian remarks that 'a system more artificial than the tribes and *trittýes* of Kleisthenes it might well pass the wit of man to devise',[36] it may be replied that, whatever we may think about it, to the Greeks of this period it was the most natural thing in the world.

The organic unit of the new system was the *dêmos*, which had originated as a clan settlement (Vol. I, pp. 326–7). It had therefore a traditional association with the clan, although, owing to the dissolution of the clan system of land tenure, this connection had been to a large extent effaced. What Kleisthenes did was to organise the men resident in each deme as a corporate body with an elective chief (*démarchos*) and several corporate functions, including the maintenance of a register in which was entered the name of every male as he came of age. Enrolment on this register carried with it the rights of citizenship. The original members of the deme were the adult males resident within it at the time when the new constitution was adopted; but in subsequent generations membership was determined by descent. No matter where he might reside, the son belonged to the same deme as his father. And so in time this unit grew into a body of genuine kinsmen, with its own chief, its own corporate life, and its own traditional attachments. Kleisthenes could not have devised a better way of filling the void left in the minds of the people by the dissolution of the clan.

The demes, which numbered altogether about two hundred, were divided into thirty groups, called *trittýes*, or ridings. As a group of demes, the riding bore the same relation to the phratry as the deme bore to the clan. It had no corporate existence at all—it was a purely geographical unit; but it provided the reformers with a cover under which they were

[36] E. M. Walker in CAH 4. 143.

able to introduce unobtrusively the really revolutionary feature of the new system. Of these thirty ridings, ten were composed of demes in or near the city, ten of demes situated in the maritime districts, ten of demes situated in the interior. The purpose of this arrangement will become clear when we see how the ridings were grouped in tribes.

Hitherto there had been four tribes. Their number was now raised to ten; and each of these ten tribes contained three ridings, one from the urban area, one from the maritime districts, and one from the interior. This meant that the urban population was entrenched in each tribe, and, since all meetings of the Assembly took place in the city, it was in a position to muster a voting power out of proportion to its numbers. Thus, the middle class of merchants and artisans secured a permanent advantage over the farmers, and the interests of the countryside were subordinated to those of the town.

The increase in the number of tribes was connected with a reform of the calendar. The old lunisolar calendar was retained in the religious life of the community, but for the purposes of state administration the year was divided into ten periods of thirty-six or thirty-seven days. At the same time the Council of Four Hundred was raised to five hundred—fifty from each of the ten tribes; and these ten tribal groups of fifty citizens acted in rotation through the year as a standing committee of the Council.

The members of the new Council were elected by lot, and the same method of election was extended a few years later to the highest officers of state, the *árchontes*. For some time, however, admission to the archonship was subject to a property qualification, which excluded the lower classes. This restriction, which reveals the middle-class character of the revolution, was only removed after a bitter struggle in 456 B.C. In this way there was created, for the first time in history, a constitution in which every citizen might share in the running of the state; and, modelled as it was on the old tribal forms, it was acclaimed by the people as a reassertion of their ancient rights, in which the conflicting forces of the preceding epoch had been reconciled.

Such was the *form* of the democratic revolution, the aspect in which it presented itself to the consciousness of those who fought for it and were inspired by it; but in *content* it was the reverse of what it appeared to be. The democrats had triumphed; their hopes had been fulfilled; yet the result was the opposite of what they had intended. By following so closely the tribal model the new constitution concealed all the more effectively the fact that the main obstacles to the growth of commodity production, and with them the last remnants of primitive social relations, had been swept away. The owners of commodities now confronted one another as equals in the 'freedom' of the open market. The watchword of democracy, *isonomia*, 'equality of civic rights', acclaimed by its supporters as 'the fairest name of all',[37] proved in the sequel to be a name and nothing more; for, as a later Greek historian remarked, 'equality before the law is futile without equality of property',[38] and there could be no equality in the private ownership of commodities. The result was that, far from being resolved, the class struggle was intensified. In place of the old conflict between noblemen and commoners, all members of the one human community, there arose a conflict between the slave-owners and the slaves, the latter being at once outcasts from society and the producers of its wealth; and this contradiction, while opening up new worlds of knowledge, destroyed democracy and created both in society and in the individual a fundamental cleavage between consumption and production, between thought and action:

> To the stage of civilisation belongs all the grandeur and beauty hitherto known by man, but also the breach at the heart of human society.[39]

[37] Hdt. 3. 80. 6.   [38] D.S. 2. 39.   [39] Torr 16.

DEMOCRATIC IDEOLOGY

1. *Social Justice*

SOLON died in 560–559 B.C., Anaximander not long after the fall of Sardeis (546 B.C.); so they were nearly contemporary. After laying down his office, Solon went abroad and travelled in many countries, including Ionia and Lydia, where he may well have met Anaximander or his master, Thales. There is, however, no direct connection between his work and theirs. The features common to both spring, as we shall see, from their common class outlook. All three belonged to old aristocratic families, with traditions inherited from the Bronze Age, which had been drawn into commercial activity and hence developed into what may be called a mercantile aristocracy, occupying an intermediate position between the ruling oligarchy of land-owners, on the one hand, and the masses of the people on the other.

In primitive thought, society and nature had been one. Thales and Anaximander succeeded in separating nature from society and presenting it as an external reality existing independently of man. Similarly, Solon succeeded in separating society from nature and presenting it as a moral order based on obligations peculiar to man. In other words, just as Anaximander objectified nature, so Solon objectified society. How this was done can best be seen by considering the development of the law of homicide.

In primitive society no distinction was drawn between intentional and unintentional homicide: that is to say, the offence was believed to inhere objectively in the nature of the act and not in the subjective attitude of the offender. At the same time a sharp distinction was drawn between the murder of a fellow clansman and the murder of one belonging to another clan. The procedure followed in each case (Vol. I, pp. 89–90, 135–7) reflects the internal solidarity of the clan and the primeval antagonism between clans. In the latter case the offence was measured objectively as a loss of man-power to be made good by compensation or retribution; in the former, the offender was treated exactly as though he had contracted a contagious disease, that is, he became an outcast (Vol. I, p. 226). He was liable to infect all who came in contact with him and to disturb the functioning of the natural order. The whole of Greece, it was said, had been afflicted with drought owing to a murder committed by Pelops;[1] Œdipus's murder of his father was followed by a plague and Alkmaion's murder of his mother by a failure of the crops.[2] In the *Oresteia* of Æschylus, the Erinyes, the mythical embodiments of the clan curse, threaten those who have given asylum to their victim with a blight on the crops and barrenness in women.[3]

With the transition from tribe to state, these practices and beliefs were adapted so as to bring the treatment of homicide under the control of the aristocratic priesthood. The idea of pollution was extended beyond the clan to cover the whole community, but at the same time its application was restricted by the new practice of purification, which was used to absolve the culprit at the discretion of the priesthood. It was as if the ruling class said to the people, We are all one kin, all children of the one fatherland, and therefore homicide is a crime against the whole community to be dealt with by the accredited authorities.

That is how matters stood when Solon was called on to reform the constitution. Under his legislation every citizen was empowered to take proceedings for offences committed against his fellow citizens, even though he was not himself an injured party, and every citizen had the right of appeal from the magistrates to the Assembly. His motive was to ensure that 'the uninjured no less than the injured should come forward and punish wrongdoers'[4] and so to create a community 'unanimous in love and hate'.[5] These enactments, and the spirit behind them, were regarded in later times as cardinal features

[1] Apld. 2. 12. 6.
[2] *Ib.* 3. 7. 5. At one time infant mortality was endemic in the Spartan Aigeidai, descended from the Kadmeioi, and it was cured after they had built a shrine to Œdipus and the Erinyes of Laios: Hdt. 4. 149.
[3] A. *Eu.* 781–96=778–92.   [4] Plu. *Sol.* 18.
[5] A. *Eu.* 985–7.

of democracy. Hence the cause of good and bad fortune is not natural or supernatural but social:

> Lawlessness brings the city most troubles, while lawfulness makes all neat and tidy and constantly shackles evildoers, smooths the rough, checks excess, humbles pride, and makes the flowers of ruin fade.[6]

'The flowers of ruin' are the harvest that is reaped when the crop has been blasted by the Erinyes. That was the old conception. What Solon is saying here is that, given the active co-operation of all its members, the community can maintain itself in a state of well-being by a system of internal control. In saying this he does not of course exclude the gods, but he means that this is the will of the gods, and that, if the city falls on evil days, the fault lies with the citizens themselves:

> Our city will never perish by the dispensation of Zeus or the intention of the blessed immortals, such a great protectress have we in Athena, who looks down on us and stretches her hands over us; but the citizens themselves choose to destroy it by their own folly and the lure of money, and the unjust purpose of the people's leaders, who yield so readily to the pride that ends in calamity.[7]

Why, then, were the citizens so perverse as to act against their own interests? In facing this question, which was forced on him by the failure of his reforms to put an end to civil strife, Solon reveals the basic contradiction of ancient democracy as seen from the standpoint of his class. He has set a limit to lawlessness, but is compelled to admit that riches 'have no limit'. He has established equality before the law (isonomía), but not equality of property (isomoiría); on the contrary, he has strenuously resisted the peasants' demand for a redivision of the land. Moreover, by making admission to public offices subject to a graduated series of property qualifications he has ensured for the rich a degree of political power proportionate to that very factor which he admits to be beyond control:

> Many bad men are rich and many good men poor; yet we will not exchange righteousness for riches, because righteousness is always secure, whereas money is constantly passing from one man to another.[8]

Consequently, while the tribal vendetta and the hereditary curse, with their train of natural calamities, have been brought

[6] Sol. 3.32–5.   [7] Ib. 3. 1–8.   [8] Ib. 4. 9–12.

to rest, the community is now agitated by a new force, the circulation of money, which releases a new conflict of opposites, the conflict between rich and poor. The rich encroach upon the poor until they impoverish themselves by ever reaching after more; the poor revolt and rob the rich, only to suffer the same fate in their turn; and so, exactly as in Anaximander's universe, they 'render satisfaction to one another for their wrongdoing according to the order of time' (p. 160).

As leader of the new middle class, Solon took his stand midway between the peasants and the landlords, granting to the former just so much power as he deemed sufficient for them and warning the latter to exercise moderation, conceding to neither side an unjust supremacy. As it became clear that his mediation had failed, he fell back on the plea that true riches are not material and objective but spiritual and sub-jective:

The man who has mules and horses, spacious lands under wheat, and plenty of silver and gold, is equal in riches to him who has no more than a feeling of comfort in belly and sides and feet.[9]

This paradox, uttered by the pioneer of Athenian democracy, foreshadows its ultimate collapse. If this be true, it might be argued, man is no better off than the animals; rather, he is worse off, because they are free from the torment of unsatisfied ambitions; this is the conclusion that was drawn in so many words by an Athenian poet some three centuries later, when the struggle between rich and poor had become more acute than ever:

Thrice blest and happy are the beasts, which have
No reason in these things, no questionings,
Nor other harmful superfluities—
Their law is their own nature; but the life
Of man is more than he can bear—he is
The slave of fancies, he has invented laws.[10]

2. Moira and Metron

In the first volume of these studies the idea of moira was traced back to primitive communism, in which each member

[9] Ib. 14.   [10] Philemo 93.

of the community received his fair share of the product of its collective labour. As mythical figures, the Moirai represented the ancestresses of the matriarchal clan, who were believed to stand for maintenance of these equal rights; and similarly the Erinyes were in origin nothing more than these same ancestresses in their negative aspect, their function being to punish those who transgressed the ancestral dispensations embodied in the Moirai. It was also shown that, in the period of transition from tribal society to the state, these figures became related and subordinated to Zeus, representing the kingship, and later to Dike (Vol. I, pp. 345–6). We are now in a position to understand more clearly the significance of Dike.

The formal evolution of the word has already been discussed: (1) 'path', (2) 'custom', (3) 'vengeance' or 'punishment', (4) 'judgment', (5) the goddess of justice, (6) the abstract idea of justice (Vol. I, pp. 134–5). The last two senses make their first appearance in the poetry of Hesiod and Solon. The significance of Dike as a substitute for Erinys can best be seen from the following lines of Solon:

> Men are tempted to enrich themselves by unjust acts; they snatch and steal from one another without sparing sacred or public property and without safeguarding themselves against the dread foundations of Justice, who takes silent note of what is happening and what was before, and comes in time to exact vengeance without fail. Then at last the whole city is visited with an incurable sickness and soon falls into servitude, which awakes war and internecine strife, so that many perish in the flower of youth.[11]

Thus, Dike intervenes in human affairs to punish wrong-doers, and her intervention affects the whole community and results in loss of life. In all this she does the same as Erinys, but with one difference. The sickness she inflicts is not physical but social: it is not pestilence or famine but oppression and civil war.

We may say, therefore, that Dike stands guard over the new order as Erinys stood guard over the old. Just as Erinys punished the violation of Moira, so Dike punishes the violation of Metron. What is Metron?

Under the landed aristocracy the tillers of the soil were bound to pay over so much of their produce to the chief. In the

[11] Sol. 3. 11–20.

Homeric poems the word *métron* is used only in the concrete senses of a measuring rod or a measured quantity of corn or oil or wine; but in Hesiod it is used also to denote a moral abstraction—'due measure' or 'moderation'.[12] The new relations of production were projected as a moral precept, which in turn invested them with an apparently external sanction. Thus, Metron is Moira in a new form, with a shift of emphasis to its negative aspect: 'nothing too much', as the proverb said. The words 'Know thyself', inscribed over the temple at Delphi, had the same meaning: man must recognise his limitations and not invite retribution by seeking to become a god. It is inherent in this outlook that all great hopes and lofty ambitions are reprehensible. Thus, while Moira had denoted the equal 'share' which constituted each man's birthright, Metron signifies that he is entitled to a limited 'measure', which he must not exceed. Such was the aristocratic conception.

Solon reinterpreted it so as to restore something of its positive aspect. In his reforms he claimed, as we have seen, to have given the people 'as much power as was sufficient' to prevent the landlords from driving them to extremes. In general, he believed that by application of this principle the conflict of opposites could be, not indeed eliminated, but kept under control. 'How hard it is,' he says in one of his fragments, 'to perceive the hidden measure of intelligence, which alone holds the limits of things!'[13] The context is lost, but his meaning is clear. It is a rationalistic approach to the class struggle. If only the contending classes can be brought to understand that unrestrained conflict must result in their common ruin, then in their own interests they will set a limit to it. This was an illusion. He had set a limit to political oppression, but none to economic exploitation, and so the political oppression broke out anew. As he himself confessed, 'Riches have no limit'.[14] In this aphorism, for all his subjective concept of economic value, he expressed an objective economic truth:

The simple circulation of commodities (selling in order to buy) is a means for carrying out a process which lies outside the domain of circulation—a means for the appropriation of use-values, for the satisfaction of wants. The circulation of money as capital, on the other hand, is an end in itself, for the

[12] Hes. *Op.* 694.   [13] Sol. 16.   [14] *Ib.* 1. 71.

expansion of value can only occur within this perpetually renewed movement. Consequently, the circulation of capital has no limits.[15]

Before pursuing the further development of these ideas we must consider how in this same period the tribal conception of Moira was being reinterpreted by the masses of the people. The Attic peasants sold into slavery had no Amos, but, together with the artisans, they played an active part in the democratic revolution, and hence made a distinctive contribution to the ideology of democracy.

3. Orphism

'The ideas of the ruling class are in every epoch the ruling ideas.'[16] The ideas of the subject class are always suppressed and distorted by the ruling class, except in revolutionary periods, when they are in process of becoming the ruling ideas. Further, since class society is based on the division between mental and manual labour, the ideas of the subject class, which is manually active but mentally passive, tend to be practical, concrete, and subjective rather than theoretical, abstract, and objective. As we have seen, the emergence of natural philosophy, in Greece and China alike, presupposed a certain intellectual development—in particular, the power of abstraction and objectification—such as could only be attained by a leisured class divorced from the labour of production; and, as we shall see later, this separation of theory from practice rapidly reached the point at which the theory itself tended to decay, being cut off from its roots in the productive process.

One characteristic of a revolutionary period, important from an ideological as well as a political point of view, is that a section of the ruling class, especially of that part of it which is concerned with the theoretical problems of its development, transfers its allegiance to the new, revolutionary class, and plays

[15] Marx C 1. 129. Cf. Arist. Pol. 1. 9. 13: 'Just as every art that is not a means to an end but an end in itself has no limit to its aims, because it is always seeking to approach more closely to that end, while those arts that pursue means to an end are not unlimited, having a limit imposed on them by their objective, so it is with money-making: there is no limit to its aim, which consists in wealth of this kind, in the possession of money.'

[16] Marx-Engels GI 39.

an active part in formulating the new ideology.[17] In this way the new ruling class takes over and develops all that is creative in the old ideas at the same time as it gives expression to its own ideas, hitherto distorted and suppressed. The new ideology is drawn from both these sources and forms a unity to the extent that the new class itself is united. In general, however, we find at such periods not one subject class but two, one which leads the revolution and another which is rallied in support of it. In these conditions it is the ideas of the leading revolutionary class that prevail—ideas which are closely akin to those of the class allied to it, being in fact derived from them, just as the leading class itself has emerged out of the other in the course of the development of the mode of production.

Applying these considerations to the period under review, we may distinguish three main trends in democratic thought. The first, represented by Anaximander at Miletos and Solon at Athens, consists of the old aristocratic tradition as modified and developed by that section of the aristocracy which had thrown in its lot with the new merchant class. This has been discussed. The second, embodying the traditions and aspirations of the dispossessed peasantry, is, from the nature of the case, not represented by any famous name; but it can be studied in the mystical cults associated with the mythical figure of Orpheus. This will occupy us for the remainder of the present chapter. The third, which may be regarded as a synthesis of the other two, is Pythagoreanism.

In keeping with his policy of mobilising popular support against the old nobility, Peisistratos gave official encouragement to the cults of Dionysus, which were then assuming new forms, although in origin they were very ancient—older, in fact, than the deity to whose name they were attached, being derived from primitive agrarian magic. It was natural that such cults should have survived among the peasantry, who tilled the soil, and not among the aristocracy, who owned it.

Peisistratos was not the first tyrant to pursue such a policy. Periandros of Corinth had entertained at his court a poet, Arion, from Methymna in Lesbos, who under his patronage invented the dithyramb, a form of choral ode addressed

[17] Marx-Engels MCP 216.

to Dionysus. The story of Arion is told by Herodotus.[18] After spending a long time at the court of Periandros, he emigrated to the west, where he made a lot of money. Desiring to return to Corinth, he hired a Corinthian ship and set sail from Taras in southern Italy. During the voyage the sailors plotted to kill him and steal his money. Arion discovered the plot and implored them to spare his life. They refused, but, anxious to hear a singer of such celebrity, they agreed to let him jump overboard after singing one last song. Attired in his ritual costume, he took up his lyre, sang his song, and leapt into the sea. There a dolphin was waiting for him and carried him safe to shore at Cape Tainaron.

This is not history but myth. Dionysus himself is said to have been kidnapped by pirates;[19] and in another myth, based on ritual, he threw himself into the sea.[20] The head of Orpheus was thrown into the river Hebros after he had been torn to pieces by the Bacchants on Mount Pangaion.[21] Cape Tainaron was one of the entrances to Hades, and it was there that Orpheus descended in quest of his wife Eurydike.[22] Yet, although mythical, the story has a historical setting. Corinth was probably the first city on the mainland to set up a tyranny, and at this time Lesbos too was under a dictator, Pittakos. There was a tradition that the head of Orpheus was cast up on the shores of Lesbos and preserved there as a sacred relic; and at Methymna in Lesbos, Arion's native town, some fishermen are said to have hauled up in their nets a mask of olive-wood representing the head of Dionysus.[23] Finally, the earliest coins of Taras, where Arion embarked on his return voyage, are engraved with a human figure riding a dolphin.[24] The coins date from the time of Pythagoras. The conclusion to which this evidence points is that the Orphic movement started in Thrace and spread in the

---

[18] Hdt. 1. 23–4.

[19] Hom. *H.* 7, cf. Apld. 3. 5. 3: 'Dionysus hired a ship belonging to Tyrrhenian pirates to convey him from Ikaria to Naxos. They carried him past Naxos and made for Asia Minor, where they intended to sell him; but he turned the oars and mast into snakes and filled the vessel with ivy and the music of flutes, and the pirates went mad and leapt into the sea and turned into dolphins.'

[20] *Ib.* 6. 130–7.   [21] Kern 33–40.   [22] *Ib.* 65.

[23] Philost. *Her.* 2. 36 Paus. 10. 19. 3.   [24] Seltman BGC 11.

wake of trade to Lesbos and Corinth, and so to Italy and Sicily. This is in keeping with the traditions relating to Orpheus himself, which are unanimous in representing him as a native of Macedonia or Thrace.[25]

The Orphics were established at Athens in the time of Peisistratos, who patronised their leader, Onomakritos, author of a book called *Initiations* (Vol. I, p. 571). It cannot be proved that the movement reached Attica direct from Thrace; but, in view of the tyrant's connections with Mount Pangaion, it seems not improbable, especially when we find that in the mining village of Semachidai there was a shrine of Dionysus, called the Semacheion, and a local tradition of the coming of the god.[26]

The hypothesis that the movement began among the peasantry receives further support when we compare Orphic literature with the Hesiodic poems. To Homer the Orphic writers owed almost nothing, but their debt to Hesiod was profound. This is significant, because, a small farmer himself, Hesiod addressed his poems primarily to the peasantry.

The Orphics had their own theogony, in several different versions, but its general affinity to Hesiod's is unmistakable. In the beginning there was Time. Then Sky (Aither) and the Void came into being, and from them Time fashioned a silver egg, out of which sprang Phanes, or Love. The parentage of Zeus is as in Hesiod, but, having come to power, he swallows Phanes and so identifies himself with him. By Persephone he became the father of Dionysus, who when still a child was seized by the Titans, torn in pieces, and devoured. This part of the myth was enacted in the Orphic rite of the *omophagía*, a form of totemic sacrament, in which the initiates, who normally abstained from meat, ate the raw flesh of a bull. When Zeus discovered what the Titans had done, he blasted them with the thunderbolt, and in some way—the tradition varies at this point—the slain god was restored to life. When the thunderbolt struck them, the Titans were still reeking with their victim's blood; and from this blend of blood and ashes was formed the human race. That is why man's nature is partly good and partly evil: it is divided against itself.[27]

[25] Kern 10–3.   [26] Philoch. 78.   [27] Orph. fr. 220, 232.

In their conception of justice, too, the Orphics followed Hesiod. In the *Works and Days* Dike sits at the right hand of Zeus drawing his attention to the wickedness of the nobles who give crooked judgments;[28] in Orphic writings likewise we find her beside the throne of Zeus looking down from heaven and watching the life of man.[29] And finally the Hesiodic conception of Love as a creative force was developed as a direct challenge to aristocratic thought. To the nobility Love was a dangerous thing, because it implied desire, ambition, discontent. The tendency of aristocratic thought was to divide, to keep things apart. To the Orphics it was a thing to be revered, because it effected the reunion of what had been severed, the recovery of what had been lost. In the philosophy of Empedokles, who had much in common with the Orphics, it is Love that brings the world together, Strife that forces it apart, and the world is best when Love overcomes Strife. The tendency of popular thought was to unite.

The core of Orphism lay in its mystical teaching, derived from agrarian magic and ultimately from primitive initiation. In the Orphic mysteries, as in the Eleusinian and Christian and indeed in all mystical religions, the form of primitive initiation was taken over and charged with a new content. Primitive initiation had been directed towards the practical task of preparing the adolescent for real life (Vol. I, p. 45). Mystical initiation is directed towards preparing the candidate, not for this world, but for the next, not for life but for death. Robbed of their birthright, the exploited and dispossessed turn away in despair from the real world towards the hope of recovering their lost heritage in an illusory world to come (Vol. I, p. 347). As an ideological weapon in the class struggle, a mystical movement of this kind has two contradictory aspects. On the one hand, in so far as it is an expression of real misery and a protest against it, it can, given revolutionary leadership, become a class-conscious political movement. On the other hand, in the absence of such leadership, it can equally well be seized on by the ruling class as a means of diverting attention from the real struggle and so perpetuating the misery from which it springs. In sixth-century Attica the first of these tendencies

[28] Hes. *Op.* 254–60.   [29] Ps. D. 25. 11 (Kern 94).

was represented by Orphism, which differed from the Eleusinian Mysteries in its immediate popular origin and its
freedom from state control; but during the following century it
lost its positive value and became one of many mystical cults—
the Mysteries of Eleusis, of Bendis, of Attis—which competed
with one another in offering patent prescriptions for salvation
in the world to come.

According to Orphic doctrine, life is a penance by which man
atones for the sin of the Titans. The immortal part of him is
encased in the mortal; the soul is imprisoned in the body. The
body is the tomb of the soul.[30] We are chattels of the gods,
who will release us, when they choose to do so, from the
prison house of life.[31] All life is a rehearsal for death. Only
through death can the soul hope to escape from its imprisonment and find deliverance from the evils of the body. Life is
death and death is life.[32] After death the soul is brought to
judgment. If it is so deeply corrupted by the body as to be past
cure, it is consigned to eternal torment in the subterranean
prisons of Tartarus. If curable, it is purged and chastised, then
sent back to earth to renew its penance. When it has lived three
lives unspotted of the body, it is released for ever and goes to
join the celestial company of the blest.[33]

Such is the doctrine as we find it in Plato. It must have taken
some time to attain its final shape, and in the sixth century, no
doubt, it was still rudimentary; but through it runs one clear
thread—the idea that man is to god and body to soul what the
slave is to his owner. The soul is by rights the ruler and master,
the body its subject and slave.[34] This dualism is something new
in Greek thought. Nowhere in Milesian philosophy, or in the
Homeric poems, is there anything that corresponds to this
conception of the soul as generically different from the body,
the one pure, the other corrupt, the one divine, the other
mortal. Its social origin has already been indicated in general
terms; and we shall now proceed to define it more precisely by
examining the traditional symbolism in which the doctrine
was expounded.

[30] Pl. *Grg.* 492–3, *Crat.* 400c, E. fr. 38, Philol. 14.   [31] Pl. *Phdo* 62d.
[32] E. fr. 638.   [33] Pi. fr. 129–33, Pl. *Phdo* 70c, 107c–114c, *Phdr.* 248c–d.
[34] Pl. *Phdo* 62b–d.

4. The Origin of Dualism

It is just in this period, when the last vestiges of tribal society are being swept away, that there arises, by the side of Moira, the Orphic figure of Ananke. This word is commonly translated 'necessity', which serves well enough in many contexts, but its real meaning is more concrete—'compulsion' or 'coercion'. In literature, Ananke makes her first appearance in the writings of Herakleitos and Parmenides, who were both influenced by Orphism. Herakleitos couples Ananke and Moira together as being virtually identical; Parmenides assigns the same attributes to Moira, Dike, and Ananke.[35] A century later, in Plato's *Republic*, Ananke usurps the place of Moira and is even equipped with her spindle.[36]

Throughout Greek literature, from Homer onwards, the ideas of *anánke*, 'compulsion', and *douleía*, 'slavery', are intimately connected, the former being constantly used to denote both the status of slavery and the hard labour and tortures to which slaves were subjected.[37] The sight of slaves harnessed for transport or toiling in chain gangs under the lash suggested the image of a yoke or drove of oxen; and hence *zygón*, 'yoke', is the metaphor traditionally associated with both *douleía* and *anánke*.[38] In an Orphic painting of the underworld we see the condemned sinner, Sisyphos, rolling his stone uphill, while over him, lash in hand, stands the slave-driver Ananke.[39] Ananke represents the principle that the labouring members of society are denied all share in the product of their labour beyond the minimum necessary to keep them labouring. When Moira became Ananke, she was transformed into her opposite.

One of the formulas which the Orphics learnt for recital in the other world was the following:

> I have flown off the wheel of misery
> And with swift feet attained the longed-for crown.[40]

[35] Heracl. A 8, Parm. 1. 14, 28, 8. 14, 30, 37, 10. 6; Vol. I, p. 345.
[36] Pl. *Rp.* 616c.
[37] *Ib.* 6. 458, Tyrt. 5. 2, A. *Ag.* 1026=1042, 1055=1071, *Ch.* 74–6 =76–7, *Per.* 590=587, E. *Hec.* 1293–5, etc.; Hdt. 1. 116, Antipho 625, etc.
[38] A. *Ag.* 228=218, *Pr.* 107–8, 698–9=671–2, S. *Ph.* 1025, E. *Or.* 1130, cf. A. *Ag.* 944=953, 1225=1226, S. fr. 532, etc.
[39] Guthrie 190.   [40] Orph. fr. 32c. 6–7; Thomson WC.

The second verse refers to the idea, derived from primitive initiation, that life is an ordeal or race (Vol. I, p. 48). It is the first that concerns us here. In the Wheel of Birth, Fate, or Necessity, as it is variously called, we recognise the totemic cycle of birth and death; but the primitive concept has been reinterpreted and expressed in a contemporary symbol. The wheel was an instrument of torture used for punishing slaves, who were bound to it hand and foot.[41] Hence, to fly off the wheel of birth was to escape from the miseries of mortality.

With these ideas in mind, let us try to envisage the labour conditions in the silver mines of Laurion.

This is Frazer's description of the mines themselves:

Such are the hills of Laurion; they extend about eleven miles north and south, and about five miles east and west. In places they are honeycombed with the shafts and galleries of the ancient silver mines, and heaps of slag and the ruins of furnaces are to be seen everywhere. More than 2000 ancient shafts have been counted. Some are perpendicular, and vary in depth from 65 to 400 feet. In the sides of these perpendicular shafts there are holes in which ladders were probably fixed. Other shafts are slanting, with steps cut in them. The shape of the shafts is almost invariably square, and they measure about 6 feet across. At a depth from 80 to 150 feet the galleries begin. The roofs of these galleries are supported by pillars consisting sometimes of pieces of the native rock left standing, sometimes of built piers. As the pillars of native rock contained ore, the proprietors were tempted by cupidity to remove them. This dangerous practice was a capital offence at law, and in the time of the orator Lykourgos the death penalty was actually inflicted on one Diphilos, who had enriched himself by this unscrupulous proceeding. In the sides both of the shafts and of the galleries niches for lamps may be seen; some of the miners' lamps, made of clay, have been found, and are exhibited in the small museum at Ergastiria or Lavrion, as the modern mining town is called. The noxious atmosphere of the mines at Laurion was remarked by the ancients, and ventilation shafts were accordingly constructed, some of which have been discovered descending to depths of 260 to 360 feet. The ore seems to have been brought to the surface partly by machinery and partly by slaves.[42]

It need hardly be explained that the machinery to which Frazer refers was so simple as scarcely to deserve the name.

[41] Pl. M. 509c, Luc. Deor. 6. 5, Anac. 54. 7, Ar. Pa. 452, Pl. 875, Andoc. 1. 43, Antipho 5. 40, D. 39. 40, Plu. M. 19e, 509b, cf. Pl. Rp. 361e, Grg. 473c; Orph. fr. 230, D.L. 8. 14.

[42] Frazer PDG 2. 4, taken from Dodwell and Leake.

At the end of the second century B.C., when there was an insurrection, the number of slaves employed in these mines ran into tens of thousands. In the sixth century the working population, servile and free, must have been very much smaller. Some idea of the labour conditions can be formed from the account by Diodoros in the first century B.C. of the Egyptian gold mines. This evidence, though indirect, is quite reliable, because the actual labour of extracting the ore, in which the majority were engaged, was entirely unskilled and therefore not likely to have altered:

On the borders of Egypt, and in the adjacent districts of Arabia and Ethiopia, there are many large gold mines worked intensively at great expense of misery and money. The rock is black with rifts and veins of marble so dazzling white that it outshines everything. This is where the gold is prepared by the overseers of the mines with a multitude of labourers. To these mines the Egyptian kings send condemned criminals, prisoners of war, also those who have fallen victim to false accusations or been imprisoned for incurring the royal displeasure, sometimes with all their kinsfolk—both for the punishment of the guilty and for the profits which accrue from their labour. There they throng, all in chains, all kept at work continuously day and night. There is no relaxation, no means of escape; for, since they speak a variety of languages, their guards cannot be corrupted by friendly conversation or casual acts of kindness. Where the gold-bearing rock is very hard, it is first burned with fire, and, when it has been softened sufficiently to yield to their efforts, thousands upon thousands of these unfortunate wretches are set to work on it with iron stone-cutters under the direction of the craftsman who examines the stone and instructs them where to begin. The strongest of those assigned to this luckless labour hew the marble with iron picks. There is no skill in it, only force. The shafts are not cut in a straight line but follow the veins of the shining stone. Where the daylight is shut out by the twists and turns of the quarry, they wear lamps tied to their foreheads, and there, contorting their bodies to fit the contours of the rock, they throw the quarried fragments to the ground, toiling on and on without intermission under the pitiless overseer's lash. Young children descend the shafts into the bowels of the earth laboriously gathering the stones as they are thrown down, and carrying them into the open air at the shaft-head, where they are taken from them by men over thirty years, each receiving a prescribed amount, which they break on stone mortars with iron pestles into pieces as small as a vetch. Then they are handed on to women and older men, who lay them on rows of grindstones, and standing in groups of two and three they pound them to powder as fine as the best wheaten flour. No one could look on the squalor of these wretches, without even a rag to cover their loins, and not feel compassion for their plight. They may be sick, or maimed, or aged, or weakly women, but there is no indulgence, no respite. All alike are kept at their labour by the lash, until, overcome by hardships, they die in their torments (*en taîs anánkais*). Their misery is so great that they dread what is to come even more than the present, the punishments are so severe, and death is welcomed as a thing more desirable than life.[43]

This passage, so plainly written from personal observation, is worthy to stand beside Sir Thomas More's description of the sufferings of the English peasantry.[44] It is the only example in classical literature of a writer who had the intellectual and moral courage to discover for himself and describe the mass of human misery on which his civilisation rested. His account of the Spanish silver mines is similar:

The workers in these mines produce incredible profits for the owners, but their own lives are spent underground in the quarries wearing and wasting their bodies day and night. Many die, their sufferings are so great. There is no relief, no respite from their labours. The hardships to which the overseer's lash compels them to submit are so severe that, except for a few, whose strength of body and bravery of soul enables them to hold out for a long time, they abandon life, because death seems preferable.[45]

Here, apparently without noticing it, Diodoros has slipped into the traditional phraseology of Orphism. Life is death and death is life.

These, then, are the realities that first inspired the imagery that underlies so many Orphic parables of this life and the next—the Platonic Cave, in which men are chained from childhood hand and foot and have never seen the daylight, and the topography of Tartarus, with its subterranean channels of water, mud, fire, and brimstone; or the upper regions, under a clear sky, where the souls of the righteous are at rest:

Those who are judged to have lived lives of exceptional purity, are liberated and delivered from the subterranean regions as from a prison, and are brought up to dwell on the surface of the earth; while those who have purified themselves sufficiently by the pursuit of wisdom, enjoy eternal life, free altogether from the body, in the fairest land of all, which would be hard to describe, even if there were time to do it. And so, Simmias, for these reasons we must do all we can to attain righteousness and wisdom while we live. It is a fine prize, and the hope is great.[46]

Plato was not a miner—far from it—but he was drawing on

[43] D.S. 3. 11.   [44] More *Utopia* Bk. I.   [45] D.S. 5. 38.
[46] Pl. *Phdo* 114c.

Orphic tradition. It was in the mines that men first thought of life as a prison and the body as the tomb of the soul.

In order to appreciate the crudity of Orphic doctrine, we have only to compare it with the work of the Milesian philosophers. Yet it would be a mistake to regard it as a retrograde step in Greek thought, for two reasons.

In the first place, the Orphics issued a challenge to the time-honoured code of aristocratic morality. Hope is dangerous, love is dangerous; it is dangerous to strive overmuch, dangerous to emulate the gods; keep measure in all things, rest content with what you have. The Orphics delivered men from these timid and intimidating lies. They could not rest content with what they had, because they had nothing, and their hopes were as infinite as their desires. All life was strife and struggle, and if only man would run the race with courage, there was none so humble and debased but he might win the prize of glory and become a god. In all this the Orphics revealed—in an inverted, mystical form—the objective potentialities of the democratic movement; and it remained for the people, aroused out of its lethargy, to translate their mysticism into action.

In the second place, although it preserves many elements derived with little change from primitive myth and ritual, Orphic thought is not primitive. It has developed out of primitive thought no less far than Milesian philosophy, but in the opposite direction. In Milesian philosophy the old content is presented in a new form; in Orphic mysticism the old form has been charged with a new content. Primitive consciousness was essentially practical. It rested on the union, at a low level, of theory and practice, corresponding to the collective character of production and consumption. That was its positive feature. Its level, however, was so low that the subject (society) and the object (nature) were indistinguishable. In the period we have now reached, with the full growth of commodity production and the division of society into consciously contending classes, that distinction is drawn, but in such a way as to sever the unity of subject and object. The Milesians presented nature as existing independently of man, excluding the subject; the Orphics presented man as existing independently of nature, excluding the object. From the one trend there arose objective (that is, deterministic) materialism, from the other subjective idealism. In the ensuing period this fundamental issue—'the basic question of philosophy'—forced itself on the consciousness of society and divided the philosophers into the two opposing camps of materialism and idealism, in which they have been ranged right down to the present day.

Part Five

PURE REASON

Who fails here to call to mind our good friend
Dogberry, who informs neighbour Seacoal that 'to
be a well-favoured man is the gift of fortune, but
reading and writing comes by nature'?

MARX

XII

NUMBER

1. *The Pythagoreans of Kroton*

PYTHAGORAS was a native of Samos and a contemporary of the tyrant Polykrates, who was executed by the Persians about 523 B.C. His father, Mnesarchos, was an engraver of gems.[1] He became interested in scientific investigation, especially the theory of number, and is said to have been the first to advance the study of mathematics beyond the needs of trade.[2] He was also a religious mystic, and believed in the transmigration of souls. In middle life he emigrated to Kroton in southern Italy. This was a prosperous commercial city, famous for its medical school, which produced just at this time two distinguished men. One of these, Demokedes, who was contemporary with Pythagoras, became physician to the Persian Emperor.[3] The other, Alkmaion, was some years younger. Here Pythagoras founded a religious order, which for some time held political power in Kroton and several other cities of the region, the wealthiest of which was Sybaris. War broke out between these two, and in 510 B.C. Sybaris was destroyed. Not long after this event Pythagoras retired to Metaponton, where he seems to have spent the remainder of his life. The Pythagoreans maintained their organisation and continued their activities, until about 450 B.C. the order was broken up and they were violently expelled. With their subsequent history we are not at present concerned. That is all we can claim to know about the life of Pythagoras. The further particulars that are available from ancient writings are poorly authenticated.

The question arises, what political programme did Pythagoras and his colleagues pursue, when they were in power in Kroton and elsewhere in southern Italy, and what was their class basis? Only vague and conflicting answers have been given. It is stated by Porphyry in his *Life of Pythagoras* that he left

[1] Heraclit. 129, Hdt. 2. 123, Clem. *Str.* 1. 62.
[2] Aristox. 81.　　　　[3] Hdt. 3. 125, 131.

Samos in order to be free from the tyranny of Polykrates, which was becoming more repressive.[4] From this it has been inferred by some that he was an aristocrat and by others that he was a democrat. The truth is that we know very little about the internal affairs of Samos at this period, and that Porphyry's

SOUTHERN ITALY AND SICILY   **MAP X**

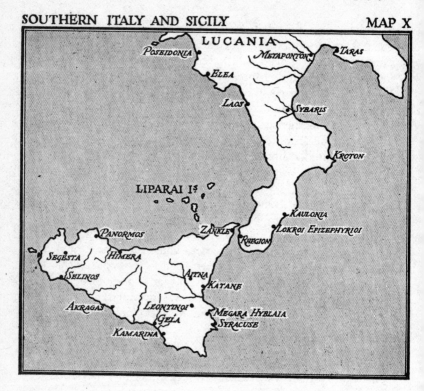

account of the matter cannot be accepted in the absence of reliable support; and therefore all we can do with this evidence is to dismiss it. It is stated by Diogenes of Laerte that at Kroton the disciples of Pythagoras 'administered the government so well (*árista*) that their rule was as it were an aristocracy (*aristokratía*)'.[5] From this it has been inferred that they represented the interests of the landed nobility. It is clear, however,

[4] Aristox. 4.   [5] D.L. 8. 3.

that the word *aristokratía* is here employed in its literal and philosophical sense of the rule of the best, and not in a political sense at all. It cannot be inferred that the Pythagoreans represented the big landowners. On the contrary, it may be regarded on general grounds as extremely improbable, if not impossible, that an emigrant from Samos should have found himself at the head of a hereditary landowning oligarchy in a state which had been founded nearly two centuries before his arrival. Finally, it is stated by Apollonios that the opponents of the Pythagoreans were two—Kylon, described as one of the leading citizens in wealth and birth, and a democrat named Ninon.[6] This suggests that they were moderate democrats, occupying a central position resembling that of Solon at Athens, except that he was a nobleman by birth, whereas Pythagoras was not. Here again, however, no conclusion can be drawn, because the evidence is unreliable.

If this were all, we should have no choice but to fall back on general considerations drawn from the content of their teaching; and any conclusion that might be reached on these grounds would be weakened by the difficulty of determining which of the doctrines expounded by later Pythagoreans can be attributed to the founder, who left nothing in writing. In this respect Pythagoras confronts us with the same problem as Confucius (p. 69). Fortunately, however, we have some archæological evidence, which, rightly understood, is decisive.

This is what Seltman has to say about the earliest coins of Kroton and its associated cities:

Mnesarchos, an engraver of stones living in Samos, had a famous son, Pythagoras. The latter, versed in metal-work, mathematics and music, a profound thinker, migrated about 535 B.C. to Kroton, where he made the coinage, introduced a philosophy, and founded Pythagorean brotherhoods which presently obtained political control in several prosperous cities; and in some of these there appeared a coinage in character like that of Kroton, but different in appearance from any other Greek money. Each piece displayed in relief the state's blazon and some letters of its name, all within a round cable border, and each piece had on its reverse side the identical picture but sunk in intaglio. The most famous of these, besides Kroton with an Apolline tripod, were Sybaris with a bull looking back, Metaponton with a big ear of

6 Iambl. *VP*. 2. 48.

barley, Kaulonia with an Apollo statue, Taras with a dolphin rider, and Poseidonia with a picture of the statue of its patron god Poseidon. All these seem to have been made in the three decades before 510 B.C.[7]

From this evidence, which is contemporary and concrete, two conclusions may be drawn.

In the first place, the period of Pythagorean rule coincided with the introduction of the coinage. That being so, the class which the Pythagoreans represented must have been 'the new class of rich industrialists and merchants'. Of course, the merchant class might have forced through such a development without actually taking power, as we know they did in Syracuse; but the new coinage described by Seltman was issued immediately after the Pythagoreans established their governments, and therefore the initiative can only have come from them. They differed, accordingly, from the Milesian philosophers, and resembled Solon, in being actively involved in the political struggle for the development of commodity production; and they differed from both them and him in being commoners and hence more closely identified with the popular movement. As we shall see, these differences are reflected in their teachings.

In the second place, they succeeded for a short time in establishing some sort of federal union embracing a number of independent city-states. What their aim was is a matter of conjecture. It may have resembled the plan which Thales is said to have proposed to the Ionians. He urged them to establish a common capital at Teos, the other cities to be reduced to the status of demes.[8] According to Herodotus, who tells us of the proposal, it was advocated as a defensive measure against

---

[7] Seltman BGC 10–1, cf. GC 76–9, PFIC. Others have argued that the coins cannot be dated much later than 550 B.C. and are therefore too early to be Pythagorean; but against this it has recently been shown that Pythagoras may have reached Italy a good deal earlier than 535 B.C.: White DST. The Pythagoreans believed that the upper and lower parts of the universe 'stood in the same relation to the centre, only reversed' (Philol. 17). This is exactly the relation between the two sides of these coins, the same design appearing on either side, but reversed. Evidently, therefore, as Seltman pointed out many years ago (GC 76–8), they were intended to symbolise the Pythagorean unity of opposites.

[8] Hdt. 1. 170.

the Persians after the fall of Sardeis; but, since in such a situation it would have been worse than useless from a military point of view, it seems more likely that it was put forward, before the Lydian hinterland had been lost to the Persians, with the object of unifying the economy of the coastal region. If the Pythagorean aim was similar, it was foredoomed to failure. A democratic federation of city-states could only have been maintained on condition that the productive forces were sufficiently developed to permit an organised division of labour between the federated cities; and this condition was precluded by the growth of slave labour. As Marx observed:

> In the ancient states, in Greece and Rome, compulsory emigration, assuming the shape of the periodical establishment of colonies, formed a regular link in the structure of society. The whole system of those states was founded on certain limits to the numbers of the population, which could not be surpassed without endangering the condition of ancient civilisation itself. But why was it so? Because the application of science to material production was utterly unknown to them. To remain civilised they were forced to remain few. Otherwise they would have had to submit to the bodily drudgery which transformed the free citizen into a slave.[9]

It is true that after the Persian Wars the Athenians succeeded in establishing the Confederacy of Delos; but this was a union based on the domination of one of its members over all the others; and it owed its cohesion to the intensity of the struggle between democrats and oligarchs, which in the fifth century attained a panhellenic scale. In Italy in the sixth century this stage had not been reached, and the Pythagorean plan, if such it was, was wrecked by the rivalry between Kroton and Sybaris. Nevertheless, the fact that an attempt at federation was made indicates that under Pythagorean rule these Italian cities were for a short time in the vanguard of the Greek-speaking world.

All that has just been said about Pythagorean politics refers to the generation of Pythagoras himself, when the Order was actually in power in Kroton and elsewhere. It stands to reason that after their expulsion their political orientation must have undergone a more or less radical change. The account that has been given here of the initial period gives precision to

[9] Marx FE 374.

the conclusions reached by von Fritz in his study of the subject:

> In the later part of their history the Pythagoreans seem always to have adhered to an extremely conservative policy. . . . Yet there must have been a time when they were newcomers and when consequently what was new in their doctrines must have come in conflict with accepted notions and traditions. The struggles which developed as a result of this situation must have been entirely different in character from those which occurred when the Pythagoreans had become more or less identified with an established régime.[10]

This is vague, but it contains the truth of the matter. The Pythagoreans of Kroton not only issued a challenge to accepted notions and traditions but also seized power from the landed aristocracy and used it to promote the development of commodity production. We may now turn to their religious and philosophical doctrines and see whether we can recognise in them their social and political objectives.

2. Pythagorean Religion

On its religious side Pythagoreanism had so much in common with Orphism that it has been said that 'the Pythagoreans were practically an Orphic community'.[11] This is an exaggeration. There were important differences between them, which correspond, as we shall see, to the differences in their class basis. But first let us see what they had in common.

Both sects were organised in what may be called secret societies or fraternities—the Orphic *thíasoi* and the Pythagorean *synédria*. Admission was obtained by some form of initiation, involving participation in secret rites and doctrines, which were not to be divulged to the uninitiated. This vow of silence was expressed in the Pythagorean symbol of 'the ox on the tongue', corresponding to the Orphic 'door on the tongue' and the Eleusinian 'key on the tongue'.[12] The Pythagoreans, in particular, made a regular practice of silent meditation.[13] The

[10] Von Fritz 97–8.   [11] Bury HG 317.

[12] Theog. 815, A. *Ag.* 36–7, Strattis 67, Hsch. βοῦς ἐπὶ γλώσσῃ, Philost. *Ap.* 1. 1, 6. 11, A. fr. 316, S. *OC.* 1052–3, Critias fr. 5. 3, *Anth. Pal.* 10. 42, 16. 132, Theog. 413, E. *Or.* 903, Ar. *Ra.* 838, Orph. fr. 245, 334, Pl. *Sym.* 218b; Thomson AO 2. 7–8.

[13] Philost. *Ap.* 1. 1, Stob. *Fl.* 34. 7, *Anth. Pal.* 10. 46, 14. 1, 16. 325–6, Greg. Naz. *Or.* 33. 535c.

subject of meditation, we may suppose, consisted of sayings of
the master. Aristotle tells us that the disciples of Empedokles
used to learn his poems by heart and could 'rattle them off' long
before they understood their meaning: for that 'time was needed,
so that they might sink in'.[14] Similarly, in language which is
clearly reminiscent of the Eleusinian Mysteries, Herakleitos
declared that his utterance was as unintelligible on first hearing
as before it had been heard.[15] All mystical doctrines have an
inner meaning into which the initiated can only penetrate by
constant repetition and reflection.

It has been mentioned above that the Orphics abstained from
meat except sacramentally. Porphyry states that a similar rule
was observed by the Pythagoreans.[16] His authority would carry
little weight in itself, but in this case it is supported by other
evidence. We know that in the third century B.C. the rule was
followed by those Pythagoreans who claimed to have preserved
the religious side of the master's teaching; and we have contemporary evidence that Pythagoras himself preached the
doctrine that after death the souls of men are reincarnated in
animals. He is said to have appealed to it in protest at the
beating of a dog.[17] If the early Pythagoreans refrained for such
reasons from beating animals, it is probable that, like the
Orphics, they also refrained from eating them.

These considerations are important, because they show that
the Orphic and Pythagorean brotherhoods preserved certain
totemic practices and beliefs (Vol. I, p. 51) and indeed were not
far removed from those magical fraternities, characteristic of
the upper stage of tribal society, which were discussed in
Chapter II (pp. 55–6). This, as we have seen, was the ultimate
origin of those hieratic traditions which gave birth in Ionia to
the Milesian school of philosophy; but, whereas in that case
the line of descent is long and devious, taking us back to
Minoan Thebes, Crete, Syria, and Mesopotamia, these Orphic
and Pythagorean brotherhoods are, we might say, only one step
removed from tribalism. Why do they stand so much closer to
their origin? The answer, in general terms, is that the subject
class, just because it is culturally more backward than the

---

14 Arist. *EN.* 1147a.   15 Heraclit. B 1.
16 Porph. *Abs.* 1. 26.   17 Xenoph. 7.

ruling class, tends to be more retentive of primitive customs and beliefs; but there are two further considerations which enable us to make this answer more precise.

In the first place, the Orphic movement started in Thrace, spread rapidly to the Greek colonies in Italy and Sicily, and flourished there more widely and longer than anywhere else in Greece. Similarly, the Pythagorean movement started in Italy. This was not an accident. It was precisely in these outlying regions—Thrace, Italy, and Sicily—that the Greeks were in close and continuous contact with more backward peoples, which had preserved their tribal institutions. In contrast to the Ionians, whose outlook was predominantly secular and rational, these westerners were noted for the religious cast of their thought and their faith in prophecy and miracles. In this they resembled the Hebrews, who also, owing to the circumstances of their history, had kept in touch with their tribal origins (pp. 98–100).

In the second place, Pythagoras was well fitted by the circumstances of his life to combine the two traditions, both because he was an Ionian who settled in Italy and because by parentage and upbringing he belonged to the new middle class. This is the significance of an important observation made by Engels. In Ionia, the new aristocracy of wealth had been 'identical from the outset with the old hereditary aristocracy', and hence was able to transmit and reinterpret the old hieratic traditions. In Italy, on the other hand, the early Pythagoreans were predominantly new men who had 'pushed the old hereditary aristocracy into the background',[18] and hence, having assimilated the achievements of Ionian philosophy, were able to merge them with the popular traditions which they shared with the common people.

The Pythagoreans observed other taboos besides abstinence from meat, and invested them with an ethical significance; for example, 'Don't step over the beam of a pair of scales'—that is, don't transgress the bounds of equity. They believed in the moral responsibility of the individual for his actions, and, when they returned home after the day's work, they said to themselves, 'Where have I erred? what have I accomplished? what have I left undone that I ought to have done?' They believed

[18] Engels OF 191.

in the immortality of the soul, and that the souls of the pure, after being freed from the wheel of birth, ascended to the upper region of Hades, while those of the impure were bound by the Erinyes in unbreakable bonds; that the air was full of guardian spirits which visited men in dreams, for the soul awakes when the body sleeps; and that the man who was possessed of a good spirit was blest. Their rites of burial were designed to secure their personal salvation.[19]

In all this they differed little, if at all, from the Orphics. But their patron god was Apollo, not Dionysus. Everywhere they went the Orphics carried with them the worship of their god, which was ecstatic and popular in contrast to the aristocratic and more restrained Apollo; but in Ionia the latter retained his dominant position, being the god of Delos (Vol. I, p. 551), whose altar Pythagoras is said to have held in special reverence. As an Ionian, therefore, Pythagoras had traditional ties with the Delian Apollo. And there is a further reason why this god was worshipped in the new brotherhood. As prophet, musician, and healer, he united under his patronage the two sides of the Pythagorean way of life (*philosophía*), the practical and the theoretical. On the practical side, they cultivated music as a means of purifying the soul from the contamination of the body; on the theoretical side, they were the first to investigate the connection between music and mathematics. The lyre-playing Apollo, leader of the Muses (Vol. I. p. 484), was the divine embodiment of this organic unity.

Finally, although derived from Orphic mysticism, the philosophy of the Pythagoreans constituted an entirely new system of ideas expressing a new outlook on man and nature, the outlook of the new class which had been brought into being by the new developments in the mode of production; and in the Greek cities of southern Italy these ideas were consciously applied to the task of transforming the social order:

New social ideas and theories arise only after the development of the material life of society has set new tasks before society. But once they have arisen they become a most potent force which facilitates the carrying out of the new tasks set by the development of the material life of society, a force which facilitates the progress of society.[20]

[19] D.L. 8. 13–35.   [20] Stalin DHM 116.

3. *Theory of Number*

It was pointed out in the last chapter that Orphic doctrine rested on the belief that there exists a fundamental difference and perpetual antagonism between body and soul.

This belief is not primitive. In primitive thought the soul is that by which things move and live; and, since no distinction is drawn between organic and inorganic matter, the possession of a soul is equivalent to the power, real or apparent, of self-movement. In the parent speech of the Indo-European languages there existed, instead of the two or three genders with which we are familiar, two grammatical classes, animate and inanimate, the names of things being assigned to the one class or the other according as they were believed to be self-moving or not.[21] This distinction was so fundamental that objects which we know to be identical might be divided between the two classes, because they manifested themselves in different aspects. Thus, of the two words for *fire*, one, represented by the Latin *ignis* (originally animate, later masculine), denoted a forest fire or a prairie fire or any fire that was beyond human control; the other, represented by the Greek *pŷr* (originally inanimate, later neuter), denoted such fire as might be created by rubbing sticks or striking flints, the sort of fire that was amenable to control. In this mode of thinking, to say of a living creature that it possesses a soul is only another way of saying that it is alive. So deeply rooted is this conception of the soul that to this day the Irish peasant, who accepts without question the Catholic doctrine that animals have no souls, will say none the less, when his cow dies, *Thuit an t-anam aiste*, 'The soul fell out of her'.

The Orphic conception springs from the self-alienation which, inherent in all forms of exploitation, reaches its extreme form in slavery. The slave has alienated not only his labour power but himself. Both the product of his labour and his own body are the property of another, to be disposed of as use values or as exchange values without regard to his will. Both alike, therefore, form part of the objective reality which confronts him as subject; and accordingly the subject consists

[21] Meillet 189–91.

solely of his disembodied self, that is, his unrealised desires. In these conditions the subject finds expression in the denial of the object. The real world is not the world in which he lives and labours, but an imaginary world in which there is neither labour nor life. Life is death and death is life. It would be incorrect to describe this doctrine as philosophical dualism, because, in the first place, it is not a philosophical theory at all, and, in the second place, it is rather an inverted form of monism, in which, after the severance of subject and object, the subject has become everything and the object nothing. In this respect it stands in direct opposition to the materialist monism of the Ionian philosophers, in which the object has become everything and the subject nothing. Nevertheless, the principle of dualism is implicit in it, and this principle was developed by the Pythagoreans.

Turning to the earliest Pythagorean accounts of the soul, we are confronted with what seems on the face of it to be a doctrine entirely different from the Orphic. According to Philolaos, a disciple of Pythagoras who fled to Greece after the dissolution of the Order and later returned to Italy, the soul is a sort of attunement of the opposites in the body—the hot and cold, wet and dry, etc.—which are held together by it in due proportions like the strings of a lyre.[22] From this it follows that the soul cannot survive the dissolution of the body any more than the attunement of the strings can survive the destruction of the lyre. Such a view is clearly incompatible with the Pythagorean theory of the transmigration of souls.

The discrepancy can, however, be explained. It will be observed that, if we set aside the musical analogy, the theory of Philolaos does not disagree with the Ionian materialist view of the soul as that which imparts life to the body. It is possible, therefore, that during his stay in Greece, where he must have met members of the Ionian school, Philolaos was concerned to accommodate Pythagorean doctrine to the theories which he

[22] Pl. *Phdo* 85e–86d. The doctrine is ascribed, not to Philolaos himself, but to his pupil, Simmias, who had studied under him at Thebes (61e); it seems, however, to have been current, not only at Thebes, but also at Phleious (88d), where there was another Pythagorean society (Burnet GP 152).

found established there. From the Pythagorean point of view the idea of attunement was much more than an analogy; it was based, as we shall see, on the numerical relations between the fixed notes of the octave, and the early Pythagoreans believed that numbers constituted the only ultimate reality. Regarded from this point of view, the theory of Philolaos appears in a very different light. The intervals of the octave constitute a numerical reality which is perfect and permanent in contrast to the partial and transitory reality of mere bodily existence.

If this reconstruction is accepted, we may recognise the original Pythagorean doctrine in some famous lines of Pindar, who belonged to the generation before Philolaos:

The body waits on the omnipotence of death, but an image of life survives, for this alone comes from the gods: while the limbs are active, it sleeps, but it gives in dreams to those that sleep the interpretation of joys and sorrows to come.[23]

This conception is expounded more fully in one of the Hippocratic treatises:

While the body is awake, the soul is not her own mistress but serves the body, her attention divided between the various bodily senses—sight, hearing, touch, walking and all bodily actions—which deprive the mind of its independence. But, when the body is at rest, the soul wakes and stirs and keeps her own house, and carries out herself all the activities of the body. In sleep the body does not feel, but the soul awake knows everything: she sees what is to be seen, hears what is to be heard, walks, touches, grieves, remembers —in a word all the functions of body and soul alike are performed in sleep by the soul. And therefore anyone who knows how to interpret these matters possesses a great part of wisdom.[24]

These two passages are clearly drawn from a common source, which is probably Pythagorean; and it is also clear that the idea of the soul enjoying freedom of action only when the body is dormant agrees with the wider Orphic doctrine that life is death and death is life.

It seems, then, that the early Pythagorean view of the relationship between soul and body was similar to the Orphic. They were antagonistic opposites, the one good and the other

[23] Pi. fr. 131, cf. A. *Ag.* 189–91 = 179–81, Ach. Tat. 1. 6.
[24] Hp. *Reg.* 4. 86.

evil. This accords with what we know in general of the Pythagorean theory of opposites.

The Pythagoreans recognised ten pairs of opposites:

Limit	Unlimited
Odd	Even
One	Many
Right	Left
Male	Female
Motionless	Moving
Straight	Crooked
Light	Darkness
Good	Evil
Square	Oblong[25]

It is obvious that the list might be extended indefinitely. The reason why the pairs were traditionally restricted to ten is simply that, as the sum of the first four integers, ten was regarded with veneration as the perfect number.[26] Further, it is clear that some of them are less fundamental than others. Excluding the less fundamental, we are left with four pairs: limit—unlimited; odd—even; one—many; good—evil. Further, since the odd, the one and the good all pertain to the limit, while their opposites pertain to the unlimited, we may say that the whole scheme rests on the basic opposition of the limit or good and the unlimited or evil. This antagonistic pair is the origin of all things, corresponding to the 'primary substance'— water, the unlimited, air—of the Milesian school. The dualism implicit in Orphic mysticism is here formulated systematically as a philosophical doctrine.

At the same time, while its inspiration is Orphic, there can be little doubt that it was formulated under the influence of Ionian monism, with which Pythagoras must have been familiar before he emigrated to Italy. In particular, it can hardly be an accident that the second member of his primary pair bears the same name as Anaximander's primary substance. The idea of a primeval unity separating out into opposites was derived, as we have seen, from the myth of creation, which in turn was in origin nothing more than the conscious reflection of the conflict of opposites inherent in all things which became

[25] Arist. *Met.* A 5.986a. 15.   [26] Burnet EGP 102–3.

manifest to man through the social relations imposed on him by the needs of material production. Thus, for Anaximander, as for the other members of this school, the world is a material, time-bound process. Pythagoras, however, in substituting for this Ionian unity his own premiss of an original duality, took the first step towards a conception of the world as something immaterial and timeless; and his premiss too was derived from social relations—the relations of a society divided into antagonistic classes.

Before proceeding, we may compare the Pythagorean opposites with the Chinese *yang* and *yin* (p. 66). The two theories have this in common, that they postulate a series of pairs, in each of which one member is morally superior to the other; and, moreover, they agree in excluding, or at least thrusting into the background, the origin of the world in time. But, although pregnant with dualism and idealism, the Chinese theory is still monistic and materialistic, the conflicting opposites being reconciled and regulated in the person of the king. The Chinese theory, therefore, is less advanced than the Pythagorean. It represents the outlook of a mercantile intelligentsia in a society in which the development of commodity production is held in check by the oriental despotism.

How, then, did the Pythagoreans explain the structure of the universe? It is possible that the statement just made, that they conceived of it as being timeless in origin, should be qualified. It has been suggested that they taught that the world grew from a seed which the Limit sowed in the Unlimited.[27] If so, we have here a link with the primitive anthropomorphic myth; but it rests on tenuous evidence, and in any case it is to be regarded as a vestigial remnant rather than an integral feature of their system. What is new and revolutionary is the postulate that the primary substance is number. The original pair, the limit and the unlimited, represents number in its two aspects of odd and even. As a material substance, number has extension in space. The universe is an aggregate of numerical quantities. How the aggregation came into being is not entirely clear; but it seems that the unlimited was equated with the void, and

[27] Raven 47.

that the first unit absorbed a portion of the unlimited, thereby limiting it and at the same time dividing itself into two; by a continuation of the same process two generated three, and so on. The first unit represented the point; the number two represented the line, extended in one dimension; three the triangle, extended in two dimensions; four the pyramid, extended in three dimensions, and so on.[28] What concerns us here is not the details of the process, which involve a good deal of sophistry, but the underlying postulate. In putting forward the theory that the material world is composed of numbers, that is, of ideas, the Pythagoreans took up, without being yet aware of what they were doing, the position of philosophical idealism.

And yet here again, although the postulate is new, it is not difficult to recognise its *point de départ* in the work of the Milesian school. It was pointed out in Chapter VIII that Anaximenes's theory of rarefaction and condensation had the effect of reducing the cosmogonical process to quantitative terms (p. 165). In other words, the world was by implication stripped of quality and presented as a quantitative abstraction. The Pythagoreans took the further step of identifying the primary substance with number, thereby stating explicitly what Anaximenes had implied.

What led them to take this step? Not simply their interest in mathematics. Rather, their interest in mathematics was only another manifestation of the same tendency. So fundamental a development in thought can only be explained if it is seen as the conscious reflection of a movement equally fundamental in the social relations of their time. What was new in ancient Greek society? This question has been answered in the preceding chapters. It was precisely in Greece of this period that commodity production came to its full growth and revolutionised the whole of previous society. Anaximenes and Pythagoras both reveal the characteristic outlook of the new merchant class, which was engaged in the exchange of commodities on a scale which appears very small by our standard but was unprecedented by theirs. The basic factor, therefore, was the growth of a society organised for the production of exchange values and

[28] *Ib.* 48.

the consequent decay of the old relations based on the production of use values. Hence the distinctive feature of their thought may be defined quite simply by reference to the essential difference, as defined by Marx, between production for use and production for exchange:

> Every useful thing, as iron, paper, etc., may be looked at from the two points of view of quality and quantity. It is an assemblage of many properties and may therefore be of use in various ways. To discover the various uses of things is the work of history. So also is the establishment of socially recognised standards of measure for the quantities of these useful objects. . . .[29]
>
> But the exchange of commodities is evidently an act characterised by a total abstraction from use value. Then one use value is just as good as another, provided only it be presented in sufficient quantity. Or, as old Barbon says, 'one sort of wares are as good as another, if their values be equal. There is no difference or distinction in things of equal value. . . . An hundred pounds' worth of lead or iron is of as great value as one hundred pounds' worth of silver or gold'. As use values, commodities are, above all, of different qualities, but as exchange values they are merely different quantities.[30]

4. The Mean

We have no proof that the doctrine of the fusion of opposites in the mean goes back to Pythagoras himself, but it may be regarded as probable, for two reasons. It was familiar to Æschylus, who was born before Pythagoras died, and, since it is based on a mathematical study of the musical scale, it provides the link between the two sides of his teaching, the mystical and the rational, the practical and the theoretical. Music is an important element in the therapeutic magic of primitive medicine (Vol. I, p. 460). For the Pythagoreans, it was to the soul what medicine was to the body, and the secret of both was to be found in mathematics.

We may, then, attribute to Pythagoras the following discovery. The Greek lyre had seven strings, of which three were pitched at different intervals according to the mode that was being played, while the other four were pitched at the same intervals for all the modes. What he discovered was that the intervals between the four fixed notes correspond to the numerical series 6—8—9—12. It is a discovery that he could easily have made by experimenting on a single string with a

[29] Marx C 1. 2.   [30] Ib. 1. 4.

movable bridge. The terms 6 and 12 are the extremes: 8 is the subcontrary or harmonic mean $(8=12-\frac{12}{3}=6+\frac{6}{3})$; and 9 is the arithmetic mean $(9=12-3=6+3)$. These are objective facts, but the Pythagoreans interpreted them in the light of preconceptions peculiar to themselves.

Anaximander had maintained that the world was brought into being by the differentiation of the opposites out of the unlimited, and that it was destroyed by their mutual encroachment and consequent fusion and dissolution. For him, the process of fusion was destructive. For Pythagoras, on the other hand, it was constructive: the conflict of opposites was resolved by their mutual interpenetration, out of which there emerged an organic unity. In this respect the theory follows the Orphic conception of Love as a unifying and creative force.

Solon had maintained that, by taking his stand midway between the contending classes and imposing 'measure' on their ambitions, which were limitless in themselves, he had achieved social justice. This was the first appearance in Greek thought of the idea of the 'mean', or 'middle', as it should rather be called (*méson*). But the Pythagorean conception was different. For Solon, the mean was the point midway between the two extremes, and it was imposed from outside. For the Pythagoreans, it was a new unity brought into being out of the very conflict which it negated.

The significance of this conception becomes still clearer when we examine the phraseology in which it was expressed. The Pythagoreans described concord in music (*harmonía*) as 'a co-ordination of opposites, a unification of the many, a reconciliation of dissentients'.[31] The words *dícha phronéo* 'dissent' and *symphrónasis* 'reconciliation' are Doric, and their Attic equivalents are *stásis* and *homónoia*, corresponding to the Latin *certamen* and *concordia*. All these words are derived from social relations: *stásis* means party strife or civil war (Latin *certamina ordinum*); *homónoia* means civil peace or concord (Latin *concordia*). Thus, the 'concord' of the Pythagoreans reflects the outlook of the new middle class, intermediate between the landed aristocracy and the peasantry, which claimed to have resolved the class struggle in democracy.

31 Philol. B 10 Diels.

If further confirmation is needed, we have only to contrast their outlook with that of Theognis, who had lived to see his native Megara pass into the control of the hated democrats:

> In our rams, asses and horses we endeavour to preserve a noble breed, and we like to mate them with a good stock. Yet the nobleman does not scruple to marry a low-born wife, so long as she brings him money, nor will a woman refuse a low-born suitor, preferring riches to nobility. What they value is money. The nobles marry into base families, the base into noble. Wealth has blended birth. So do not wonder that the breed of the citizens is dying out; for noble is being blended with base.[32]

Theognis was not a philosopher; he is merely describing, as one bitterly opposed to them, the social changes he saw in his time; and what did he see? He saw the opposites, *esthloí* and *kakoí*, whom as an aristocrat he wanted to keep apart, being blended by the money of the new middle class.

This interpretation is so clear that it may be regarded as corroborating the view that the doctrine in question goes back to the Pythagoreans of Kroton. Such a doctrine could only have arisen at a time when the new middle class was in the ascendant. The same conclusion is to be drawn from the work of Æschylus, who died in 456 B.C., just about the time when the Pythagorean Order was overthrown. It is expressly stated by Cicero, who had studied at Athens, that Æschylus was a Pythagorean;[33] and the authenticity of this tradition is confirmed by a study of his plays. We need not, of course, infer that he was actually a member of the Order, although he paid several visits to Sicily and might well have joined it there; but he was undoubtedly acquainted with its teachings, with which, as a moderate democrat, he felt a natural sympathy. His earliest plays date from the beginning of the fifth century B.C., when Pythagoras may have been still alive; and, as I have shown in my *Æschylus and Athens*, the type of drama which he created—the trilogy—embodies, in form and content alike, the idea of the fusion of opposites in the mean. The progress of mankind, as he regarded it, had consisted of a struggle between rival powers, through which man had slowly raised himself out of barbarism into civilisation—a struggle which had been resolved during his own

[32] Theog. 189-92.   [33] Cic. TD. 2. 23.

lifetime in the new unity represented by democratic Athens, the most brilliant city the world had ever seen.

To this Æschylean and Pythagorean view of man's social evolution there is a close parallel in the view put forward a generation later by Hippokrates:

If the sick had benefited by the same diet and regimen as the healthy, if there had been nothing better to be found, the art of medicine would never have been discovered or sought after, because there would have been no need for it. Men were driven to seek and find medicine by force of circumstances, because the sick do not benefit by the same regimen as the healthy, and never did. Furthermore, I maintain that our mode of life at the present day would never have been discovered, if men had been content with the same food and drink as the animals, such as oxen and horses, which feed and grow up and thrive on fruit and wood and grass without pain and without the need for any other diet. In the beginning, I believe, this was the diet of man himself. Our present mode of life, in my opinion, is the outcome of a long period of invention and elaboration. So long as men partook of crude foods, strong in quality and uncompounded, their brutish diet subjected them to terrible sufferings—the same as they would suffer now, attacked by acute pains and diseases quickly followed by death. In former ages, it may be, they suffered less, because they were used to it, but severely even then. Many, whose constitutions were too weak to stand it, naturally perished, but the stronger resisted, just as now some men dispose of strong foods without difficulty, others only with severe pain. And that I think is the reason why men sought a diet in harmony with their constitutions until they discovered that which we use now.[34]

Hippokrates was not a Pythagorean, but his work and that of his school was deeply influenced by the Pythagorean idea that health represented a fusion (Greek *krâsis*, whence our 'temperament') of the opposites in the body—an idea attributed, in its earliest recorded version, to Alkmaion of Kroton, a younger contemporary of Pythagoras himself (p. 249):

Health consists in the enjoyment by the powers—the wet and dry, the hot and cold, the bitter and sweet, and so on—of equal rights (*isonomía*), while the monarchy of one or other of them is conducive to sickness.[35]

Just as Æschylus reveals Athenian democracy in the light of the Pythagorean theory of musical concord, so Alkmaion describes physical health in terms of a democratic constitution. In the human body, as in the body politic, well-being flows from the resolution of internal contradictions.

[34] Hp. *VM*. 3.   [35] Alcmaeo B 4 Diels.

That this conception has something in common with modern dialectics is clear, but there is one fundamental difference. Lenin wrote:

The unity (coincidence, identity, resultant) of opposites is conditional, temporary, transitory, relative. The struggle of mutually exclusive opposites is absolute, just as development and motion are absolute.[36]

In the Pythagorean doctrine of the fusion of opposites in the mean this relationship is inverted. The unity is absolute, the struggle is relative. The conflict between the opposites culminates in their fusion in the mean, which, once established, is assumed to be permanent. There is no suggestion that the achievement of unity will be followed by the renewal of conflict at a higher level. This limitation emerges clearly in the work of Æschylus, who at the same time reveals its class origin. At the end of the *Oresteia*, having reconciled the Erinyes, standing for tribal society, with Apollo, standing for the landed aristocracy, by assigning to both antagonists an appropriate part in the new democratic constitution, the goddess of Athens promises her citizens that their city shall stand for ever, on one condition:

> Only let them not tamper with their laws;
> For none can drink from springs befouled with mire.
> I bid my people honour and uphold
> The mean between the despot and the slave.[37]

The new constitution, representing the mean, is to remain unchanged. This shows that Æschylus was opposed to the policy of the radical democrats, who were bent on changing it. He failed to see that his fusion of opposites was only a transitory unity, out of which new opposites must arise.

The application of this principle to ethics must have been a central feature in the teaching of the early Pythagoreans, because all their theoretical studies—cosmology, mathematics, music, medicine—were pursued with the practical aim of providing them with a rule of life that would ensure the welfare of their souls. On this point our best witness is, again, Æschylus, for whom ethics were inseparable from politics:

[36] Lenin D 81.   [37] A. *Eu.* 696–700=693–7.

> Times there are when fear is well;
> Yes, it must continually
> Watch enthroned within the soul.
> Needful, too, straits to teach humility.
> Who of those that never nursed
> Wholesome fear within the heart,
> Be they men or cities, shall
> Show respect to righteousness?
> Choose a life despot-free,
> Yet restrained by rule of law. Thus and thus
> God doth administer, yet hath appointed the mean
>   as the master in all things.[38]

This conception of the mean as a moral principle was passed on from the Pythagoreans through Plato to Aristotle, who defined virtue as follows:

I am speaking of moral virtue. This is concerned with feelings and actions, in which one can have excess or deficiency or the mean. Thus, one can feel fear, courage, desire, anger, pity, and in general pleasure and pain, either too much or too little, in both cases wrongly. To have these feelings at the right time, on the right occasion, towards the right people, for the right purpose, in the right manner, is the best, or the mean, which pertains to virtue. In the same way there can be excess, deficiency and the mean in regard to actions. Now, it is with feelings and actions that virtue is concerned, and in them excess and deficiency are errors, while the mean is commended and constitutes success, and commendation and success pertain to virtue. Virtue, then, is a sort of middle attitude in that it aims at the mean. Further, while there are many ways of failing (for, in the imagery of the Pythagoreans, evil belongs to the unlimited, good to the limited), there is only one way to success (hence it is easy to fail, hard to succeed—easy to miss the mark, hard to hit it)—so this is another reason why excess and deficiency belong to vice and observance of the mean to virtue.[39]

A century before Aristotle, Tzu Ssu, grandson of Confucius, had defined virtue in similar terms:

Confucius said, 'The man of true breeding is the mean in action. The man of no breeding is the reverse. The relation of the man of true breeding to the mean in action is that, being a man of true breeding, he consistently holds to the mean. The reverse relationship of the man of no breeding is that, being what he is, he has no sense of moral caution.'
The Master said, 'I know the Way is not pursued. The learned run to excess and the ignorant fall short. I know why the Way is not understood. The good run to excess and the bad fall short.'[40]

[38] *Ib.* 520–34 = 516–30.   [39] Arist. *EN.* 1106b.   [40] Hughes 33.

The similarity arises from the fact that both Pythagoras and Confucius expressed the outlook of a new middle class, intermediate between the nobility and the peasantry, which had arisen through the emergence of commodity production within a primitive agrarian economy.

XIII

BECOMING

1. *Herakleitos: his Political Position*

THE democratic revolution marked a turning-point in Greek society. It was the culmination of the struggle between the landed nobles, on the one hand, and the merchants and peasants, on the other, and it was only brought to a successful issue by the development of slave labour. For the merchant class, who saw in it the realisation of their aims, it represented the final achievement of social justice, leaving nothing to be desired. In fact, it was nothing of the kind. Rather, it was the political expression of the radical transformation in the class structure of society which has been described in Chapter IX. It was the first form of state adapted to a commodity-producing community of slave-owners and slaves.

From this it must not, of course, be inferred that the struggle within the citizen body, between rich and poor citizens, ceased; but it assumed a new form, subordinate to the struggle between slave-owners and slaves. Even the poor citizens, most of them, owned at least one or two slaves. Their aim, therefore, was not to unite with the slaves in a struggle to abolish slavery, but on the contrary to extend the exploitation of slave labour so as to secure a greater share of it for themselves. In this way they were caught in a vicious circle. No matter how energetically they might strive to redress the inequalities between themselves and the rich, the effect was only to deepen the cleavage from which those inequalities arose. Hence the struggle between democrats and oligarchs continued with ever-increasing violence and a growing sense of desperation, because it was incapable of any solution, within the limits of the city-state, other than the common ruin of the contending classes.

The democratic revolution took place in different cities at different dates, ranging from the beginning of the sixth century to the fourth; but in the country as a whole the movement culminated in the period of the Persian Wars, which ended in 479 B.C. This period fell within the lifetime of Herakleitos and Parmenides, whose work, as will appear in this and the following chapters, marks a turning-point in the evolution of Greek thought.

Herakleitos belonged to the nobility of Ephesos (p. 135). His outlook was anti-democratic, as is shown by his violent denunciation of the people for banishing his brother and his contempt for the worship of Dionysus.[1] We have already had occasion to mention another class-conscious aristocrat, Theognis of Megara (p. 223). The views of these two noblemen, separated by one of the most eventful centuries in Greek history, make an instructive contrast. Theognis had denounced the effect of money in blending the opposites, the nobles and the commoners, which, as a nobleman, he wished to keep apart. This attitude belonged to the early stages of the democratic movement, in which slavery was undeveloped. Against it the Pythagoreans, representing the men of money, put forward the idea of the fusion of opposites in the mean. Then the Pythagorean doctrine is challenged by Herakleitos, who affirms that the world is held together, not by fusion, but by tension, not by harmony, but by strife. As if to drive the point home, he borrows his imagery from the Pythagorean Apollo, god of the bow and lyre:

> They do not understand how it agrees by differing—a concord of contrary tensions as in bow and lyre.[2]

In negating the Pythagorean doctrine, Herakleitos does more than reaffirm the old aristocratic attitude. He invests it with a new meaning, corresponding to the new alignment of classes. In standing for tension or strife as against fusion or reconciliation, he is at one with Theognis; but the opposites are no longer the same. His opposites are not noblemen and commoners but freemen and slaves. This is clear from his own words:

> War is father of all and lord of all, and has made gods and men, freemen and slaves.[3]

For him, therefore, strife is absolute, unity relative. This is true dialectics. The main question with which we are confronted in studying his work is, what were the conditions which rendered possible so brilliant a contribution to human thought?

[1] Heraclit. B 14–5, 121.   [2] *Ib.* 51.   [3] *Ib.* 53.

2. Herakleitos and the Mysteries

If Pythagoreanism may be described as having been produced by the impact of Ionian rationalism on Orphic mysticism, we may say that the work of Herakleitos represents the impact of Pythagoreanism on Ionian rationalism. He speaks with contempt of Pythagoras and of the popular cults of Dionysus; yet, unlike his predecessors of Miletos, he is deeply concerned with the welfare of the soul, and he seeks in the structure of the universe a guide to the conduct of life. His outlook was, however, aristocratic and exclusive. He had a body of disciples, the Herakleiteioi, but without any programme of social or political reform, and they had no influence comparable with that of the Pythagorean brotherhoods. In this respect he anticipates the individualism of Sokrates, Demokritos, and Epicurus.

He wrote a book, which he deposited in the temple of the Ephesian Artemis. From it there survive about 130 fragments, mostly short and disconnected, but sufficient to give us a general idea of the form and content of his teaching. It has been shown in Chapter VI that his prose style is hieratic and liturgical, in keeping with his position as a member of the royal family, which held a hereditary priesthood of Demeter Eleusinia (p. 135); and it was suggested that his book consisted of a discourse presented in the manner of the Orphic *hieroi lógoi* and the *legómena* of the Eleusinian Mysteries (p. 132). This suggestion is confirmed by an examination of the introductory paragraphs, which have survived more or less intact:

It is wise to hearken, not to me, but to the Word, and to agree that all things are one.

Of this Word, which is for ever, men have no more understanding on first hearing than before they have heard it. Though all things come to pass according to this Word, men seem to be without experience when they experience such words and facts as I expound, dividing everything according to its nature and showing how it is. The rest of mankind know not what they do when they are awake, just as they forget what they do when they are asleep.

They are like the deaf, having listened without understanding. The proverb testifies of them that they are present, yet absent.

Eyes and ears are bad witnesses for men, if they have barbarian souls.[4]

[4] *Ib.* B 1, 34, 107.

The meaning of *lógos*, translated as 'the Word', will be discussed presently. Here it carries the idea of a mystical discourse (*hieros lógos*). Men are divided into three categories: those who have heard and understood the Word, like Herakleitos himself; those who have heard it for the first time but not yet understood it; and those who have not heard it.[5] Those who have heard and understood belong to the second grade of initiation, known as *epopteía*; those who have heard but not yet understood belong to the first grade (*mýesis*), the newly initiated; and those who have not heard are the uninitiated (*amýetoi*). That this was the writer's intention is clear from the following considerations.

First, the special sense of *epopteía*, with reference to the second grade of the Mysteries, was so familiar that in later Greek literature, from Plato onwards, we find the second or more advanced stage of almost any study or pursuit constantly described as though it were the second grade in the progress of the initiate.[6] Secondly, the word *asýnetos*,[7] applied here to those who are 'without understanding' of the Word, was commonly employed of those who were 'without understanding' of the mystical secrets, that is, the uninitiated. Thirdly, barbarians were excluded from the Mysteries on the ground that their speech was unintelligible (*asýnetos*). The meaning of the last sentence, therefore, is that those who are without understanding of the Word can place no reliance on the evidence of the senses. Finally, as Cornford observed, the phrase 'without experience of such words' recurs in a passage of the *Frogs*, where Aristophanes parodies the official proclamation issued annually at Athens before the celebration of the Eleusinian Mysteries. The words of Aristophanes are as follows:

Let him hold his peace and stand aside from our company, whoever is without experience of such words or is not pure in heart.[8]

It is not necessary to suppose that Herakleitos was alluding

[5] Cf. Pascal *Pensées* 6: 'There are but three classes of men: those who have found God and serve him; those who busily seek him but find him not; and those who pass their lives neither seeking nor finding.'

[6] Lobeck 127–31; Thomson AO 2. 204, WC 10.

[7] Lobeck 15–190; Thomson AO 2. 111–12.

[8] Ar. *Ra.* 354–5; Cornford PS 113.

specifically to the Athenian formula, because there is evidence
that a similar procedure was followed in the Orphic Mysteries.
Thus, one of the *hieroi lógoi* begins with the words, 'I will sing
to those who understand', and the hymn to Dionysus in the
Bacchants of Euripides opens as follows:

Who is there? who approaches? Let him go hence, let him leave us, and let
all lips be at rest, hushed in silence! We shall now praise Dionysus in accord
with long custom.

Blessed are they that lead pure lives and have learnt by God's grace
mysteries, sanctified, made clean, joined in a holy band which roams on the
hills with fleet foot, filled with the breath of Bacchus.[9]

Thus, Herakleitos presented his account of the universe in the
form of a mystical discourse based on the hieratic traditions
which formed part of his family heritage; and in this he was
following the example of the Pythagoreans, who organised
themselves in mystical brotherhoods, similar to the Orphic.
Like them, he was concerned not merely with the world of
nature external to man, but also with man as part of nature.
At the same time he rejected their dualism and reaffirmed
in a new form, consciously elaborated, the monism of the
Milesian school.

3. The Lógos

The principal senses covered by the word *lógos*, as used by
Herakleitos, are three: discourse, reason, ratio. It may be
defined as the correct exposition of the true understanding of the
universal law which governs nature, including god and man. It
is not a historical law, or law of evolution; on the contrary, it
is timeless, just as the world in which it operates is eternal,
though subject to perpetual change. Nor is it a natural law in
the sense of excluding the supernatural or divine; rather, it is
itself identified with the divine, inasmuch as it is an immaterial
abstraction representing all that is general and absolute in the
universe as opposed to all that is particular and relative. It is in
this sense that 'all things are one'. Things are many in the
sense that each thing is what it is and not something else: but
this identity of a thing with itself is transitory and relative,
because everything is always in process of being transformed

[9] Orph. fr. 334. E. *Ba.* 68–77.

into its opposite. The only thing that is permanent and absolute and therefore divine—'immortal and imperishable', like
Anaximander's unlimited—is this conflict of opposites, or
rather the law which underlies it, the law of perpetual change.

Such being the truth, it is of necessity hard to discover. Not
that it is transcendental; on the contrary, it pertains to a
material reality perceptible to the senses. 'The things that can
be seen, heard and learnt are what I prize the most.'[10] The five
senses and the faculty of reason exist in all men: 'Thought is
common to all.'[11] Hence it is to be apprehended by reason
through observation of the external world. It is *not* to be apprehended, as the Pythagoreans assert, through dreams, which are
not a true reflection of the external world: 'The waking have
one common world, but those that sleep turn aside each into a
world of his own.'[12] To reject the evidence of the senses is 'to
act and speak like men asleep'.[13] Such men 'disagree with that
with which they are most intimate'.[14] Hence, 'we must follow
the common; yet, though my Word is common, the many live
as though they had a wisdom of their own'.[15] That is because
they follow false teachers. 'Hesiod is most men's teacher; they
are sure he knew many things; yet he did not know that day and
night are one.'[16] Much knowledge is not enough. 'The learning
of many things does not teach understanding, or it would have
taught Hesiod and Pythagoras.'[17] Pythagoras, who 'practised
inquiry beyond all other men', laid claim to a wisdom
which was mere 'erudition and deception'.[18] So with all the
rest: 'Homer should be turned out of the lists, and Archilochos
too.'[19] These false teachers thrive on human folly: 'The
fool is fluttered at every word.'[20] The wise man 'evades
recognition through disbelief', and 'dogs bark at those they do
not know'.[21]

Wherein have these false teachers erred? Not simply in the
accumulation of knowledge. That is desirable and necessary:
'Men who love wisdom must acquire knowledge of many
things.'[22] But they have been content with superficial observations and unverified conjectures: 'We must not make random

[10] Orph. fr. 334. E. *Ba.* 55.   [11] Heraclit. B 113.   [12] *Ib.* 89.
[13] *Ib.* 73.   [14] *Ib.* 72.   [15] *Ib.* 2.   [16] *Ib.* 57.   [17] *Ib.* 40.
[18] *Ib.* 129.   [19] *Ib.* 42.   [20] *Ib.* 87.   [21] *Ib.* 97.   [22] *Ib.* 35.

guesses about the greatest matters.'[23] The seeker after truth must take infinite pains: 'Those who seek gold dig up much earth and find a little.'[24] He must make careful observations, so that he may penetrate into the essence of things. 'The many take no heed of such things as come their way, nor do they mark them when taught, though they think they do';[25] and consequently they fail to perceive the truth, which does not lie on the surface of things: 'Nature loves to hide herself.'[26] Hence the truth is different from what it seems to be: 'If you do not expect the unexpected, you will not find it; it is baffling and hard to discover.'[27] From this it follows that it cannot be expounded in language that is immediately intelligible, but only indirectly and enigmatically, like the Delphic Oracle: 'The Lord to whom belongs the Oracle of Delphi neither speaks nor hides, but signifies.'[28] It is for this reason that men cannot expect to understand the truth when they hear it for the first time, just as the newly initiated are at first overcome with fear and wonder at what they see and hear. Only after taking to heart what has been revealed to them and pondering over it many times will they begin to understand it.

In what, then, does wisdom consist? 'Wisdom is one thing only, willing and unwilling to be called by the name of Zeus.'[29] It is willing to be called by the name of Zeus (*Zenós*), because it is the principle of life (*zên*); unwilling, because life is death. 'Wisdom is one—to know the purpose with which all things are piloted through all things.'[30] This 'purpose' or governing principle is stated as follows: 'The world, which is the same for all, has not been made by any god or man; it has ever been, is now, and ever shall be ever-living fire, kindled by measures, quenched by measures.'[31]

Thus, the primary substance, according to Herakleitos, is fire, corresponding to the water, unlimited and air of the Milesian school. But his fire is not primary in the sense of being original. His world has no origin. It has existed always. At this point Herakleitos parts company with his predecessors. They had all started from the traditional postulate, derived from mythology and through mythology from society, of a

---

[23] *Ib.* 47.   [24] *Ib.* 22.   [25] *Ib.* 17.   [26] *Ib.* 123.   [27] *Ib.* 18.
[28] *Ib.* 93.   [29] *Ib.* 32.   [30] *Ib.* 41.   [31] *Ib.* 30.

universe which had evolved in time. His universe is timeless and self-regulating. Hence, the fire with which he identifies it is only primary in the sense of symbolising the fundamental law of its existence—the law of perpetual change and the strife of opposites. Such a law is appropriately symbolised by the element which is always visibly in motion and transmutes everything with which it comes in contact. But this is a symbol only; the reality is an abstraction. In Herakleitos, therefore, the primary substance of Milesian cosmology has been divested of its concrete value and become an abstract idea.

The 'measures' by which this universal fire is alternately kindled and quenched constitute a self-regulating cycle of change, which is uniform as a whole but subject to a series of alternating and inexorable fluctuations. The cycle is fire—air—water—earth—water—air—fire: 'Fire lives the death of air, and air lives the death of fire; water lives the death of earth, and earth lives the death of water.'[32] Thus, 'the way up and the way down are the same'.[33] It is this eternal cycle that maintains the world in being. 'In the circumference of a circle the beginning and the end are common.'[34] Every beginning is an end, and every end a beginning; therefore there is no beginning and no end; the world is everlasting.

It is clear, however, that, if the elements were always gaining from one another neither more nor less than they lost to one another, this ever-changing world would remain outwardly the same. But this is not the case. From time to time the fire takes more than it gives, and so is increased to excess; but, since it is fed by the other elements, the increase is followed later by a corresponding diminution, and so with the other elements. 'Fire is want and surfeit.'[35] Thus, each of the elements is constantly encroaching on the next and surrendering to it in turn. There are several of these fluctuations, small and great, which explain the periodicities of nature: day and night, morning and evening; summer and winter, spring and autumn; waking and sleeping, prophesying and dreaming; life and death, childhood and old age. Life, sleep, and death correspond to fire, water, and earth; the sun in the world at large corresponds to the soul in man. Everything that lives dies, and

[32] *Ib.* 76.   [33] *Ib.* 60.   [34] *Ib.* 103.   [35] *Ib.* 65.

everything that dies is born again; man becomes god and god man.[36]

This perpetual strife of opposites, without which the world could not exist, is not an injustice, as Anaximander had said, but justice: 'We must know that war is common to all and strife is justice.'[37] And again: 'Homer was wrong to pray that strife might perish from the earth; for, if his prayer were granted, all things would pass away.'[38] Nothing can exist without its opposite; or rather this conflict of opposites is inherent in the nature of things: 'Couples are wholes and not wholes, agreement disagreement, consonance dissonance.'[39] Similarly, 'it is sickness that makes health pleasant, evil good, hunger plenty, weariness rest'.[40] Hence, although 'men hold some things to be wrong and some things right', the truth is that 'to God all things are fair and good and right', for 'good and evil are one'.[41] This is the 'hidden harmony' of things, which only the wise man understands.

In so far as their material relations are concerned, the elements are equal, but they are arranged in a hierarchy of value, with fire at the top. Just as sleep is superior to death and waking to sleep, so water is superior to earth and fire to water. But, as has been pointed out, this fire is far more than the material process known by that name: it is the living, the intelligent, the divine. The divinity is not to be identified with one of any pair of opposites, as Pythagoras had taught, but on the contrary with the unity of all opposites: 'God is day and night, summer and winter, war and peace, surfeit and hunger.' Thus, the *lógos* may be described, on the one hand, as the rate of exchange between the elements, or more generally as the law of the interpenetration of opposites, and, on the other hand, as the understanding of that law, which is attainable to some degree by man but is perfect only in God.

This conception of the universe as an organic unity of mind and matter presupposes a distinctive mode of reasoning, which is also part of the *lógos*. The logic of Herakleitos may be defined retrospectively as a denial of the rules of formal logic. Historically speaking, it would be more correct to describe the rules

[36] *Ib*. 62, 88.   [37] *Ib*. 80.   [38] *Ib*. A 22.
[39] *Ib*. B 10.   [40] *Ib*. 111.   [41] *Ib*. 102.

of formal logic as a denial of the logic of Herakleitos; and we shall have something to say about ancient logic after we have discussed the work of Parmenides. Here we are merely concerned to note the contrast.

Criticising from the standpoint of modern dialectical materialism the laws of formal logic, Caudwell remarked:

> Logical laws are social. They are approximate rules which must be obeyed if language is to fulfil a social function. But they are in no way true of the nature of reality. . . . It is not true that a thing is either A or not-A. Yesterday it was A; to-day it is not-A. It is not true that a thing cannot both be and not be A. To-day I am alive, some day I will be dead. To-morrow I will or will not be dead. Both alternatives are equally true. The use of the verb 'is' gives a spurious truth to the methodological rules of logic: it implies a universal instant; but this we know from relativity physics to be impossible. There is only a social instant.[42]

All this, except the last sentence, is implied by Herakleitos. 'The sea is the purest and the impurest water.'[43] 'It is the same thing in us that is quick and dead, awake and asleep, young and old.'[44] 'We step and we do not step into the same river; we are and we are not.'[45] Herakleitos knew nothing of relativity physics; yet he denied the possibility of a universal instant. He was able to do this, because such a possibility was alien to primitive thought. In its place he affirmed the principle, implicit in primitive thought but never before stated, of the unity of opposites.

4. Objective Dialectics

Commenting on the fragment referring to 'the ever-living fire' (p. 277), Lenin wrote: 'A very good account of the elements of dialectical materialism.' This brings us back to the question, how was it that Herakleitos was able to come so close to the position of modern dialectical materialism?

The answer is implicit in the following observation of Engels:

> When we reflect on nature, or on the history of mankind, or on our own intellectual activity, the first picture presented to us is of an endless maze of relations and interactions, in which nothing remains what, where and as it was, but everything moves, changes, comes into being and passes out of

[42] Caudwell FSDC 252–3.   [43] Heraclit. B 61.
[44] Ib. 88.   [45] Ib. 49a.

existence. This primitive, naïve, yet intrinsically correct, conception of the world was that of ancient Greek philosophy, and was first clearly formulated by Herakleitos: everything is and also is not, for everything is in flux, is constantly changing, constantly coming into being and passing away. But this conception, correctly as it covers the general character of the picture of phenomena as a whole, is yet inadequate to explain the details of which this total picture is composed; and, so long as we do not understand these, we also have no clear idea of the picture as a whole. In order to understand these details, we must detach them from their natural or historical connections, and examine each one separately, as to its nature, its special causes and effects, etc. This is primarily the task of natural science and historical research— branches of science which the Greeks of the classical period, on very good grounds, relegated to a merely subordinate position, because they had first of all to collect materials for these sciences to work on.[46]

Dialectical materialism is the distinctive outlook of the class-conscious proletariat, as opposed to the metaphysical outlook, materialist or idealist, of the bourgeoisie; and, since it is the historical destiny of the proletariat to abolish exploitation and so put an end to the class struggle, its outlook is characterised by the reunion of theory and practice. In pre-class society theory is so closely united with practice as to be scarcely distinguishable from it, being little more than its passive reflection. Primitive consciousness is practical rather than theoretical, just as primitive knowledge is perceptual rather than rational. Nevertheless, the outlook of pre-class society is intuitively dialectical and materialistic. Motion, change, conflict are accepted as self-evident truths. With the division of society into classes, theory develops, but not in society as a whole, only in the ruling class, and consequently it tends to become divorced from practice, just as the ruling class is divorced from the labour of production.

Like his predecessors of the Milesian school, Herakleitos belonged to the old hieratic aristocracy; like them, he preserved the materialist content of the old tribal traditions, and like them he presented that content in a new form. His work marks an advance on theirs, because, while the content remains essentially unchanged, the form in which it is presented is more elaborate, more theoretical, more abstract. It belongs to a higher level in the development of abstract thought. Now, this

[46] Engels AD 26-7.

development was, as we have seen, rendered possible and determined by the development of commodity production; and in the work of Herakleitos it has been applied with such mastery that its economic basis is almost self-evident. His concept of a self-regulating cycle of perpetual transformations of matter is the ideological reflex of an economy based on commodity production. In his own words, 'all things are exchanged for fire and fire for all things as goods are exchanged for gold and gold for goods'.[47] In his cosmology fire stands to other forms of matter in exactly the same relation as money stands to other commodities: it has been abstracted from them in order to serve as the universal equivalent. Accordingly, if we compare his system with the primitive myth of the separation of heaven and earth, from which it is descended, we see that it represents the socially necessary false consciousness of a society in which the ties of kinship have been replaced by the nexus of commodity exchange.

Further, if Herakleitos excels Pythagoras in his grasp of dialectics, this too must be ascribed to his class· position. As one opposed to democracy, he was quicker to discern its internal contradictions, by which it was destined to be destroyed, and so was enabled to perceive the truth that only conflict, motion, change are absolute. *Alles, was besteht, ist wert, dass es zugrunde geht.*

5. Tragedy

Herakleitos was the first philosopher to propound a comprehensive theory of causality. His law of the interpenetration of opposites has revealed itself under analysis to be a projection on to nature of the forms in which the new relations of production were reflected in the human consciousness. It is a social image. This does not mean that it is lacking in objective truth. On the contrary, all such theories must of necessity contain a certain measure of truth, just because they are social images; for society is part of nature, and the categories in which man acquires knowledge of nature are necessarily social. Indeed, the theory of Herakleitos contains a great truth, which he was able to grasp precisely because his powerful intellect penetrated the

[47] Heraclit. B 90.

traditional world view, inherited from his Ionian predecessors, more deeply with the new social categories.[48] His system, worked out in conscious opposition to Pythagorean dualism, was the *ne plus ultra* of materialist monism. After him Greek philosophy split into two opposed camps, consisting of monist idealism on the one hand and pluralist materialism on the other. This was the final break with the outlook of primitive communism.

In the last chapter a comparison was drawn between Pythagoras and Æschylus. It is possible to draw a similar comparison between Herakleitos and Sophokles. In the evolution of drama Sophokles stands to Æschylus in the same relation as Herakleitos to Pythagoras in the evolution of philosophy. In Sophokles, as in Herakleitos, the centre of interest has shifted from the reconciliation to the conflict. Sophokles brought to maturity the form of drama which we call tragedy. In Aristotle's *Poetics* tragedy is defined as the representation of an action involving a reversal of fortune brought about unintentionally through some error on the part of the protagonist. The reversal is normally catastrophic: it is in Aristotle's words, a 'transformation of the action into its opposite'.[49] It is the dramatic expression of the Heraclitean law of the interpenetration of opposites. It was brought to perfection by Sophokles, and its finest example is his masterpiece, the *King Œdipus*.

Œdipus belonged to the Kadmeioi. Just as their cosmogonical myths were rationalised, so their genealogical myths were humanised—first by the epic poets (Vol. I, pp. 555–6) and later by the dramatists. That is why the Greek myths are so much more attractive to our minds than the Mesopotamian and Egyptian, which are for the most part inhuman.

[48] Caudwell CP 25: 'The greater the genius, the more profoundly he will be penetrated with the qualities of his experience. In science this means the greater the genius, the more penetrative of nature the categories of society will become in his hands. . . . Hence the genius does not escape from the categories of his age, any more than man escapes from time and space, but the measure of his genius consists in the degree to which he fills these categories with content—a degree which may even result in their explosion. This explosion is, however, in turn dependent on a certain ripeness in the categories.'   [49] Arist. *Poet.* 1452a.

Laios and Jocasta were king and queen of Thebes. To the south of Thebes lies Corinth; to the west, the Delphic Oracle of Apollo, on whose temple were inscribed the words, 'Know Thyself'. A son was born to them, Œdipus, of whom it was predicted that he would murder his father and marry his mother. Rather than rear such a child, they gave it to one of their slaves, a shepherd, with instructions to leave it to perish in the hills. The shepherd took pity on it and gave it to another shepherd, a Corinthian, who took it home with him. The king and queen of Corinth, whose slave he was, were childless, so they reared it as their own.

Twenty years later the young Œdipus was taunted with not being the true son of his supposed parents. They tried to reassure him without revealing the truth, but, not to be put off, he went to Delphi and consulted the god. The only reply he got was a reaffirmation of the old prophecy, of which he heard now for the first time, that he was destined to murder his father and marry his mother. Resolving never to set foot in Corinth again, he took the road that led in the opposite direction—the road to Thebes. At this time the Thebans were suffering from the ravages of the Sphinx, a female monster which took a daily toll of human lives till someone could be found to answer the riddle she had set them. Laios was now on his way to Delphi to consult the Oracle about it. He was driving a chariot, and one of his attendants was his slave, the shepherd. Meeting Œdipus, he tried to force him off the track. Œdipus resisted. Laios struck at him with his whip. Œdipus struck back and killed him. He killed the attendants too—all except the shepherd, who took to his heels and brought back to Thebes the panic-stricken story that the king had been murdered on the road to Delphi by a band of robbers.

Œdipus reached Thebes, and the first thing he did was to seek out the Sphinx, whose riddle was this:

> A thing there is whose voice is one,
> Whose feet are four and two and three;
> So mutable a thing is none
> That moves in earth or sky or sea;
> When on most feet this thing doth go,
> Its strength is least, its pace most slow.[50]

[50] Sheppard OTS xvii.

Œdipus guessed the answer: man. He knew himself. And yet he did not know himself, as the sequel was to show.

The grateful people acclaimed him as their deliverer and made him king. At this point the shepherd, who had recognised him but decided to keep the truth to himself, obtained leave from Jocasta to spend the rest of his days in retirement in the hills. The new king married the widowed queen. The years passed, and children were born to them. Then the Thebans were again afflicted, this time with a plague. Determined not to fail them, Œdipus sent a special emissary to consult the Oracle. The reply was that the plague would cease when the murderer of Laios had been expelled. The search for the unknown criminal was led by Œdipus, who pronounced a curse on him.

There was one other besides the shepherd who knew the truth—the blind prophet, Teiresias. He, too, had decided to keep it dark. Questioned by Œdipus, he refused to answer. Œdipus flew into a passion and accused him of disloyalty. Then Teiresias lost his temper too and denounced Œdipus as the murderer. The quarrel was brought to an end by the intervention of Jocasta. In reply to her husband's questions, she told him what she knew of the death of Laios: he had been murdered on the road to Delphi by a band of robbers. The road to Delphi —Œdipus remembered. But a band of robbers—he had been travelling alone. She assured him that the second point could be proved by sending for the sole survivor, the old shepherd in the hills. This Œdipus instructed her to do, in the hope that his evidence would clear him.

At this juncture a messenger arrived from Corinth with the news that the king of that city was dead and that Œdipus had been appointed to succeed him. Œdipus was now at the height of fortune—king of two cities. Jocasta acclaimed the news as proof that the old prophecy was false: his father had died a natural death. Reassured on this point, Œdipus nevertheless insisted that he would never return to Corinth for fear of marrying his mother. Eager to reassure him on this point too, the messenger explained that he was not their true son but a foundling. Meanwhile the old shepherd had arrived. He recognised the messenger from Corinth as the shepherd he had met

long ago in the hills. He did his best to evade the king's
questions, but was forced to answer by threats of torture. The
truth was out at last. Œdipus rushed into the palace and put
out his eyes with a brooch torn from the dead body of his
mother, who had already hanged herself.

> Ah, generations of men!
> I count your life as nothing.
> None that mortal is hath more
> Of happiness than this—
> To seem and not to be, and then, having seemed,
>   to fail.[51]

Since the beginning of the play nothing has changed objectively, but subjectively everything has changed. All that has
happened is that Œdipus has learnt what he is as opposed to
what he seemed to be. He ends life as he began it—as an outcast. The interval was only seeming. And yet, if seeming is
being, this outcast who became a king, this king who became
an outcast, has twice become the opposite of what he was. And
these strange mutations have been brought about against the
intention, yet through the unconscious agency, of all concerned.
The parents exposed the child to save it and them from a life
worse than death. The shepherd rescued it out of pity, so that
it grew up ignorant of its parentage. When doubt was cast on
his parentage, the young man consulted the Oracle; and, when
the Oracle revealed his destiny, he sought to escape from it
along the road to Thebes. He killed his father in self-defence.
When the shepherd recognised him, he said nothing, and so
left him free to marry his mother. When the Oracle demanded
the expulsion of the murderer, Œdipus led the search and
followed up each clue until he was brought face to face with
himself. The prophet would not have denounced him if he had
not denounced the prophet. His charges against Teiresias were
unjustified. His vehemence at this point was the error that
brought about his fall. And yet this error was but the excess of
his greatest quality—his zeal in the service of his people. And,
finally, the old shepherd, summoned to disprove the charge
that he had killed his father, played into the hands of the
Corinthian messenger, who, by seeking to relieve him of the

[51] S. *OT.* 1186–92 tr. Sheppard.

fear of marrying his mother, proved that what he feared to do he had already done. This persistent transmutation of intentions into their opposites is carried on to the catastrophe with the terrifying automatism of a dream.

Who, then, is Œdipus, and who is Apollo, the invisible god who has caught him in his toils? Œdipus is man, the new man, the individual owner of commodity-producing society, cut off from his kin, independent, free, yet caught as by some super-human power, elusive and inescapable, in a 'network of social relations spontaneous in their growth and entirely beyond the control of the actors' (p. 176). Just as the fire of Herakleitos is 'the universal equivalent', so the Sophoclean Apollo is 'the radical leveller' who 'does away with all distinctions',[52] entangling the lonely stranger in abominable relations with his nearest kin.

[52] Marx C 1. 108.

XIV

BEING

1. *The Eleatic School*

ELEA was a colony on the coast of Lucania, founded about
540 B.C. by emigrants from Phokaiai who had fled to the west
after the Persian conquest of Ionia.[1] It lay some thirty miles
south of Poseidonia, which belonged to the Pythagorean confederacy. One of the earliest coins so far discovered in the west
is from Elea.[2] It is an isolated specimen, and does not conform
to the coin types used by the Pythagorean cities, but at least it
suggests that Elea was not behind them in the development of
trade; and Elea, too, was the cradle of a new philosophy.

The founder of the Eleatic school, according to tradition, was
Xenophanes of Kolophon, who had also emigrated to escape
Persian rule. Like Theognis, he was an easy-living nobleman
and an accomplished after-dinner singer. From the fragments
of his songs we learn that he believed in 'one god, the greatest
among gods and men, resembling mortals neither in shape nor
understanding; he sees all over, thinks all over, hears all over,
and sways all things by his intelligence without effort'.[3] It is
doubtful, however, how closely he was connected with Elea and
how strictly he should be regarded as a philosopher, although
his views may well have had an influence on Parmenides, who
was a native of Elea and more probably the real founder of the
school.

Xenophanes was acquainted with the teachings of Pythagoras,
and his own teachings were known to Herakleitos. Parmenides
was born in the last quarter of the sixth century B.C., and so
was a somewhat younger contemporary of Æschylus. He was
active in politics and drew up a code of laws for his native city.
In his early days he was a close friend of a Pythagorean named
Ameinias, and it is very likely that he was himself a member
of the Order; but later he broke away and composed a long

---

[1] Hdt. 1. 167.   [2] Seltman BGC 6, 10.
[3] Xenoph. 23–5.

poem, putting forward his own philosophical views as a direct challenge to Pythagoreanism and all previous systems.

2. *Parmenides and the Mysteries*

The poem opens with an introduction (*prooímion*), modelled on the hymns prefaced to the recitals of epic lays (Vol. I, p. 490):

My horses carried me as far as my heart's desire on the road of the goddess who conducts the man of understanding from city to city. On this road clever horses drew my chariot, maidens leading the way; and the blazing axle sang between the flying wheels, after the daughters of the Sun had left the house of Night and drew the veils from their faces as they sped me towards the light. There stands the gateway of Day and Night, with a lintel above and a stone threshold below, high in the air, and closed by great doors, whose keys are kept by the goddess of Justice. The maidens spoke to her, and at once she unbolted the gates. The doors swung back, opening a broad thoroughfare, through which the maidens led the chariot and horses; and the goddess grasped my right hand and greeted me and said: 'Welcome, young man, brought to my dwelling-place by these immortal charioteers! It is no misfortune, but right and justice that have carried you so far from the beaten paths of men, and you shall learn all things, both the stedfast heart of rounded truth and human fancies, in which there is no true belief.'[4]

All this is taken from the Mysteries. The 'man of understanding' is the initiate, as in Herakleitos (p. 274). The chariot is the mystical chariot of Æschylus, Sophokles, Plato, and many later writers, pagan and Christian.[5] The veils of the daughters of the Sun are those worn by candidates for initiation during the rite of purification.[6] One of the most celebrated features of Eleusinian ritual was the moment when torches were brought in and scattered the darkness in a blaze of light[7]—just like the candles lit at midnight on the modern Greek Easter Saturday.[8] The gates represent the doors of the

[4] Parm. 1, cf. Bowra PP.

[5] A. *Ch.* 790–5=795–9, 939–41, 1020–2=1022–4, S. *El.* 680–763, Pl. *Phdr.* 247a–256e, Plu. *M.* 561a, 593d–e, Clem. *Pr.* 12. 93 P, DS. 3. 937 P, Porph. *Abs.* 1. 30, N. T. *Ep. Hebr.* 12. 1–2; Thomson AA 124–5.

[6] Thomson AA 122, 273.

[7] A. *Ch.* 960=961, S. *OC.* 1048–50, Ar. *Ra.* 154–5, Plu. *M.* 81e, *Anim.* 6. 4, D.C. 1. 387 R, *Philosoph.* Cruice 170, Firm. *Err. Pr. Rel.* 22; Thomson AO 2. 240, 382–3, AA 123.

[8] Sikelianos 3. 209.

inner sanctuary, within which were performed the ceremonies reserved for initiates of the second grade.[9]

This passage should not be treated as an allegory, but rather as a truthful account of a religious experience which had taken the traditional form of mystical initiation. As a Pythagorean, Parmenides had been trained in the duties of a secret society which was at once religious and scientific. It is true that modern treatises on logic have little in common with the literature of divine revelation; but for one who may be regarded as the founder of the science such work can hardly have appeared in any other light. Further, in so far as the poem was designed as a refutation of Pythagoreanism, it must have been intended as a declaration of faith held with the same fervour as the doctrine to which it was opposed.

The remainder of the poem, following the introduction, falls into two parts, the Way of Truth and the Way of Seeming. In the Way of Truth Parmenides gives his own theory of the nature of the universe. One of its most original features is the categorical denial of the evidence of the senses. In the Way of Seeming, which follows, the evidence of the senses is accepted. It is put into the mouth of the same goddess who has expounded the Way of Truth; she admits that it is deceptive, yet assures Parmenides that, when he has heard it, no man's intelligence will ever overtake him. The surviving fragments show that it contained a cosmology of the established type, neither Pythagorean nor Ionian but apparently an invention of Parmenides himself, and yet incompatible in all respects with the theory expounded in the Way of Truth. How is this anomaly to be explained?

The answer given by Simplicius, an Athenian philosopher of the early Byzantine period, is probably on the right lines. In his view, the Way of Truth refers to the intelligible world, the Way of Seeming to the sensible world.[10] It is true, as Burnet pointed out, that this is an anachronism in the sense that Parmenides cannot have distinguished the two worlds in these terms.[11] At the same time, he was

---

[9] Plu. M. 81e, Heliod. 9. 9, Ath. 167f., Themist. Or. 570–1, Walz Rh. Gr. 114; Thomson AO 2. 240, WC 10.

[10] Simpl. Phys. 39. 10.   [11] Burnet EGP 183.

obviously aware that the world of sense perception, whose reality he denied in the Way of Truth, had at least an illusory existence, of which some accounts might be more plausible than others; and in the Way of Seeming he gave what he believed to be the most plausible. This is the interpretation now generally accepted, and it is confirmed by an examination of the surviving fragments from the standpoint of mystical initiation.

According to the Way of Seeming, the universe is composed of two contrary and incompatible substances, light and darkness; and in its centre resides the goddess of Necessity (Ananke), who 'directs the course of all things'. This distinction between light and darkness, introduced at the beginning of the Way of Seeming, must surely be intended to recall the Way of Truth, which opens with the young man's arrival at the gateway of Day and Night. Having entered the gateway, he is welcomed by the goddess of Justice (Dike), in whom we may recognise the goddess of Necessity, but seen now as she really is, and from her he learns that the world is not divided between day and night, light and darkness. That is an illusion of the senses. The truth is, there exists nothing but light, which is only another name for what *is*. Thus, the Way of Seeming may be regarded as a preparation for the Way of Truth. It is the best account of the world of the senses, because it is the best calculated to lead the inquirer to recognise that it is only an illusion and so prepare him for the revelation of the truth. It is a stage in the progress of the mystic.

3. *The One*

We turn to the Way of Truth, in which Parmenides put forward his own theory, framed in opposition to all his predecessors. He was undoubtedly conversant with the work of the Milesian school, and probably also with that of Herakleitos; but, since he had himself been an adherent of Pythagoreanism, the school which dominated the Greek-speaking Italy of his time, we shall not be surprised to find that the teaching of Pythagoras is his main target of attack. This is indeed rendered virtually certain by an allusion at the beginning of the Way of

Seeming, where, introducing the principles of light and darkness, he says:

> They have decided to name two forms, one of which should not be named, and that is where they have gone astray.[12]

This is clearly a denial of Pythagorean dualism. According to Parmenides, opposites are mutually exclusive. If there is light, there can be no darkness; if good, no evil; if being, no not-being. Thereby he becomes involved in a contradiction; for from this postulate it should follow that, if there is truth, there can be no falsehood. He endeavours to meet this difficulty by identifying falsehood with not-being. The Way of Seeming is false, and therefore it does not really exist. It is already clear that in Parmenides, for the first time in the history of western thought, we have to deal with a *metaphysical* conception of being, contradicting the *dialectical* conception of becoming, which had prevailed hitherto without question.

Accordingly, he opens his Way of Truth by affirming the postulate that *it is*, and denying its contrary that *it is not*:

> Come, I will tell you, and take heed of my words: there are only two ways of enquiry to be conceived of. The one, that *it is*, and that it cannot *not be*, is the way of persuasion, for truth is its companion. The other, that *it is not*, and that it must needs *not be*, is, I say, a path utterly undiscoverable; for you cannot know or speak of that which *is not*; it is impossible. . . . It is the same thing that can be thought of and that can be.[13]

This passage shows that Parmenides had not grasped the distinction, attributed to him by Simplicius, between the sensible and the intelligible. He is still under the influence of the primitive notion that things which have no names do not exist (p. 142).

The object of this attack on not-being is to refute the doctrine that *it is and it is not*:

> This is the first way of enquiry from which I hold you back. The second is one which men imagine for themselves, two-faced in their ignorance; for helplessness guides their straying thoughts, and they are swept along in amazement, deaf and blind, an undiscerning multitude, holding that it is and it is not the same and not the same, and that all things turn back in their tracks. . . . It shall never be proved that the things which are not are; so keep your thoughts from this way of enquiry, and be not constrained by

[12] Parm. 8. 53–4.   [13] *Ib.* 4.

force of habit to cast along this path an aimless eye or ringing ear or tongue; but judge by reason, when you have heard it from me, the much-contested proof.[14]

In the 'undiscerning multitude' we recognise the disorderly crowd of the uninitiated, to which there are many allusions in mystical literature.[15] This second way of inquiry is that of Herakleitos, who believed in the interpenetration of opposites, and of Pythagoras, who believed in the fusion of opposites in the mean, and indeed of all his predecessors, all of whom believed that things come into being and pass away, accepting the evidence of the senses. According to Parmenides, the truth cannot be apprehended by the senses—the 'aimless eye and ringing ear and tongue'—but only by 'reason' (*lógos*), that is, 'pure reason'. In these words he establishes his claim to be the first philosopher of 'pure reason', the first metaphysician.

There remains the Way of Truth:

> One path only is left to tell of, that *it is*. There are many signs that what *is* is unborn and imperishable; for it is uniform, motionless, endless. It was not, neither shall be, for it *is*, all together, now, one, continuous.[16]

These attributes of the One are then elaborated.

First, it is timeless. It has neither past nor future but exists wholly in the present; therefore it is subject to neither birth nor death, neither beginning nor end:

> What birth will you seek for it? how and whence could it have grown? I shall not permit you to say or think that it grew out of nothing, for it cannot be said or thought of anything that it is not.[17]

It is probable that this argument is directed against the Pythagoreans, who believed that the world was formed by the Limit drawing in the Unlimited from the surrounding void. According to Parmenides, there can be no void. There is no such thing as empty space: for empty space *is not*. He goes on to argue that, even if it could have arisen out of nothing, it would still be impossible to explain why it should have arisen at one time rather than another; and, further, if it had arisen

[14] *Ib.* 6–7.
[15] Orph. fr. 233, Hom. *H.* 2. 256–7, Ps. Pyth. *Aur. Carm.* 55, Plu. *Anim.* 6. 3, cf. Parm. 1. 3.
[16] Parm. 8. 1–6.   [17] *Ib.* 8. 7–9.

out of something, we should have to believe in the existence of something else in addition to what *is*:

And, if it did begin out of nothing, what need could have made it grow sooner or later? Thus, it must either be altogether or not be at all. Nor will the force of belief suffer to arise out of what is not something else besides what is. Hence Justice does not relax her fetters and suffer anything to come into being or to perish, but holds it fast; and our judgment on the matter lies in this question, is it, or is it not? Our judgment is, then, of necessity, to dismiss the one way as nameless and inconceivable (for it is not true), and to hold that the other way *is* and is true. How could that which is be hereafter? how could it come into being? If it came into being, it is not, nor is it, if it is yet to be.[18]

Secondly, it is indivisible:

Nor is it divisible, because it is all alike, with no more of it here than there to prevent it from holding together, nor less of it: it is all full of what is. Hence it is all continuous; being touches being.[19]

Thirdly, it is motionless:

It is immovable in the confines of great fetters, without beginning or ceasing, because coming into being and perishing have been cast out by true belief and driven far away. It is the same, resting in the same place, lying by itself, and so remaining constant; for powerful Necessity holds it in the bonds of the limit that constrains it on either side.[20]

It is motionless and unchanging because it is one, and, being one, it is limited. In other words, the fundamental error of the Pythagoreans was to postulate the many as the opposite of the one and the unlimited as the opposite of the limit. In each case the opposite is excluded. Further, being limited, it must be spatially finite; for, if it were infinite, it would be unlimited. It is spherical; for the sphere resembles the circle in that, although limited, it has no beginning and no end (p. 163):

Since, then, it has a furthest limit, it is complete on every side, like a round spherical mass poised equally from the centre outwards in all directions; for it cannot be greater or smaller in one direction or another.[21]

The Way of Truth ends with a recapitulation of the argument:

To think of a thing and the thing that is thought of are the same; for you will not find thought without that which is, in which the thought is named.

[18] Parm. 8. 9–21.
[20] *Ib.* 8. 25–31.
[19] *Ib.* 8. 22–4.
[21] *Ib.* 8. 42–5.

There is not, and never shall be, anything besides what is, because Moira has bound it to be whole and immovable. Therefore all those things which mortals have laid down, believing them to be true, such as coming into being and perishing, being and not being, changing place and colour, are empty names.[22]

Our next task must be to analyse the preconceptions which underlie this remarkable conclusion.

4. *The Second Isaiah*

First of all let us consider an analogy which is not really so remote as it may seem.

The foundation of Elea in the far west was a consequence of the fall of Sardeis, which was captured by Cyrus, king of the Medes and Persians, in 546 B.C. Leaving the conquest of Ionia to his general, Harpagos, Cyrus turned east, and seven years later he entered Babylon. There he was welcomed by the exiled Jews, who had never ceased to pray for their restoration, and in 538 B.C. they made the journey across the desert, over forty thousand of them, back to their native land. Never in their history had the future seemed so bright; yet once more their hopes were disappointed. It was not merely that they were received with suspicion by their neighbours, the Edomites, Moabites, and Samaritans, so that unexpected difficulties were encountered in the rebuilding of Jerusalem; but they soon found themselves divided once more by class antagonisms, whose development was now accelerated by the introduction of the coinage. There arose a new merchant class, which maintained itself, on the one hand, by taking full advantage of the commercial opportunities open to it under Persian rule, and, on the other, by organising the common people in a theocratic community controlled by priests of a new type, who used their great intellectual gifts to remould the old tribal traditions into a system of beliefs predominantly abstract and metaphysical. The new conception of Jehovah has been thus described:

The old idea of group unity becomes that of universal solidarity. Jehovah is represented as the sole creator, the only and eternal God. . . . He is omniscient, incomparable, and all-powerful over nature and man. He is absolutely holy and righteous.[23]

[22] *Ib.* 8. 34. 41.   [23] S. A. Cook in CAH 3. 489.

This conception may be illustrated from some well-known passages of the Second Isaiah:

> Hast thou not known, hast thou not heard? The everlasting God, the Lord, the Creator of the ends of the earth, fainteth not, neither is weary; there is no searching of his understanding.[24]

In this he resembles the 'one god' of Xenophanes, who 'sways all things by his intelligence without effort' (p. 288).

> All flesh is grass, and all the goodliness thereof is as the flower of the field: the grass withereth, the flower fadeth, because the breath of the Lord bloweth upon it: surely the people is grass. The grass withereth, the flower fadeth; but the word of our God shall stand for ever.[25]

That is to say, the material world is transitory and relative; only God is permanent and absolute.

> Remember this, and show yourselves men; bring it again to mind, O ye transgressors. Remember the former things of old; for I am God, and there is none else; I am God, and there is none like me; declaring the end from the beginning, and from ancient times things that are not yet done.[26]

Men forget the past, but in God past, present, future merge together.

> But we are all become as one that is unclean, and all our righteousnesses are as a polluted garment; and we do all fade as a leaf; and our iniquities, like the wind, take us away.[27]

Moral values are relative, no less than the material world itself; and, being relative, they are constantly changing into their opposites. In the real world everything is involved in the flux of perpetual change:

> Every valley shall be exalted, and every mountain and hill shall be made low; and the crooked shall be made straight, and the rough places plain; and the glory of the Lord shall be revealed, and all flesh shall see it together; for the mouth of the Lord hath spoken it.[28]

What, then, is this God? The answer has been given by Frankfort:

> The God of the Hebrews is pure being, unqualified, ineffable. He is *holy*. This means that he is *sui generis*. It does not mean that he is taboo, or that he is power. It means that all values are ultimately attributes of God alone. Hence all concrete phenomena are devaluated.[29]

[24] Isaiah 40. 28.   [25] *Ib*. 40. 6–8.   [26] *Ib*. 46. 8–10.
[27] *Ib*. 64. 6.   [28] *Ib*. 40. 4–5.   [29] Frankfort BP 241–2.

Thus, notwithstanding all the differences in the cultural traditions of the two peoples, we may recognise in Jehovah the
Hebrew counterpart of the Parmenidean One. Both are abstract
conceptions of pure being created by stripping the material
world of everything concrete and qualitative; both, therefore,
are products of the new mode of thinking brought into being
by the social relations arising out of a monetary economy. It
is necessary to add, however, one qualification. While it is true
that in the Second Isaiah all flesh is grass and only the word of
our God shall stand for ever, that word includes the destiny of
His chosen people; and to this extent Jehovah is still a tribal
god, embodying the popular aspirations voiced by Amos (pp.
100-1):

> The poor and needy seek water and there is none, and their tongue faileth
> for thirst; I, the Lord, will answer them, I the God of Israel will not forsake
> them. I will open rivers on the bare heights, and fountains in the midst of the
> valleys; I will make the wilderness a pool of water, and the dry land springs
> of water.[30]

In this he may be contrasted with the much more sophisticated
figure of the Sophoclean Apollo, who carries out his subversive
operations without regard to right or wrong, seizing with
deadly accuracy on his victim's best intentions.

5. Parmenides and Herakleitos

Next, we must consider more closely the relationship in
which Parmenides stood to Herakleitos. Which of them was
the earlier? In the preceding pages it has been assumed that the
floruit of Herakleitos is to be placed in the closing years of the
sixth century B.C., when Ionia was under Persian rule. This is
the tradition preserved by Diogenes, and it is supported by the
letters he is supposed to have written to King Dareios. These
letters are forgeries, but that does not invalidate their evidence
on this point; for their author, who shows himself to be well
acquainted with his subject, was naturally concerned to make
them conform with the known facts. Further support is forthcoming from Parmenides himself, who condemns the vulgar
notion that 'it is and it is not the same and not the same'

[30] Isaiah 41. 17-8.

(p. 292). It is true that this notion is implicit in the very idea of *becoming*, which had been taken for granted by ordinary people, and also by the Milesian philosophers; but Herakleitos was the first to state it in this challenging form, which brings out the contradiction inherent in it; and therefore it is natural to suppose that Parmenides was referring to him.

Against this, there is a tradition, preserved by Eusebios, which puts the *floruit* of Herakleitos some fifty years later, making him a contemporary of Zenon, who was a pupil of Parmenides. This date has been accepted by some authorities, who quote in support of it the following passage from Plato:

> In our part of the world the Eleatic set, who hark back to Xenophanes or even earlier, unfold their tale on the assumption that what we call 'all things' are only one thing. Later, certain Muses in Ionia and Sicily perceived that safety lay rather in combining both accounts and saying that the real is both many and one, and is held together by enmity and friendship.[31]

The 'Muses in Ionia and Sicily' are Herakleitos and Empedokles respectively; of that there is no question. Parmenides, however, is not mentioned; only Xenophanes. There is nothing in this passage to show that Parmenides preceded Herakleitos. The statement of Eusebios is therefore to be rejected.

I have dwelt on this point, because the later date has recently been reaffirmed by Szabó in an otherwise excellent article on early Greek dialectics. Szabó maintains that the development of thought from Parmenides to Herakleitos reveals the following sequence. First, we have the popular belief that reality is many (thesis); this was controverted by Parmenides, who held that reality is one (antithesis); and this in turn was controverted by Herakleitos, who held that reality is both one and many (synthesis). A pretty formula, but it does not fit the facts; for, apart from the chronological evidence, it takes no account of Pythagoras, who held that reality is two. Moreover, it rests, as it seems to me, on an incorrect assessment of the place of Herakleitos in the evolution of Greek thought.

Since the standpoint of Herakleitos is so close to that of dialectical materialism, we are tempted to infer that his work

[31] Euseb. 81. 1–3, Pl. *Soph.* 242d; Reinhardt 155–6, 221–3.

marks the culmination of early Greek philosophy; and there is a certain sense in which this is true. We must, however, take care not to be misled by the modern analogy. We must remember that the general trend of ancient philosophy was from materialism to idealism, whereas modern philosophy has moved in the opposite direction—from idealism to materialism. There is thus a certain affinity between Herakleitos and Hegel. Each of them stands at a turning-point. But, whereas Hegelian dialectics represents that which is new and developing, the dialectics of Herakleitos represents that which is old and dying away. This distinction is vital. In Herakleitos the dialectics of primitive thought, which had been formulated for the first time by the Milesian school, received, under the impact of Pythagoreanism, which marked a further stage in the development of abstract thinking, a stage leading to idealism, its full and final expression. Yet, for this very reason, the dialectical materialism of Herakleitos is already pregnant with its opposite. As we have observed, his ever-changing yet everlasting fire is an abstraction; and the very regularity of the changes to which it is subject invites the objection that really there is no need to postulate any change at all. This step was taken by Parmenides. In denying the reality of change, he did no more than draw out the implication inherent in his predecessor's theory of perpetual change by carrying still further the process of abstraction and substituting for the fire of Herakleitos his own absolute One. Thus, we may say that the transition from Herakleitos to Parmenides marks the passage from quantity to quality in the evolution of idealism. It is his work, therefore, rather than that of Herakleitos, which signalises the emergence of what was new and developing in ancient thought—the moment at which the ideological fetters of primitive society were finally swept away.

6. Ideology and Money

We are now at the end of our survey of early Greek philosophy, from Thales to Parmenides. What is its underlying tendency, and how is that tendency to be related to the development of the society that produced it? Our answer to these questions may be stated provisionally as follows.

Aristotle wrote:

> Most of the earliest philosophers regarded as beginnings of things only those in material form. That from which all things that are derive their being, that out of which they first come into being, and into which they finally pass away, its substance persisting despite changes of conditions—this they call the beginning or principle of things, and hence they consider that it neither comes into being nor perishes, since its nature, being such as has been described, is always preserved.[32]

Aristotle is here summarising their views in his own words, which they would scarcely have recognised; yet what he says is essentially true. As we pass from Thales to Anaximander and Anaximenes, from the Milesians to Pythagoras and Herakleitos and finally to Parmenides, we find the concept of matter becoming progressively less qualitative and concrete, until Parmenides confronts us with a pure abstraction, timeless and absolute. The Parmenidean One represents the earliest attempt to formulate the idea of 'substance'—an idea which was developed by Plato and Aristotle, but only brought to maturity in modern times by bourgeois philosophers. What was the origin of this conception?

Remembering that the society in which these philosophers lived and worked was characterised by the rapid growth of a monetary economy, let us turn to Marx's analysis of commodities:

> If then we leave out of consideration the use-values of commodities, they have only one property left, that of being products of labour. But even the product of labour itself has undergone a change in our hands. If we make abstraction from its use-value, we make abstraction at the same time from the material elements and shapes that make the product a use-value; we see in it no longer a table, a house, yarn, or any other useful thing. Its existence as a material thing is put out of sight. Neither can it any longer be regarded as the product of the labour of the joiner, the mason, the spinner, or any other definite kind of productive labour. Along with the useful qualities of the products themselves, we put out of sight both the useful character of the various kinds of labour embodied in them and the concrete forms of that labour; there is nothing left but what is common to them all; all are reduced to one and the same sort of labour, human labour in the abstract.
>
> When they assume this money shape, commodities strip off every trace of their natural use-value and of the particular kind of labour to which they owe their creation, in order to transform themselves into the uniform, socially recognised incarnation of homogeneous human labour.[33]

[32] Arist. *Met*. 983b. 6.   [33] Marx C 1. 4–5, 82–3.

In *Capital* Marx gave the first scientific analysis of those mysterious things called commodities. A commodity is a material object, but it only becomes a commodity by virtue of its social relation to other commodities. Its existence *qua* commodity is a purely abstract reality. It is at the same time, as we have seen, the hall-mark of civilisation, which we have defined as the stage at which commodity production 'comes to its full growth'. Hence, civilised thought has been dominated from the earliest times down to the present day by what Marx called the fetishism of commodities, that is, the 'false consciousness' generated by the social relations of commodity production. In early Greek philosophy we see this 'false consciousness' gradually emerging and imposing on the world categories of thought derived from commodity production, as though these categories belonged, not to society, but to nature. The Parmenidean One, together with the later idea of 'substance', may therefore be described as a reflex or projection of the substance of exchange value.

In order to establish this conclusion, it would be necessary to discuss systematically some fundamental problems of modern as well as ancient philosophy; and that cannot be attempted here. That is why I have described it as provisional. Nevertheless, enough has, I think, been said to indicate that the money form of value is a factor of cardinal importance for the whole history of philosophy.

MATERIALISM AND IDEALISM

1. *Philosophy and Science*

WITH Parmenides we leave behind the realm of primitive thought and enter a new phase in Greek philosophy, which, apart from some general considerations, lies beyond the scope of the present volume. Philosophy, as he left it, contained certain crudities—fragments of the chrysalis out of which it had emerged; but these were quickly brushed away, and in the work of his successors it took flight into the realm of 'pure reason', where it has sustained itself down to our own day. During its history it has assimilated knowledge from science and made contributions to science, but the union has never been stable, and to-day the gulf is so wide that, as we remarked in the first chapter, most bourgeois philosophers, while claiming to be specialists in the study of thought, continue their disputations without regard to what scientists have learnt about the actual mechanism of the human brain.

In primitive society there was no such gulf, for the simple reason that philosophy and science did not exist. Primitive consciousness was practical and concrete, not theoretical and abstract. The development of theoretical and abstract reasoning was dependent on the division between mental and manual labour, and that in turn on the division of society into classes; and even after these conditions had been created, it was retarded for a long time by the survival in distorted forms of primitive modes of thought, which served to disguise the realities of class exploitation. This is not to say, of course, that technical discoveries were not made, which from a purely practical point of view might be described as scientific achievements; on the contrary, the technical achievements of the early Sumerians and Egyptians were immense. In this respect they have far more to their credit than the Greeks, who may be said to have built on the foundations which their predecessors had laid. Indeed, that is precisely the relation between them. With the important exception of the coinage, the technical basis of ancient society was created, for the most part, in Mesopotamia and Egypt; what the Greeks did was to reorganise, on the basis of a monetary economy, the political and ideological superstructure. It is in Greece, therefore, that we find the beginnings of philosophy and science, united in the form of natural philosophy. And yet they had scarcely appeared when they began to part company. The scientific achievements of the Greeks belong mainly to the Hellenistic age. The most notable development of the preceding period was in medicine, in which important advances were made as early as the sixth century B.C. This calls for a brief discussion here, because it illustrates the nature of the conflict between science and philosophy.

Herodotus says that the Greeks differed from other peoples in being 'cleverer and freer from silly nonsense'.[1] This sweeping statement cannot be accepted without reserve, but it is true of medicine. In Mesopotamia and Egypt the art of healing the sick never emancipated itself from magic. In Mesopotamia especially the patient was commonly believed to be possessed by an evil spirit, and therefore the treatment applied to him was magical rather than medical. In Greece, too, certain diseases, especially 'the sacred disease', that is, epilepsy, were popularly attributed to possession and treated accordingly; but in the Hippocratic treatise on the subject, which dates probably from the latter years of the fifth century, this superstitious attitude is held up to ridicule:

This is a treatise on the sacred disease. It seems to me to be no more sacred or divine than any other. It has a natural cause, and people only regard it as divine because of its peculiar character, which arouses wonder. . . . But, if it is to be regarded as divine just because it is wonderful, there must be many sacred diseases, because, as I shall show, there are others no less wonderful which nobody regards as sacred. . . . My own belief is that a sacred character was first attributed to this disease by men who made pretensions to exceptional piety and superior knowledge, like the magicians, purifiers, charlatans and quacks of our own day.[2]

In Greece, as elsewhere, medicine had developed out of magico-religious practices and beliefs, particularly athletics and divination. Public festivals, derived from the clan feast, were a universal feature of social life in the Greek city-states; and in

[1] Hdt. 1. 60. 3.   [2] Hp. *Morb. Sacr.* 1–2.

them an important function fell to the athlete, whose training included a controlled diet, and to the sacrificial priest, who inspected the entrails of the victim with a view to predicting the future. Nowhere else in the ancient world do we find so much attention to questions of diet, the recording of symptoms, and the compilation of case-histories. On this basis the Greek physicians established, in general terms, some fundamental truths. Thus it was known to Alkmaion of Kroton (p. 249) that the seat of consciousness is the brain, and that man differs from the animals in that his consciousness is not only sensory but conceptual. This he expressed by saying that 'man differs from the other animals in that he alone understands, whereas the others feel but do not understand'.[3] Taken in conjunction with the idea, already a commonplace in his time, that man is distinguished from the animals by the faculty of reason or speech (*lógos*), this may be regarded as a genuine contribution to scientific knowledge.

After Alkmaion, the centre of medical studies shifted from Kroton to Kos, the birthplace of Hippokrates. The Hippocratic school must have owed a great deal to the Crotonian, because its literature reveals many signs of Pythagorean influence, which must presumably have been transmitted to it through the work of Alkmaion. In fact, it was probably a continuation of the same tradition. The best evidence for this is to be found in the treatise *Airs Waters and Places*, which is believed to have been written by Hippokrates himself.

This, for all its crudities, may fairly be described as a treatise in social medicine. It begins as follows:

The man who wishes to make a proper study of medicine should proceed thus. First, he should consider the seasons of the year and the effects of each; for they differ greatly both in themselves and in the transitions from one to the next. Secondly, he should consider the hot and cold winds, first those that are universal and then those peculiar to each country. He should also consider the different influences of waters, which differ from one another in weight and taste. Then, on arrival at a city which he has not visited before, he should examine its situation in relation to the prevailing winds and the rising sun. Each aspect—northern, southern, eastern, western—has a different influence. In addition to all this, he must consider how they are off for water, whether they drink soft marshy water or hard water from high or rocky

[3] Alcmaeo B 1a.

ground, or whether it is brackish and rough; and so with the soil, whether bare and waterless or wooded and watered, low-lying and stuffy or high and cool; and also the mode of life which the inhabitants find congenial, whether they are lazy, drinking heavily and eating more than one full meal a day, or fond of exercise and athletic, eating well but drinking little.[4]

The conception of the physician's task put forward in this treatise was a product of the age of colonisation. In the course of innumerable seafaring expeditions the Greeks had learnt from experience that to establish a colony overseas with any prospect of success was a formidable undertaking, which involved careful planning, not merely determining the number of settlers, selecting them, and preparing for their departure, but also surveying the territory to be settled, fixing the site of the new city, and dividing the arable into the requisite number of lots, with due regard to the lie of the land, the accessibility of water, the climate, and other environmental factors. Operations of this kind were being carried out throughout the seventh and sixth centuries B.C., largely from Ionia, and directed mainly to the coasts of southern Italy and eastern Sicily. It was in these conditions that Greek medicine took on its scientific character; and in such circumstances it is easy to understand why the oldest medical school belonged to one of the main colonial areas.

Thus, Greek medicine was a product of the same social movement as Greek philosophy; yet already in the fifth century B.C. we find them in conflict. The treatise on *Ancient Medicine*, which probably goes back to the time of Hippokrates, if not to Hippokrates himself, was written to protect medical theory, as established by the observation and experience of organised practitioners, from the unwelcome attentions of the philosophers, who were concerned mainly to demonstrate the truth of their preconceived dogmas and only incidentally to cure the patient:

Those who in setting out to speak or write on medicine proceed from a postulate of their own, such as the hot, cold, wet, dry, or whatever it is they fancy, and thereby reduce the basic cause of disease and death to the same for all cases, making it depend on one or two postulates, are not only obviously mistaken in their account of the facts, but their mistake is particularly culpable because it concerns a craft to which people have recourse on the most serious occasions, holding in special esteem its skilled practitioners.

[4] Hp. *Aer.* 1.

There are good and bad practitioners, and this would not be the case, if there was no such craft, the subject of observation and discovery. Then everyone would be equally ignorant and inexperienced in it, and the treatment of the sick would be entirely a matter of chance. In fact, however, there is just as much variety of skill in the theory and practice of medicine as there is in any other craft; and consequently it does not stand in need of any empty postulates, as do such obscure and difficult studies as astronomy and geology, in which one must proceed from postulates. Whatever account may be given of such matters, it cannot be proved to be true or false; for there is no test that can be applied to it. . . .[5]

I am at a loss to understand how those who make the craft dependent on postulates, instead of following the traditional method, apply their assumptions to the treatment of the patients. So far as I am aware, they have not discovered an absolute hot or cold or dry or moist, which partakes of no other form. They have, I imagine, at their disposal the same foods and drinks as the rest of us, but at the same time they attribute to them the properties of being hot, cold, dry or moist; because obviously it would be futile to instruct a patient to take 'the hot': he would at once ask 'What?' Hence they are bound to have recourse to one of these known substances, or else talk nonsense. . . .[6]

Some philosophers and physicians assert that in order to understand medicine it is necessary to know what man is. This is a question for philosophy, for those who, like Empedokles, have written about man, his nature, origin and structure. My own opinion is that what physicians and philosophers have written on this subject has no more to do with medicine than it has with painting; and further I consider that the only source from which a true understanding of these matters can be acquired is medicine, and then only when medicine has been properly understood—without that it is impossible—an exact knowledge, I mean, of what man is and the causes of his evolution and so on.[7]

The writings of these medical practitioners are animated by a spirit at once scientific and humane, which gives them a unique place in ancient literature; and yet, although they put up a determined fight against the philosophers, they not only failed to advance their science but steadily lost ground. It is important to understand why.

This controversy was not a straight fight between science and ideology, between 'open-minded observation' and 'a priori premises'. On the contrary, like all branches of science in all epochs of class society, Greek medicine contained within itself an ideological element consisting of social preconceptions identical with those which shaped the course of Greek philosophy.

[5] Hp. VM. 1.   [6] Ib. 15.   [7] Ib. 20.

The growth of scientific medicine was limited first and foremost by the low level of the productive forces. In the absence of all but the crudest instruments, even the keenest observation was inadequate to accumulate a thorough knowledge of anatomy or to do more in tending the sick than assist the course of nature. This deficiency, however, was inherent in the structure of ancient society, which rested on slave labour; and it was this, more than anything else, that hampered the advance of medicine.

One does not need to read far in the Hippocratic writers to realise that the treatment which they prescribe is such as could only have been followed by people who could afford to be ill. In this they are at one with Plato:

'When a carpenter is ill,' said Sokrates, 'he asks the doctor for a quick remedy—an emetic, purge, cautery, or the knife—that is all. If he is told to diet or wrap up his head and keep warm, he replies that he has no time to be ill, that there is no good going on living just to nurse his disease if he can't get on with his work. So he says good-bye to the doctor and returns to work, and either gets over it and lives and carries on with his livelihood, or else dies and is put out of his misery that way.'

'I understand,' said Glaukon 'and of course that is the proper use of medicine for a man in his walk of life.'[8]

The result was not merely to give free rein to the spread of infectious diseases, which recognise no class distinction—for that one might quote modern parallels—but to degrade the physician himself. He too was a craftsman, and that in a society in which craftsmanship as such was falling into contempt as an occupation which no citizen should undertake. It is true that the medical practitioner seems to have survived this stigma more successfully than other manual workers, no doubt because his work brought him into intimate relations with even the wealthiest of his fellow-citizens; nevertheless Aristotle informs us that in his time there were three types of physician—the manual worker, the superintendent, and the educated amateur.[9] The outcome has been thus described by W. H. S. Jones:

The transcendent genius of Plato, strong in that very power of persuasion the use of which he so much deprecated, won the day. The philosophic fervour which longed with passionate desire for unchanging reality, that felt a lofty contempt for the material world with its ever-shifting phenomena,

8 Pl. *Rp.* 406; Farrington HHAG 35-6.   9 Arist. *Pol.* 1282a.

that aspired to rise to a heavenly region where changeless Ideas might be apprehended by pure intelligence purged from every bodily taint, was more than a match for the humble researches of men who wished to relieve human suffering by a patient study of those very phenomena that Plato held of no account.[10]

There was, however, one philosopher who drew on the Hippocratic tradition. Aristotle, founder of the biological sciences, was the son of a physician, a member of the Asklepiadai (Vol. I, p. 333).

2. The Atomic Theory

After Parmenides the basic question of philosophy—the issue of materialism versus idealism—was brought to a head. This did not happen all at once. The issue on which his immediate successors concentrated their attention was the problem of motion. If the reality of the perceptual world was to be re-established, it was necessary to find a cause of motion. Hitherto it had been assumed that motion was a property of matter; but from now on there was a growing tendency to make the contrary assumption, that matter is inert in itself and only moves under the impact of some external force, such as the Love and Strife of Empedokles, the Mind of Anaxagoras, and Aristotle's First Mover. The new assumption reflects the principal contradiction in the new stage of Greek society—the antagonism between freeman and slave. According to Aristotle the principle of subordination is a universal law of nature. As the slave is to his master, so the wife is to her husband, body to soul, matter to mind, the universe to God. His First Mover is an ideological expression of the ownership of the homogeneous slave labour embodied in ancient commodity production.

Empedokles of Akragas was a leading democrat and at the same time a prophet and miracle-worker who claimed to be a god incarnate.[11] His religious teaching is hardly distinguishable from Orphism, and he seems also to have had some connection with the Pythagorean Order.[12] He made a special study of medicine; yet, although he must have been acquainted with the work of the Crotonian school, he did not carry it forward but, on the contrary, retreated from the stand taken by Alkmaion.

[10] W.H.S. Jones 1. 8.   [11] Emped. B 112 Diels.
[12] Tim. 81, Suid. s.v., Ath. 5e.

Whereas Alkmaion had distinguished between thought and sensation, and identified the organ of thought as the brain, Empedokles drew no such distinction and believed that man thinks with his blood.[13] It was his views in particular that the Hippocratic writers had in mind when they protested at the intrusion of philosophical preconceptions into their craft. According to him, the universe is not indivisible and motionless, as Parmenides had maintained, but is composed of four 'roots'—earth, air, fire, and water—which are constantly moving in and out of one another and so effect changes in its structure. They are kept in motion by the two opposed forces of Love and Strife, being drawn together by Love and driven apart by Strife. As we learn from Aristotle, he failed to explain whether these two forces were substances like the four elements, or, if not, what.[14] In fact, they are figures drawn from the world of mythology. Like many primitive ideas, they contain the germ of a scientific truth, but the form in which they are conceived is still mythical.

Anaxagoras of Klazomenai settled at Athens, where he enjoyed for many years the patronage of Perikles. About 450 B.C. Perikles's opponents charged him with irreligion, on the ground that he believed the sun to be a molten mass of metal. He was forced to leave Athens, and settled at Lampsakos, a colony of Miletos. There he spent the rest of his life, and after his death a memorial dedicated to Mind and Truth was set up in his honour in the market-place.[15] In his system the number of elements, or 'seeds' as he calls them, is infinite, and each of them contains more or less of all the opposites—the hot and cold, the wet and dry, and so on—so that 'even snow is black' and 'there is a portion of everything in everything'.[16] To this general law there is one exception. One of the seeds, the finest and lightest of them all, is unmixed; and it is this element, called Mind, which by penetrating the others sets them all in motion, mixing them up and sifting them out, and by means of these combinations and separations bringing about what men mistakenly describe as the process of coming into being and passing away.[17] This was the Ionian answer to Parmenides.

[13] Emped. B 105.   [14] Arist. *Met.* 1075b. 3.   [15] Arist. *Rhet.* 1398b. 15.
[16] Anax. B 6, 11, A 97 Diels.   [17] Anax. B 17.

Anaxagoras agrees with Herakleitos in believing that all things consist of a unity of opposites and that one of the elements is superior to the rest; but he differs from him in postulating a cause of motion and from both him and the Milesians in denying an original unity. Like Empedokles, he is a pluralist.

These systems were both designed to maintain the reality of the perceptual world without falling into the pitfalls of Eleatic logic. In the meantime, however, the Eleatics were defending the standpoint of Parmenides. Zenon of Elea contended with a dialectical skill fully equal to his master's that, so far from improving matters, the pluralists had involved themselves in an endless series of logical contradictions. His arguments will be considered presently. The Parmenidean theory was re-affirmed, with certain modifications, by another member of the same school, Melissos of Samos, who argued:

> If things were many, they would have to be of the same kind as I say the one is. If there is earth and water, air and iron, gold and fire, if one thing is living and another dead, if things are black and white and all that people say they are: if all this is so, and if we see and hear aright, then each one of these things must be as we have decided; it cannot be changed or altered, but must be just as it is. Now, we declare that we do see and hear and understand aright, and yet we believe that the warm becomes cold and the cold warm, that the hard becomes soft and the soft hard, that the living dies and that things are born from what is without life, and that all these things have changed, and that what they are is altogether different from what they were. . . . Now these beliefs do not agree with one another. We have said that things are many and eternal, with forms and strength of their own, and yet we imagine that they are all subject to change, and that they have altered each time we see them. From this it is clear that we do not see aright after all, and that we are wrong in believing that all these things are many. If they were real, they would not change; each would be just what we believed it to be, for there is nothing stronger than true being. If it has changed, what was has passed away, and what was not has come into being. Therefore, if things were many, they would have to be of the same nature as the one.[18]

This argument provided the logical starting-point for the atomic theory, which had already been foreshadowed by Anaxagoras. Taking Melissos at his word, and borrowing the 'seeds' from Anaxagoras, Leukippos of Miletos argued, first, that the universe is composed of an infinite number of particles, each of which has the properties of the Parmenidean One, and,

[18] Meliss. B 8.

secondly, that these particles are constantly combining and separating in the course of their movements in empty space, which he identified with the not-being of Parmenides.[19] These ideas were developed by Demokritos (460–360 B.C.), a wealthy citizen of Abdera in Thrace, who in the encyclopædic range of his philosophical investigations was surpassed only by Aristotle. Postulating an infinite number of atoms, indivisible, indestructible, without weight, falling through the void, colliding and combining to form the world, including ourselves, he elaborated on this basis a deterministic theory of the universe in which every event is the product of necessity (*anánke*). In his system the idea of Ananke has shaken off its mythical associations and become an abstract idea like the modern scientific concept of natural law. And finally Epicurus of Athens (342–268 B.C.), who, like Thucydides, belonged to the Philaidai (p. 205), modified this system to the extent of attributing to the atoms the property of weight, so that they contained in themselves the cause of their own motion, and he also postulated that they possessed, in. addition to the vertical, an oblique motion or swerve from the straight line.[20] In this way necessity (*anánke*) was supplemented by chance (*týche*); the atoms became free.

Epicurus lived in the period of the dissolution of the Greek city-states. He and his disciples renounced their part in a society which had ceased to conform to reason, and preached the self-sufficiency of the individual. Their atomism was the complement of their individualism. The very word *átomon* means both 'atom' and 'individual'. They made the elements of the universe impassive and imperturbable, because, in a society torn by discord, that is what they themselves strove to become. Their renunciation of public life, whereby they hoped to achieve freedom from everything that disturbed their spiritual tranquillity, was an act of free will; and that is why they introduced into the determinism of Demokritos the element of chance.

Ancient Greek atomism has been described by Farrington as 'the culmination in antiquity of the movement of rational speculation on the nature of the universe begun by Thales'.[21] This description is correct. It is true above all of what the

---

[19] Leuc. A 7.   [20] Marx DDEN.   [21] Farrington GS 1. 60.

atomists had to say about the nature of human society. Thus, rejecting Plato's idealist conception of absolute justice, Epicurus wrote:

There never has been an absolute justice, but only a contract established in social intercourse, and differing from place to place and from time to time, for the prevention of mutual wrongdoing. . . . All those elements in what is legally recognised as just possess that character in so far as the necessities of social intercourse prove them to be expedient, whether they are the same for everybody or not; and if a law turns out to be incompatible with the expediencies of social intercourse, it ceases to be just; and, even though the expediency expressed in the law corresponds only for a time with that conception, nevertheless for that time it is just, so long as we do not trouble ourselves with empty phrases but look simply at the facts.[22]

Of human progress he wrote:

We must understand that human nature has been taught much by the sheer force of circumstances, and then, taken over by the reason, these lessons have been elaborated and augmented by fresh discoveries, the rate of progress varying among different peoples and in different periods.[23]

There is nothing like that in Egyptian or Babylonian literature.

The same may be said of atomist cosmology, although here we must make an important reservation. The resemblance of the atomic theory of Demokritos and Epicurus to the atomic theory of modern physics is superficially so striking that we are tempted to regard the work of those philosophers as scientific. This is a mistake. Ancient atomism is not science but ideology. It is, no less than Parmenidean monism and Platonic idealism, an exercise of 'pure reason' reflecting the structure of the society in which it was generated. As I have remarked, it was an ideological expression of the individualism which characterised one section of the ruling class in the period of the dissolution of the city-state. This was indicated long ago by Marx in his thesis on the subject.

The deviation of the atom from the straight line is not an accidental feature in the physics of Epicurus. On the contrary, it expresses a law which penetrates his whole philosophy, but naturally in such a way as to manifest itself in a particular form determined by the sphere in which it is applied. . . . Just as the atom frees itself from its relative existence, the straight line, by setting it aside, by withdrawing from it, so the whole Epicurean philosophy withdraws from the limitative mode of being, wherever the abstract notion of

[22] D.L. 10. 150–2.   [23] Ib. 10. 75.

individuality, autonomy, and the negation of relativity in all its forms find expression in it. Thus, the end of action is abstraction, effacement before pain and everything that may agitate us, imperturbability.[24]

If, in the ancient world, atomism in physics was an ideological reflection of individualism in society, how are we to explain its resemblance to the modern scientific theory? The answer is that the modern theory, like all scientific theories in class society, contains an ideological element which in this case reflects an analogous feature of bourgeois society. The first to draw attention to this important truth was Caudwell:

> We now understand how it is that the Newtonian world presents such a strange likeness to bourgeois society *as the bourgeois envisage it*. It is atomistic. It is composed of individuals who merely proceed on their own right lines doing what the immanent force of each makes necessary. Each particle is spontaneously self-moving. It corresponds to the 'free' bourgeois producer as he imagines himself to be.[25]

At the same time, the modern atomic theory is from the beginning immeasurably superior to the ancient in that, within the framework of these ideological premises, it embodies a vast store of truth tested in practice; and, as it continues to grow, this body of knowledge is constantly bursting the bonds of bourgeois ideology. That is how science advances. But the ancient atomic theory, restricted as it was by the economic basis and intellectual level of slave society, was not capable of developing in this way. It was a purely ideological construct.

The philosophy of Epicurus is the culmination of ancient philosophical materialism. His sense of dialectics, revealed in his conception of the interdependence of necessity and chance, of the relation between man and nature, and of the uneven development of human progress, invites comparison with the intuitive dialectics of Ionian materialism, which culminated in Herakleitos; and to that extent he may be regarded as bringing to maturity the most positive elements in primitive thought. On the other hand, his materialism, like that of Demokritos, is passive rather than active. The Epicureans did not seek to

[24] Marx DDEN 29.
[25] Caudwell CP 48–9. The particle derives its mobility from the divine impulse, just as the individual liberty of the bourgeois is a gift from God.

change the world, but to withdraw from it. Their ethics aimed at the self-negation of the subject. They formed a closed circle of friends, devoted to one another and to the pursuit of happiness in the present life, but cut off from the rest of the world so far as that was possible. Their renunciation of the city-state was a bold repudiation of slave-owning society expressed in the categories of the society which it condemned. It was the negative counterpart of the Stoic affirmation of world brotherhood, which expressed in positive form the tendencies making for the unification of the Mediterranean world.

For these reasons it may be claimed that Aristotle rather than Epicurus stands in the true line of progress; for, although an idealist, he did not turn away from the world, but, on the contrary, examined it in concrete detail with a view to analysing its inner purpose. He denied that matter could move of itself, and ascribed motion to the agency of a First Mover, motionless, immaterial, divine; but this did not prevent him from affirming that matter is in perpetual motion. For him A may be not-B and yet contain the potentiality of becoming B. His system is teleological. It is a reaffirmation of Ionian evolutionism, materialist in content, idealist only in form.

3. Subjective Dialectics

Dialectics, according to Lenin, is 'the study of the contradictions in the nature of objects themselves: it is not only appearances that are shifting, flowing, passing away, but also the essences of things'. In keeping with this definition, dialectics may be regarded from two aspects. First, there is the conflict of opposites which exists objectively in the external world, independent of our consciousness. This is the dialectics of the object—objective dialectics. Secondly, since the human consciousness is a social image of the external world, the contradictions inherent in that world are necessarily reflected in it. To quote again from Lenin: 'Man's ideas are not immovable but in perpetual motion, passing and flowing into each other; only so do they reflect real life.'[26] This is the dialectics of human thought—subjective dialectics.

[26] Lenin PN 181, 187–8.

Reviewing the history of Greek philosophy with this distinction in mind, we see that the work of Parmenides marks a turning-point. His predecessors had been concerned to give a true account of the natural order, including man himself as part of it. The question they had set themselves was one which they had inherited from the beginnings of class society: how has the world come to be what it is? With the consolidation of the class structure of society and the growth of commodity production their answer to this question became progressively more theoretical, abstract, rational; and at the same time the question itself began to change its character: what is the world made of? what is the nature of reality? In this way the conditions were created for the formulation of an entirely new question, marking a new stage in the development of abstract thinking: how do we *know*?

This question was not asked by Parmenides, but arose in consequence of his work. Whereas the Ionian philosophers had assumed that man is part of nature, and therefore subject to her laws, he maintained that nature, as perceived by the senses, is an illusion, because it is contrary to reason. Clearly, this concept of reason does not correspond to anything in the external world of nature. Rather, just as his universe of pure being, stripped of everything qualitative, is a mental reflex of the abstract labour embodied in commodities, so his pure reason, which rejects everything qualitative, is a fetish concept reflecting the money form of value. This theory, far from reflecting the external world, rejects it: it is the negation of the object. And yet it is in practice impossible to reject the world in which we live. Parmenides himself was constrained to recognise this; for, as we have seen, he provided his students with a Way of Seeming for their probationary period, to be discarded later, like Wittgenstein's ladder. The eventual outcome of this line of reasoning was Plato's theory of Ideas, in which the material world was allowed to enjoy a derivative existence as an imperfect image of the ideal. In the meantime important advances were being made in the study of knowledge.

The conclusion of Parmenides, that motion and change cannot exist because they are contrary to reason, was reaffirmed in opposition to the pluralists by his disciple, Zenon of Elea, in a series of paradoxes. The best-known is the following:

Achilles will never overtake the tortoise. He must first reach the point from which the tortoise started out. By that time the tortoise will be some way ahead. He must then cover that distance, but by that time the tortoise will be still further ahead. He is always getting nearer, but he never catches up.[27]

The premiss is that a line consists of an infinite number of points, which, being infinite, cannot be traversed in a finite time. He used similar reasoning to argue that a flying arrow does not move:

The flying arrow is at rest. For, given that everything is at rest when it occupies a space equal to itself, and that what is in flight at a given moment always occupies a space equal to itself, then it cannot move.[28]

Zenon dismissed the concept of motion as an illusion, because it contains a contradiction; for, like his master, he maintained that only what is free from contradictions is real. The truth is, of course, that, just because it contains a contradiction, the concept of motion is a faithful reflection of reality. If we examine motion, not in abstraction, but as we encounter it in reality, we find that it is the mode of existence of matter:

Pure distance is a meaningless conception, because it is unknowable. Distance can only be known by the motion of something between relata, for physical distance involves a physical relation. Such a relation must be motion. In this sense distance is secondary to motion; motion is a prerequisite for spatial relations as such. Motion is therefore existence; the contradiction rooted in it, the inner activity of what constitutes the space and time in it, is the existence of the atom.[29]

So with the concept of infinity:

It is clear that the infinity which has an end but no beginning is neither more nor less infinite than that which has a beginning but no end. . . . The whole fraud would be impossible but for the mathematical usage of working with infinite series. Because in mathematics it is necessary to start from definite, finite terms in order to reach the indefinite, the infinite, all mathematical series, positive or negative, must start from 1, or they cannot be used for calculation. The abstract requirements of a mathematician are, however, very far from being a compulsory law for the world of reality. . . .

[27] Arist. *Phys.* 239b. 14.   [28] *Ib.* 239b. 30.
[29] Caudwell CP 171.

Infinity is a contradiction, and is full of contradictions. From the outset it is a contradiction that an infinity is composed of nothing but finites, and yet this is the case. The finiteness of the material world leads no less to contradictions than its infiniteness, and every attempt to get over these contradictions leads, as we have seen, to new and worse contradictions. It is just *because* infinity is a contradiction that it is an infinite process, unrolling endlessly in time and in space. The removal of the contradiction would be the end of infinity. Hegel saw this correctly, and for that reason treated with well-merited contempt the gentlemen who subtilise over this contradiction.[30]

The Eleatic paradoxes were countered in ancient times by Protagoras of Abdera: 'Man is the measure of all things; of the things that are, that they are; of things that are not, that they are not.'[31] From this we understand, in the first place, that knowledge is a relation between two terms, knower and known, subject and object. Moreover, the object of knowledge is the perceptual world. If we reject the evidence of the senses, there can be no knowledge of anything. Hence the Eleatics knew nothing. That this is what Protagoras meant is clear from his attitude to the gods. The gods are not normally perceptible to the senses, though some men have claimed to have seen or heard them. Are they, or are they not? Protagoras did not know: 'Concerning the gods, I cannot know either that they exist nor that they do not exist, nor what shape they have; for there are many obstacles to knowledge, such as the obscurity of the subject and the brevity of human life.'[32] In the second place, in so far as both man himself and the world around him are subject to change, to that extent all knowledge is necessarily relative. The same thing will appear different to the same person at different times and at the same time to different persons. This, however, is far from being pure relativism. Thanks to our common humanity, including speech, which enables us to exchange our experiences, we have a large measure of common ground. Thus, knowledge is a *social* product.

This was the stage at which the term 'dialectics' was invented. The Greek *dialektiké*, from *dialégomai*, 'converse' or 'discuss', means 'the art of discussion'. The democratic city-state offered unlimited opportunities for discussion in the assembly and the law-courts, and there arose a new type of

[30] Engels AD 61.   [31] Pl. *Tht.* 151e–152a.
[32] Pl. *Rp.* 600c sch.

318   STUDIES IN ANCIENT GREEK SOCIETY   XV

philosopher, the sophist, a professional teacher who imparted
to his pupils a general education with special attention to public
speaking and debate, including the study of grammar. This 'art
of discussion' was invented by Zenon and developed by
Sokrates and Plato. Its best-known products are the Platonic
dialogues. The procedure is that a proposition is stated by one
of the two principals, opposed by the other, and finally either
rejected altogether or else re-stated in a form acceptable to both
parties. Thus the discussion proceeds to its conclusion by the
resolution of contradictions.[33] This is only a summary description of the procedure, but no more is needed, because it is only
mentioned here as preparing the way for the subjective
dialectics of Plato and Aristotle.

Plato agreed with Parmenides that only what is free from
contradictions is knowable, and that, since both motion and
change contain contradictions, therefore the sensible world is
not knowable. In working out this theory he made some
important advances, not in the study of the material world,
but in the study of ideas. Some of the sophists had argued that
man cannot learn anything:

It is not possible for a man to enquire after either what he knows or what
he does not know. He would not enquire after what he knows, because he
knows it already and does not need to enquire; nor would he enquire after
what he does not know, because he does not know what to enquire after.[34]

Here the sophists were applying to the theory of knowledge the
Parmenidean conception of being. Just as being excludes not-
being, so knowledge excludes ignorance and ignorance excludes
knowledge. They excluded learning, the transition from ignorance to knowledge, by the same reasoning as Zenon excluded
motion: it involves a contradiction. Plato's solution of the
problem was as follows. Knowledge is a faculty of the soul,
which is immortal. When it is incarnated in a human body, its
knowledge is overlaid through contact with the body and
temporarily forgotten, but it can be recovered, even in life, by
theoretical study and above all by the pursuit of philosophy,
which is designed to free the soul from the contamination of the
body. Thus learning is the recovery of knowledge that has been

[33] Burnet GP 134–5, 164.   [34] Pl. Mno 80e.

lost. Hence, a man who is learning something may be said both to know it and not to know it. Thus the idea of learning contains a contradiction; it is a unity of opposites.

Another problem of the same kind was, how can a man communicate his experiences to others? You have your experience and I have mine; your experience cannot be mine. If we are capable of sharing our experiences with one another, it must be that they are not only different for each of us, but also somehow the same. Each concrete case differs from every other. A_1 is A_1 and not A_2; A_2 is A_2 and not A_3; and so on. And yet they are all A. They are the same and not the same. This is the unity of the particular and the universal, which was recognised by Plato, though in an idealist form. He believed that different houses exist only in so far as they all participate in the idea 'house', which exists absolutely, because, being abstract and universal, it is exempt from motion and change. Thus, in place of the Parmenidean world of being, opposed to the world of seeming, which does not really exist at all, Plato postulated two worlds, the world of ideas, corresponding to the Parmenidean world of being, and the sensible world, which differs from the Parmenidean world of seeming in that it is not pure illusion but exists as an imperfect copy of the ideal. This misconception of the relation between ideas and things was corrected by Aristotle, who wrote, in opposition to Plato: 'We should not suppose that "house" exists apart from certain houses.'[35] In other words, the universal does not exist apart from the particulars. And this is the position of dialectical materialism, as explained by Lenin:

The opposites (the particular as opposed to the general) are identical: the particular exists only in the connection that leads to the general. The general exists only in and through the particular. Every particular is (in one way or another) a general. Every general is (a fragment or a side or the essence of) a particular. Every general comprises only approximately all the particular objects. Every particular enters into the general incompletely, etc. etc. Every particular is connected by thousands of transitions with other *kinds* of particulars (things, phenomena, processes), etc. *Here already* we have the elements, the germs, the concepts, of *necessity*, of objective connection in nature, etc. Here already we have the contingent and the necessary, the appearance and the essence; for when we say 'John is a man', 'Fido is a dog', 'This is a leaf

[35] Arist. *Met.* 3. 4. 8–9.

of a tree' etc., we *disregard* a number of characteristics as *contingent*; we separate the essence from the appearance, and put one in opposition to the other.[36]

How far Plato had advanced towards this comprehension of the unity of opposites represented by the general and the particular, may be judged from the following passage:

—Dividing according to kinds, not taking the same form for a different one or a different form for the same—is not that the business of the art of dialectics? Yes.—And the man who can do that discerns clearly *one* form everywhere extended throughout many, where each one lies apart, and *many* forms, different from one another, embraced from without by one form. . . .[37]

On this passage Taylor remarked:

Logic is here, for the first time in literature, contemplated as an autonomous science with the task of ascertaining the supreme principles of affirmative and negative propositions (the combinations and 'separations').[38]

It is an open question, which need not be discussed here, whether the invention of formal logic should be credited to Plato or to his pupil Aristotle.[39] All that concerns us for our present purpose is to note that it was something new.

Thus, the dialectical nature of being, which had been recognised by Herakleitos in the material world, and then denied by Parmenides, was reasserted by Plato, but only in the realm of ideas. And yet his work was an advance; for, whereas Herakleitos had only been able to express his sense of dialectics in the semi-mystical form of the *lógos*, Plato's dialectical method was a systematic procedure of synthesis and analysis. It is not an accident, therefore, that the term 'dialectics' was invented for the study of the ideas in which the external world is reflected rather than for the study of the external world itself.

Again we ask, how had this advance been effected? And, following our general principle, that men's ideas are determined by their relations of production, we look for the answer in the further development of those relations which we have already seen to be decisive in the history of philosophy. The fire of Herakleitos serves in his system as universal equivalent; but how does this universal stand in relation to its particular embodiments, and how do these particulars stand in relation to one

---

[36] Lenin D 83.
[37] Pl. *Soph.* 253c.
[38] Taylor 387.
[39] Cornford PTK 264.

another? To these questions Herakleitos could only give the general answer, that they are transformed into one another 'as goods are exchanged for gold and gold for goods'. Plato's answer is much subtler, and in order to understand it historically we must turn once again to Marx's analysis of commodities:

Let us look at the matter a little closer. To the owner of a commodity, every other commodity is, in regard to his own, a particular equivalent, and consequently his own commodity is the universal equivalent for all the others. But since this applies to every owner, there is in fact no commodity acting as universal equivalent, and the relative value of commodities possesses no general form under which they can be equated as values and have the magnitude of their values compared. So far, therefore, they do not confront each other as commodities, but only as products or use-values. In their difficulties our commodity-owners think like Faust: *Im Anfang war die Tat*. They therefore acted and transacted before they thought. Instinctively they conform to the laws imposed by the nature of commodities. They cannot bring their commodities into relation as values, and therefore as commodities, except by comparing them with some other commodity as universal equivalent. That we saw from the analysis of a commodity. But a particular commodity cannot become the universal equivalent except by a social act. The social action, therefore, of all other commodities sets apart the particular commodity in which they all represent their values. Thereby the bodily form of this commodity becomes, by this social process, the specific function of the commodity thus excluded by the rest. Thus it becomes—money.[40]

The power of abstraction embodied in the Platonic theory of Ideas and in Aristotelian logic was an intellectual product of the social relations created by the abstract process of commodity exchange. In saying that the rules of logic are socially determined, we do not impugn their objective truth, but, on the contrary, affirm it; for truth is a social product.

4. *The Battle of Gods and Giants*

The basic question of philosophy, wrote Engels, 'is that concerning the relation of thinking to being':

The answers which the philosophers gave to this question split them into two great camps. Those who asserted the primacy of spirit to nature and therefore in the last instance assumed world creation in one form or another (and among philosophers—Hegel, for example—this creation often becomes even more intricate and impossible than in Christianity) comprised the camp of idealism. The others, who regarded nature as primary, belong to the various schools of materialism.[41]

[40] Marx C 1. 58.   [41] Engels LF 31.

The Ionians and the Atomists were materialists. The position of Pythagoras and Parmenides was transitional. The Pythagoreans taught that matter is composed of numbers; the Eleatics denied that it was perceptible to the senses. The first to assert the primacy of spirit to matter was Plato, the founder of philosophical idealism.

Idealism has nothing in common with science. It is a product of 'ideology' in the special sense of that term used by Marx to denote the metaphysical mystification of reality which is a constantly recurring phenomenon in the thought of class society. His study of this subject, which has a direct bearing on the Platonic theory of ideas, deserves to be read in full; but here it must suffice to give the bare outline of his argument.

Ideology begins by removing from beings and things the reality that belongs to them and confers it on abstractions; then it sets out from these abstractions to reconstruct the world, producing from them concrete being and reality. Take the idea of *fruit*. If we reduce all the different fruits—apples, pears, peaches, and so on—to the concept *fruit*, and if we consider that this concept, existing apart from them, constitutes their essence, we have then established this concept as the 'substance' of the fruit; and consequently we may describe apples or pears as nothing more than modes of existence of that substance. Accordingly, the essence of the apple or pear does not reside in its concrete being but in the abstract entity or concept which we have substituted for it. Real, particular fruits are only apparent fruits; their essence is the substance, the fruit considered in itself. If fruit, which exists really only as substance, appears under different forms—a fact which contradicts the unity of substance—the reason is that fruit considered as a concept is not an abstract idea but a living entity, of which the varieties of fruit are only different manifestations. Real fruits, such as apples and pears, are only different degrees of development of the concept *fruit*. And so, having reduced real objects to a substance, we recreate them by treating them as incarnations of that substance. The idea of a thing has become its reality, and the thing itself has become an idea.[42]

[42] Marx HF 228.

Plato worked out his theory of Ideas in conscious opposition to materialism. In the *Sophist* he wrote:

—Why, this dispute about reality is a sort of Battle of Gods and Giants. One side drags everything down to earth, literally laying hands on rocks and trees, arguing that only what can be felt and touched is real, defining reality as body, and if anyone says that something without body is real, they treat him with contempt and will not listen to another word.

—Yes, they are clever fellows: I've met a lot of them.

—So their opponents in the heights of the unseen defend their position with great skill, maintaining forcibly that true existence consists in certain intelligible, incorporeal forms, describing the so-called truth of the others as a mere flowing sort of becoming, not reality at all, and smashing their so-called bodies to pieces. On this issue there is a terrific battle always going on.[43]

The Giants are the materialists. The Gods are, of course, the idealists, including Plato. In the *Laws* he shows that his interest in the controversy is not merely theoretical:

—They say that earth, air, fire and water all exist by nature or chance, not by art, and that by means of these wholly inanimate substances there have come into being the secondary bodies—the earth, sun, moon and stars. Set in motion by their individual properties and mutual affinities, such as hot and cold, wet and dry, hard and soft, and all the other combinations formed by necessity from the chance admixture of opposites—in this way heaven has been created and everything that is in it, together with all the animals and plants, and the seasons too are of the same origin—not by means of mind or God or art but, as I said, by nature and chance. Art arose after these and out of them, mortal in origin, producing certain toys which do not really partake of truth but consist of related images, such as those produced by painting, music and the accompanying arts, while the arts which do have some serious purpose, co-operate actively with nature, such as medicine, agriculture and gymnastics; and so does politics too to some extent, but it is mostly art; and so with legislation—it is entirely art, not nature, and its assumptions are not true.

—How do you mean?

—The Gods, my friend, according to these people, have no existence in nature but only in art, being a product of laws, which differ from place to place according to the conventions of the lawgivers; and natural goodness is different from what is good by law; and there is no such thing as natural justice; they are constantly discussing it and changing it; and, since it is a matter of art and law and not of nature, whatever changes they make in it from time to time are valid for the moment. This is what our young people hear from professional poets and private persons, who assert that might is

[43] Pl. *Soph.* 246a–c.

right; and the result is, they fall into sin, believing that the gods are not what the law bids them imagine them to be, and into civil strife, being induced to live according to nature, that is, by exercising actual dominion over others instead of living in legal subjection to them.

—What a dreadful story, and what an outrage to the public and private morals of the young![44]

And how did Plato propose to rescue the young from this godless materialism? By bringing them up on lies. In the same dialogue, having demonstrated to his own satisfaction that the unjust life—that is, the life which does not conform to his legislative programme—is actually less agreeable than the just life, he is at pains to dispel any doubt that may linger in the reader's mind about the efficacy of this conclusion:

—And even if this were not true, as our argument has proved it to be, could a legislator, who was any good at all and prepared to tell the young a beneficial falsehood, have invented a falsehood more profitable than this, more likely to persuade them of their own free will to do always what was right?

—The truth is a fine thing and lasting; yet it is not easy to make people believe it.

—Well, was it hard to make people believe the myth of Kadmos, and hundreds of others equally incredible?

Which do you mean?

—The sowing of the dragon's teeth and the appearance of the warriors. What an instructive example that is to the legislator of his power to win the hearts of the young! It shows that all he needs to do is to find out what belief is most beneficial to the state and then use all the resources at his command to ensure that throughout their lives, in speech, story and song, the people all sing to the same tune.[45]

Scrap the achievements of Ionian natural philosophy and back to mythology—that was Plato's final remedy for the evils of the dying city-state. No wonder he admired the petrified culture of the Egyptians, still living in the mentality of the Bronze Age:

—What are the legal provisions for such matters in Egypt?

—Most remarkable. They recognised long ago the principle we are discussing, that the young must be habituated to the use of beautiful designs and melodies. They have established their norms and displayed them in the temples, and no artist is permitted in any of the arts to make any innovation or introduce any new forms in place of the traditional ones. You will find

[44] Pl. *Lg.* 889b–90b.   [45] *Ib.* 663d–4a.

that the works of art produced there to-day are made in the same style, neither better nor worse, as those which were made ten thousand years ago —without any exaggeration, ten thousand years ago.

—Very remarkable.

Rather, I should say, extremely politic and statesmanlike. You will find weaknesses there too, but what I have said about music is true and important, because it shows that it *is* possible for a legislator to establish melodies based on natural truth with full confidence in the result. True, it can only be done by a god or a divine being. The Egyptians say that the ancient chants which they have preserved for so long were composed for them by Isis. Hence, I say, if only the right melodies can be discovered, there is no difficulty in establishing them by law, because the craving after novelty is not strong enough to corrupt the officially consecrated music. At any rate, it has not been corrupted in Egypt.

Yes, this evidence seems to establish your point.[46]

Those who denounce communism as immoral would do well to ponder these sayings from the father of philosophical idealism.

Some scholars have sought to extenuate Plato's educational programme on the ground that, when he wrote the *Laws*, he was a disillusioned and embittered old man. This is true enough, but it should not be overlooked that his disillusionment resulted from his failure to realise in practice the very similar ideas which he had already advocated in the *Republic*. A word about the 'noble lie' of the *Republic* is necessary here in order to counter a recent attempt to whitewash it on the principle *Plato veritate amicior*.

Having divided the governing class of his ideal state into two sections, the Rulers, in whom the governing authority is vested, and the Auxiliaries, whose duty it is to see that their decisions are enforced, Plato goes on:

—Well, said I, how can we contrive one of those expedient falsehoods we were speaking of just now, one noble falsehood, which we may persuade the whole community, including the Rulers themselves, if possible, to accept?

—What sort of thing?

—Nothing new; one of those Phœnician stories of what has happened before now in many parts of the world, if the poets are to be believed, and they *are* believed; but it has not happened in our day, and it would be hard to persuade anybody that it could.

—You seem to be hesitating.

—Yes, and with good reason, as you will see when I tell you what it is.

[46] *Ib.* 656d–657b.

—Tell me; don't be afraid.

—Well, I will tell you, though I don't know how to find the heart or the words to do it. I shall try to persuade first of all the Rulers and the soldiers and after them the rest of the community, that all this upbringing and education they have had from us was really nothing but a dream; that really they were beneath the earth all the time, being shaped and nursed and their weapons and the rest of their equipment manufactured for them, until at last the earth their mother released them all complete into the light of day; and therefore they must take thought for their country and defend it against aggressors as their mother and nurse, and treat their fellow-citizens as their earth-born brothers.

—No wonder you were ashamed to tell your falsehood.

—Yes, but wait till you have heard the end of the story. All of you, we shall tell them, are brothers; but, when God was fashioning those of you who are fit to rule, he mixed in some gold, so these are the most valuable; and he put silver in the Auxiliaries, and iron and bronze in the farmers and other craftsmen. Since you are all akin, your children will mostly be like their parents, but occasionally a golden parent may have a silver child or a silver parent a golden child, and so on; and therefore the first and foremost task that God has laid upon the Rulers is, of all their functions as Guardians, to pay the most careful attention to the mixture of metals in the souls of the children, so that, if one of their own children is born with an alloy of iron or bronze, they must not give way to pity but cast it out among the craftsmen and farmers, thus assigning it to the station appropriate to its nature; and conversely, if one of these should produce a child with silver or gold in it, they must promote him to the Guardians or Auxiliaries, according to his value, in the belief that it has been foretold that, if ever the state should fall into the keeping of a bronze or iron guardian, it will be ruined. That is the story. Can you suggest any device by which we can get them to believe it?

—Not the first generation, but perhaps their sons and descendants and eventually their whole posterity.

—Well, even that would help to make them care for one another and for the community. I think I see what you mean.[47]

The only significant difference between this passage and the one already quoted is that, whereas in the *Laws* he condones the use of lies without any apparent scruple, here he still shows a certain hesitancy.

The opening words of this passage are translated by Cornford as follows:

Now, said I, can we devise something in the way of those convenient fictions we spoke of earlier, a single bold flight of invention, which we may induce the community in general, and if possible the Rulers themselves, to accept?[48]

[47] Pl. *Rp.* 414b–415d.   [48] Cornford RP 103.

He attempted to justify this version in a footnote:

This phrase *gennaíon ti hen pseudoménous* is commonly rendered by 'noble lie', a self-contradictory expression no more applicable to Plato's harmless allegory than to a New Testament parable or the Pilgrim's Progress, and liable to suggest that he would countenance the lies, for the most part ignoble, now called propaganda.[49]

It is regrettable that so fine a scholar should have lent his name to this perversion of the Greek. The word *gennaîos* means (1) true-born, high-born, noble; (2) honest, genuine; (3) of good quality, high-grade; (4) whole-hearted, intense, vehement. There is no evidence that it could mean 'on a generous scale', as he asserted, and the phrase *mázas gennaías*, which he cited from another passage of the *Republic* in support of this interpretation, means probably something equivalent to our 'plain bread and butter', just as we say 'good honest beer', *mâza* being the traditional type of the simple diet, as I have shown in my commentary on the *Oresteia*.[50] The expression is certainly self-contradictory, but expressions of this kind are familiar to every Greek student under the name oxymoron (p. 135, n. 14), and the present example is merely a variant of the proverbial *kalòn pseûdos*, a lie which brings an immediate advantage, but is nevertheless unprofitable, because it cannot last.[51] What Plato wants is a falsehood which will be both profitable and lasting. Cornford adduced no evidence to show that *pseûdos* could mean 'allegory', or indeed anything else but 'falsehood'; and in any case this fable cannot be so described. It is of the very nature of an allegory that it does not, as such, require to be believed: it is merely a symbolical illustration of an alleged truth. But Plato admits that it will take several generations before the people can be got to accept this *pseûdos*, which shows that he wants them to accept it, not as an allegory, but as a fact. And he admits himself it is not a fact. It is, therefore, a lie, and noble only to those who share his class prejudices.

In an earlier chapter, after referring to Cornford's claim that the Ionian philosophers 'made the formation of the world a natural and no longer a supernatural event' and that 'this has

[49] *Ib.*
[50] Thomson AO 2. 109–10.
[51] A. *Ag.* 625–6=620–1, S. fr. 59, Theog. 607–9; Thomson AO 2. 73–4.

become the universal premiss of all modern science', it was pointed out that Cornford failed to explain why some of their successors, including Plato, renounced this premiss and reverted to the supernatural. It is now clear what the reason was. As a member of the old nobility who was bitterly opposed to democracy, Plato could see no hope for society except to undo all that had been done by the merchant class and re-establish the rule of the landed aristocracy: in other words, to restore the past in such a way that it will remain henceforth as it was and suffer no further change. His whole philosophy is inspired by this antipathy to change, and hence it is not surprising that he felt such an admiration for the Egyptian priesthood, which had succeeded so well in laying a dead hand on the cultural development of their people. He and his fellow oligarchs would have done the same for Athens. As Caudwell has said:

> Such a culture shores up the past in which they were strong. This ideal past does not bear much resemblance to the real past, for it is carefully arranged so that, unlike the real past, it will not again generate the present. For Plato this past is idealised in his *Republic*, ruled by aristocrats and practising a primitive communism which is the way Plato hopes to undermine the trade by which the rival class has come to power.[52]

Granted that in his theory of Ideas Plato made important contributions to epistemology, and that all his writings (except the *Laws*) are presented with superb literary skill, his philosophy expresses the reactionary outlook of a selfish oligarchy clinging blindly to its privileges at a time when their social and economic basis was crumbling away. It is a philosophy founded on the denial of motion and change and hence of life itself.

5. *The End of Natural Philosophy*

During the fifth century B.C. there grew up in the country immediately to the west of the Strymon a kingdom which resembled in some respects the early military monarchies of the type described in the Homeric poems. The dominant people was the Macedonians, who were closely akin to the Greeks, and, after consolidating their hold over their neighbours, the Illyrian and Thracian tribes, they extended their sway along the

[52] Caudwell IR 47.

whole north coast of the Ægean and began to expand southwards into Greece. In 360 B.C. Philip became their king. Thirty years later his son, Alexander the Great, had made himself master of Greece, Anatolia, and Mesopotamia. The Persian Empire lay at his feet. In 323 B.C. he died of a fever at thirty-three years of age, having extended his empire as far as Upper Egypt in the south and the Indus valley in the east.

In Greece itself, the Macedonians were opposed by the ruling clique in each city, who had a vested interest in maintaining the autonomy of these petty states. They succeeded because their expansionist policy provided the only means whereby the Greek propertied class of money-lending landowners could maintain their wealth and power against the pressure of the poor freemen, who, afflicted by mass unemployment, 'went about as armed rovers, attached to no city, hiring themselves out to any state that needed fighting men, a constant menace to society'.[53] The urgency of the problem and its solution were seen very clearly by Isokrates (436–338 B.C.), who was born eight years before Plato and died only sixteen years before Aristotle. He was a mediocre thinker and a tedious orator, but he was more alert than either of the philosophers to the interests of his class:

> This is the only war preferable to peace, being more like a pilgrimage than a campaign, and beneficial alike to lovers of fighting and lovers of quiet, enabling the former to make fortunes abroad and securing for the latter the enjoyment of what they have.[54]

The military conquests of Alexander the Great were followed by developments in the technique of production more rapid and radical than any the world had seen since the beginning of the Bronze Age. New cities sprang up throughout the Middle East, all the territories of the old Persian Empire being now open to the free circulation of commodities. The movement of economic expansion was not essentially different from that which had radiated from the Ægean in the seventh century B.C., but its scale was much larger; and, since it included Egypt and Mesopotamia, these ancient centres of civilisation were now united for the first time politically and culturally with Greece. The product of this unification was the civilisation called

[53] Bury HG 714.   [54] Isoc. 4. 182.

Hellenistic, in which, although it comprised many different peoples, who continued to use their own languages among themselves, the Greek language was recognised as the international medium for administration, commerce, and culture. It was in this period that science broke loose from the apron-strings of natural philosophy.

As Plato's pupil and Alexander's tutor, the giant figure of Aristotle stands astride the transition from the old era to the new. He was the last of the great philosophers, except Epicurus, and he was the first great scientist. His philosophical studies reveal his gradual but incomplete emancipation from Platonic idealism. His unique claim to greatness is one that his master would have despised. He organised and conducted systematic research into biology, zoology, botany, history, and economics. In his zoological treatises he describes several hundred different species of animals according to the specimens collected and dissected by himself and his fellow-workers. His analysis of the function of money is without parallel in antiquity. It is referred to repeatedly by Marx, who acclaimed him as 'the great thinker who was the first to analyse so many forms, whether of thought, society or nature, and amongst them also the form of value'. As the function of money is vital to the history of philosophy, it is worth while to recall Marx's estimate of his contribution to this subject:

There was, however, an important fact which prevented Aristotle from seeing that to attribute value to commodities is merely a mo · of expressing all labour as equal human labour, and consequently as labour of ̣ qual quality. Greek society was founded upon slavery, and had therefore for its natural basis the inequality of men and of their labour powers. The secret of the expression of value, namely, that all kinds of labour are equal and equivalent because and so far as they are human labour in general, cannot be deciphered until the notion of human equality has already acquired the fixity of a popular prejudice. This, however, is possible only in a society in which the great mass of the produce of labour takes the form of commodities, in which, consequently, the dominant relation between man and man is that of owners of commodities. The brilliancy of Aristotle's genius is shown by this alone, that he discovered in the expression of the value of commodities a relation of equality.[55]

Aristotle founded a school, the Lyceum, which produced, in the two centuries following his death, several scientists

[55] Marx C 1. 29.

comparable with himself and a mass of research covering, in addition to the subjects mentioned, mechanics, mathematics, astronomy, music, and grammar. These men may be regarded as pioneers of experimental science. Only one of them concerns us here, Theophrastos of Lesbos, who succeeded Aristotle as head of the Lyceum. He attacked the basic assumptions of the natural philosophers, idealist and materialist alike. As against the idealists, he reasserted the truth that motion is a property of matter. As against the materialists, he showed that the doctrine of the four elements, as employed by them, could not be correct. He did this by arguing that fire is not a substance at all, like earth or air or water, but a 'form of motion':

The other elements are self-subsistent; they do not require a substratum. Fire does—at least such fire as is perceptible by our senses. . . . Flame is burning smoke. A coal is an earthy solid. It makes no difference whether the fire is in the sky or on the earth. In the first case fire is burning air; in the second case it is either all the other three elements burning or two of them. Speaking generally, fire is always coming into being. It is a form of motion. It perishes as it comes into being. As it leaves its substratum, it perishes itself. That is what those ancients meant who said that fire is always in search of nutriment. They saw that it could not subsist of itself without its material. What is the sense then of calling fire a first principle if it cannot subsist without some material? For, as we have seen, it is not a simple thing, nor can it exist before its substratum and material. One might of course assert that in the outermost sphere there exists a kind of fire which is pure and unmixed heat. If so, it could not burn, and burning is the nature of fire.[56]

This, and other similar conclusions equally well founded, did not of course prevent the philosophers from carrying on their disputations; but, so far as the discovery of truth was concerned, their occupation was gone. They turned their attention increasingly to ethics, by which they understood the knowledge required by a man of leisure, whose material needs were provided by his slaves, to lead a tranquil life devoted to intellectual pursuits, indifferent to the sufferings of all but his personal friends. Even for Epicurus, the study of nature was only a means to this end:

If we were not troubled by the misgivings aroused by celestial phenomena, or the fear that death may mean something to us after all, or neglect of the limits of pains and desires, we should have no need to study nature. . . .

[56] Theoph. *Ign.*, tr. Farrington GS 2. 25–6.

> Given a certain degree of security against our fellow men, we may, with the power to support ourselves and with affluence in its most genuine form, enjoy the security of a quiet life secluded from the multitude.[57]

Whereas the Epicureans studied nature in order to rid themselves of their fears of the supernatural, the Stoics studied her in order that they might discover her underlying law and live their lives in conformity with it:

> Zenon of Kition was the first to designate as the end living in agreement with nature, that is, living according to virtue, for nature leads us to virtue. . . . And this is why the end is living consistently with the nature of the universe and of ourselves, a life in which we refrain from all actions commonly forbidden by the universal law, that is, the right reason pervading all things, which is the same as Zeus, who is the supreme administrator of the world. Herein lies the virtue of the happy man and the smooth course of his life, when all his actions tend to bring his indwelling spirit into harmony with the will of the lord and governor of all.[58]

Whether materialist or idealist, these philosophers had one thing in common—their abstract aloofness from the labour of production.

Two centuries after Alexander had reached the Indus, the impetus which his conquests had given to the world was well-nigh exhausted, and, under Roman rule, the slave-states of the Mediterranean and the Middle East entered into their last period of decline. The causes which brought about the decay of Hellenistic civilisation have been well summarised by Walbank:

> Once slavery has spread from the home to the mine and the workshop, it appears to rule out the development of an advanced industrial technique. For the kind of slaves employed in the big productive processes, such as agriculture or mining, are not capable of operating complicated machinery or advanced methods of natural exploitation, still less of improving them. Hence slavery militates against the development of mechanical power; and at the same time it brings few advantages in the concentration of industry, and therefore offers little opposition to the tendency of production to fly outwards to the periphery of the economic area. Furthermore, when slaves are there as an alternative, the producer has no incentive to economise labour; and the bargaining power of the poor free worker is automatically reduced where the two classes are in competition, as they frequently were in the Hellenistic Age.[59]

[57] D.L. 10. 142–3.   [58] Ib. 7. 87–8.   [59] Walbank 16.

The profits made from the exploitation of slave labour were not, for the most part, reinvested in production, because, being fixed on a slave basis, the mode of production was incapable of expansion. They were simply spent. The ruling class entered on a career of disgusting luxury and extravagance, from which the philosophers turned away politely without protest. They had no more to offer to the masses of the people than had the official religion, with which indeed they became closely identified, with its threadbare puppets and stale Olympian myths.

The hope of the future lay then, as always, with the people, who, in virtue of their status as manual labourers, preserved from primitive society one precious asset, which their sophisticated masters had lost—the capacity to apprehend reality 'as sensuous human activity, as practice'—and together with this an instinctive sense of dialectics drawn from their own experience of the class struggle:

> My soul doth magnify the Lord,
> And my spirit hath rejoiced in God my Saviour.
> For he hath looked upon the lowliness of his handmaiden:
> For behold, from henceforth all generations shall call
>   me blessed.
> For he that is mighty hath magnified me;
> And holy is his name.
> And his mercy is on them that fear him
> Throughout all generations.
> He hath shewed strength with his arm;
> He hath scattered the proud in the imagination of their
>   hearts.
> He hath put down the mighty from their seats,
> And hath exalted the humble and meek.
> The hungry he hath filled with good things,
> And the rich he hath sent empty away.
> He, remembering his mercy, hath holpen his servant
>   Israel,
> As he promised to our forefathers,
> Abraham and his seed for ever.[60]

Christianity started as only one creed among many, and, in the form in which we know it, it is a complex product of many diverse cults—Egyptian, Syrian, Mesopotamian. It began in Palestine as an expression of the Jewish national movement,

[60] Luke I, 46–55.

which, as has been explained in the foregoing pages, was a unique phenomenon in the ancient world, and was now stimulated to renewed activity through contact with Greek political ideas. Thus, as the combined product of Judaism and Hellenism, the two most distinctive cultures of the Mediterranean world, opposed to one another in many ways and hence complementary, Christianity was the proper ideological outcome of the whole course of ancient civilisation. Later, as it was taken over by the ruling class, it absorbed, mainly from Greek philosophy and rhetoric, many ideas originally alien to it; but the primitive dialectics could not be effaced and survives to this day embalmed in the liturgy, pouring scorn on the philosophers who are incapable of grasping a truth so simple and self-evident as the unity of opposites:

Hail, room confining boundless God; hail, door to holy mysteries!

Hail, doubtful rumour of the infidel; hail, undoubted glory of the faithful!

Hail, holy chariot of him who rides the Cherubim; hail, excellent mansion of him who mounts the Seraphim!

Hail, thou who hast brought the opposites together; hail, thou who hast coupled chastity with childbirth!

Hail, thou through whom transgression is redeemed; hail, thou through whom Paradise is opened!

Hail, key to Christ's kingdom; hail, hope of eternal bliss!

Hail, bride unwed!

The whole nature of Angels was amazed at thy great work of incarnation; for they saw their unapproachable God a man approachable to all, living with us and thus addressed by all:

Alleluia!

We see the wordy orators like dumb fishes before thee, Virgin, for they are at a loss to tell how being still a Virgin thou hadst power to bear a child; but we, in wonder at the Mystery, cry faithfully:

Hail, receptacle of God's wisdom; hail, treasury of his providence!

Hail, thou who hast refuted the philosophers; hail thou who hast struck the clever speakers speechless!

Hail, thou who hast confounded the subtle debaters; hail, thou who hast fooled the false myth-makers!

Hail, thou who hast torn the weavings of the Athenians; hail, thou who hast filled the fishermen's nets!

Hail, thou who hast dragged us out of the depths of ignorance; hail, thou who hast illuminated many in knowledge!

Hail, frigate of those who wish to be saved; hail, haven of life's seafarers!

Hail, bride unwed![61]

[61] From the *Akathistos Imnos*: Cantarella 1. 90–1.

In the Middle Ages, when slave society had been superseded by feudalism, some of the schoolmen, experts in ecclesiastical doctrine, raised the question, whether matter could think? Of them Marx and Engels wrote:

> Materialism is the natural son of Great Britain. Already the British school-man, Duns Scotus, asked, 'whether it was impossible for matter to think?' In order to effect this miracle he took refuge in God's omnipotence, *i.e.* he made theology preach materialism.[62]

Thus, in its modern form, as in the ancient, materialism came into being within the bosom of Mother Church.

[62] Marx-Engels HF (SW 1. 395).

XVI

FALSE CONSCIOUSNESS

1. *Theory and Practice*

J. E. RAVEN, in his *Pythagoreans and Eleatics*, gives this estimate of early Greek philosophy:

Perhaps the most remarkable feature of early Greek thought is the extent of its reliance on dogmatic reasoning alone. With a cheerful ignorance of the conditions of scientific knowledge, it seeks nevertheless to expound a theory of the objective world. The evolution of that theory, culminating in the atomism of Leukippos and Demokritos, presents a gradual approximation to the truth; and that approximation, not the least astonishing achievement of the Greek genius, was effected not so much by minute observation of phenomena as by the continual exchange of conflicting and equally arbitrary opinions. Greek thought during the fifth century resembles, therefore, a prolonged symposium; and though we may grant, in the light of later knowledge, that the atomists had the last word, it can hardly be doubted that the most important contribution to the debate is to be found in the conflict, the details of which we have now explored, between the Pythagoreans on the one hand and the Eleatics on the other. It remains only to recapitulate the main points of the dispute, and to see how the modified Pythagoreanism that emerged from it contributed towards, and yet fell far short of, the Platonic doctrine with which it was soon to be fused.[1]

The first comment to be made on these observations is that, granted that in the light of later knowledge the Atomists had the last word, how is it that 'the most important contribution to the debate' is found to lie, not in their work at all, but in the controversy which prepared the way for the Platonic doctrine of Ideas? Raven expands this conclusion at the end of his book:

The Pythagoreans had, by their theory of numbers and harmony, introduced a crude and undeveloped 'science of measurement'; and to this extent Plato was in their debt. They had, however, failed to distinguish the two 'widely different' species that fall under the genus *metretiké*. It was the achievement of Sokrates to turn men's minds towards the 'measuring of things against the mean, the due and morally right'; and it was the achievement of Plato, by his theory of Ideas, finally to distinguish that class of measurement from the other, and to establish it as the mistress of which the other is but the handmaid.[2]

[1] Raven 175.   [2] *Ib.* 187.

Raven reveals here the same confusion as Cornford, whose pupil he was. It is admitted that the Ionian materialists sought 'to expound a theory of the objective world', but then they were ignorant 'of the conditions of scientific knowledge'; it is admitted that the later materialists, in the atomic theory, did approximate to the truth, but they too neglected 'the minute observation of phenomena'; and so, having disqualified the materialists, we are free to award the palm to Plato's theory of Ideas, which has no claim to be considered scientific at all. It is, rather, anti-scientific, being so conceived as to discredit the minute observation of phenomena and hence to deny the possibility of scientific knowledge. And this is the theory to which after paying lip-service to science Raven asks us to give the last word.

The second point inviting comment is his apt designation of early Greek philosophy as a 'prolonged symposium' or debate. This comparison shows up both its positive and its negative aspects. On the one hand, there was at that time no other country in the world where such debates were being held, or could have been held, with the single exception of China. The distinctive character of early Greek philosophy, as compared with Mesopotamian or Egyptian thought, is that it was *not* dogmatic, in the sense of being restricted by a consciously imposed and accepted body of theological doctrine; on the contrary, it was rational, pursued for the most part with the conscious aim of excluding the supernatural. Hence, although it fell short of scientific knowledge, it was an important step towards the development of science. On the other hand, having little foundation in observation and none at all in experiment, it *was* dogmatic in the sense that it proceeded from *a priori* premises accepted as self-evident.

In both these aspects it reflected the structure of society as determined by the development of the productive forces. It was the work of a ruling merchant class based on slave labour. Without the leisure created for them by the workers, the intellectuals of the ruling class would have had no time for symposia. True, a leisured class had existed long before in Mesopotamia and Egypt, but this was a priest-ridden class of landowners preoccupied with the struggle to control those economic forces which eventually brought the merchant class to power. The Bronze Age states of the East had been monarchical and theocratic, whereas the new Greek cities of the Iron Age were almost from the beginning republican—first oligarchical and then democratic. At the same time, as members of a leisured class, these intellectuals had no part in the labour of production, and consequently their theories were divorced from practice. Hence their neglect of observation and experiment, and their 'arbitrary' assumptions. In this connection, however, it should not be overlooked that in the fifth century B.C. something like a science of medicine did begin to emerge, being based on the systematic observation of actual cases; and, as we have seen, the medical writers protested vigorously against the arbitrary assumptions of the philosophers (pp. 305–6). In them we hear for the first time the authentic voice of scientific inquiry.

Above all, however, early Greek philosophy expresses the outlook of a class engaged in the exchange of commodities. This does not mean, of course, that every philosopher was a merchant, although some of them were, and many of them were politicians actively engaged in promoting their class interests. Moreover, we must be careful not to exaggerate the development of ancient commodity production. Restricted as it was by slave labour, it was never strong enough to abolish entirely the old households, based on a self-sufficient natural economy. Hence individual merchants were constantly being absorbed into the landowning class and, in the Hellenistic age, faced with mass revolts of the slaves, the two classes became virtually one. Nevertheless, it was a basic factor in the rise of Greek philosophy. Small in volume though it was, its development was so rapid as to shatter at one blow, so to speak, the primitive tribal ideology, which, owing to their relatively late development, had persisted among the Greeks into the period of the democratic revolution. This explains why, following the invention of the coinage, the spread of money made so deep an impact on Greek life and thought. How, then, does early Greek philosophy reflect the new economic and social relations brought into being by the circulation of money? This question has been constantly before us in the preceding chapters. It is raised again here in order to recapitulate the main thesis of this book.

Primitive society was based on the production of use values. The means of production were communally owned, and both production and consumption were collective. There were only rudimentary divisions of labour, and social relations were simple and direct, being based on kinship. In keeping with these conditions, primitive consciousness was uniformly subjective, concrete, practical. Being only very imperfectly aware of the objectivity of the external world, man was also ignorant of the objective limits to his power to change it. It appeared to him therefore as an assemblage of sensible qualities, as a field for the satisfaction of his desires through the exercise of his will organised in the collective labour of production. And, since his knowledge of it, such as it was, was obtained entirely through production, which alone had enabled him to surpass the purely sensory consciousness of the animals, the categories of his knowledge were of necessity social categories, being determined by the level of development of the productive forces and by the social relations into which he had entered for the purpose of production. Hence, in so far as he was able to think of the external world as something separate from himself, he thought of it as a social order. Nature and society were one. Accordingly, just as his social relations were subject to the collective control of the community, so also the world of nature, as he imagined it, could be controlled by collective action; and, since the human community was composed of totemic kinship groups related by common descent, so also was the community of nature. These rudimentary conceptions of nature found expression, on the one hand, in the form of magic, which served as an illusory technique of production supplementing the deficiencies of the real technique, and, on the other, in the form of myths, which began as nothing more than the oral accompaniment to the magical act, but developed gradually into a rudimentary theory of reality.

With the division of society into classes, which began as a division between the producers and the organisers of production, between manual and mental labour, the conditions were created for immense advances, not only in the technique of production, but also in the organisation of society and in the enrichment of the human consciousness, leading to the emergence of civilisation. At the same time, just as society was divided within itself, so also was the human consciousness. These internal contradictions, kept in constant motion by continuous developments in the forces of production, have been the driving force of history. Without them the polarisation of wealth necessary for the creation of a leisured class, free to devote itself to theoretical pursuits, such as the abstract sciences and philosophy, would have been impossible; yet, with this division between intellectual and manual labour, theory was continually being drawn apart from practice and so losing touch with reality. Without it there could have been no development of abstract thinking, and hence no philosophy or science; with it, the intuitive dialectics of primitive society, springing from the union between theory and practice, was continually being effaced by metaphysical mystifications of the kind described by Marx (p. 322). Such metaphysical views of the world are indeed a reflection of reality; but the reality which they reflect is not simply, as it purports to be, the world of nature; it embodies also the class structure of society as seen by the ruling class, which cannot maintain itself without fostering the illusion that its power is a product, not of history, but of nature. And yet, since the social relations, from which these illusions spring, are constantly changing and developing in response to developments in the productive forces, so all the intellectual products of class society also change and develop, driven forward by their internal contradictions. This is the secret historical logic which, unknown to the debaters, presided over the 'prolonged symposium' of Greek philosophy.

The characteristic feature of class society as opposed to primitive communism is the development of the production of exchange values, that is, of commodity production. The effect of commodity production was to break down the primitive relations, based on the production of use values and regulated by the palpable, personal ties of kinship, and to create a new nexus of relations based on the market, which brings men together simply as individuals, as owners of commodities; and, since the laws governing the market are beyond their understanding and control, the relation between them appears to them as a relation, not between persons, but between things:

Whence, then, arises the enigmatical character of the product of labour, so soon as it assumes the form of commodities? Clearly from this form itself. The equality of all sorts of human labour is expressed objectively by their products all being equally values; the measure of the expenditure of labour-power by the duration of that expenditure, takes the form of the quantity of value of the products of labour; and finally, the mutual relations of the producers, within which the social character of their labour affirms itself, takes the form of a social relation between the products. A commodity is therefore a mysterious thing, simply because in it the social character of men's labour appears to them as an objective character stamped on the product of that labour, because the relation of the producers to the sum total of their own labour is presented to them as a social relation existing not between themselves but between the products of their labour.[3]

Having recognised the significance of commodity production for the history of thought, we have no difficulty in understanding why it was that philosophy, as distinct from mythology, emerged for the first time in Greece and China with the invention of the coinage. In the Bronze Age states of Egypt and Mesopotamia commodity production had never penetrated further than the upper strata of society, which accordingly had preserved, in a modified form, the personal relations and mythical ideology of primitive communism. In Greece and China, however, the old relations and ideas were dissolved and replaced by new relations and ideas, which, being based on money, were abstract. This was the origin of philosophy. In both countries the development of these new relations and ideas was subsequently arrested, but, especially in Greece, only after the concept of 'pure reason', reflecting the relations of a monetary economy, had achieved its classical formulation. In this way, man, the subject, learnt to abstract himself from the external world, the object, and see it for the first time as a natural process determined by its own laws, independent of his will; yet by the same act of abstraction he nursed in himself the illusion that his new categories of thought were endowed with an immanent validity independent of the social and historical conditions which had created them. This is the 'socially necessary false consciousness', which, on the one hand, has provided the epistemological foundation of modern science right down to our own day, and, on the other, has prevented

[3] Marx C 1. 42–3.

philosophers from recognising the limitations which are inherent in their 'autonomy of reason' in virtue of its origin as the ideological reflex of commodity production.

2. *The Illusion of the Epoch*

It is characteristic of the ruling class in each epoch of class society to regard the established social order as a product, not of history, but of nature. This is what Marx and Engels called 'the illusion of the epoch'. It corresponds to the concept of 'socially necessary false consciousness', and it follows from the Marxist principle that 'it is not the consciousness of men that determines their being, but, on the contrary, it is their social being that determines their consciousness'.

Each epoch has introduced a new illusion, determined by the new class relations, the new relations of production. Thus the mode of exploitation characteristic of ancient society was slavery; and slavery was justified by Aristotle on the ground that the slave is naturally inferior to the freeman.[4] The mode of exploitation characteristic of feudal society was serfdom; and serfdom was justified by John of Salisbury on the ground that 'according to the law of the universe all things are not reduced to order equally and immediately, but the lowest through the intermediate and the intermediate through the higher'.[5] The mode of exploitation characteristic of capitalist society is wage labour, the labourer being 'free' to sell his labour power, just like any other commodity, on the open market; and this 'free competition' was justified by Rousseau's *contrat social*, 'which makes naturally independent individuals come in contact and have mutual intercourse'.[6]

These 'illusions' are inevitably reflected in the philosophical and scientific theories of the ruling class. The world of nature and of man is interpreted on the basis of certain assumptions which are accepted without question as absolute truths, although in fact they are historically determined by the position of the given class in the given epoch.

In ancient society freedom was believed to consist in the

---

[4] Arist. *Pol.* 1254b.   [5] John of Salisbury *Polycraticus* 6. 10.
[6] Marx CCPE 266.

conscious domination exercised by the slave-owner over the slave. His domination was socially complete, being limited only by the physical capacities of the slave. This relation gave rise to teleological theories of the universe, which is set in motion and directed by a 'divine master' or 'first mover' without any physical effort on his part but simply by an act of will. There was no conception of natural law. Its place was taken by the idea of *anánke* or 'coercion', which connoted the relation between slave-owner and slave.

In feudal society freedom was still believed to consist in the conscious domination of man by man, that is, of the lord over the serf; but the domination is no longer socially complete, being restricted by the feudal system of 'degrees', which include the serf as a full member of the community. Accordingly, the Aristotelian system, which was accepted as the foundation of medieval theology, was modified at certain points. In particular, the divine master operated within the self-imposed limits of his own appointed 'laws'. This marks the beginning of the concept of natural law.

With the removal of feudal restrictions on 'free competition', the domination of the capitalist over the proletarian became veiled by the relations of commodity exchange; and, stripped of their divine sanction, the universal laws of feudal society became natural laws. It was only in this epoch that science, in the full sense of the word, came into being:

Science is thus conceived for the first time as the field of laws which connect phenomena in a mutually determining way, and are sufficiently explained by exhibiting the structure of that determinism.[7]

Just as the capitalist system expanded and developed by constantly revolutionising its instruments and relations of production, so in this epoch of society we have witnessed the growth of science on a scale without precedent in the history of the world. At the same time, however, since the relations of production are now veiled by the market, the laws of bourgeois science differ from the 'universal laws' of feudal ideology in that they tend to exclude society. The natural sciences make great advances; the social and historical sciences lag behind. Nature and history are counterposed. Nature is regarded as the

[7] Caudwell FSDC 162.

realm of necessity, standing outside of man—a realm which man can operate according to his will, provided that he understands its laws; but man himself is somehow 'free', his freedom being seen 'as a product, not of history, but of nature'. In bourgeois society, as Frankfort has so candidly remarked, 'man does not quite succeed in becoming a scientific object to himself' (p. 94). Hence the limitations of bourgeois science:

The weak points in the abstract materialism of natural science, a materialism that excludes history and its process, are at once evident from the abstract and ideological conceptions of its spokesmen, whenever they venture beyond the bounds of their own speciality.[8]

It is one of the achievements of Marxism to have overcome this limitation. In contrast to earlier forms of materialism, which were all confined to the contemplation of the world as an external object, dialectical and historical materialism embraces man himself, the subject, and thus reunites theory with practice. In this, of course, it expresses the outlook characteristic of the proletariat, the new class which, by abolishing the private ownership of the means of production, is putting an end to the class struggle, and hence also to the division between mental and manual labour.

Reviewing the whole process, we may say that in primitive society the individual was barely conscious either of himself or of his natural environment as existing separately from the social environment of his clan or tribe. The capacity of objectifying the external world developed as the bonds of kinship which united the tribal group were dissolved by divisions of labour, exchange between individuals, and production for exchange. With the growth of commodity production these tribal ties were replaced by ties of a new kind, which, on the one hand, served to define the subjective self-sufficiency of the individual, and, on the other, to bind him objectively to other individuals in a nexus of relationships which, since they lay beyond his understanding and control, presented themselves to his consciousness, not as they really were, but as absolute truths founded on abstract reason. Hence, as Sohn-Rethel has well said, 'the discovery of nature as a physical cosmos is correlated with man's discovery of himself as man':

[8] Marx C 1. 367.

In 'pure thought', arising out of a monetary economy, man becomes aware of himself as distinct from the rest of nature, but only by severing himself from practice, by separating himself from nature. Hence his self-discovery is also his self-deception. The power of pure thought and abstract reasoning, which he attributes to the mind, is really due to the fact that commodity exchange has become the nexus of society. The timeless, absolute concepts of pure thought, in terms of which the mind is framed, are based on the elimination of everything that relates to usage. Hence it comes about that, while the bodily part of us, which, measured in terms of human history, is unchanging, appears as timebound and transient, that part of us which arises directly out of our history, our mind, appears as timeless and unoriginated.[9]

These concepts, which constitute the Kantian 'autonomy of reason', are the mental reflex of the social relations brought into being by commodity production, which has been a feature of the economic basis of class society in all its successive epochs. They belong to those 'common forms or general ideas' of which mention is made in the *Communist Manifesto*:

Does it require deep intuition to comprehend that man's ideas, views and conceptions—in one word, man's consciousness—change with every change in the conditions of his material existence, in his social relations and his social life?

What else does the history of ideas prove than that intellectual production changes its character in proportion as material production is changed? The ruling ideas of each age have ever been the ideas of its ruling class. . . .

The history of all past society has consisted in the development of class antagonisms—antagonisms that assumed different forms at different epochs. But, whatever form they may have taken, one fact is common to all past ages, *viz*. the exploitation of one part of society by the other. No wonder, then, that the social consciousness of past ages, despite all the multiplicity and variety it displays, moves within certain common forms, or general ideas, which cannot completely vanish except with the total disappearance of class antagonisms.

The communist revolution is the most radical rupture with traditional property relations; no wonder that its development involves the most radical rupture with traditional ideas.[10]

Through this revolution man is at last enabled to see the world, including himself, as it really is, and hence, having healed the breach at the heart of human society, to shape his own destiny, master of both society and nature. 'Beauty is truth, truth beauty'. This has long been the dream of

[9] Sohn-Rethel IML.   [10] Marx-Engels MCP 226.

philosophers, prophets and poets, but for the most part they have placed its realisation in an imaginary world beyond the grave. So Plato:

There the seasons are tempered so that men live without sickness and much longer than here; and in sight, hearing, understanding and all other faculties they are as far superior to us as air is in purity to water and ether to air; and they have sacred groves and shrines there, in which the gods really dwell, and divine voices and oracles and intuitions and other forms of direct intercourse with the gods; and they see the sun, moon and stars as they really are, and in every respect enjoy all the happiness that follows from this.[11]

And so St. Paul:

For now we see in a glass darkly, but then face to face; now I know in part, but then shall I know even as I have been known.[12]

Or, if the vision is realised in this life, it is only for a moment, at the point of death, as when the blinded Faust, imagining himself to stand with a free people engaged in creative labour in an earthly paradise, utters the cry that brings on him his doom: *Verweile doch, du bist so schön!*

In modern times, however, with the rise of the proletariat, bourgeois poets have reflected, some dimly and some more clearly, the growing determination of the workers to build the promised land with their own sweat and blood 'here where men sit and hear each other groan'. Only then, freed of illusions, will man become fully 'self-knowing'. So Keats:

> 'High Prophetess,' said I, 'purge off,
> Benign, if it so please thee, my mind's film.'
> 'None can usurp this height,' returned that shade,
> 'But those to whom the miseries of the world
> Are misery, and will not let them rest.'[13]

So Shelley:

> The loathsome mask has fallen; the man remains
> Sceptreless, free, uncircumscribed, but man,
> Equal, unclassed, tribeless and nationless,
> Exempt from awe, worship, degree, the king
> Over himself.[14]

[11] Pl. *Phdo* 111b–c.   [12] 1 Cor. 13. 12.   [13] Keats *Hyperion*.
[14] Shelley *Prometheus Unbound* 3. 4.

And so Hardy:

> But—a stirring thrills the air
> Like to sounds of joyance there
>   That the rages
>   Of the ages
> Shall be cancelled and deliverance offered from the
>   darts that were,
> Consciousness the Will informing, till It fashion all
>   things fair![15]

So long as man is ignorant of the laws which govern his existence, he is their slave, and they appear to him as the will of a superior being; but, in so far as he understands them, he can master them and make them serve his will.

Lastly, the material basis of these poets' visions has been analysed by Marx and presented as a scientific theory, the truth of which is now being demonstrated in practice:

The life process of society, which is based on the process of material production, does not strip off its mystical veil until it is treated as production by freely associated men and is consciously regulated by them in accordance with a settled plan.[16]

[15] Hardy *The Dynasts*, *ad fin.*: see Thomson THP.   [16] Marx C 1. 51.

BIBLIOGRAPHY

Where an English translation of a foreign work is specified, the references are to its pages and not to those of the original. A list of periodicals, with the abbreviations used for them, will be found at the end of the Bibliography.

ALBRIGHT, W. F. 'The Phœnician Inscriptions of the Tenth Century B.C. from Byblos.' JAO 67. 153.

ALEXANDROV, G. F., and others. История философии. ТОМ 1. Moscow/Leningrad, 1941.

ANDERSEN, J. C. *Myths and Legends of the Polynesians.* London, 1928.

ANTONIADIS, S. *La place de la liturgie dans la tradition des lettres grecques.* Leiden, 1939.

AVDIEV, V. I. История древнего востока. Moscow/Leningrad, 1948.

BANCROFT, H. H. *Native Races of the Pacific States of North America.* London, 1875–6.

BARNETT, R. D. 'The Epic of Kumarbi and the Theogony of Hesiod.' JHS 45. 100.

BOAS, F. *Handbook of American Indian Languages.* ARB 40. Washington, 1911–22.

BOWRA, C. M. 'The Proem of Parmenides.' CP 39. 97.

BRIFFAULT, R. *The Mothers.* London, 1927.

BRUGMANN, K. *Die Syntax des einfachen Satzes im Indogermanischen.* Berlin/Leipzig, 1925.

BÜCHER, K. *Arbeit und Rhythmus.* 5 ed. Leipzig, 1919.

BURNET, J. *Early Greek Philosophy.* 4 ed. London, 1930.

— *Greek Philosophy, Thales to Plato.* London, 1914.

BURY, J. B. *History of Greece.* 3 ed. London, 1951.

Cambridge Ancient History. Cambridge, 1925–39.

CANTARELLA, R. *I poeti bizantini.* Milan, 1948.

CASSIRER, E. *Philosophie der symbolischen Formen.* Berlin, 1923–9.

CAUDWELL, C. *The Crisis in Physics.* London, 1938.

—— *Further Studies in a Dying Culture.* London, 1949.

—— *Illusion and Reality.* 2 ed. London, 1947.

—— *Studies in a Dying Culture.* London, 1938.

CHERNISS, H. *Aristotle's Criticism of Presocratic Philosophy.* Baltimore, 1935.

CHILDE, V. G. *What Happened in History.* London, 1942.

CLARK, G. *From Savagery to Civilisation.* London, 1946.

CLAY, S. *The Tenure of Land in Babylonia and Assyria.* London, 1938.

CODRINGTON, R. H. *The Melanesians.* Oxford, 1891.

COOK, R. M. 'Ionia and Greece.' JHS 66. 67.

COOKE, G. A. *The Book of Ezekiel.* Edinburgh, 1936.

CORNFORD, F. M. *From Religion to Philosophy.* Cambridge, 1912.

—— 'The Origin of the Olympic Games.' Harrison T 212.

CORNFORD, F. M. *Plato's Theory of Knowledge*. London, 1935.

—— *Principium Sapientiæ*. Cambridge, 1952.

—— *The Republic of Plato*. Oxford, 1941.

CURR, E. M. *The Australian Race*. Melbourne, 1886–7.

CUSHING, F. H. 'Outlines of Zuni Creation Myths.' ARB 13. 368.

DAWSON, J. *The Australian Aborigines*. Melbourne, 1881.

DORSEY, J. O. *Siouan Sociology*. ARB 15.

DURKHEIM, E. *Les formes élémentaires de la vie religieuse*. 2 ed. Paris, 1912.

DURKHEIM, E., AND MAUSS, M. 'De quelques formes primitives de classi-fication.' AS 6.

DUSSAUD, R. *Prélydiens, lydiens et achéens*. Paris, 1953.

EBERHARD, W. *History of China*. London, 1950.

EHRENBERG, V. *Aspects of the Ancient World*. Oxford, 1946.

—— 'Isonomia.' Pauly-Wissowa Suppl. 7. 293.

—— 'Origins of Democracy.' H 1. 515.

—— *The People of Aristophanes*. 2 ed. London, 1953.

ENGELS, F. *Anti-Dühring*. London, 1934.

—— *Dialectics of Nature*. London, 1940.

—— 'On Historical Materialism.' Marx SW 1. 395.

—— *Ludwig Feuerbach*. London, n.d.

—— *Origin of the Family, Private Property and the State*. London, 1940.

ENGNELL, I. *Studies in the Divine Kingship in the Ancient Near East*. Uppsala, 1945.

Εὐχολόγιον τὸ Μέγα. Rome, 1863.

FARNELL, L. R. *Cults of the Greek States*. Oxford, 1896–1909.

FARRINGTON, B. *Greek Science*. London, 1944–9.

—— *Head and Hand in Ancient Greece*. London, 1947.

FITZGERALD, C. P. *China*. 2 ed. London, 1950.

FOTHERINGHAM, J. K. 'Cleostratus.' JHS 39. 179.

FOWLER, W. W. *Roman Festivals*. London, 1899.

FRAENKEL, H. *Parmenidesstudien*. Berlin, 1930.

FRANKFORT, H. *Kingship and the Gods*. Chicago, 1948.

FRANKFORT, H., AND H. A., AND WILSON, J. A., AND JACOBSEN, T. *Before Philosophy*. London, 1949.

FRAZER, J. G. *Pausanias's Description of Greece*. London, 1898.

—— *Totemica*. London, 1937.

—— *Totemism and Exogamy*. London, 1910.

FRITZ, K. VON. *Pythagorean Politics in Southern Italy*. New York, 1940.

FUNG YU-LAN. *History of Chinese Philosophy*. Princeton, 1937–53.

GARDINER, A. *Egyptian Grammar*. 2 ed. Oxford, 1950.

GASTER, T. H. *Thespis*. New York, 1950.

GIGON, O. *Der Ursprung der griechischen Philosophie*. Basel, 1945.

GLEZERMAN, G. 'Basis and Superstructure.' CoR 1951.

GLOTZ, G. *Le travail dans la Grèce ancienne*. Paris, 1920. *Ancient Greece at Work*. London, 1926.

GRANET, M. *La civilisation chinoise*. Paris, 1929. *Chinese Civilisation*. London. 1930.

—— *La pensée chinoise*. Paris, 1934.

GURNEY, O. R. *The Hittites*. London, 1952.

GÜTERBOCK, H. G. 'The Hittite Version of the Hurrian Kumarbi Myths.' AJA 52, 123.

—— *Kumarbi*. Istanbuler Schriften 16. Istanbul, 1946.

GUTHRIE, W. K. *Orpheus and Greek Religion*. London, 1935.

HARRISON, J. E. *Prolegomena to the Study of Greek Religion*. 3 ed. Cambridge, 1922.

—— *Themis*. Cambridge, 1912.

HASEBROEK, J. *Staat und Handel im alten Griechenland*. Tübingen, 1928. *Trade and Politics in Ancient Greece*. London, 1933.

HASTINGS, J. *Encyclopædia of Religion and Ethics*. Edinburgh, 1908–18.

HEAD, B. V. *Historia Numorum*. 2 ed. Oxford, 1911.

HOLLITSCHER, W. 'The Teachings of Pavlov.' CoR 1953.

HOOKE, S. H. (editor). *The Labyrinth*. London, 1935.

—— *Myth and Ritual*. Oxford, 1933.

HUGHES, E. R. *Chinese Philosophy in Classical Times*. London, 1942.

Ἱερὰ Σύνοψις καὶ τὰ Ἅγια Πάθη. Athens, n.d.

JACOBSEN, T. 'Primitive Democracy in Ancient Mesopotamia.' JNE 2. 159.

JONES, A. H. M. 'The Economic Basis of Athenian Democracy.' PP 1. 13.

JONES, W. H. S. *Hippocrates*. London/New York, 1923–31.

KARSTEN, R. *The Civilisation of the South American Indians*. London, 1926.

KERN, O. *Orphicorum Fragmenta*. Berlin, 1922.

KÖHLER, W. *The Mentality of Apes*. 2 ed. London, 1927.

KORNILOV, K. N., AND SMIRNOV, A. A., AND TEPLOV, В. М. Лсихология. Moscow, 1948.

KRAMER, S. N. 'Sumerian Mythology.' APS 21.

KUZOVKOV, D. V. Об условиях, породивших различия в развитии рабства, и его наивышее развитие в античном мире. VDI 1954. 1.

LANGDON, S. 'The Babylonian Conception of the Logos.' JRAS 433.

—— *The Babylonian Epic of Creation*. Oxford, 1923.

—— *Babylonian Menologies and Semitic Calendars*. London, 1935.

LANGE, H. O. 'Magical Papyrus Harris.' Danske Videnskabernes Selskab, Hist. Fil. Med. 14. 2. 1927.

LEFEBVRE, G. 'L'œuf divin d'Hermopolis.' ASA 23. 65.

LE GROS CLARK, W. E. *History of the Primates*. London, 1953.

LENIN, V. I. *Aus dem philosophischen Nachlass*. Vienna, 1932.

— - 'On Dialectics.' SW 11. 81.

—— Конспект книги Гегеля: наука логики. Ленинский Сборник IX. Moscow/Leningrad, 1931.

—— 'Materialism and Empirio-criticism'. SW 11.

—— *Selected Works*. London, n.d.

—— 'State and Revolution'. SW 7.

—— 'War and Peace.' SW 7. 283.

—— 'What the Friends of the People Are.' SW 11. 413.

LEWY, J., AND H. 'The Origin of the Week and the Oldest West Asiatic Calendar.' HUC 17. 1.

LILLEY, S. *Men, Machines and History*, London, 1948.

LOBECK, C. A. *Aglaophamus*. Königsberg, 1825.

LYSENKO, T. D. 'On the Situation in Biological Science.' Proceedings of the Lenin Academy of Agricultural Sciences of the USSR, July–August 1948.

MAKEMSON, M. W. *The Morning Star Rises: an Account of Polynesian Astronomy*. New Haven, 1941.

MALINOWSKI, B. *Coral Gardens and their Magic*. London, 1935.

MAO TSE-TUNG. *Selected Works*. London, 1954.

MARÓT, K. 'Die Trennung von Himmel und Erde.' ActAnt 1. 35.

MARX, K. *Capital*. Vol. I: London, 1946. Vols. II–III: Chicago, 1909–33.

—— *Contribution to the Critique of Political Economy*. Calcutta, 1904.

—— *Critique of Hegel's Philosophy of Law*. Marx-Engels Gesamtausgabe.

—— 'Forced Emigration.' Marx and Engels OB.

—— *Formen die der kapitalistischen Produktion vorhergehen*. Berlin, 1952.

—— *Die heilige Familie*. Marx-Engels Gesamtausgabe 1. 3.

—— *Selected Works*. London, 1942.

—— *Ueber die Differenz der demokritischen und epikurischen Naturphilosophie*. Marx-Engels Gesamtausgabe 1. 1.

—— 'Wage Labour and Capital.' SW 1.

MARX, K., AND ENGELS, F. *Correspondence*. 2 ed. London, 1936.

—— *The German Ideology*. London, 1938.

—— 'Manifesto of the Communist Party.' SW 1. 189.

—— *On Britain*. Moscow, 1953.

MATHEW, J. *Eaglehawk and Crow*. London, 1899.

McPHERSON, A. 'Recent Advances in Conditioned Reflexes.' Society for Cultural Relations with the USSR: Science Section, 1949.

MEILLET, A. *Introduction à l'étude comparative des langues indo-européennes*. 8 ed. Paris, 1937.

MEISSNER, B. *Babylonien und Assyrien*. Leipzig, 1920–5.

MENDELSSOHN, I. *Slavery in the Ancient Near East*. New York, 1949.

MITCHELL, P. C. *The Childhood of Animals*. London, 1912.

MOMMSEN, A. *Feste der Stadt Athen*. Leipzig, 1898.

MONDOLFO, R. *Il pensiero greco*. Florence, 1950.

MOORE, G. F. *Descriptive Vocabulary of the Language in Common Use amongst the Aborigines of Western Australia*. London, 1842.

MORGAN, L. H. *Ancient Society*. 2 ed. Chicago, 1910.

NEEDHAM, J. *Science and Civilisation in China*. Vol. I. Cambridge, 1954.

NEUGEBAUER, O. *The Exact Sciences in Antiquity*. Princeton, 1952.

NILSSON, M. P. 'Die Entstehung und religiöse Bedeutung des griechischen Kalenders.' 1. 14. 21. *Lund Universitets Arsskrift*.

—— *Griechische Feste mit religiöser Bedeutung mit Auschluss der attischen*. Leipzig, 1906.

—— *Primitive Time Reckoning*. Lund/Oxford, 1911.

—— 'Sonnenkalender und Sonnenreligion.' ARW 30. 141.

—— *Studia de Dionysiis atticis*. Lund, 1900.

NORDEN, E. *Agnostos Theos*. Leipzig/Berlin, 1913.

—— *Die antike Kunstprosa*. Leipzig/Berlin, 1898.

OAKLEY, K. P. *Man the Tool-maker*. London, 1949.

OLIVA, P. *Raná řecká Tyrannis.* Prague, 1954.

'Ωρολόγιον τὸ Μέγα. Venice, 1876.

PARKER, R. A. *The Calendars of Ancient Egypt.* Chicago, 1953.

PARROT, A. *Ziggurats et Tours de Babel.* Paris, 1949.

PAULY, A., AND WISSOWA, G. *Realencyclopädie der klassischen Altertumswissenschaft.* Stuttgart, 1894–1937.

PAVLOV, I. P. *Lectures on Conditioned Reflexes.* London, 1927.

—— *Selected Works.* Moscow, 1955.

PEI WEN-CHUNG. 'New Light on Peking Man.' ChR 3. 4. 33.

PRENANT, M. *Biologie et Marxisme.* Paris, 1936. *Biology and Marxism.* London, 1938.

RADIN, P. *The Winnebago Tribe.* ARB 37.

RAVEN, J. E. *Pythagoreans and Eleatics.* Cambridge, 1948.

REINHARDT, K. *Parmenides und die Geschichte der griechischen Philosophie.* Bonn, 1916.

ROBERTSON, D. S. *Greek and Roman Architecture.* Cambridge, 1929.

ROBINSON, T. H., AND OESTERLEY, W. O. *History of Israel.* Oxford, 1932.

ROHDE, E. *Psyche: Seelencult und Unsterblichkeitsglaube der Griechen.* Freiburg, 1898.

ROSCHER, W. H. *Ausführliches Lexikon der griechischen und römischen Mythologie.* Leipzig, 1884–1937.

RYTKHEU. 'Ten Days in the Train.' ASJ 15. 2.

SAPIR, E. *Selected Writings.* Berkeley/London, 1949.

SCHAEFFER, C. F. A. *Cuneiform Texts of Ras Shamra.* London, 1939.

SCHÄFER, H. 'Weltgebäude der alten Aegypter.' Ant 91.

SELTMAN, C. T. *Athens, its History and Coinage.* Cambridge, 1924.

—— *A Book of Greek Coins.* London, 1952.

—— *Greek Coins.* London, 1933.

—— 'The Problem of the First Italiote Coins.' NC 9. 1.

SERGEIEV, V. S. История древней Греций. Moscow/Leningrad, 1948.

SHEPPARD, J. T. *The Œdipus Tyrannus of Sophocles.* Cambridge, 1920.

SIKELIANOS, A. Λυρικὸς βίος. Athens, 1946–7.

SINCLAIR, W. A. *The Traditional Formal Logic.* London, 1937.

SINGER, C. *Greek Biology and Greek Medicine.* Oxford, 1922.

SKINNER, J. *A Critical and Exegetical Commentary on Genesis.* 2 ed. Edinburgh, 1930.

SMYTH, R. B. *The Aborigines of Victoria.* London, 1878.

SOHN-RETHEL, A. *Intellectual and Manual Labour.* Unpublished.

SOMMERFELT, A. *La langue et la société.* Oslo, 1938.

SPENCER, B., AND GILLEN, F. H. *The Arunta.* London, 1927.

—— *Native Tribes of Central Australia.* London, 1899.

SPINDEN, H. J. *Ancient Civilisations of Mexico and Central America.* New York, 1928.

SPIRKIN, A. G. 'Учение И. В. Павлова о второй сигнальной системе: естественно-научная основа учения И. В. Сталина о языке'. Известия АН СССР, Отделение историй и философий. ТОМ 8, no. 3, 1951: pp. 221–36. Moscow, 1951.

STALIN, J. V. 'Dialectical and Historical Materialism.' *History of the Communist Party of the Soviet Union*, Chapter IV. Moscow, 1939.
—— *Concerning Marxism in Linguistics.* London, 1950.
—— *Economic Problems of Socialism.* Moscow, 1953.
—— 'On the Problems of Leninism.' *Leninism* 118. London, 1940.
STEVENSON, M. C. *The Zuni Indians.* ARB 23.
SZABÓ, A. 'Beiträge zur Geschichte der griechischen Dialektik.' ActAnt 1. 377.
TAYLOR, A. E. *Plato, the Man and His Work.* 2 ed. London, 1927.
THOMSON, G. *Æschylus and Athens.* 2 ed. London, 1946.
—— *Æschylus, Oresteia.* Cambridge, 1938.
—— 'The Greek Calendar.' JHS 63. 52.
—— Письмо в редакцию. VDI 1954. 4. 107.
—— 'From Religion to Philosophy.' JHS 73. 77.
—— *Studies in Ancient Greek Society.* Vol. I: *The Prehistoric Ægean.* 2 ed. London, 1954.
—— 'Thomas Hardy and the Peasantry.' CoR August 1949.
—— 'The Wheel and the Crown.' CR 59. 9.
TOD, M. N. *Greek Historical Inscriptions.* Oxford, 1933–48.
TORR, D. 'Productive Forces: Social Relations.' CoR May 1946.
TRITSCH, F. J. 'Die Agora von Elis und die altgriechische Agora.' JOA 27. 63.
TYLOR, E. B. *Primitive Culture.* 2 ed. London, 1891.
URE, P. N. 'Diakrioi and Hyperakrioi.' CR 29. 155.
—— *Origin of Tyranny.* Cambridge, 1922.
VAILLANT, G. C. *The Aztecs of Mexico.* London, 1950.
VALETAS, G. Ἀνθολογία τῆς δημοτικῆς πεζογραφίας. Athens, 1947–9.
VENDRYES, J. *Le langage.* Paris, 1921. *Language.* London, 1925.
VLASTOS, G. 'Equality and Justice in Early Greek Cosmologies.' CP 42. 156.
—— 'Isonomia.' AJP 74. 337.
—— 'Solonian Justice.' CP 41. 79.
WALBANK, F. W. 'The Causes of Greek Decline.' JHS 64. 10.
WEILL, R. *Phœnicia and Western Asia.* London, 1940.
WENIGER, L. 'Das Hochfest des Zeus in Olympia.' K 5. 1.
WESTERMANN, W. L. 'Athenæus and the Slaves of Athens.' *Athenian Studies Presented to W. S. Ferguson.* Cambridge, Mass., 1940.
WHEELER, W. M. *The Social Insects.* London, 1928.
WHITE, M. 'The Duration of the Samian Tyranny.' JHS 74. 36.
WINTON, F. R., AND BAYLISS, L. E. *Human Physiology.* 3 ed. London, 1948.
WOOLLEY, L. *Abraham.* London, 1935.
—— *A Forgotten Kingdom.* London, 1953.
—— *The Sumerians.* Oxford, 1928.
WU TA-KUN. 'An Interpretation of Chinese Economic History.' PP 1. 1.
YOUNG, J. Z. *Doubt and Certainty in Science.* Oxford, 1951.
ZIMMERN, A. E. *Solon and Crœsus.* London, 1928.
ZUCKERMAN, S. *The Social Life of Apes and Monkeys.* London, 1932.

PERIODICALS

ActAnt	*Acta Antiqua.* Budapest.
Ant	*Die Antike.* Berlin.
AJA	*American Journal of Archæology.* Concord, U.S.A.
APS	*Memoirs of the American Philosophical Society.*
ARB	*Annual Reports of the Bureau of Ethnology.* Washington.
AS	*Année sociologique.* Paris.
ASA	*Annales du service des antiquités.* Paris.
ASJ	*Anglo-Soviet Journal.* London.
ARW	*Archiv für Religionswissenschaft.* Freiburg.
CP	*Classical Philology.* Chicago.
CoR	*Communist Review.* London.
CR	*Classical Review.* Oxford.
ChR	*China Reconstructs.* Peking.
H	*Historia.* Baden-Baden.
HUC	*Hebrew Union College Annual.* Cincinnati.
JAO	*Journal of the American Oriental Society.* Baltimore.
JHS	*Journal of Hellenic Studies.* London.
JNE	*Journal of Near Eastern Studies.* London.
JOA	*Jahresheft des österreichischen archäologischen Institutes.* Vienna.
JRAS	*Journal of the Royal Asiatic Society.* London.
K	*Klio.* Leipzig.
MDA	*Mitteilungen des deutschen archäologischen Instituts: Athenische Abteilung.* Berlin.
NC	*Numismatic Chronicle.* 6th series. London.
PP	*Past and Present.* London.
VDI	Вестник древней историй. Moscow/Leningrad.

GENERAL INDEX

(Roman figures refer to the Maps)